SHAKESPEARE STUDIES

EDITORIAL BOARD

Harry Berger Jr.
The University of California, Santa Cruz

Catherine Belsey
University of Wales College of Cardiff

Michael Bristol
McGill University

S. P. Cerasano
Colgate University

Jonathan Dollimore
York University

Barry Gaines
The University of New Mexico

Jean E. Howard
University of Pennsylvania

Lena Cowen Orlin
University of Maryland, Baltimore County

John Pitcher
St. John's College, Oxford

Maureen Quilligan
Duke University

Alan Sinfield
The University of Sussex

Peter Stallybrass
The University of Pennsylvania

SHAKESPEARE STUDIES
VOLUME XXX

EDITED BY
LEEDS BARROLL

BOOK REVIEW EDITOR

Susan Zimmerman
Queens College
City University of New York

Madison • Teaneck
Fairleigh Dickinson University Press
London: Associated University Presses

© 2002 by Associated University Presses, Inc.

All rights reserved. Authorization to photocopy items for internal or personal use, or the internal or personal use of specific clients, is granted by the copyright owner, provided that a base fee of $10.00, plus eight cents per page, per copy is paid directly to the Copyright Clearance Center, 222 Rosewood Drive, Danvers, Massachusetts 01923 [0-8386-3962-3/02 $10.00 + 8¢ pp, pc.]

Associated University Presses
2010 Eastpark Boulevard
Cranbury, NJ 08512

Associated University Presses
16 Barter Street
London WC1A 2AH, England

Associated University Presses
P.O. Box 338, Port Credit
Mississauga, Ontario
Canada L5G 4L8

The paper used in this publication meets the requirements of the American National Standard for Permanence of Paper for Printed Library Materials Z39.48-1984.

International Standard Book Number 0-8386-3962-3 (vol. xxx)
International Standard Serial Number 0582-9399

All editorial correspondence concerning *Shakespeare Studies* should be addressed to the Editorial Office, *Shakespeare Studies,* University of Maryland (Baltimore County), Baltimore, Maryland 21250. Manuscripts submitted without appropriate postage will not be returned. Orders and subscriptions should be directed to Associated University Presses, 2010 Eastpark Boulevard, Cranbury, New Jersey 08512.

Shakespeare Studies disclaims responsibility for statements, either of fact or opinion, made by contributors.

Contents

Foreword	9
Contributors	11

Forum: The Idea of History in Renaissance Studies

Introduction Dympna Callaghan	23
Readers, Evidence, and Interdisciplinarity Frances E. Dolan	26
Parliament and the Theater of State: The Construction of Texts Chris R. Kyle	31
Afterlife Crystal Bartolovich	36
The Promise of History John Parker	43
Atomic Shakespeare Jonathan Gil Harris	47

Symposium: "Mere Archaeology": Theater History Updates

Introduction S. P. Cerasano	55
Hyper-Revels in Cyberspace Sally-Beth MacLean and Alan Somerset	62
Archaeology Update: Four Playhouses and the Bear Garden Simon Blatherwick	74

Early London Pageantry and Theater History Firsts 84
ANNE LANCASHIRE

John Brayne and His Other Brother-in-Law 93
HERBERT BERRY

Domestical Matters 99
R. A. FOAKES

Sir John Astley and Court Culture 106
JOHN H. ASTINGTON

Two Playhouses, Both Alike in Dignity 111
ROSLYN L. KNUTSON

Playhouses Make Strange Bedfellows: The Case of Aaron and Martin 118
WILLIAM INGRAM

Some Recent Dramatic Manuscript Studies 128
GRACE IOPPOLO

Articles

"Crack'd Crowns" and Counterfeit Sovereigns: The Crisis of Value in *1 Henry IV* 137
JESSE M. LANDER

"Awake Remembrance of these Valiant Dead": *Henry V* and the Politics of the English History Play 162
ALISON THORNE

Anachronistic Italy: Cultural Alliances and National Identity in *Cymbeline* 188
PETER A. PAROLIN

Reviews

Dympna C. Callaghan, ed., *A Feminist Companion to Shakespeare* 219
LISA HOPKINS

Kent Cartwright, *Theatre and Humanism: English Drama in the Sixteenth Century* 220
SHEILA T. CAVANAGH

Contents

Frances E. Dolan, *Whores of Babylon: Catholicism, Gender, and Seventeenth-Century Print Culture* 224
JEFFREY KNAPP

Katherine Eggert, *Showing Like a Queen: Female Authority and Literary Experiment in Spenser, Shakespeare, and Milton* 228
COPPÉLIA KAHN

Peter Erickson and Clark Hulse, eds., *Early Modern Visual Culture: Representation, Race, and Empire in Renaissance England* 232
JERRY BROTTON

Jonathan Goldberg, *Desiring Women Writing: English Renaissance Examples* 234
JUDITH BUTLER

Bruce Gordon and Peter Marshall, eds., *The Place of the Dead: Death and Remembrance in Late Medieval and Early Modern Europe* 242

Peter C. Jupp and Clare Gittings, eds., *Death in England: An Illustrated History* 242
KATHERINE O. ACHESON

Kenneth Gross, *Shakespeare's Noise* 247
MARSHALL GROSSMAN

Graham L. Hammill, *Sexuality and Form: Caravaggio, Marlowe, and Bacon* 254
DENISE ALBANESE

Martin Harries, *Scare Quotes From Shakespeare: Marx, Keynes, and the Language of Reenchantment* 258
JOHN DRAKAKIS

Richard Helgerson, *Adulterous Alliances: Home, State, and History in Early Modern European Drama and Painting* 271
CLARK HULSE

Cynthia Herrup, *A House in Gross Disorder: Sex, Law, and the 2nd Earl of Castlehaven* 274
RICHARD RAMBUSS

Peter Hulme and William H. Sherman, eds., *"The Tempest" and Its Travels* 282
BRUCE AVERY

Ann Rosalind Jones and Peter Stallybrass, *Renaissance Clothing and the Materials of Memory*   284
  FRANCES E. DOLAN

David Scott Kastan, *Shakespeare after Theory*   288
  KIERNAN RYAN

Arthur L. Little Jr., *Shakespeare Jungle Fever: National-Imperial Re-Visions of Race, Rape, and Sacrifice*   294
  RICHARD BURT

Naomi J. Miller and Naomi Yavneh, eds., *Maternal Measures: Figuring Caregiving in the Early Modern Period*   300
  MARY BETH ROSE

Lena Cowen Orlin, ed., *Material London, ca. 1600*   304
  CYNTHIA WALL

Christopher Pye, *The Vanishing: Shakespeare, the Subject, and Early Modern Culture*   309
  SCOTT WILSON

Katherine Rowe, *Dead Hands: Fictions of Agency, Renaissance to Modern*   313
  TALIA SCHAFFER

James Schiffer, ed., *Shakespeare's Sonnets: Critical Essays*   318
  LYNNE MAGNUSSON

Barbara Howard Traister, *The Notorious Astrological Physician of London: Works and Days of Simon Forman*   326
  S. P. CERASANO

Luke Wilson, *Theaters of Intention: Drama and the Law in Early Modern England*   333
  CONSTANCE JORDAN

Susanne Woods, *Lanyer: A Renaissance Woman Poet*   337
  BARBARA K. LEWALSKI

Index   341

Foreword

SHAKESPEARE STUDIES is very pleased to offer in Volume XXX its second Symposium, "*Mere Archaeology*": *Theater History Updates,* conceived and organized by S. P. Cerasano, whose introductory essay reviews the major currents of thought regarding the material apsects of London theaters. Other theater historians in the Symposium write on such topics as recent studies in dramatic manuscripts, and the current state of archaeology in regard to four playhouses and the Bear Garden. The results are of some importance to scholars for whom the London theater backgrounds their own thinking about the role of plays in early modern English society.

In addition to the Symposium, Volume XXX presents our sixth Forum, organized by Dympna Callaghan: "The Idea of History in Renaissance Studies." Discussing the difficulties inherent in the move to "contextualize" the literary text, Callaghan presents five scholars who address such topics as "Readers, Evidence, and Interdisciplinarity," and "Parliament and the Theatre of State." Volume XXX also features three essays contributed by Jesse M. Lander, Alison Thorne, and Peter A. Parolin on subjects ranging, respectively, from early modern English coinage and the concepts it evoked, to a fresh approach to the politics of the English history play, to a scrutiny of the "Italy" presented in *Cymbeline.* The balance of Volume XXX, as customary, is devoted to (twenty-four) substantial reviews of important new scholarly work.

Plans for Volume XXXI, to appear in fall 2003, include the first in a new series, *Vistas of the Early Modern: Seen and Unseen.* Assuming that what was happening in the arts outside of Shakespearean England during the early modern period is increasingly relevant to our current historicism, this series will present three to five short essays focusing on non-English cultural traditions. The first such "Vista" will feature current scholarship on dramatic practices in Spain, France, Japan, and, hopefully, China, circa

1560–1630, along with some description of available resources on the subjects. Volume XXXI will also include essays on early modern Morocco and on the Renaissance notion of "hysteria," among others.

LEEDS BARROLL

Contributors

KATHERINE O. ACHESON is Associate Professor of English at the University of Waterloo. Editor of *The Diary of Anne Clifford* and author of articles on various topics in English Renaissance studies, she is presently at work on a project about seventeenth-century visual rhetoric.

DENISE ALBANESE is Associate Professor of English and Cultural Studies at George Mason University. Author of *New Science, New World* (1996), she has also published on Shakespeare, film, and performance, as well as on humanism and early modern mathematics. She is completing *Extramural Shakespeares,* a study of Shakespeare in perimillennial public culture.

JOHN H. ASTINGTON is Professor of English and Drama at the University of Toronto. He is the author of *English Court Theatre 1558–1642.* He is currently at work on various aspects of the history of the Shakespearean stage.

BRUCE AVERY is Associate Professor of English at San Francisco State University. He recently completed editing four of Shakespeare's plays for iLrn, an on-line Shakespeare edition.

CRYSTAL BARTOLOVICH is Associate Professor of English at Syracuse University. Currently she is working on a book-length project entitled *Britain Translated.*

HERBERT BERRY is Emeritus Professor of English at the University of Saskatchewan.

SIMON BLATHERWICK is a Director of the Rose Theatre Trust and a principal archaeologist with Gifford & Partners Ltd. (London). He co-directed the excavation of the Rose Theatre in the late 1980s and has recently directed an "evaluation" to the east of the Rose Theatre, within the Little Rose Estate. This provided further evidence of the high quality of archaeological preservation within the historic property boundaries and located a post- and plank-lined ditch, thought to be the eastern boundary ditch of the estate on which the Rose was built. In addition to managing archaeological work on large infrastructure and development projects within the southeast of England, he is presently working on further documentary and archaeological assessment of London's Tudor and Stuart playhouses.

JERRY BROTTON is Lecturer in English at Royal Holloway, University of London. He is the author of *The Renaissance Bazaar: from the Silk Road to Michelangelo* (2000). He is currently working on the art collection of Charles I.

RICHARD BURT is Professor of English at the University of Massachusetts, Amherst. He is author of *Unspeakable ShaXXXspeares: Queer Theory and American Kiddie Culture* (1998), and *Licensed by Authority: Ben Jonson and the Discourses of Censorship* (1993); and editor of *Shakespeare After Mass Media* (2002). He is currently working on two books: *Ever Afterlives: Reanimating the Renaissance and the Loss of History,* and *Dumb Love: A Loser's Guide.*

JUDITH BUTLER is Maxine Elliot Professor in the Department of Rhetoric and Comparative Literature at the University of California, Berkeley. She is the author of several books and numerous articles on philosophy and on feminist and queer theory. Her most recent book is *Antigone's Claim: Kinship Between Life and Death* (2000).

DYMPNA CALLAGHAN is William P. Trolley Distinguished Professor in the Humanities at Syracuse University. She has authored *Shakespeare Without Women* (2000), and edited *John Webster's The Duchess of Malfi: Contemporary Critical Essays* (2000), as well as *The Feminist Companion to Shakespeare* (2000), winner of Choice Award for Outstanding Academic Title. Her contextual edition of *Romeo and Juliet* is forthcoming with Bedford Books.

SHEILA T. CAVANAGH is Associate Professor of English, and Associated Faculty in Women's Studies and Violence Studies at Emory University. She is author of *Cherished Torment: The Emotional*

Geography of Lady Mary Wroth's Urania (2001), and *Wanton Eyes and Desires: Female Sexuality in* The Faerie Queene (1994).

S. P. CERASANO is Professor of English at Colgate University. Her most recent publication is "The Patronage Network of Philip Henslowe and Edward Alleyn" in *Medieval and Renaissance Drama in England,* Volume 13 (2001). She is currently working on a study of Henslowe's *Diary.*

FRANCES E. DOLAN is Professor of English at Miami University of Ohio. She is the author of *Whores of Babylon: Gender, Catholicism, and Seventeenth-Century Print Culture* (1999), and *Dangerous Familiars: Representations of Domestic Crime in England, 1550–1700* (1994); and editor of *The Taming of the Shrew: Texts and Contexts* (1996). She is currently working on a study of representations of marital conflict in seventeenth- and twentieth-century England and America.

JOHN DRAKAKIS is Professor of English Studies at the University of Stirling. He is the General Editor of the Routledge *New Critical Idiom* and the editor of the New Arden *The Merchant of Venice.* His current project is entitled *Shakespearean Discourses.*

R. A. FOAKES is Professor Emeritus at UCLA. Most recently he has edited *King Lear* for the Arden Shakespeare, Series 3, while his latest book, *Shakespeare and Violence,* is forthcoming.

MARSHALL GROSSMAN is Professor of English at the University of Maryland. His publications include *"Authors to Themselves": Milton and the Revelation of History; The Story of All Things: Writing the Self in English Renaissance Narrative Poetry; Aemelia Lanyer: Gender, Genre, and the Canon* (a collection of essays by diverse hands), and numerous articles in Renaissance literary history.

JONATHAN GIL HARRIS is Robert Ryan Professor of the Humanities at Ithaca College. The author of *Foreign Bodies and the Body Politic: Discourses of Social Pathology in Early Modern England* (1998), and the co-editor, with Natasha Korda, of *Staged Properties in Early Modern English Drama* (2002), he is currently at work on a book called *Etiologies of the Economy: Dramas of Mercantilism and Disease in the Age of Shakespeare.*

LISA HOPKINS is Reader in English at Sheffield Hallam University. Her most recent publication is *Christopher Marlowe: A Literary Life* (2000). She is presently at work on a book called *Shakespeare on the Edge.*

CLARK HULSE is Professor of English and Art History and Dean of the Graduate College at the University of Illinois at Chicago. His most recent book is *Early Modern Visual Culture: Representation, Race, and Empire in the English Renaissance* (edited with Peter Erickson, 2000).

WILLIAM INGRAM is Emeritus Professor of English Language and Literature at the University of Michigan.

GRACE IOPPOLO teaches at the University of Reading. She is the author of *Revising Shakespeare* (1991) and editor of *Shakespeare Performed: Essays in Honor of R. A. Foakes* (2000). She has edited plays by Shakespeare and Middleton, has published widely on manuscript and textual studies, and is currently finishing a book on the circulation of the dramatic manuscript.

CONSTANCE JORDAN is Professor of English at Claremont Graduate University. She is author of *Renaissance Feminism: Literary Texts and Political Models* (1990), and *Shakespeare's Monarchies: Ruler and Subject in the Romances* (1997). She is currently working on a book on *Concepts of Property in the Atlantic World, 1585–1680.*

COPPÉLIA KAHN is Professor of English and Gender Studies at Brown University. Her most recent book is *Roman Shakespeare: Warriors, Wounds, and Women* (1997).

JEFFREY KNAPP is Associate Professor of English at the University of California, Berkeley. His second book, *Shakespeare's Tribe: Church, Nation, and Theater in Renaissance England,* was published in spring 2002.

Contributors

ROSLYN L. KNUTSON is Professor of English at the University of Arkansas at Little Rock. Her most recent publication is *Playing Companies and Commerce in Shakespeare's Time* (2001). Currently her long-term project is a search for the narratives behind lost plays in Henslowe's diary.

CHRIS R. KYLE is Associate Professor of the Humanities at Syracuse University, New York. Author of a number of articles on early Stuart Parliaments, he edited *Parliament, Politics, and Elections, 1604–48* (2001), and with Jason Peacey, *Parliament at Work* (2002). He is currently writing a book on public access and the role of Parliament in sixteenth- and early seventeenth-century England.

ANNE LANCASHIRE is Professor of English at the University of Toronto and author of *London Civic Theatre: City Drama and Pageantry from Roman Times to 1558* (forthcoming, 2002).

JESSE M. LANDER is Assistant Professor of English at the University of Notre Dame. He has published essays on Shakespeare in print, Foxe's *Acts and Monuments,* and Heywood's *Edward IV.* He is presently writing a book on print technology and religious polemic in early modern England.

BARBARA K. LEWALSKI is William R. Kenan Professor of History and Literature and of English Literature at Harvard University. Her most recent book is *The Life of John Milton: A Critical Biography* (2000).

SALLY-BETH MACLEAN is General Editor of the Records of Early English Drama series and co-author, with Scott McMillin, of *The Queen's Men and their Plays* (1998). Her essay on "Tracking Leicester's Men: the patronage of a performance troupe" will be published this year in *Shakespeare and Theatrical Patronage in Early Modern England,* eds. Paul Whitfield White and Suzanne Westfall.

LYNNE MAGNUSSON is Professor of English at Queen's University in Canada. She is the author of *Shakespeare and Social Dialogue: Dramatic Language and Elizabethan Letters.* Currently she is writing a book on Elizabethan women's letters and editing *Love's Labour's Lost.*

JOHN PARKER is Assistant Professor of English at Harvard University. He is presently at work on a book-length project dealing with the theological lineage of Shakespearean aesthetics.

PETER A. PAROLIN is Assistant Professor of English at the University of Wyoming. He most recent publication is "'A Strange Fury Entered My House': Italian Actresses and Female Performance in *Volpone*," in *Renaissance Drama*, n.s. 29 (1998). He is presently co-editing a collection of essays, *Beyond the All-Male Stage in Early Modern England: Women Players 1500–1660*.

RICHARD RAMBUSS is Professor of English at Emory University. He is author of two books, *Spenser's Secret Career* and, more recently, *Closet Devotions*. He has also published numerous articles on Chaucer, Spenser, Shakespeare, Donne, Crashaw, and Milton.

MARY BETH ROSE is Professor of English and Director, Institute for the Humanities, University of Illinois at Chicago. Her most recent book is *Gender and Heroism in Early Modern English Literature* (2002).

KIERNAN RYAN is Professor of English Language and Literature at Royal Holloway, University of London, and a Fellow of New Hall, University of Cambridge. The third revised and enlarged edition of his book *Shakespeare* was published in 2002. He is currently completing a study of Shakespearean comedy and romance.

TALIA SCHAFFER is Assistant Professor of English at Queens College, CUNY. She is author of *The Forgotten Female Aesthetes: Literary Culture in Late-Victorian England* and co-editor, with Kathy A. Psomiades, of *Women and British Aestheticism*. She has published numerous articles on nineteenth-century writers, gender politics, and material culture. Her current work traces the connection between the mid-Victorian domestic handicraft movement and the realist novel.

ALAN SOMERSET is Professor of English at the University of Western Ontario. He is the editor of *Shropshire* for Records of Early English Drama (1994, 2 vols.), and author of *The Stratford Festival Story* (1991), as well as numerous articles. He is currently completing his edition of Staffordshire and Warwickshire for REED.

ALISON THORNE is Lecturer in English Studies at the University of Strathclyde (Glasgow). She is author of *Vision and Rhetoric in Shakespeare* (2000) and has edited *Shakespeare's Romances* for the New Casebook series (2002). She is currently working on a monograph provisionally entitled *Shakespeare and the Culture of Literacy.*

CYNTHIA WALL is Associate Professor of English at the University of Virginia. Primarily an eighteenth-century scholar, she studies the rebuilding of London after the Great Fire in *Literary and Cultural Spaces of Restoration London* (1998). She is currently working on the historically changing role of description in early modern narrative space.

SCOTT WILSON is Director of the Institute of Cultural Research at Lancaster University and co-editor (with Michael Dillon) of *Cultural Values: The Journal for Cultural Research.* His most recent books (co-authored with Fred Botting) are *The Tarantinian Ethics* (2001) and *Bataille* (2001). He is currently working on a genealogy of addiction from the early modern period to the present.

SHAKESPEARE STUDIES

FORUM
The Idea of History in Renaissance Studies

FORUM

Introduction

Dympna Callaghan

"The past," writes Michael Neill in the introduction to his important collection of essays, *Putting History to the Question*, "can be as eloquent in its troubling familiarity as it is taciturn in alterity and . . . the business of historical criticism is to trade as tactfully as possible between these contraries" (5). In a sense, Renaissance historicism—especially in the Renaissance itself in its encounter with both pagan classicism and nascent modernity—has always been a matter of negotiating between the present and the past. This encounter was precipitated in part by political struggle—namely, the flight of Greek scholars to Italy after the fall of Constantinople in 1453. The process of textual recovery had already begun with Manuel Chrysoloras's presence in Florence and translations of Plato. Nor was this neutral knowledge. For example, Pico della Mirandola's introduction of hermeticism and cabbalah made him a prime target of the Inquisition. Crucially, too, knowledge of the Ancients emerged from the peripatetic wanderings of scholars displaced by war, by the necessity of seeking patronage, or driven to seek refuge from other forms political strife. In other words, the past is always possessed of a present, something all the contributors to this forum (four literary scholars and one historian) acknowledge.

History becomes most problematic when the object of inquiry is not what is beyond the perimeters of the text but inherent in the text itself and in the often messy procedures of its making. Literary texts in particular do not record the "facts" of history. Rather, like Freud's view of the psyche, they register not "real" events but the mental representation of those events. Literature perhaps records at the level of culture what Freud described at the level of the individual psyche, and as such literature resists and even contradicts the claims of empiricism. Further, unlike other types of historical documents—the receipt, the sessions roll, and so on—literature has not just *meaning* in the present but also *function*. The impetus of the aesthetic does not end with its designated function at the historical moment of its composition, even if it lies unread on the library shelf, unperformed on the stage. That is, *Othello* has an afterlife that the ticket to see the play in Stratford in 1977 does not. I would venture to say that the literary does not share the innate propensity to become inert that is characteristic of most matter from the past. Perhaps because the aesthetic, the ornament to daily living, is never solely defined by a practical purpose (you do not need it—if needs are defined in purely material terms—for the maintenance of life), it never loses its capacity to function. That said, I have argued (in an article in Jean Howard and Scott Shershow's anthology, *Marxist Shakespeare*) that the aesthetic itself is something of a presentist category, only emerging as an entity completely separate from the practices of daily life *after* the Renaissance. This is because the literary and the aesthetic are contiguous but not identical categories, and the aesthetic is a very specific and loaded definition of a vast cultural array of literary practices across social classes.

In the face of these well-nigh insurmountable definitional difficulties, a now almost orthodox method of approach is to "contextualize" the literary text, a move that seeks to challenge the notion of an absolute distinction between the literary and the sociohistorical. But what does it mean, for example, to contextualize a passage of such lyrical intensity as the following from *Romeo and Juliet*?

> Come night. Come, Romeo. Come thou day in night;
> For thou wilt lie upon the wings of night
> Whiter than new snow upon a raven's back.
> (3.2.17–19)

Should we address ourselves to the problem of inadequate street lighting in the early modern city, or to the health hazard posed by raven droppings at the Tower of London? This would, of course, reduce these lines to absurdity because they are not really *about* the images they invoke. Literary texts, then, are not simply allegories of their social and historical contexts any more than they are islands hermetically sealed off from the main. All we can do perhaps is "trade as tactfully as possible" between them.

The following position pieces do just that. Frances Dolan suggests that the "aesthetic" is an empty category, one that defines only our interpretive relation to the text, our point of access to it, and not the text itself. For her, it is crucial if uncomfortable to straddle that much-contested boundary between the disciplines of literature and history, especially if we are to uncover the lives of women. Chris R. Kyle (the lone historian represented) takes issue with the way his own discipline addresses parliamentary history. He argues that Parliament needs to be read through the process by which its texts were produced, by MPs scribbling on tablets on their knees in a cramped chamber with the door wide open, and not in terms of the conveniently complete and polished texts bequeathed to posterity, which is the prevailing fiction of the institution. Crystal Bartolovich comes to the defense of Ben Jonson's universalism arguing that his statements were radical in early modern England even though they might now be retrograde. In other words, she argues, we must "always historicize," not just when we agree with the sentiments being expressed. John Parker is both wary of and enamoured by the lure of the aesthetic. Beauty is what lures us into the trash-heap of history; we want to excavate its origins, wallow in its lyricism, and so we find ourselves, Casaubon-like, entombed in the archive. He suggests that it would be easier if we could admit that only love makes us do such strange things. Gil Harris addresses himself to the current vogue for the object in studies of Renaissance material culture by examining the prevailing Lucretian theory of materialism in the period. Lucretius, it emerges, employed a more dynamic model of matter than current criticism. We are still, Harris argues, learning from the past.

Readers, Evidence, and Interdisciplinarity

Frances E. Dolan

At conferences and other academic gatherings, I often face a question that reveals just how uneasy many academics remain about interdisciplinary work: "Do you think of yourself as a literary critic or an historian?" My answer is simple: I don't think about this at all. What interests me about the question is the implied necessity of choosing. One can be a literary critic or an historian, but certainly not both. Working in the "both/and" space, it sometimes feels as if others are determined to conclude that what you accomplish is "neither/nor"—readings of texts are suggestive but underdeveloped; historical claims are insufficiently supported resulting in "historicizing" or "history lite," it is claimed, but not history. Perhaps because I often make gender a central category of analysis in my work, and women's studies has always been an interdisciplinary enterprise, I am more interested in the shared assumptions and methods shaping recent work on women and gender in early modern England than I am in whatever disciplinary distinctions divide the various people laboring in these fields.

The widely used method of examining most texts as, to some extent, stories—directed to a particular audience, indebted to particular traditions, and shaped by particular conventions—is resulting in a broader range of materials consulted, considerably more interesting readings of those materials, and messier but more productive conceptualizations of them. This interdisciplinary approach is certainly more interesting than the tired "prescription vs. practice" debate, in which we all admonished one another on how to read conduct books and sermons. It is now a truth universally acknowledged that while these texts offer insight into how people were supposed to (or were told to) act, they should not be taken as evidence of how they actually acted. Increasing attention to literacy and reading is complicating our understanding of how prescriptions operate in a culture. People interacted with what they read in erratic ways; they might resist or revise what they read or insert themselves into available narratives unpredictably. While prescription and practice should not be confused with one another, they are not wholly discreet either. Scholars are reading print and archival sources in relation to one another rather than viewing them as prescription on the one hand and practice on the other, or as the representational and the real. If many kinds of texts purport to tell stories, whether or not they present them as true, it is most useful to attend to the position of the storyteller, the resources he/she had available, the purpose behind the story, the venue and audience, rather than to waste time denoting some texts as literature and others as non-, extra-, or subliterary. Many scholars are finding that compelling cultural analyses require one to look outside the usual suspects that have been enshrined in anthologies of "literature" (even though these are themselves changing). As a consequence, genre is commanding renewed attention as a category of analysis, and its boundaries are being expanded to include the pamphlet, the trial account, or the sermon as well as the tragedy or the sonnet.[1]

Some of the most exciting work of rereading focuses on court records. For Natalie Davis, in her pioneering work, what it meant to argue that she had found fictions in the archives was that she had found evidence that "authors shape the events of a crime into a story," and that in this very shaping they created testimony that would strike their readers as "true"—true because it was recognizable and conventional. The law directed certain narratives: include this but not that, emphasize this and suppress that; a context of storytelling and listening shaped speakers' sense of what made for a good story. What would speakers' status and circumstances, audience, and venue bring to the shaping of testimony? Since evidence suggests that witches and vagrants shaped their testimony, and that servants angled their testimony to exonerate or incriminate an employer, it is ill-advised to assume that such shaping is too "sophisticated" for some speakers.[2] The line between shaping and lying was a difficult one to draw then; it continues to be a conundrum now. Our research puts us in the oddly uncomfortable position of legal personnel; like them, we assess these narratives, looking for just the right balance of the conventional and the particular/peculiar. But the "heads-up" effect of the odd detail is worth questioning. If listeners would find most plausible a story that was most conventional, can we simply just reverse that process, finding most plausible those stories that are least conventional? We must also scrutinize the significance of our own belief. What does it mean, for instance, when, in response to a man's statement, Miranda Chaytor says: "I believe him"?[3] Where does this certainty come from? What is it based on? How is it produced? What role should it play in our assessments of evidence?

Many have built on Davis's initial insight, extending and elaborating on it. Yet many who work on court records first acknowledge and then repress the complex mediations through which these records were composed. Chaytor explains that clerks "wrote at the plaintiffs' dictation, changing nothing and omitting nothing. Or so the internal evidence of these narratives suggests."[4] Garthine Walker offers a more detailed and, to me, convincing assessment of mediating factors: how deponents played to the legal definition of what constituted rape, and to an all male audience of legal officials; the complexities of memory and narration more generally. Yet she, too, concludes: "My own view is that depositions were likely to have been transcribed by clerks more or less verbatim."[5] So these texts are both mediated and accurate. How these scholars repress their awareness of mediation is especially striking in the decision both make to "return" depositions to the first-person singular. Erasing a disorienting distance in the language of the depositions themselves, both Chaytor and Walker insert an accessible, self-possessed person into the depositions, despite their claims to be analyzing narratives, not real people. This change makes the quoted texts much more engaging and compelling. The "I" here is an enabling and animating fiction, but it should be acknowledged that it is not a "return" to an origin but a creation. That is, both Chaytor and Walker create an " 'I' that speaks" and then analyze its operations.[6] Many scholars interested in the early modern period share this desire for an " 'I' that speaks"—one that speaks to us, although this desire is often muffled or repressed. Assessing and theorizing why we want this, what it will afford us if discovered or invented, is a project that can bring scholars together across disciplinary lines. Can the voice conferred on historical subjects speak across the gap of time? Why would one want to speak to the dead, as Stephen Greenblatt so famously claimed he longed to do? What is it that we hope they can tell us?

Many a grave gapes empty and tongueless. To borrow from Marvell, the grave's a fine and private place, but none I think do there expound upon their subjectivities. Many students of the early modern period are therefore reading the historical record for what is not there. Chaytor and Walker both show that, in depositions in rape cases, the experience of rape itself is missing; Laura Gowing argues that, while accounts of legitimate births describe labor and delivery, accounts of illegitimate births do not; Mary Beth Rose has assessed how many aristocratic women autobiographers omit their bodily histories, especially pregnancies and births, from their life stories.[7] Why is what we would think of as the heart of the matter—the bodily experience of pain—missing? More generally, in their history of *Women in Early Modern England*, Sara Mendelson and Patricia Crawford employ "techniques of reading against the grain, of asking where women are absent as well as present in the documents"; "we need to be sensitive to the silences in discourse as well as the stated words."[8] But what do we do with them once we notice them? As Margaret Ferguson has asked: "How does one theorize the gaps in one's evidence?"[9] My hope in this brief reflection is that we will theorize what we can find and what we cannot in as generous, interdisciplinary, and collaborative a way as possible.

Notes

1. See, for instance, Mario DiGangi's work on dramatic forms in *The Homoerotics of Early Modern Drama* (Cambridge: Cambridge University Press, 1997) or Marion Gibson's work on the witchcraft pamphlet as a genre in *Reading Witchcraft: Stories of Early English Witches* (New York and London: Routledge, 1999).

2. Natalie Zemon Davis, *Fiction in the Archives: Pardon Tales and Their Tellers in Sixteenth Century France* (Stanford, CA: Stanford University Press, 1987), 2; Jodi Mikalachki, "Women's Networks and the Female Vagrant: A Hard Case," in *Maids and Mistresses, Cousins and Queens: Women's Alliances in Early Modern England*, ed. Susan Frye and Karen Robertson (New York: Oxford University Press, 1999), 52–69.

3. Miranda Chaytor, "Husband(ry): Narratives of Rape in the Seventeenth Century," *Gender & History* 7, no. 3 (1995): 378–407, esp. 399.

4. Chaytor, "Husband(ry)," 381.

5. Garthine Walker, "Rereading Rape and Sexual Violence in Early Modern England," *Gender & History* 10, no. 1 (1998): 1–25, esp. 8.

6. Chaytor, "Husband(ry)," n. 1; Walker, "Rereading Rape," n. 4; Chaytor, 379; Walker, 19.

7. Laura Gowing,"Secret Births and Infanticide in Seventeenth-Century England," *Past & Present* 156 (August 1997): 87–115; Mary Beth Rose, "Gender, Genre, and History: Seventeenth-Century English Women and the Art of Autobiog-

raphy," in *Women in the Middle Ages and the Renaissance*, ed. Mary Beth Rose (Syracuse, NY: Syracuse University Press, 1985), 245–78.

8. Sara Mendelson and Patricia Crawford, *Women in Early Modern England* (Oxford: Clarendon Press, 1998), 9, 17.

9. Margaret W. Ferguson, "Moderation and Its Discontents: Recent Work on Renaissance Women," *Feminist Studies* 20, no. 2 (1994): 349–66, esp. 359.

Parliament and the Theater of State: The Construction of Texts

Chris R. Kyle

SEEKING TO RECONSTRUCT and understand the past through its documents has provided scholars in all disciplines with one of their most difficult tasks. The selection of texts made by the historian or literary critic informs the reader of the nature of the inquiry as well as providing the reviewer with an easy entrée to criticism and judgment. Shakespearean scholarship has long been concerned with the so-called bad quartos and, more recently, with the problematical constructs of representation and meaning influenced by theorists such as Foucault, Derrida, and Lacan. For political historians the problem is often the reliance on one type of document to the marginalization of others. Despite this, analysis of political texts is still, in most cases, a function of selection rather than reconstruction and representation. Parliamentary historians seeking to reconstruct the institution and workings of Parliament, especially its textual output, have tended to concentrate upon the problem of the reliability and accuracy of sources. But rather than placing value judgments upon the individual diaries, I want to ask: How were they written, and what was the culture that produced them? Thus, positing the question "What do MPs writing diaries tell us about early Stuart political culture?" allows us to ask "How does the construction of parliamentary texts affect our understanding of the institution?"

The printing of early-seventeenth-century parliamentary diaries has consumed veritable forests of paper in the twentieth century—seven large volumes comprises the output of the 1621 Parliament alone and more will be required when 1624 is published. The immediate impression of this decries both a revisionist understanding that Parliament decreased in importance—why otherwise would so many people bother to take notes? And that despite the contemporary commentators view that the proceedings of Parliament were *arcana sacra*, many MPs and peers spent their parliamentary time scribbling in books and on papers. The processes that they applied to these texts are difficult to discover even if we know the reasons for their construction.

Parliament, when in session, served as both the center and the physical fulcrum of notetaking in Westminster. St Stephen's Chapel, in which the House of Commons sat after 1547, was surrounded by institutions in which the writing of script formed an important part of their existence. The major central law courts—Common Pleas, King's Bench, Chancery, Wards, Star Chamber, and Requests—enveloped it while in Westminster Hall booksellers and hawkers plied their trade. Both legal education and the procedures of the courts relied upon writing down the words spoken in courts, either for a formal record or as part of the learning process. The legal institutions were themselves housed in small and open areas, often a single small room (Star Chamber, Requests), two chambers (Wards), or open wooden structures within Westminster Hall (Common Pleas, Chancery, King's Bench). Parliament was thus immersed in a space and a culture in which both formal record-keeping and informal scribbling were part of the everyday milieu. Proximally and functionally they occupied an overlapping space. Both the Lords and the Commons used the courts and other adjacent rooms as committee chambers and MPs and peers transited Westminster Hall and the court rooms to reach the Commons and the Lords. The relationship was symbiotic in more than one way—lawyers who were MPs plead cases in the Courts while Parliament was in session, and the cases were presided over by those judges who had been called as legal assistants in the Lords. Naturally, in the litigious society of early modern England, MPs, their families and servants held intimate if often unwanted knowledge of the surrounding legal processes.

Parliament had long functioned as a court in its own right with an official written record—the Parliament Roll. During the sixteenth and early seventeenth centuries the journals kept by its clerks (clerk of the Parliament in the Lords and underclerk in the Commons) became more formalized and part of the official record of the house. This was also reflected in the contiguous relationship between these officers of the house and those interested in the proceedings or procedures of Parliament. MPs copied speeches from the Commons Journal while the clerks occasionally relied on diarists and those who had spoken to fill in what they had missed. MPs took notes for a variety of reasons—some to provide their patrons in the Lords with information on the proceedings of the "other house"; some no doubt for circulation among family members and friends at home; and many for their own benefit—be it simply as a record of proceedings or for future reference. Trained in the art of rhetoric in grammar schools, MPs listened carefully and copied down the arguments as well as classical and biblical references of their fellow members. But Parliamentary diaries as a form of writing were no different from any other type of diary—some such as those of John Pym in the 1620s were neatly drawn into legible, seamless books while others were the hasty hurried notes of a member busy trying to scrawl down every word. These were often riddled with gaps where the author planned to fill in the names and speeches later but never did so. Some MPs started with full annotations and then tailed away as the length of the session and physical requirements wore down the writer. Members—John Hawarde is the obvious example—employed devices such as Law French and types of shorthand or abbreviations of common words to ease their task. Hasty scrawlings over the page, barely legible writing, and shorthand leaves the modern-day reader with the difficult task of reading the diaries as well as the impression of a court—the theater of state—in action.

This can further be illustrated by the amount of extant material. In 1621 over three thousand pages have been printed of diaries alone. Even leaving aside other forms of material relating to Parliament (newsletters, separates, drafts of legislation, petitions), some of which were written and copied for sale, the surviving numbers of diaries gives rise to a view of the Commons awash in a sea of papers and scribbling MPs. Many of the diaries were kept in small notebooks, which seem to have been purchased just for that purpose, although some were drafted on individual sheets of paper and bound together afterwards. The way in which the diarists took notes varied from those who scribbled comments over parliamentary documents such as breviates of acts, petitions, or separates to those who attempted to record diligently every word. Some annotations were made in pencil, including more than the odd doodle or caricature during tedious speeches, while others used pen and ink. The latter form of writing must have been a very public and possibly cumbersome activity. Even the small writing cases of the seventeenth century needed to hold the usual implements—pen, ink, knives for sharpening quills, and sand for erasing or blotting. The clerks of the Parliament had their own tables to write upon, but MPs would have been balancing their writing material on their knees while sitting on cramped benches. The task was made more difficult as this was theater in which the MPs were participants/actors as well as the audience. They came and went from the chamber, interjected in speeches, talked to each other, and occasionally yelled and hawked at other speakers. Throughout the 1620s, to this noise and confusion was added the sound of over a dozen pens scratching on paper as the clerks and members took notes. This effect of sound and movement added a dimension to the chamber that is far removed from static representations that have come down to us today through woodcuts and other images of "Parliament at Work."

Parliament and Westminster Hall were public theaters whose audiences paid admission only for state trials such as that of the Gunpowder Plotters. At other times they were a view of a political world and legal culture in which the individual and the state were on display. The public nature of the opening procession to Parliament and the image of the monarch gave way only to a different form of public activity: that of speeches, debate, argument, the coming and going of the principal actors and the walk-on parts of the remainder of the cast—actors, actresses, and animals (in 1605 a mouse-colored spaniel wandered into the House). Those fulfilling the minor roles included legal counsel, witnesses called to attend (including women), and other interested spectators. The view the audience and participants had was of a scribal culture—a political society immersed in recording its activities in a variety of ways for both public and private consumption. This view can be reinforced by the intimate size of the chamber. Measuring a tiny sixty feet by thirty-two feet, it was possible to see and hear much of the proceedings of the Commons. Unless specifically ordered closed, the door of the Chapel remained open and thus the activity able to be observed by the public. The writing culture was also a visible presence in the lobby outside the chamber to which the public had access. Times, places, and lists of committee members were tacked to a post, and the assistant of the clerk of the Commons often sat there, perhaps recording the proceedings when he was able to hear, more often serving as a scrivener for those who wanted copies of documents or arranging for their copying elsewhere.

Viewing Parliament through the eyes of the construction of texts produced in it allows us to consider a more a sophisticated representation of the institution. It offers for the viewing audience a picture of MPs actively engaged in the work of the nation, aware of their responsibilities and partaking in them. It also illustrates the function of Parliament as a court, observing scribal rituals that were mimicked in the adjacent courts. It challenges a revisionist reliance on what documents say, by seeing political material culture as part of a wider sociology of early modern texts, important not only for their content but also their production. With this approach the texts can be viewed as part of a writing culture of Parliament—one witnessed by participants and spectators rather than as simply part of an isolated and institutionalized body where the hands are stylistically separated from the rest. For those innumerable MPs engaged in the practices of writing, it was an activity that provided them with an intimate physical connection to the debates as an aide memoire, as scribes for their patrons and as information gatherers. It was an activity that bespoke the implicit and explicit importance of the events taking place inside the chamber. Those who stood and watched at the door or were in the environs of the Palace of Westminster saw "their representatives" carrying writing boxes to and from the chamber, perhaps purchasing writing materials from stalls in Westminster Hall, and copying down the words spoken in the political nation. They could not fail to understand that this political society was not a dead institution, marginalized by the absolutist nonparliamentary tendencies of James and Charles, but a vibrant and living political body voraciously consuming paper, ink, and pens in the pursuit of legislation, the easing of public grievances, and perhaps, even on occasion, justice.

Afterlife

CRYSTAL BARTOLOVICH

ASKED TO COMMENT on how literary critics might best "use history" or "think historically" today, I will here attempt to illustrate a response to these questions by way of an engagement with a much-discussed and familiar text that is widely perceived to be ahistorical in its claims. Ben Jonson's commendatory verse for the First Folio, "To the Memory of My Beloved, The Author, Mr William Shakespeare, And What he Hath Left Us," has been rebuked frequently in recent years for its ostensibly "humanist assumptions" about the (geographical and historical) transcendence of great literary themes and values. Many critics have pointed out the investment in "afterlife" of Jonson's poem in lines such as "[Thou] art alive still while thy book doth live," or "He [Shakespeare] was not of an age, but for all time!" and argued that such claims are inherently ahistoricizing and otherwise suspect. As one recent essay muses, surveying the criticism: "it is difficult to think of any famous critical pronouncement which is less fashionable." One critic has even wittily reversed the emphasis of Jonson's famous line so that it reads: "Not for all time, but for an age," a quip much-repeated in subsequent commentary on the poem. While these recent discussions have provided a needed corrective to ahistorical textualist readings, I want to insist nevertheless that much of the critique is misplaced, and that Jonson's gesture is not only understandable in its originary context, but actually commendable. Through this argument, I hope to show the importance of carefully situating poetry simultaneously in its moments of writing *and* reading, including—irreducibly—the living critic's moment; a *historical* approach as I enact it here, then, recognizes that not only literature but also the critic inhabits time.

While this is not an especially surprising position for a critic to take today, it is going rather against the grain to claim that Jonson's poem seems to suggest such a position as well. However, "To the Memory of My Beloved" exhibits the keenest possible awareness of changing valuations of poetry over time and, thus, the importance of ongoing critical commentary (such as Jonson's own) to the endurance of literature. This is not, I would suggest, the strategy of a critic who believes in timeless and transcendent poetry but one who, to the contrary, understands that poets are "made, as well as born"—and made, in part, by how they are *read*. While the poem is adamant, to be sure, that Shakespeare's work is "*not* of an age" as the current criticism emphasizes, it is equally insistent that this continuous timeliness (not timelessness) won't happen all on its own, since the past is dependent on successive readings to keep it alive:

> Thou art a monument without a tomb,
> And art alive still while thy book doth live,
> *And* we have wits to read, and praise to give.
> (emphasis added)

The afterlife of poetry, then, is not a function of the "book" alone but of its readers as well.

This insistence on a collective responsibility for Shakespeare's preservation at first seems to contradict the opening sixteen lines of the poem where—in typical Jonsonian fashion—the persona utterly rejects most people as proper readers of the Shakespearean text, and actually appears to insist that Shakespeare does not "need" collective approbation at all. The difficulty is resolved only when we realize Jonson is not referencing a synchronic readership in his "we" who "have wits to read," but a diachronic one. The opening lines of the poem establish (as does Jonson's criticism more generally) that there are very few proper readers, but that proper reading is nonetheless crucially important to the preservation of a text. While this is an elitist view, it is certainly not necessarily an ahistorical one. Jonson's own "judgement," he emphasizes, is not merely "of years" to be sure, but this does not mean that it is time*less*. Rather, his text refuses to restrict itself to his present (and situating Shakespeare only among his coevals) because it aspires to continue to accompany the Shakespearean text—collected as it is with it—to promote it to potentially doubting future readers. As the aggression of images such as the Shakespearean "issue" (the plays) rising up to "shake . . . a lance . . . at ignorance" suggests, Jonson foresees an ongoing struggle against "ignorance," a quite historicized perspective. There is no reason to assume from the poem that it is even always the same ignorance and insufficiency that the text will meet as it wends its way through time.

Jonson is surely aware after all that to make grandiose claims for Shakespeare's stature—against prevailing global politics of literary value that took no account of Shakespeare whatsoever—he actively asserts the changing fortunes of literary figures in time rather than claiming immortality as an absolute. He knows full well that without a change in prevailing norms, there can be no place for Shakespeare to endure. The most emphatic critical claim in Jonson's poem, thus, is his announcement that Shakespeare has put the ancients in their place, which is to say the land of the dead, and thus that English subordination to the ancients—as well as to the continental writers who claimed closer ties and affinity to their legacy—comes to an end in him. Jonson's persona first commands Shakespeare to "rise" then "call[s] forth . . . to life again" his ("dead") classical rivals from "insolent Greece or Haughty Rome," who are shown to be no competitors after all:

> The merry Greek, tart Aristophanes,
> Neat Terence, witty Plautus, *now* not please,
> But *antiquated* and *deserted* lie
> As they were not of nature's family.
>
> (emphasis added)

Elsewhere these lines might easily be read as Jonsonian assessment of the general bad taste of the "age" into which he (and Shakespeare) had the misfortune of being born. In this poem, however, they have a specific role to play in the assertion of England's international prominence through Shakespeare's accomplishments: "Triumph, my Britain, thou hast one to show / To whom all scenes of Europe homage owe." The subtext of these lines is not only an attempt at reversal of the lack of cultural prestige England suffered in relation to the continent—manifestly the case—but also an attempt to assert that it is the critic who "call[s] forth . . . to life again" and who can, conversely, pronounce a poet dead. To insert Shakespeare into the "scenes of Europe," Jonson imagines killing off the tradition, which has denied or derided English contributions to it. Jonson's much-critiqued "universalism" must be read in this context to be fully understood.

Although Jonson's poem now reads like a textbook case of Anglocentrism at its worst, it is important to remember how truly preposterous his words would have appeared in the international context of 1623. That claims such as Jonson's were not immediately successful in raising Shakespeare's stature on the continent (much less beyond it) is evident from the ignorance of, or deeply ambivalent attitude toward, Shakespeare outside of England well into the latter half of the eighteenth century. Voltaire famously wonders, for example, how Samuel Johnson could have the audacity to defend Shakespeare's considerable weaknesses—from his point of view—against the critique of foreign detractors. He goes on, reluctantly, to proclaim Shakespeare a "genius," but he also makes it clear that he understands why "Italians, Frenchmen, men of letters from all countries who have not lived for a time in England [as Voltaire himself had], take him only as a kind of marketplace dramatist . . . as a farceur many notches below Harlequin, as the most miserable clown who ever amused the populace." Voltaire's observation is interesting because it indicates he is willing to entertain the possibility that English culture in its particularity—however odd it may appear to outsiders—might rise to universality ("truth, nature herself speak their own language here") if understood—at least partly—on its own terms (hence his reference to the need to live in England "for at time"). Before Voltaire's moment, such a position does not appear to have been thinkable in any sustained or influential way on the continent. Indeed, earlier, the contempt was even greater, because it extended to the whole language of English, and thus there was no continental opinion of Shakespeare to speak of at all. Hence a great deal of ink is spilt through the sixteenth and seventeenth centuries in England—Jonson's poem prominently included—attempting to assert "The Excellency of English," in Richard Carew's words—in its *particularity*—against tidal waves of European indifference and disdain, and substantial local insecurity and doubt as well.

Although Voltaire does not appear to have read Jonson's poem, it is very much to future critics like him that the poem seems to make an appeal. Jonson Anglicizes "Nature," the great arbiter of the "universal"—rendering England not just an exemplar but *the* exemplar of it. She is described as being delighted "to wear the dressing of Shakespeare's lines" at a time in which costume (or lack thereof)—as the decorative borders of countless period maps illustrate—was widely viewed as one of the principle markers of cultural difference. He even claims exclusivity: "Since [Shakespeare] she [Nature] *will* vouchsafe no other wit." With such lines Jonson attempts to keep at bay future potential competitors to Shakespeare (as Jonson's use of future tense "will" here implies) not only in hopes of rendering the monopoly of the continent on cultural authority defunct but of setting English claims to prestige on less easily overturned foundations than the classical poets, who have just been cast out of "nature's family" by Jonson. This is not, however, we must recall, the haughty gesture of a confident, self-assured world power, but the defiant assertion of a subaltern nation.

Indeed, given the context in which Jonson wrote, it seems to me that good radical critics should be applauding him for defending local cultural value against the oppressive weight of tradition and the global balance of power, at a time in which English was not yet what it would become. Perhaps the greatest anachronism of much criticism of Jonson's poem today is treating a statement of the 1600s as if it already carried the force of a similar statement made in the 1800s. By charging Jonson's poem with "universalist" offenses, current critics are at fault in two respects it seems to me: firstly, in assuming a continuity in the force of Jonson's words, and, secondly, in assuming that "universalism" must—however theorized—be a bad thing. At a moment in which even critics as fiercely patriotic as Francis Meres cannot bring himself to make so preposterous a claim as that English can be listed among the "famous and chief languages of the world," Jonson defiantly says what Meres cannot. By inserting Shakespeare, with his "small Latin and less Greek," in Nature's place, Jonson renders particular English *universal*. As Slavoj Žižek has recently argued, the despised, excluded, and marginalized must always make precisely such a gesture against the pretension of the guardians of a (false) universal that would exclude them. From this perspective it is not a crime in 1623 to propose English language and culture—even via Shakespeare—against overwhelming global counterforce as universal. The crime, rather, is that once Britain's "triumph" was material rather than rhetorical, its elites came to believe that the universal ended in them rather than being an ongoing project. If we remember the global struggle for cultural recognition out of which Jonson's poem emerges rather than just the words, we can, however, reclaim the possibility that the universal remains an incompleted project. As English once more becomes a site in which global cultural prestige is worked out, it is crucial for us to hear this part of the poem, as well as critique of universalism that comes so easily to current critics.

Around the globe, after all, those who have inhabited subalternized nations are not so willing to give up the concept of the universal—albeit recognizing at the same time that it must be a differently conceived "universal" than the Eurocentric tool that has predominated in the history of modern imperialism. Samir Amin, for example, has advocated for some time a "true universalism," and Gayatri Spivak has emphasized the importance of a project to "bring humanism [attention to the "ways human beings are similar"] and difference together" in the current quest for global social justice. Whatever such a quest is called, however, the point is that much attention has been returned recently to the once thoroughly disparaged concept of "universalism," though this shift has not been reflected in the criticism of Jonson's poem. The absence of any recognition of the unrealized utopian possibilities of "To the Memory of My Beloved" is no mere problem of "keeping up" with theory, however, but rather of failing to situate the poem in a current situation that it still speaks to as a living poem: English as a contested site.

Since the end of World War II, with the onset of decolonization and the speed up of globalization, "English" has been proliferating rapidly as a "world language"—and as a site of struggle. In this context, questions and concerns multiply: to what extent (and how) could English ever be a "common language"? How are hierarchies of linguistic prestige and dispersion related to political, economic, and military power? I do not raise these questions to answer them here, but in order to insert Jonson's poem into a living problematic—the work of a properly historical criticism in the materialist sense of the term. Jonson's poem, when situated in "its" originary moment, a time in which English was, as John Florio put it, "worth nothing past Dover," can be seen as performing a crucial gesture of cultural assertion—a refusal to be excluded from the universal. Understood thus, its most compelling afterlife would be to direct us to listen for the voices that make such claims now—within or even against the English language that Jonson worked so hard to promote. Both "English" and the universal, his poem emphasizes, are in process. Lest we contribute to the reification of either, a "historical" criticism must be equally willing to understand both the irreducibility of process, and that metropolitan voices are certainly not the only—or even the primary—ones that need be heard on the subject of the politics of language and culture, any more than in Jonson's day the continental arbiters of taste were. Hence, I close (or rather open out) with a voice other than my own, Gayatri Spivak's, as she complains: "There are countless languages in which women all over the world have grown up and been female or feminist, and yet the languages we keep on learning are the powerful European ones, sometimes the powerful Asian ones, least often the African ones." Jonson's poem asserted that the particularity of the "least" of his day be recognized in the "universal"; I have tried to make this part of the poem once again audible, since we need to do the same if, as Spivak continues, we are not to misunderstand "solidarity" by discovering it always—and only—in English.

The Promise of History

John Parker

Literary critics make their own history, but they do not make it just as they please. The less pleasing the literature's historical context (it used to be), the more prestigious the scholar. One knew genuine erudition by his unflagging patience, his technical expertise, the endless reserve of masochism that kept him wheezing in the stacks till after dark, red-eyed from book-dust. History for literary critics has always been what hurts, penance for staking their lives on a frivolous pasttime in defiance of the factual. Over the last century Renaissance studies has swung from penitent to defiant and back again, a pendulum in step with the literature's own facticity and its implicit claim, as fiction, to rise above mere facts. An old teacher of mine once spoke derisively of an eminent, older-school Shakespearean, his *Doktorvater* of years before, who had a personal key to Widener and every detail of Shakespeare's theater committed to memory: "What did he know about poetry? Nothing." That is the voice of the New Criticism, and only as a reaction against it, among those of us who never really grasped the agony of Old Historicism, could historicism become at this late date again fashionable.

The New varieties differ from the Old in the following realization: literature's context obeys no clear boundaries and includes, along with all the exotic anecdotes culled from obscure sources, the present. This strikes me as a tremendous advance, but its disadvantages are many. Faced with a literary form or text whose history was not forthcoming from immediate appearances, historicists used to resort in the main to scansion, philology, and bibliography. They could establish if nothing else authenticity, provenance, dates. Their throwbacks still produce indispensable apparati. Today's more up-to-date practitioner like myself, steeped in theory rather than paleography and falling at random on a tract from the *Short-*

Title Catalogue, resorts to "interrogation." Does the frequency of this term in certain quarters not suggest a secret nostalgia for the Elizabethan police state? The Jamesonian impulse to establish through historicism some solidarity with the past despite its resistance succeeds too often as an academic recapitulation of the tactics of Francis Walsingham. If only we could *interrogate* whatever has lured us into this livelihood—the forced march through reams of tedious, non-, or sub-literary documents in search of literature's "complicity" when the literature itself refuses to confess—we might in a single act of punishment both spare ourselves the tedium of the search and bring those responsible for it to a final account. O for the days that Foucault anatomized, when the author was whomever the authorities chose to torture! Historicists have always been masochists, good old English empiricists. Sadists have since joined the ranks with the blessing of the French.

What unites historicisms old and new is a strong disinclination to inquire very far into aesthetics, that strange membrane separating literature from the materials that surround it, from the sea of sermons and tax rolls and official communiqués between heads-of-state, a membrane thin and porous like a cell wall but no less essential. Frankly I do not know what literature is, but I notice we tend to bestow the title on the kind of document whose relation to the facts of history traditional historians are trained to doubt. Basically historical, literary texts on their own seem somehow incapable of transmitting their basis reliably—otherwise who would need historicism? Not without enormous and almost incalculable mediation does literature reflect what is. Among the various mediating factors perhaps the most fundamental to the aesthetic domain is the constant interference of what is not. Theorists have a lot of useful names for this type of confusion: ideology, fantasy, repression. A preferable, more inclusive term for the early modern period might be *religion,* to which a number of critics have recently turned their attention in hope of locating Renaissance literature's historical bias. Deborah Shuger makes the point, however, bucking the dominant trend, that the discourses grouped under this heading are not simply allegories for the coded depiction of existing social forces; they concern also God and the soul. This is true, granted the further provision that for all anybody knows, God and the soul do not exist: "Nothing in the world appears more deceptive than the Word of God and faith, nothing more empty than hope in the promise. In short, nothing seems to be more nothing than God Himself." *Also sprach Luther*. Even highly profane forms could flourish in proximity to such a religion, whose negativity vis-à-vis the real world they encoded formally, most of all when the art form was itself the target of religious antipathy, as with the drama. It takes a consummate antihistoricist like Harold Bloom to puzzle over the persistence in Shakespeare of the word *nothing*, as though from the airy zeros of the poet's brain to the great wooden O there were perhaps some evidence of nihilism in the heart of humanity's gentle "inventor." But Shakespeare's nothingness and Bloom's bardolatry together mark the failure of even the period's most secular genre to detach itself entirely from devotion. The God of the mysteries likewise began *ex nihilo*.

And to nothingness he returned the world at cycle's end in fulfillment of the final promise. Because of its apparent theological cast, the nineteenth-century historicist concern with the apocalyptic end of history has not enjoyed the same veneration in literary studies as putatively secular issues. Theology seems most absurd where we approximate its catastrophic fulfillment. At one time Armageddon was the fantastic concoction of a superstitious people, pure mythology. It took hundreds of years of skeptical enlightenment to make the myth a likely possibility, but with the cleverness that is our lone divine spark, somehow we engineered it. One should bear in mind how much the historicist emphasis on the radical alterity of previous cultural forms is merely the conviction that things must change, or cease. To view the past as entirely different, though still containing a germ of ourselves, is secretly to hope that the future will be more than extinction while in it the present will have nonetheless expired. This hope current historicism attributes to a text's political or theological content when in fact it springs most powerfully from form. "*It is* radiates wordlessly from artworks, against the foil that *it*—the unredeemable grammatical subject—*is not*," Adorno writes. "It can be referred demonstratively to nothing in the world that already exists. In the utopia of its form, art bends under the burdensome weight of the empirically given, from which, as art, it steps away." Such utopias are as empty as hope in the Promise, but no one would say religion lacks power for being a fraud, and neither does art. The social transformations promised by it, however—occasion for much laborious historicist inquiry under the rubric of "subversion"—are supremely difficult to gauge owing to the simultaneity of art's insistence on change and its own aloofness from the mechanisms that would bring change about. When less aloof, art's insistence devolves into the hectoring clamor of a sermon, the threat of a royal proclamation, the dumb clarity of a sales receipt. It is a small, as-yet ineffectual miracle that those drawn to literature for their lives' work could ever be prompted by the beauty of an inscrutable literary artifact to turn to such detritus as though it were teeming with literary significance. History is garbage. We have been drawn into the desert of its compulsions by a mirage: freedom from all compulsion, which is the apparition of the aesthetic.

Atomic Shakespeare

Jonathan Gil Harris

Fredric Jameson's well-known injunction, "Always historicize!," has long been the shibboleth of materialist literary critics. These days, however, the slogan is increasingly accompanied by calls to get "material" in a new way—by embracing physical objects as the stuff of history.[1] The current vogue for so-called "material culture" represents the culmination of historicism's attempts to break free from formalism's prison-house of language: for the new scholars of the object, figures of speech tend to be shunned as somehow less "material," and hence less "historical," than (say) figures of clay. Against this critical tide, however, we might do well to remember Barthes's famous apothegm: "a little formalism turns one away from history, but . . . a lot brings one back to it."[2] Barthes's point is illustrated particularly well by Jameson's impressive body of work from the 1970s, whose abiding preoccupation is the historicity, and materiality, of literary form.[3] In a similar vein, I'd like to think briefly about how Shakespeare engages an antique tradition of materialist philosophy so as to underscore history's double helix of matter and form—a double helix that entails both the materiality of figures and, just as importantly, the figurality of matter.

For the pre-Socratic philosophers Leucippus, Democritus, and Epicurus, the universe was composed of tiny particles, which they named "atoms" (the Greek term for "indivisible"). They also called these particles "forms" and "figures"; yet they never regarded the atom as just an ideal, unchanging form in the later Platonic or Aristotelian sense. This much is clear from the Roman poet Lucretius's homage to and adaptation of Epicurus in his extraordinary six-volume poem *De Rerum Natura*. The first two books of the poem elaborate Lucretius's version of atomic theory, which is fundamentally grounded in the principle of change. Here he presents atoms as minute particles in perpetual motion, maneuvering and colliding like specks in a beam of sunlight.[4] With his emphasis on motion, Lucretius invites a very different understanding of materialism from that which we find in much recent scholarship on "material culture." Where the latter has tended to fasten onto physical things as synecdoches for synchronically conceived historical "moments," Lucretius understands atoms diachronically, in terms of their movement through space and time. To this extent, Lucretius's atoms exemplify Aristotle's—and Marx's—conception of matter as potentiality (*dynameos*), presuming and inducing a future.[5]

During the middle ages, Lucretius disappeared beneath a veil of almost total obscurity; *De Rerum Natura* survived into the Renaissance in only one manuscript version, which lay forgotten in an Italian library before its rediscovery in the fifteenth century. The poem wasn't translated into English until the mid-seventeenth century—and then only begrudgingly by Lucy Hutchinson, who was appalled by its atheism. By then, however, Lucretius was already well known to English writers.[6] Ben Jonson owned, and heavily marked up, a Dutch edition of *De Rerum Natura*; Shakespeare had access to Lucretius through Montaigne, who quoted the Roman poet copiously in his essays. English writers may have absorbed Lucretian ideas also from the work of Girolamo Fracastoro, the Veronese physician who proposed that disease was not a humoral state but a migratory *semina* or seed that entered the body through its orifices. Whether or not Shakespeare was directly acquainted with the latter theory, Fracastoro's as well as Montaigne's adaptation of Lucretian philosophy resonates with a noteworthy materialist strand in his plays.

Shakespeare never uses the term "atom." But he does use its close derivative, "atomy," on four occasions.[7] He (mis)uses it as a synonym for "anatomy" in *2 Henry IV* (5.4.33); but in *As You Like It*, he twice employs it in its more traditional philosophical guise as a figure for irreducible smallness. Celia remarks that "it is as easy to count atomies as to resolve the propositions of a lover" (3.2.230–31), and Phebe notes that "eyes . . . are the frail'st and softest things, / Who shut their coward gates on atomies" (3.5.12–13). Phebe's remark hints at the materialist dimension of Lucretian atoms; they are not simply small but also in perpetual motion, producing friction in eyes. This motile, pathological property is yet more evident in *Romeo and Juliet*'s sole reference to atoms. Mercutio's famous speech about Queen Mab takes wing with the following powerful image:

> She is the fairies' midwife, and she comes
> In shape no bigger than an agate stone
> On the forefinger of an alderman,
> Drawn with a team of little atomi
> Over men's noses as they lie asleep.
>
> (1.4.54–58)

Prominent in Mercutio's description of Mab and her "atomi" is their alacrity of movement. Later in this speech, Mercutio again registers this dynamic property in pathological terms that hint at Fracastoro's understanding of disease: as a result of her peregrinations, he exclaims, "the angry Mab with blisters plagues" the lips of ladies (1.4.75).

But there is a further, crucial dimension to Shakespeare's version of Lucretian materialism. It's important to remember that Mercutio's fantasy of atomi in motion *is* a fantasy, a figment of his fevered imagination: "Thou talk'st of nothing" (1.4.96), Romeo tells him. This quip contains a bawdy quibble, of course: the sexualized "nothing" of women serves as a misogynist figure for the insubstantiality of matter, an association that also pervades *Hamlet*.[8] In the process, however, Romeo's quip foregrounds the sheer *figurality* of matter. Indeed, figurality pervades Mercutio's speech: for all the mercurial materiality of his vision, he notably ensnares Mab in the formal freeze-frame of simile ("in shape no bigger than an agate stone / On the forefinger of an alderman"). This apprehension of dynamic matter in figural or formal terms is hardly Shakespeare's innovation. The pre-Socratics did not regard atoms as the positive entities that they later became for nineteenth-century physicists; Epicurus called atoms "figures," after all. The figurality of pre-Socratic atoms also struck Montaigne, who wrote that "I cannot really convince myself that Epicurus, Plato and Pythagoras genuinely wanted us to accept their Atoms, Ideas and Numbers as valid currency.... Each of these great figures strove to bring some image of light into the dark ignorance of the world ... '*unicuique ista pro ingenio finguntur, non ex scientiae vi*' " [such theories are fictions, produced not from solid knowledge but from individual wits].[9]

How are Shakespeare's atoms useful for thinking about history? For one, they can remind us of a dynamic, diachronic dimension of materiality that is often lacking in recent work on "material culture" (which, given the synchronic bias of its investment in physical objects, is ironically closer to what Aristotle would have regarded as "formal culture"!). This dimension is a recurrent theme in Shakespeare; think of Ulysses' remark to Ajax that "things in motion sooner catch the eye / Than what stirs not" (*Troilus and Cressida*, 3.3.183–84). Interestingly, "things in motion" is also the phrase used by anthropologist Arjun Appadurai to designate what he regards as the proper "object" of object studies—that is, the social lives of things through space and time.[10] But Shakespeare's "things in motion" do far more than proleptically ventriloquize Appadurai's anthropology. What is most striking about Mercutio's fantasy of Mab and her migratory atomi, I have suggested, is the attention it draws to the factitiousness of narrating motion and, hence, of narrating history. To become intelligible, materiality—just like the Epicurean atom—cannot escape the idealizations of the figure. Mab and her team of atomi are thus split between the diachronic and the synchronic, between the material and the figural. Shakespearean atomism is most interesting, perhaps, inasmuch as it rhetorically splits the atom three centuries before the fact. Yet this split is equally a splicing. Shakespearean atomism, after all, recognizes what recent object criticism has stealthily worked to efface—the double helix of matter and form that is the very condition of history.

Notes

1. Fredric Jameson, *The Political Unconscious: Narrative as a Socially Symbolic Act* (Ithaca: Cornell University Press, 1981), 9. For examples of the new object criticism in Renaissance studies, see Margreta de Grazia, Maureen Quilligan, and Peter Stallybrass (eds.), *Subject and Object in Renaissance Culture* (Cambridge: Cambridge University Press, 1996); Lisa Jardine, *Worldly Goods: A New History of the Renaissance* (New York: Nan A. Talese, 1996); and section one, "Materials," of Patricia Fumerton and Simon Hunt (eds.), *Renaissance Culture and the Everyday* (Philadelphia: University of Pennsylvania Press, 1999).

2. Roland Barthes, *Mythologies*, transl. Annette Lavers (London: Paladin, 1973), 112.

3. For Jameson's groundbreaking work on literary form and history, see *Marxism and Form: Twentieth-Century Dialectical Theories of Literature* (Princeton: Princeton University Press, 1971) and *The Prison-House of Language: A Critical Account of Structuralism and Russian Formalism* (Princeton: Princeton University Press, 1972).

4. Lucretius, *De Rerum Natura*, 6 vols., ed. M. F. Smith (Cambridge: Harvard University Press), 2.114.

5. Aristotle, "De Anima," *The Basic Works of Aristotle*, trans. Richard McKeon (New York: Random House, 1941), vol. 2, 555; Karl Marx, "Theses on Feuerbach,"

in *Writings of the Young Karl Marx on Philosophy and Society*, trans. Lloyd D. Easton and Kurt H. Guddat (New York: Doubleday, 1967), 400. I have discussed the "material" of "material culture" elsewhere; see Jonathan Gil Harris, "The New New Historicism's Wunderkammer of Objects," *European Journal of English Studies* 4, no. 3 (2000): 111–23; and "Shakespeare's Hair: Staging the Object of Material Culture," *Shakespeare Quarterly* 52, no. 4 (2001): 479–91.

6. On the Renaissance afterlife of Lucretian materialism, see Jacques Lezra, *Unspeakable Subjects: The Genealogy of the Event in Early Modern Europe* (Stanford, CA: Stanford University Press, 1997).

7. All references to Shakespeare's works are to G. Blakemore Evans, et al. (eds.), *The Riverside Shakespeare*, 2nd ed. (Boston: Houghton Mifflin, 1997).

8. See Margaret W. Ferguson, "Hamlet: Letters and Spirits," in Geoffrey Hartman and Patricia Parker (eds.), *Shakespeare and the Question of Theory* (London and New York: Methuen, 1985), 292–309.

9. Michel de Montaigne, "An Apology for Raymond Sebond," in *The Complete Essays*, trans. M. A. Screech (Harmondsworth: Penguin, 1993), 571.

10. Arjun Appadurai, "Introduction: Commodities and the Politics of Value," in Appadurai (ed.), *The Social Life of Things: Commodities in Cultural Perspective* (Cambridge: Cambridge University Press, 1986), 3–63.

SYMPOSIUM
"Mere Archaeology": Theater History Updates

Introduction

S. P. Cerasano

E. K. CHAMBERS'S MONUMENTAL study, *The Elizabethan Stage* (1923), and G. E. Bentley's (equally monumental) sequel, *The Jacobean and Caroline Stage* (1941–68), set a precedent for mapping the early English theater; but Chambers's approach was not that which was commonly thought of as a "history of theater" at the time that his monument was published. Instead, when Chambers began *The Elizabethan Stage* he purposely set out to write something very different from a history of dramatic literature. Specifically, he decided to concentrate upon the diverse conditions that shaped the production of the drama and the personalities who surrounded that enterprise, using literary evidence only "as documents helping to throw light upon the history of the institution which produced them" (*ES*, 1.1.viii). In preparing their monuments, both Chambers and Bentley addressed many of the same areas of inquiry, organizing their evidence topically in order to investigate issues relating to players and playing companies, playhouse construction and theater economics, staging methods, censorship, and the politics of control. In addition, Chambers introduced his study with a thorough discussion of the court during the reigns of Elizabeth I and King James, highlighting the workings of the royal household and the Revels Office. To date, Chambers's and Bentley's monuments remain more comprehensive than any other account of the theater. Yet Chambers was extremely modest in his claims. In the preface to *The Elizabethan Stage* he characterized much of the content of his volumes as "mere archaeology" (1.1.vii). Nevertheless, it is the careful parsing of documentary evidence that remains not only the major interest but the major strength of contemporary revisionist historians.

Throughout the years many scholars have supplemented the vast storehouse of Chambers's enterprise. The many "Collections" volumes published by the Malone Society reproduced some of the

Lord Chamberlain's records and the Jacobean and Caroline Revels accounts. They probed records relating to the Blackfriars and records of the Inns of Court. One "collection" gathered together the patents for playing companies, while another presented material from the City of London archives, documents from the "remembrancia" and pageants prepared for various lords mayor. While a few of the "Collections" volumes supplemented *The Elizabethan Stage* simply by virtue of the fact that they followed Chambers's tomes into print, in fact all of the "Collections" series is supplementary in another sense: their purpose was to provide transcriptions of original source materials that could be consulted alongside histories such as Chambers's.

Moreover, even today many individual treatments of playhouses, companies, players, and theater owners are thoroughly grounded in documentary scholarship. For instance, Herbert Berry's *The Boar's Head Playhouse* (1986) or William Ingram's *A London Life in the Brazen Age* (1978) both fall well within the "Chambers tradition," as do many other studies (too numerous to mention here) that investigate particular aspects of the theater. In addition, during the past thirty years scholars have returned to large-scale projects that employ Chambers's methods. To cite an obvious example, the editors of the Records of Early English Drama project have been working through documents in every county in England to locate and present material that might help to reshape the history of drama and entertainment, more generally speaking. The series of their publications already includes records from York, Coventry, Cambridge, Bristol, Hereford, Worcester, and Sussex, with many more volumes in various stages of preparation.

Nor have scholars stopped here. Quite recently, Glynne Wickham, Herbert Berry, and William Ingram have underscored the importance of scrutinizing archival evidence by publishing *English Professional Theater, 1530–1660* (2001), their contribution to a series undertaken by Cambridge University Press, entitled "Theatre in Europe: A Documentary History." Despite the volume's hefty seven hundred pages, the editors sound apologetic in their introduction: so many documents relating to the professional stage in England have survived that they were faced at the outset with having to decide whether the space allotted would or would not permit them to include even a fraction of the extant material (7-8.) Consequently, the editors of *English Professional Theatre, 1530–1660* have concentrated their efforts on three fundamental areas: players and playing, playhouses (1560–1660), and documents of control (1530–1660). With limited introductory essays and few annotations, the archival material is preeminent in this collection.

The authors who contributed the nine essays that follow in this volume of *Shakespeare Studies* were each asked to write brief updates that would demonstrate, either by example or by implication, the many ways in which theater history continues to be rewritten. Beyond this general charge no other promptings were given. Yet, interestingly, each author returned to the Chambers-Bentley model in some way, either by using their broad assertions as a backdrop against which to examine their own evidence and observations; or alternately by attempting, like Chambers and Bentley, to build more general claims from specifics culled from archival sources. Although most scholars would agree that the infrastructure provided by Chambers and Bentley remains sound, happily there are many related structures to be built. In this, theater history remains vital, delivering fresh insights and information. The essays included here help to demonstrate, in a limited but fundamental way, how incredibly much remains open to investigation.

For obvious reasons theater historians are quick to class themselves as "archival positivists"; but despite their time in the archives locating new evidence, or reexamining known evidence, the investigation is far from solitary. In fact, few uninitiated readers probably comprehend—without reviewing the last century's worth of background scholarship—how absolutely this research reflects the sort of concentric interrelations that grow out of many years of ongoing conversation and debate. This is so much the case that the essays represented here seem to share interests, even as they are framed around radically different topics. Although the subjects of their research are unique, the scholarly interests exemplified in them continually overlap. Generally defined, these interests center on "origins," the processes of narrative in relating the history of the theater and the "ongoing processes" that seemed to shape various changes within the theatrical enterprise.

Owing to the longstanding question of whether the theater was in any way "evolutionary" in its development the act of establishing "origins" remains an important locus for scholarly investigation. In her essay, entitled "Early London Pageantry and Theatre History Firsts," Anne Lancashire engages questions relating to London's civic ceremonies for Richard II in order to ask "how far back" civic ceremony can be traced. William Ingram ("Playhouses Make

Strange Bedfellows") probes the origins of a specific document—in this case, a petition seemingly written by actor Martin Slater to the Privy Council around 1605–6 referring to a playhouse that has yet to be identified with certainty. Herbert Berry ("John Brayne and His Other Brother-in-Law") traces the origins of a legal dispute involving the man who was part-owner of the Theatre along with James Burbage. As he explains, the early theater was defined by personalities and their legal dilemmas. Every time historians think that they finally have the last word on a playhouse such as the Theatre, more material turns up that seems to extend or alter our perceptions. It is forever an ongoing process.

"Ongoing processes" define the interests of Sally-Beth MacLean and Alan Somerset as well, as they push ahead on an impressive new database that seeks to delineate and trace patronage networks ("Hyper-revels in Cyberspace"). Planned as a "research tool," the project will "make available for the first time our cumulative databases of itinerary, patrons and performance information for professional entertainment activities before 1642." Given the computer's ability to contain, search, and display a vast collection of data, the MacLean-Somerset project will be able to accommodate new information as long as it becomes available, "retrieving and analyzing information from across counties and boroughs." Similarly, Simon Blatherwick, in his research, is involved in the ongoing bricks-and-mortar investigations of the material remains of the Elizabethan stage. His essay ("Archaeology Updates: Four Playhouses and the Bear Garden") describes the current state of play regarding the technical investigations of archaeologists into the Rose, Globe, Hope, and Boar's Head playhouses, as well as the Bear Garden. Additionally, Blatherwick charts some of the influences on archaeological investigation "outside of the pit," suggesting the many complexities that have developed between institutions such as English Heritage and the private owners of the sites that archaeologists study. In a very practical sense these owners and agencies have become the modern "patrons of dramatic enterprise." After all, it is they who determine what archaeological investigation will ultimately be done. "As archaeologists,' Blatherwick notes, "we work within a commercial environment serving the interests of the client, the archaeology and the public."

Still, an interest in patronage networks—whether ancient or modern—isn't restricted to the MacLean-Somerset database. In "Sir John Astley and Court Culture" John Astington's researches into

Sir John Astley, appointed Master of the Revels in 1622, pose questions similar to those of MacLean and Somerset. Astington asks: Who were Astley's patrons? Can historians think of him as a courtier who, like the duke of Buckingham, "danced his way to favour" in the royal masques? What do Astley's literary associations suggest about his activities in the last decade of Elizabeth's reign? Astington intrigues us with new information that potentially connects Astley with Lord Hay's circle, the countess of Warwick's circle, and with poets such as Edmund Spenser and Sir John Harrington. Further, he opens up debate on methodological grounds, connecting the many ways in which Astley seems to have made his way at court. Contrary to our impulse to see patronage as linear, Astington reminds us that it more frequently involved multifaceted associations.

The personalities behind other historical moments are researched by Berry, Ingram, and R. A. Foakes. In all cases these historians are "returning" to persons who have been researched earlier, sometimes by the authors who now find additional threads to follow. When Herbert Berry returns to his earlier work on the Burbage-Brayne family, he learns that several other families, chief amongst them the Stowers and Warrisons, are involved in disputes related to Brayne; and these occur at just about the time that Brayne was winding up business with the Theatre. R. A. Foakes similarly returns to biographical issues that have emerged from his earlier editing of Henslowe's *Diary* and the Henslowe papers. In examining Henslowe with fresh eyes, Foakes underscores the personal nature of Henslowe's account book, which has been seen by many readers as a record through which Henslowe held the Admiral's Men to strict standards of repayment, fostering an antagonistic atmosphere between himself as financier and the players to whom he loaned money. Yet there is no indication, Foakes argues, that Henslowe's relationship with the players was anything but symbiotic. He concludes: "Fussy he may have been, and keen to put things in writing, but mainly for his private satisfaction or as a record for the company."

While personalities, money, and property are common focal points, so are playing companies and playhouses. In "Two Playhouses, Both Alike in Dignity" Roslyn Knutson questions the longstanding assumption that after the King's Men acquired the lease of the Blackfriars they alternated between their two houses, using the Globe in the summer and the Blackfriars in the winter. Knutson suggests that this neat equation doesn't finally explain patterns of performance. Indeed, there were periods when the Globe playhouse was more important commercially than has generally been believed; and the pattern of closures does not suggest the early superiority of the Blackfriars.

Sharing this interest in openings and closures is William Ingram, whose essay raises a variety of questions involving Aaron Holland, the established owner of the Red Bull playhouse, and Martin Slater, a stage player and manager. In the petition submitted to the Privy Council, Slater asks to resume construction on an inn that was in the process of conversion to a playhouse (c. 1605–6). With some sense of urgency he argues that resuming construction is critical because he had been asked to put together a company of players for the duke of Holstein, the brother of Queen Anna of Denmark. (And this company presumably needs somewhere to perform.) But where precisely was this playhouse? And what can historians finally do to solve this mystery? In reexamining this enigma Ingram demonstrates, amongst other things, that even "dead letters" are worth opening, if only to clarify what historians know or need to seek out; though in his conclusion he sounds resigned to the fact that the gray area surrounding Slater's petition is destined to remain so. Toward the end of his essay Ingram remarks: "One can perhaps be forgiven for wishing that this document would simply go away." However, in this suggestion he, of course, only ends up recreating interest in Slater's petition. An old story, newly told, is often a different story; but even when it is not, an engaging narrative can offer a fresh approach to even the murkiest evidence.

Finally, no survey of current trends would be complete without an examination of the resurgence of work on dramatic manuscripts. Here, Grace Ioppolo's thoughtful overview ("Some Recent Dramatic Manuscript Studies") suggests that vigorous research and conversation is taking place in three venues: at the expanding number of manuscript conferences, in journals devoted specifically to manuscripts studies, and in recent publications that represent the directions of individual scholars working in manuscript studies. While the research projects mentioned in this summary are fascinating, in and of themselves, what is equally interesting is that a singular vision seems to be emerging. Ioppolo notes that there is a voice running throughout these venues and studies, one that "admonishes scholars to return to manuscripts, rather than invent[ing] theory in order to make persuasive arguments relating to the practices of Renaissance authors."

Introduction

In the process of writing such unique, seemingly unrelated investigations, the nine authors featured hereafter have demonstrated that ultimately they are writing with one purpose in mind: to revise or corroborate what we already know about the theatrical enterprise in early modern England. Furthermore, they have chosen to do so by returning to archival sources as their basis, whether that "archive" concerns a resurrected document, a new "find," or the foundation stones of an actual playhouse built in the "Jacobethan era." In this way, having underlined the primacy of archival evidence in rewriting the early modern theater, each has returned, full circle, to Chambers's "mere archaeology."

Hyper-Revels in Cyberspace

Sally-Beth MacLean and Alan Somerset

THIS JOINT ARTICLE describes the goals of the Records of Early English Drama (REED) Patrons, Performances and Playing Places Multimedia Research Tool, a project sustained by a grant, which we gratefully acknowledge, from the Social Sciences and Humanities Research Council of Canada.[1] The reader should visit our website, at http://eir.library.utoronto.ca/reed/, which has samples (for Lancashire, our "pilot" county) of some of the components that we plan to include in the project's final design. It will be a flexible, web-based interdisciplinary tool for teaching and research, which will make available for the first time our cumulative database of itinerary, patrons, and performance information for professional entertainment activities (except for those undertaken in London theaters or at court) before 1642.

The microcomputer revolution (ever faster, higher-capacity, lower-priced) and the accompanying development of the media-rich, hyperlinked Internet are essential to the project. Since the mid-1980s, REED has maintained databases to abstract, from its successive volumes, all information about professional performances. The volumes contain a wealth of detailed information about provincial entertainment, but retrieving and analyzing information from across the counties and boroughs can be a tedious process of moving from index to index, page to page. This is the kind of work that a database can complete in microseconds; the powers of analysis and comparison that become available to a researcher allow one to transcend space and time. A database, on the face of it, is the dullest thing in the world, simply a structured collection of systematic information, arranged in rows and columns, and related within itself in various ways. However, the more that a database is developed and analyzed, the more varied and intriguing are the questions one may ask of it. As we have worked with and developed the capacities of the databases, we've been increasingly struck by the analogy between provincial performance data and the nature of the Internet itself. This is one reason why we are planning to make our project freely available on the Internet as a website, updated whenever necessary (in response to users' suggestions, or for corrections) and augmented upon publication of each new REED volume. We hope that this will make the research most widely available, as an adjunct to the REED project as it continues towards completion.

Like the Internet, provincial performance activities can be surveyed in multiple ways, but they are essentially an unstructured web of often unrelated, often spontaneous playing, a web of patronage-relationships, audience expectations, tour routes, civic sponsorships, and the like, which made possible the flourishing of the touring professional theater. This web of activities was carefully nurtured over time. One can see this "web" graphically represented on the maps that accompany, the website (to be described later). We've attempted, in our design, to allow the user to start from any place on the site; one can work from any locality, any chronological starting point, any type of activity, and from there one can create multiple directions of user-constructed enquiry. Of course (and paradoxically) this capacity for serendipity results from careful overall design, and from attempting to anticipate the sorts of enquiries that users will want to construct. The first part of this essay discusses the overall design, and looks at some of the information that is forthcoming from the database tables themselves (necessarily incomplete at this point, containing about four thousand records). In the second part we look at maps, along with visual and architectural information relevant for the study of performance spaces, the venues used by these entertainers.

The databases have three main components: (1) a database of records; (2) a database of patrons; and (3) a database of localities and venues (including their images, described below). The "records" are derived directly from the pages of the REED volumes, and each record may (and usually does) contain links to the other databases. At random, here is a sample record, a payment for performance, from Worcester in 1625–26: "Payed and Given to the Lord Dudleys Players xs."[2] Before we can compare this record with others we have to analyze it closely, including in the record-entry several indicators that the user of the Internet site will never see. First, of what is this a record? We named it a "payment for performance." Lacking any indication to the contrary, and because it is a single payment to a single company, this seems safe enough, and the money recorded can be used in calculations of the income of the company, or the annual budget of the city of Worcester for entertainment. There are other types of record that need to be carefully distinguished, such as:

- Composite payments: payments to more than one company, or grouped payments of miscellaneous expenses (not all necessarily performance-related) at any point in a year.
- End-of-year summary payment records of all entertainer payments.
- Anecdotal or other allusions to performances. For example, the trial of a resident of Evesham revealed that he sent his servant to a play performed in the evening on New Year's Day, 1583, to clear the way to murder a neighbor![3]
- Permissions: troupes licenced to perform under certain conditions or for certain periods.
- Court evidence-records, arising from disturbances at performances, forged licences, etc.
- Dismissals: troupes ordered not to play, sent away without playing, or otherwise discouraged (sometimes with payments, sometimes not).
- Prohibitions: decisions by borough authorities that playing henceforth was to be forbidden or controlled.

This list illustrates the range of activities that can be isolated and compared by locality, place, date, and so forth. A second consideration for analysis: how much is the payment? Not all users will have familiarity with "old money" (£ s. d.) used before decimalization in 1972, and fewer still are comfortable with marks, nobles, royals, groats, and farthings. How do you compare, say, 42d. with 3s. 4d.? Teaching the computer "old money" to deal with the (so far) 271 amounts and designations has been challenging! We pass over a third consideration, the often-vexed question of dating, and onto a fourth question that links the records to the patrons.

The database of records will include all activities by professional entertainers, including the many records where the patron(s) are unspecified or imperfectly identified. Imperfectly identified patrons occur in records like the following, from Worcester in 1596–97: "money gyven to the Quenes players, and to Certen noble mens players . . . ," and unidentified patrons occur in the 1589–90 record from the same city: "money given to players."[4] However, in most records the patrons are specified, and we can discern much about these troupes and their patrons, the extent of their activities and comparative fortunes. (In the illustrations that follow, we deal only with patronized companies and evidence from the first eighteen REED volumes. Figures will change with each successive REED publication!) Over 500 companies in the database appear fewer than ten times, only 35 companies receive, in total, over £10, and 118 companies have a total income of 1s. or less. "Playing" (including minstrelsy and other activities) was often a local event, a sometime thing. Remarkably, even after James I limited allowable patrons to the royal family (thereby making noble or gentry troupes supposedly illegal) they continued to flourish: 75 of the 131 troupes recorded thereafter received only a single payment and had "illegal" patronage.

Sixty companies in the databases are rewarded over ten times, and we turn up a surprise when we compare average payments! Readers will recall that Philip Henslowe shared the following gossip by letter with Edward Alleyn, in the summer of 1593:

> As for my lorde a Penbrockes which you desier to knowe wheare they be they ar all at home and hausse ben this v or sixe weackes for they cane not saue ther charges with trauell as I heare & weare fayne to pane ther parell for ther carge.[5]

The databases allow us to isolate and examine the fortunes of Pembroke's Men in relation to other companies active to the same degree (ten records or more) and at the same time (1591–92 to 1600–1601). Table 1 (p. XX) presents the evidence, rounded to the nearest penny (dates are given when the company is not recorded through the whole period of comparison). One can also do another analysis, looking at the companies in Table 1, and the average payment to each, in the eight locations where Pembroke's men were paid (see Table 2—we've used the patron numbers to save space; a blank indicates no records of payments.) We see that Pembroke's men were respectably active through the whole decade (visiting more places than any company save the Queen's Men), and they come virtually at the top of the heap, although we note that the Queen's Men were often paid more in the same locations. So, might we now wish to ask Henslowe what he was talking about in his letter to his son-in-law? Can an eyewitness be misleading? Perhaps professional jealousies? Lord Strange's Men (Alleyn's troupe) records eight appearances, in 1592–93, with an average reward of only 19s. This example, while not conclusive, suggests that much fresh analysis of troupes' histories and their comparative fortunes will become possible. Equally valuable, for questions of patronage, is the wealth of data that we are carefully collecting about each patron. This will allow a man such as the above-named "Lord Monteagle" to be investigated to ascertain the "fit" between his spheres of influence, offices, residences, and familial relations, and the areas of activity of his performers. Included in the patrons' residences are known or presumable playing venues, which brings us to consider the third major database being constructed.

Where did performances take place? There are two answers; first and most obviously they occurred within the boroughs, monasteries, and other places (including households) whose records fill the REED volumes. When you begin to ask questions about individual locations, however, the variety of the records becomes problematic. Which localities spent most on travelling professional entertainers? Raw figures tell little, but the databases, again, allow for further comparative analysis. Taking the period 1524–1600, Table 3 compares boroughs whose average rewards are generous and where performances occurred fairly regularly. This table, while not definitive, does intrigue us with possibilities for analyses of activities, payment amounts, and the like, which space forbids here but which the research tool will enable.

The second answer about places of performance (which we cannot always discover) concerns venues within a borough, monastery, household, and so on, where performances occurred, and the evidence that survives about these venues. There is direct evidence, from the records themselves, of approximately one hundred named venues (so far)—churches, boothalls, guildhalls, and other public and private spaces. As well, there are further playing places not directly named as such, which we may reasonably identify and will include in our venues database.

We are producing modern maps to illustrate the tours and performance locations of our performers and the spheres of their patrons' influence. Our first overview map of England with all known public and private locations visited by touring performers is on our website. The outline of England is derived from the digital chart of the world (DCW, 1:1 million), and county maps are based on such sources as the Victorian one-inch Ordnance Survey series and the modern Ordnance Survey Landranger Series (1:50,000). The tour routes are largely drawn from research and sources outlined in a previous article for *Medieval and Renaissance Drama in England*.[6]

The overview maps will be hyperlinked with more detailed regional or individual county and city maps to locate a variety of sites: performance locations, patrons' residences, and locations associated with their provincial offices. At the county level, more geographic details such as rivers and topographical contours will be included. The pilot map of Lancashire displays samples of many map variations, and there are features that theater historians will find especially valuable. Distances between locations can be calculated, either in kilometers or miles, and, more dynamically, route maps for individual troupes can be customized and printed out upon request.

The results of new research by the team will be linked with both the locations on the map and related architectural data to illustrate the performance venues, many of which survive in some form. We are visiting each surviving site to photograph, measure, and document its architectural history, as well as to consult with local experts. Many demolished sites can be partially retrieved from antiquarian descriptions, drawings, or early photographs.[7] These, as well as ground plans, will be included.

In the Lancashire pilot website, the links between maps, databases, and performance venue data are in place, allowing the user to view images and concisely presented architectural and historical details relating to locations visited by entertainers touring the northwest. Most of these likely performance venues were not in towns but in private households. Along the Ribble Valley lay the Shuttleworth family's Jacobean home, at Gawthorpe, and the Shireburns' grander establishment at Stonyhurst. Further south survive the somewhat haunted remains of the once powerful Botilers' home at Bewsey near Warrington; and in the southeast stand the Sherringtons' home at Wardley Hall and the Shuttleworths' renaissance home at Smithills, outside Bolton.[8]

Smithills illustrates some complexities facing the researcher. Evolving from an original medieval hall in the north range, it became a home with four wings on a courtyard plan by the seventeenth century.[9] The Great Hall, which has been previously identified as the indoor performance space used by touring companies, is in the late-fourteenth-century wing, now open to the public.[10] The Radcliffe family may well have enjoyed the company of minstrels in this hall in the later medieval period, but their records do not survive. In the early sixteenth century the Radcliffe heiress Cecilia married Andrew Barton, who built the east wing. Sir Richard Shuttleworth, palatine judge in Cheshire, married the widow of Robert Barton in 1582. The surviving evidence comes from his accounts from 1582–1603, before the family relocated north to Gawthorpe.[11]

We may find the medieval great hall charming, but would a wealthy member of the Lancastrian gentry have found it so? It might well have seemed a small, outmoded space, with its central open fireplace, when compared to the commodious Renaissance space in the east wing. It seems likely that a host of Shuttleworth's status would have preferred the more modern and congenial withdrawing room, distinguished by some of the earliest linenfold panelling in Lancashire, as well as by its fashionable bay window and more generous dimensions.[12] Its present appearance belies its former greater splendor; on the website appear details of later architectural alterations and intrusive Victorian adjustments (in Smithills's case, a chapel vestry was added at the upper end, thereby reducing its size significantly).

Outdoor performance spaces present other problems for illustration. In Shropshire at Shrewsbury, for example, there was an outdoor performance site in the former marketplace of the town, called the Cornmarket or the Apple Market, used by the Queen's Men in 1589.[13] The market area has now been significantly altered by later building and street realignment, and most particularly by the demolition of the mid-fifteenth-century Boothall, which originally closed off the north end next to the high street. We can document and depict the Boothall in antiquarian sources, but we cannot recover the Elizabethan look of this outdoor space, even though today it does retain some of its intimate character.[14]

Both the Shrewsbury Boothall and the Cornmarket are recorded as performance venues, but there are also probable venues that we will include, indicating them as such. These include town or guildhalls that were typically used for official civic events.[15] The weight of evidence suggests that performers preferred indoor locations that offered protection from bad weather, more easily controlled entrances, and more dignified and comfortable ceremonial seats for the mayors and councils at civic-sponsored performances. Sometimes hitherto unacknowledged evidence in the databases themselves makes speculation more convincing. At Coventry there survives a truly remarkable venue, St. Mary's Hall, built at the turn of the fifteenth century and an astonishing survival in the midst of the modern city. It is approached through an arched entrance in Bayley Lane directly across from the cathedral ruins—the hall is on the upper floor in the west range of the courtyard. Its dimensions are approximately 72 by 30 feet, with a roof height of 33 feet.

The hall still has much of its original character and some of its fittings, so we can appreciate the rich visual surroundings it provided for renaissance performances. It is built of red sandstone with splendid windows and an intact minstrels' gallery at the lower end. The high end is dominated by a late-fifteenth-century tapestry of the Assumption of the Virgin, with an impressive stained-glass window above commemorating Henry VI, who granted the city status as a county in its own right. The timber-panelled roof with heraldic bosses and angel musicians is late medieval, restored after fire damage during the bombing. A similar blend of sacred and secular iconography was likely featured in the large stained-glass windows along the east and west walls. Angels in the tracery of some windows remain intact, and fragmentary remains of others suggest that some windows depicted historical figures significant for Coventry's urban development.[16]

This hall was most likely to have been used for performances by the numerous touring entertainers who visited the city, but there survives no record that specifically names it as such.[17] However, the records database for venues in Coventry yields up "the Council House," the name sometimes given to the whole building and sometimes to the old council chamber (and former pantry) used for meetings at the lower end of St. Mary's Hall. When the king's players from the Blackfriars were paid there by the wardens in 1636, we may reasonably suggest that their performance was staged in the much larger adjacent hall, while their reward of 20s. was presented in the smaller room afterwards.[18] St. Mary's Hall will therefore be included as a probable performance venue in the database, hyperlinked with architectural and visual data that we have collected.

To sum up, individual occurrences become important when they can be considered in their rich complexity of personal and architectural detail, and when they may be compared, measured and evaluated over time and space. The pilot site is the entry point to what we hope will be a useful and innovative research and teaching tool. We invite our readers (and our users) to engage with this web of hyperlinked visual and textual data and to participate in the construction of the full publication by sending us comments, criticisms, and suggestions.

Table 1. The Fortunes of Playing Companies 1591–1601

Patron Identity	Appearances	Average Payment
(1) Henry Herbert, earl of Pembroke	17	27s. 9d
(2) Queen Elizabeth	71	26s. 9d.
(3) Henry Howard, Lord Admiral	17 (1592–1600)	17s. 10d.
(4) Earl of Derby	11 (1594–1598)	17s. 8d.
(4) Earl of Worcester	20	15s. 9d.
(5) William Parker, Lord Monteagle	13	13s. 9d.
(6) Edward Parker, Lord Morley	11	11s. 11d.
(7) Lord Ogle	12 (1592–1596)	10s. 11d.
(8) Lord Chandos	15	9s. 6d.

Table 2. Average Payments of Playing Companies 1591–1601

Patron	Bath	Bewdley	Bristol	Coventry	Ludlow	Newcastle	Shrewsbury	York
(1)	16s. 9d.	15s.	32s. 6d.	20s.	20s.	53s. 4d.	40s.	20s.
(2)	19s. 6d.	6s. 9d.	23s. 11d.	22s. 2d.	17s. 2d.	47s. 6d.	18s. 3d.	46s. 9d.
(3)	11s. 2d.		23s. 4d.	16s. 3d.		20s.	10s.	
(4)	8s. 11d.		30s.	9s. 2d.				
(5)	15s. 6d.		26s. 9d.	8s. 6d.	6s. 6d.	43s. 4d.		25s.
(6)	10s.			8s. 6d.		30s.		20s.
(7)			10s.	8s. 9d.		20s.		
(8)				9s. 4d.		20s.		
(9)	10s. 10d.		10s.	10s.	10s.			10s.

Table 3. Payments to Playing Companies vs. Other Entertainers (9 boroughs)

Name	Other Entertainers	(# Visits)	Players	(# Visits)
Newcastle	9s. 8d.	(11)	30s. 10d.	(32)
York	22s. 6d.	(13)	30s. 4d.	(44)
Norwich	19s. 4d.	(11)	21s.	(113)
Shrewsbury	7s. 10d.	(81)	17s. 2d.	(26)
Bristol	6s. 8d.	(30)	16s. 6d.	(120)
Exeter	7s. 1d.	(71)	14s. 4d.	(46)
Gloucester	13s. 3d.	(16)	13s. 3d.	(111)
Coventry	6s. 6d.	(106)	12s. 6d.	(158)
Cambridge	5s. 3d.	(30)	9s. 10d.	981)

Notes

1. We are also very grateful to acknowledge past grants from the Academic Development Fund, University of Western Ontario; the Dean, Faculty of Arts and Science, University of Toronto; and the Provost's Information Technology Courseware Development Fund, University of Toronto, which have supported the project up to this time.

2. David N. Klausner, ed., *Herefordshire / Worcestershire*, REED (Toronto: University of Toronto Press, 1990), 455.

3. *Herefordshire / Worcestershire*, 372.

4. *Herefordshire / Worcestershire*, 449, 448.

5. E. K. Chambers, *The Elizabethan Stage* (Oxford: Clarendon Press, 1923), 2:128.

6. Sally-Beth MacLean, "Tour Routes: 'Provincial Wanderings' or Traditional Circuits?" *Medieval and Renaissance Drama in England* 6 (1993): 1–14.

7. Examples of such resources would include the remarkable nineteenth-century drawings by three generations of Buckler artists now in the British Library (Add. MSS 36356–97). The sample photos of the Stonyhurst hall interior on the current website come from an early twentieth-century article in *Country Life* (23 July 1938); these are preferable to the photos taken in the summer of 1999, when the hall was under extensive repair—and they are happily out of copyright, an issue that we must always bear in mind.

8. The dramatic records for these locations have been edited by David George in *Lancashire*, REED (Toronto: University of Toronto Press, 1991).

9. See further *The Victoria History of the Counties of England: A History of the County of Lancashire*, ed. William Farrer and J. Brownbill, vol. 5 (London, 1911), 15–18. The south wing of Smithills was demolished in the early nineteenth century.

10. See David George, "Jacobean Actors and the Great Hall at Gawthorpe, Lancashire," *Theatre Notebook* 37 (1983): 111, 119, 121.

11. See *Lancashire*, 166–70.

12. On hall design in the period see, for example, Maurice Howard, *The Early Tudor Country House: Architecture and Politics 1490–1550* (London: George

Philip, 1987), 112. The dimensions of the Withdrawing Room are presently 47 feet long by 17 feet, 4 inches wide, with a generous bay, 11 feet, 7 inches deep and 9 feet across. In the sixteenth century the room would have been much longer. The "Great Hall" on the other hand, is a smaller square space, 27 feet, 6 inches long and 25 feet wide.

13. See J. Alan B. Somerset, ed., *Shropshire,* REED, vol. 1 (Toronto: University of Toronto Press, 1994), 247.

14. Alan Somerset includes a surviving sketch of the original Boothall and an extract from Thomas Phillips's antiquarian description in the introduction to his volume; see *Shropshire,* vol. 2, 385–86.

15. See further Robert Tittler, *Architecture and Power: The Town Hall and the English Urban Community c. 1500–1640* (Oxford, 1991).

16. See Joan C. Lancaster, *St Mary's Hall, Coventry: A Guide to the building, its History and Contents,* 2nd ed. (Coventry, 1981).

17. For details of the relevant manuscripts see R.W. Ingram, ed., *Coventry,* REED (Toronto: University of Toronto Press, 1981), xxxii–xxxiii.

18. For this record and another the following year made in the Council House, see *Coventry,* 439, 440.

Archaeology Update: Four Playhouses and the Bear Garden

Simon Blatherwick

THIS ARTICLE AIMS to provide a brief update on archaeological activity on the sites of London's Tudor and Stuart playhouses. It is intended that it will provide readers with an understanding of the current situation with regard to archaeology and the playhouses and to create a wider awareness of the various forms of archaeological work that has taken place but is not always reported on. A bibliography at the end of this article will provide details of all reports referred to.

The history of archaeological activity in relation to London's playhouses begins with the Museum of London's excavations at the site of the Rose playhouse in 1988–89. Prior to the discovery of the remains of the foundations of the Rose, the main forms of evidence concerning the type of structures in which plays were performed consisted of maps, panoramic drawings, and building accounts, coupled with the written accounts of contemporary travelers. The image that appeared from these forms of evidence was, at best, confusing and often contradictory. Whilst the evidence from the Rose excavation has not dispelled debate about these early structures, it has provided dramatic evidence of the foundations of one such playhouse and provides an invaluable tool to aid interpretation of the records of (among others) Philip Henslowe and the maps of John Norden.

The uncovering of the remains of the Rose had a profound effect on the theater world and a similar one on the way in which archaeology is conducted in England. The Rose excavation (and the furor that surrounded it) resulted in the Department of Environment (1990) publishing planning guidance—Planning Policy Guidance 16, colloquially known as PPG 16—providing guidance on how archaeological remains should be dealt with in the planning and development process. As a result of this, archaeology is now a material consideration in the granting of planning consent, with most archaeological work paid for by commercial developers in advance of and during the course of development. The principle of the "polluter" paying for archaeology has lead to the increased privatization of archaeological work, the awarding of archaeological contracts primarily by competitive tender, and a move towards preservation in situ to avoid time-consuming (and sometimes expensive) archaeological excavation. This philosophy of preservation in situ (also conceived as a result of the backlog of unpublished material from excavations in the 1970s and 1980s) should provide a framework for the comprehension of policies followed on sites to be discussed in this article.

PPG 16 provides planning authorities with a staged approach to the consideration of archaeological remains that may survive on a proposed development site and states that where there are "nationally important archaeological remains . . . that are affected by a proposed development there should be a presumption in favour of their physical preservation" (DoE 1990, A8). Preservation in situ of archaeological remains does not, however, mean that they are preserved and available for public viewing and consumption but that they are often "entombed" beneath building foundations without the development impacting on the remains.

After discussing the Rose, the article will move on to look at work on the sites of the Globe, the Bear Gardens, the Boar's Head, the Hope, and the steps taken towards protecting the sites of London's other Tudor and Stuart playhouses.

The Rose

The story of the excavation of the Rose and the political fallout surrounding the excavation have been dealt with elsewhere (Blatherwick 2000, Bowsher & Blatherwick 1990, Bowsher 1998, Eccles 1990), and it is not the focus of this article to deal with issues already reported on. It is worth, however, looking at the preservation of the Rose and the future that the site holds.

When the developers received their final planning consent in the summer of 1989, their new building (now named Rose Court) was designed in such a way as to ensure that it straddled the majority of the remains and that the pile foundations had minimal impact on known archaeological deposits. It was also designed so that a basement space was created in which the remains of the Rose were preserved.

The preservation of the archaeological remains was not a straightforward issue, as the site is located on the alluvial soils of Bankside, which contain layers of peat originating from a prehistoric regression of the Thames. This damp, anaerobic environment was one that ensured the organic survival of the Rose but one that had been affected by archaeological intervention. The problem facing conservators and soil specialists, therefore, was not only that of preventing the deterioration of the organic material related to the structure of the Rose (e.g., wooden planks forming part of the foundation of the stage, timber drains running under the stage area, etc.) but of preventing the deterioration of the alluvium on which the site was based. One of the biggest concerns was that the alluvium and peat (which had been open to the environment during archaeological work) might have been affected by that exposure to such an extent that it would deteriorate once the site was reburied. The challenge, therefore, was to design a protective reburial regime that would not only protect the remains of the Rose during construction work but would also rehydrate the exposed archaeology and soils. At the same time, it was necessary to introduce a monitoring system that would allow for checks to be made to ensure that the protection was working. Although only intended as a relatively short-term measure, the last thing wanted was to rebury the Rose and then find out (on reopening) that it had decayed. Such a procedure had never been undertaken in Britain before.

The scheme eventually devised to preserve the remains of the Rose during and after the construction of Rose Court was that they were sealed under a protective layer of terram (an inert geotextile). The terram was then covered with a layer of salt and lime-free sand, with the sand being held in place by thick polythene sheeting and then secured by a weak mix of concrete. The concrete, while visually unattractive, served the purpose of preventing the evaporation of water and the movement of sand, while also providing a hard crust during the construction program. Water was slowly reintroduced to the archaeology and soils by a leaky-pipe system (normally used by horticulturists) being installed throughout the sand, with the water flow being controlled by a ballcock. This is still in place to maintain the water content of the clays. Saturation of the remains is achieved by the concrete cover being partially submerged under a pool of water.

To provide a means of checking that the protection was working, monitoring tubes were installed in the protective sand projecting out of the concrete cover. These enable regular monitoring of the Rose to be undertaken—as it now has been for the past decade. Results from this monitoring program (which looks as water level, chemical composition of the water, and so on, in an attempt to assess whether any decay is taking place) indicate that the remains of the Rose have been stabilized. This analytical conclusion has also been enhanced by visual inspection undertaken when monitoring tubes have been replaced: the visual inspection indicating that the alluvial clays (cracked and fissured when the site was reburied) have rehydrated.

The planning consent included a condition that the developer deposit a sum of money, in the keeping of Southwark Council, for the excavation of the site of the Rose to be completed and the remains put on display. However, the calculated costs of completing the excavation and developing an exhibition space greatly outweigh that sum. With this in mind, Southwark Council released some of the money to the Rose Theatre Trust (a charity established in 1990 with the aims of preserving the remains of the Rose and of making those remains accessible to the public by the completion of the excavation) to establish a temporary public exhibition on the site. The exhibition opened in April 1999 and is (at the time of writing) open for public access. It has succeeded in raising public consciousness about the Rose but has been disappointing in terms of revenue; the Rose Theatre Trust is now looking elsewhere for the capital funding required to complete the excavation of the site and put its archaeological remains on permanent display.

This autumn (2001) will probably see the temporary closure of the exhibition as activity on site moves into a new phase with the excavation of a trial pit on the eastern side of the Rose site against the foundations of Southwark Bridge. The work is to be funded by English Heritage and has the dual purpose of assessing the survival of archaeological remains contemporary or associated with the Rose and assessing the geotechnical/engineering options for ensuring that the site can be made watertight for exhibition purposes. This work will be managed by the author.

The Globe

Subsequent to the 1989 archaeological evaluation of the Anchor Terrace site (then in the ownership of Hanson plc), on which the partial remains of the Globe were discovered (Blatherwick 2000, Blatherwick & Gurr 1992, McCudden 1989 & 1990), the remains of the Globe were covered with similar protection as that installed at the Rose. Further archaeological work was also undertaken within the basement of Anchor Terrace building. This consisted of trial pits and geophysical surveys, with the dual purpose of examining archaeological and geotechnical/engineering conditions on the site to assess the state of archaeological survival beneath the building and the structural integrity of the Listed Anchor Terrace building (Mackie et al. 1996, McCann 1998). Due to the national and international importance of the known archaeological remains on the site, planning guidance recommending the presumption in favor of their physical preservation provided the framework for approaches to the site.

The archaeological trial pits within the basement indicated that remains, possibly associated with the Globe, did survive beneath the Anchor Terrace building despite the fact that it was sitting on a massive concrete raft foundation. A tentative diameter for the Globe playhouse was forwarded (Blatherwick & Gurr 1992) and quickly dismissed as presenting a scheme encompassing a stair turret leaning against the frame "like a drunk clinging to a lamp post" (Orrell 1992, 333).

A geophysical survey undertaken in 1990 failed to recognize that Anchor Terrace sat on a huge concrete raft foundation, but ground penetrating radar had undertaken in 1996 (Mackie et al. 1996) indicated that the (GPR) optimum correspondence between recorded anomalies and potential structural elements associated with the Globe lay within a projected diameter of 77 to 87 feet. A further ground-penetrating radar survey with improved techniques and data processing was undertaken within the basement of Anchor Terrace in February 1998, and concurred with the preliminary conclusions, in relation to building diameter, from the 1996 survey. The 1998 report went further in its conclusion stating that "possible significant remains of the Globe have been identified beneath Anchor Terrace and that these are more likely to have been associated with a structure whose external diameter was close to 72 feet rather than anything larger" (McCann 1998, 26). Geophysical survey does not provide "concrete" evidence and it is known that "tightly constrained sites in city centres do not offer suitable conditions for geophysical techniques, with the possible exception of GPR" (David 1995, 7), but it is hoped that another phase of geophysical survey will take place within the basement of Anchor Terrace in the future.

During the mid-1990s Hanson plc sold the Anchor Terrace site and its adjacent parking lot to a development company based in north Southwark. As a result of their development proposals for the site (refurbishing the Listed Building, constructing new flats on the eastern side of the site and protectively burying—with no development above—the remains of the Globe), they received consent for the work to go ahead. In addition to the protective burial of the site, the development company undertook to mark out the recorded remains of the Globe on the ground and mount a notice-board display on the Park Street frontage of the site. The development proceeded with the display providing an introduction to the archaeology of the site.

The Bear Gardens

In 1995 the Museum of London began a program of archaeological work in advance of development on a site known as Benbow House (immediately east of "Shakespeare's Globe"). The work had the aims of uncovering evidence of medieval buildings known to front the Southwark waterfront, and also to examine evidence for the survival of two possible animal-baiting arenas.

Due to planning control on the development site, a program of evaluation and excavation was designed with the development designed in such a way as to have reduced impact on the site's archaeology. During the course of the archaeological work (Mackinder & Blatherwick 2000), remains of medieval buildings fronting the Thames were recorded along with remains though to be associated with the Bear Gardens. These remains provisionally interpreted as being of a polygonal structure and approximately 16 meters (52 feet, 6 inches) in diameter were not fully excavated and have been preserved in situ beneath the new development. Deposits containing both horse and dog bones showing butchery marks were found associated with the remains as was evidence of the site's development and change to industrial uses.

The Boar's Head

In advance of development proposals for the site of the Boar's Head, desk-based assessment work (Blatherwick 1999a) indicated that post-medieval archaeological deposits were likely to survive on the site. On site evaluation work has taken place but the results are not known to the author. The site still remains undeveloped to date.

The Hope

Recent work by the Museum of London Archaeology Service is interpreted as having located remains associated with the Hope—the playhouse that Philip Henslowe contracted Jacob Meade and Gilbert Katherens to build for him. Henslowe's instructions to the men were to demolish the existing Bear Gardens and erect a playhouse modeled on the Swan.

Although there has been doubt over the location of the Hope in relation to the demolished Bear Gardens, archaeological work would appear to confirm that Henslowe's builders moved the new playhouse to the south of the Bear Gardens so that it was built on land within one ownership (Braines 1924, 98). Documentary evidence of successive property leases (Blatherwick 1999b) may indicate that the land available for the construction of the Hope was only 80 feet wide on its north-to-south axis.

To date the only public report on the archaeological work at the Hope is in *The Sunday Telegraph* (22 April 2001). The site has subsequently been protectively backfilled and redeveloped with the remains being preserved in situ.

English Heritage Report

As a result of archaeological work, particularly at the sites of the Rose and Globe, two major outcomes became apparent:

- that archaeological remains relating to London's Tudor and Stuart playhouses did survive despite successive generations of development

- the massive public interest generated by the survival of these sites.

With this in mind, English Heritage commissioned this author (then working as a freelance archaeologist) to undertake a "desk-based assessment" of the known sites of London's Tudor and Stuart playhouses and to assess their potential to survive as archaelogical sites. Desk-based assessments are (as a result of *PPG 16)* a common tool in the archaeology/development world with the Institute of Field Archaeologist's (1999) defining an assessment as a collation of written and graphic evidence to identify the likely character, extent, quality, and worth of the known or potential archaeological resource. The purpose of an assessment is to gain information about the potential archaeological resource on a site, in order to be able to assess the likely impact of a proposed development, enable strategies for the archaeological resource to be formulated and inform professional judgments. In addition an assessment should aim to assess the impact that previous centuries of development may have had on a site.

The report presented to English Heritage in 1998 (Blatherwick 1998) addressed the sites of twenty-two playhouses (plus the Davies Bear Garden) with locations, provided documentary and historical background to them, interpreted archaeological evidence from archaeological sites work within the vicinity of each location, and provided an assessment of potential for the archaeological survival of each playhouse. One of the striking aspects of the report was the "discovery" that of the known playhouse locations where archaeological remains are expected to survive, apparently only the Rose survives within property boundaries that has not been subject subsequent division. Other sites have been subject to division which would mean that even if development were to take place, the entire historic sites would not be available for study. In that sense along, the Rose would appear to be unique.

The report is used by English Heritage to enable them to make informed comment should any of these sites be earmarked for development or ground works activity.

Conclusion

Since 1989 there has been a huge increase in the amount of archaeological information available in relation to the study of London's Tudor and Stuart playhouse, and it is hoped that this article provides a brief introduction and review to the existing state of knowledge. As archaeologists, we work within a commercial environment serving the interests of the client, the archaeology, and the public. Development now provides the opportunity for professional archaeologists to examine sites but invariably does not provide that opportunity to the interested and informed public or academic researcher. "Sufficient interest" (Gurr 1992) to be involved with aspects of our cultural heritage is a commercial consideration.

Bibliography

The bibliography consists of published and unpublished sources. The unpublished sources are reports that have been commercially produced for clients and are not publicly available. They often provide the raw data for the material used in published sources and (as such) are referenced her.

Published Sources

Blatherwick, S. 2000. "The Archaeology of Entertainment: London's Tudor and Stuart Playhouses." In *London Underground: The Archaeology of a City,* ed. I. Haynes, H. Sheldon, and L. Hannigan. Oxford: Oxbow Books.

———. 1997. "The Evaluation of the Globe Theatre." In *Shakespeare's Globe Rebuilt,* ed. J. R. Mulryne, and M. Shewring, 66–80. Cambridge: Cambridge University Press.

Blatherwick, S., and A. Gurr. 1992. "Shakespeare's Factory: Archaeological Evaluations on the Site of the Globe Theatre." *Antiquity* 66, no. 251: 315–28. Also published in *The Design of The Globe,* ed. A. Gurr, R. Mulryne, and M. Shewring, (London: International Shakespeare Globe Centre, 1993).

Bowsher, J. M. C. and Blatherwick, S. 1990. "The Structure of the Rose." In *New Issues in the Reconstruction of Shakespeare's Theatre* ed. F. J. Hildy; 55–78. Proceedings of the conference held at the University of Georgia, February 16–18, 1990. Oxford: Peter Lang.

Bowsher, J. 1998. *The Rose Theatre: An Archaeological Discovery.* London: Museum of London.

Braines, W. W. 1924. *The Site of the Globe Playhouse Southwark.* London: Hodder & Stoughton.

David. A. 1995. *Geophysical Survey in Archaeological Field Evaluation: English Heritage.* Research and Professional Services Guideline No. 1.

Department of the Environment. 1990. *Planning Policy Guidance 16. Archaeology and Planning.*

Eccles. C. 1990. *The Rose Theatre.* London: Nick Hern Books.

———. 1992. "Cultural Property and 'Sufficient Interest': The Rose and Globe sites." *International Journal of Cultural Property* 1:9–25.

Institute of Field Archaeologists. 1999. *Standard and Guidance for Archaeological Deskbase assessment.* 2nd ed.

Mackinder, A., and Blatherwick, S. 2000. *Bankside: Excavations at Benbow House, Southwark, London SE1.* Archaeology Studies Series III. Museum of London Archaeology Service.

McCudden, S. 1990. "The Discovery of the Globe Theatre." *London Archaeologist* 6: 143–44.

Orrell, J. 1992. "Spanning the Globe," *Antiquity* 66, no. 251: 329–33.

Sunday Telegraph. "Elizabethan theatre found under car park concrete," 22 April 2001.

Unpublished Sources

Blatherwick, S. 1999a. *Hotel and Other Associated Uses, Middlesex Street, London E1.* London: Museum of London Archaeology Service.

———. 1999b. *Empire Warehouse, 1 Bear Gardens, 2 Rose Alley and 58 Park Street, Southwark, London SE1. An Archaeological Desk-Based Assessment.*

———. "London's Pre-Restoration Purpose-Built Theatres of the Sixteenth and Seventeenth Centuries." Unpublished report produced for English Heritage.

———. 1992. *Anchor Terrace Car Park. The Archaeological Considerations in Relation to Redevelopment.* London: Museum of London.

———. 1991. *Report on the Archaeological Evaluation at 1/15 Anchor Terrace, Southwark Bridge Road, London SE1.* London: Museum of London.

Mackie, P.C., McCann, W.A., and Brown, A. 1996, *The Globe Theatre Site. A Geophysical Survey: Assessment of Potential for Further Analysis.* London: Museum of London Archaeology Service.

McCann, W. A. *Site of the Globe Theatre: A Geophysical Survey.* London: Museum of London Archaeology Service.

McCudden, S. 1989, *Report on Evaluation at Anchor Terrace Car Park, Park Street, SE1.* London: Museum of London, Department of Greater London Archaeology.

Early London Pageantry and Theater History Firsts

Anne Lancashire

In 1392, in a reconciliation with the City of London after a quarrel involving money, Richard II and his queen Anne of Bohemia made a triumphal formal entry into the city. For the entry the London authorities provided not only formal ceremonies, music, and gifts but also elaborate street pageantry involving maidens scattering gold coins, like leaves or flowers, from the top of Cheapside's Great Conduit onto the royal and civic procession as it passed, and a constructed castle or tower, further along Cheapside at the Standard, suspended on cords and from which an angel and a maiden descended through the air in clouds to the king and queen, offering them crowns and a cup of wine, and then reascending. Another elaborate device, of God and angels, was located at the western end of Cheapside near St. Paul's cathedral, and yet another, a wilderness with beasts, St. John Baptist, and another descending angel, was positioned at Temple Bar.[1] We know a great deal about the pageants (constructed theatrical displays) because of a contemporary descriptive poem on the entry by Richard Maidstone (or Maydiston), providing more detail than is given in the chronicle-history accounts of the occasion.[2] The entry has been much discussed and analyzed as the first truly elaborate London royal entry; and it has been seen as developing from two earlier, seemingly simpler London entries: the coronation entry of Richard II in 1377 and the coronation entry of his queen, Anne of Bohemia, in 1382.[3] The 1377 entry is normally thought of as the first English civic entry to have included a constructed street pageant, and also performers.[4]

In 1377 Richard II was formally received through London as part of the ceremonial leading up to his coronation at Westminster; and in the chronicles, as is well known, we do find descriptions of what appears to be a simpler version (though perhaps only in quantity—of pageants, gifts, and the like) of his 1392 entry. (Holinshed, however, in describing only one elaborate 1377 entry pageant, also refers to other pageants and shows not described, and so it is possible that our kinds of information differ, for the 1392 and 1377 entries, more than did the actual entries themselves.[5] We have no surviving descriptive poem, for example, on the 1377 entry; and the chroniclers Holinshed, Grafton, and Fabyan all deal with only one pageant in 1392's entry, while Maidstone's poem deals with four.) In 1377, the chronicles tell us, Richard encountered, as his procession passed through Cheapside, a castle with four towers, from each of which a maiden dressed in white blew leaves of gold and scattered imitation gold coins down upon the king and his train, and from a higher tower in the center a golden angel leaned down to the king with a crown. Wine ran from two of the castle's sides; and the maidens must also have descended from their towers in some way, spectacularly or otherwise, since they are said to have offered the king and his nobles wine from gold cups filled from the castle's spouts.[6] Five years later, for the entry of Anne of Bohemia through London for her coronation at Westminster, a Cheapside castle was also constructed: although we know about this not from the chronicles—which comment only briefly on Anne's entry—but instead from the early surviving accounts of the Goldsmiths' Company, a wealthy London craft guild also responsible for the castle in the 1377 entry, for which entry some costs have also survived in the company's accounts. The Goldsmiths' accounts provide little information about the 1377 pageant beyond that it was a constructed castle (the expenses for which included ropes), and that there were maidens;[7] without the chronicles we would not know about the four towers, gold leaves and coins, angel with a crown, and cups of wine. The company's accounts provide a bit more information about the 1382 pageant: but since the chronicles are silent about it, in the end we do not know as much about it as about 1377's. Nevertheless in 1382—the accounts inform us—there was also a castle in Cheapside, suspended/hanging in which were three virgins to scatter leaves.[8] Whatever the simplicity, complexity, or extent, then, of the 1377 and 1382 entries, since the 1392 Cheapside castle involved suspension as well, and the angel in 1377 bent down with a crown, it seems that a typical Cheapside royal entry pageant from 1377 to 1392 not only was a castle but also included some kind of unusual or spectacular effect of movement and/or suspension, with a special-effects, seemingly mechanical descent taking place at least in 1392 (a "vice" was involved, according to Grafton) and perhaps in 1377 as well. (Perhaps the maidens in 1382 descended too; but we can only speculate.) In all three entries, though on a structure apparently separate from the castle in 1392, maidens scattered gold leaves and/or coins. Repetition with variation appears to have been an important design principle governing the construction of Cheapside pageants from 1377 to 1392; and it has been suggested that some materials were also recycled from one entry to another.[9]

But given this principle of repetition, and given also the possibility of multiple pageants even in 1377, was the 1377 royal entry castle really the first such constructed Cheapside pageant, and also the first royal entry with performers? In considering this question, we should also keep in mind that, if the Goldsmiths' accounts for 1382 had not survived, despite the chroniclers' statements about the passage of Anne of Bohemia through London we would not know about any castle, suspension, or virgins scattering leaves. Too often we tend to assume that where we have no chronicle descriptions explicitly of pageants, or only scanty information on pageants, we also have no pageants, or only minimal ones; but early chroniclers did not aim at creating historically accurate and full accounts of the events of their times or of earlier times. They appear, rather, to have described what they personally found to be of interest or importance about these events, rather than what we today might think to be important.[10] Their descriptions of events often vary, and can frequently be seen to be partial only. Another point to keep in mind is that the terms used in early chronicle descriptions and in records do not always mean what we assume today that they mean. Holinshed, Grafton, and Fabyan, for example, for the 1392 entry all use the word "stage" for what Maidstone in his poem calls a castle; and the 1382 entry involved—according to our only information source with pageant detail, the Goldsmiths' accounts—a "summer castle:" a term that, according to the full *Oxford English Dictionary,* meant c. 1400 (1) a movable tower used in sieges (first usage example, 1400) or (2) an elevated structure on a ship (first usage example, 1346). A "castle" with towers or turrets, as in the 1377 entry, may thus not be what was provided after all in 1382 but, rather, merely a tower with a suspension device, although indeed a "castle" as in 1377 may after all have been represented, the writer of the Goldsmiths' accounts merely using a term more practically than representationally descriptive of what was provided. (The military/ nautical term suggests use of military or shipbuilding construction or rigging techniques; and Richard Osberg has suggested that the "castles" in both 1377 and 1382 were built on the model of a siege tower.)[11]

What the 1377 and 1382 entries had in common, in short, as far as we can be sure, were a Cheapside structure (devised and presented by the Goldsmiths) involving one or more towers, maidens scattering leaves (presumably of gold in both cases), and some kind of special effect involving movement and/or suspension. In 1392 these various elements were repeated, with an actual descent (in clouds) and re-ascent specified in our most lengthy account of the entry, and a repetition also from 1377 of the special angel with a crown: a display element that is not mentioned in the 1382 Goldsmiths' accounts but is not in their 1377 accounts either and so may well have been present in 1382 as in 1377.

What happens, then, if we look at royal entries before 1377, not for explicit records of or references to a constructed "castle" pageant, but instead for indications of an earlier use of a Cheapside tower, maidens scattering gold, or some kind of movement or suspension device? 1377 would seem late for the start of elaborate constructed pageants (and also with human performers) in London's streets, given that we have references to royal entries into London, with elaborate display, from at least the thirteenth century on, given that portable symbolic pageants were used in London civic processions with royalty at least as early as 1313, and given that elaborate royal tournaments with role-playing also took place in the London area well before 1377.[12] The earlier that one looks, the fewer the records that have survived; also the earlier the chronicles, the less descriptive detail they tend to provide about royal entries. But if we look back only twenty years from 1377, in 1357 Edward the Black Prince, son of Edward III, returned to England and London from military victories in France, leading with him the captured King John of France, John's younger son, and a number of members of the French nobility; and London devised for the occasion, at Edward III's command, a formal entry that is described in several chronicles. The major English chroniclers we read most often today for this period—Holinshed, Grafton, Fabyan, Stow— merely tell us that the citizens received the entrants honorably;[13] but at least three lesser-known chroniclers go beyond the basics. Of these three, Henry Knighton makes the entry sound entirely like a military display;[14] but the Latin *Chronicon Anonymi Cantuariensis* and the Anglo-Norman *Anonimalle Chronicle* together tell us that there was something in Cheapside, devised and built by the Goldsmiths (again), which sounds from the chronicle descriptions very similar to the 1377, 1382, and 1392 Cheapside castle and/or maidens pageants. *Chronicon Anonymi Cantuariensis* states that there was a platform/scaffold holding two beautiful maidens who scattered gold and silver leaves onto the heads of the members of the passing procession; and the *Anonimalle Chronicle* tells us more about the maidens' appearance (they had uncovered heads, and shining hair falling down above their shoulders; did they represent angels?) and that they were suspended.[15] Did 1357's suspension involve some kind of tower, as in 1377 (not necessarily with suspension), 1382, and 1392? And was this 1357 platform (or possibly tower) practical only, or was it a kind of castle representation? The effect of the 1357 suspended maidens, in any case, is described by the *Anonimalle Chronicle* as marvellous; and although this could be argued to reflect wishful thinking, public relations, or a chronicle formula for entry descriptions, at least the constructed display must have been an attempt at something out of the ordinary, and probably *was* spectacular, given that London had been devising royal entries since the thirteenth century. It was also located in more or less the same part of Cheapside (west from the Great Conduit, towards St. Paul's, near the area which would later be called Goldsmiths' Row) as the 1377 and 1392 castles.[16] We do not know where the 1382 castle/tower was placed, but chances are, given its Goldsmith sponsors, that it too was in or around the Goldsmiths' area of Cheapside.

In short, in moving back only twenty years from 1377, we find another royal entry that comparative analysis suggests could be argued to be the "first" with a constructed pageant (including a movement/suspension device of some sort, and possibly a tower/castle), with human "performers" (the maidens), and also with symbolic meaning. (Maidens scattering gold leaves or coins, in later entries, have been interpreted as part of overall typical entry representation of London as a New Jerusalem, and suspension, as referring to a descent from heaven.[17]) There is even a chance that more "performance" than simply scattering gold and silver leaves took place, since the maidens, as already noted, might have represented angels,[18] and also we do not know whether these were actual maidens or actors. In 1392's castle/tower pageant the "maiden" accompanying the angel was apparently, like the angel himself, played by a boy actor.[19] Now, having thus moved back twenty years from 1377 to 1357 for various possible "firsts" in London royal entry pageantry, to what yet earlier date might we move, after further investigation of even earlier London royal entries?

A comparative look, then, at specific London royal entries of 1377, 1382, 1392, and 1357, and at the kinds of information we do and do not have for all four, and from what sources suggests that in early London theater history calling anything, however carefully defined, a "first" is dangerous, since we are dealing with a period for which comparatively few records of and references to theater, including the theater of civic street pageantry, have survived, and for which the records and references that we do have are neither full nor always of the same kind or number. Indeed, even for somewhat later periods, seemingly safe "firsts" can be misleadingly shifting sands upon which to build histories of theatrical development: a fact of which theater historians became painfully aware in 1983 when legal historian Janet Loengard published the record, by now extremely well known, of a purpose-built playhouse in the London area—the Red Lion in Stepney—constructed nine years earlier (in 1567) than what had been until then supposed to be the first purpose-built London playhouse.[20]

Theater historians in general are cautious people; and as the twenty-first century begins, our assumptions about early theater in general are becoming increasingly tentative, as we look more closely not only at the kinds of information we have but also at the kinds we do not have—and at the uncertainties and possibilities lying in the gaps between the two.

Notes

1. Gordon Kipling has suggested that there may have been two more pageants as well: see his "Richard II's 'Sumptuous Pageants' and the Idea of the Civic Triumph," in *Pageantry in the Shakespearean Theater*, ed. David M. Bergeron (Athens: University of Georgia Press, 1985), 100, n. 12.

2. See Maidstone's poem in Thomas Wright, ed., *Political Poems and Songs*, 2 vols., Rolls Series #14 (London: HMSO, 1859–61), 1.282–300 (for the pageants, see 290–97, and also the Maidstone excerpts, translations, and summaries in Glynne Wickham's *Early English Stages 1300–1660*, 3 vols. [London and New York: Routledge & Kegan Paul/Columbia University Press, 1959–81], 1.69–71.) See also Raphael Holinshed, *Chronicles of England, Scotland, and Ireland*, 6 vols. (London: J. Johnson et al., 1807–8), 2.819–20, Richard Grafton, *Chronicle*, 2 vols.

(London: J. Johnson et al., 1809), 1.459, and Robert Fabyan, *The New Chronicles of England and France* (London: F. C. and J. Rivington, et al. 1811), 537–38—all three of whom mention and describe only the castle pageant (perhaps conflating it with the Conduit display) and locate it at the Standard. (Maidstone does not name the Great Conduit for the display of maidens, but his description seems to apply to it.) Stow, *Annales of England* [1592; RSTC #23334], 483, focuses on gifts, saying nothing about pageants. Some additional information is provided in Helen Suggett's "A Letter Describing Richard II's Reconciliation with the City of London, 1392," *English Historical Review* 62 (1947): 209–13, and in Robert Withington's *English Pageantry*, 2 vols. (Cambridge: Harvard University Press, 1918–26; rpt. New York: Arno Press, 1980), 1.130 (quoting from Bodleian MS. Ashmole 793).

3. For analyses, see, for example, Withington, *English Pageantry*, 1.131 (now outdated), Kipling, *passim,* and Lawrence Manley, *Literature and Culture in Early Modern London* (Cambridge: Cambridge University Press, 1995), 242–43. Both Kipling and Manley see the 1392 pageant as developed from 1377's (and, for Kipling, also from 1382's).

4. Withington, for example, includes the 1377 entry in *English Pageantry*, 1.128, as the first with a constructed, stationary pageant; Kipling has called it "the first known civic triumph" (88), with "the earliest recorded appearance of actors and pageantry at a royal entry" (84), and with its constructed castle a "first attempt" (88), followed by a second castle in 1382. Manley, 242, has discussed the typological symbolism of the English royal entry, in general, as having begun with the 1377 constructed pageant.

5. See Holinshed, *Chronicles,* 2.713: although the word "pageant" could be used, both in Holinshed's time and earlier, simply for an elaborate display of some sort; the term did not necessarily refer to a theatrical construction.

6. See Holinshed, *Chronicles,* 2.713, and Thomas Walsingham, *Historia Anglicana,* ed. Henry Thomas Riley, 7 vols., Rolls Series #28 (London: HMSO, 1863–76), 1.331–32. Walsingham's account is partially reproduced and translated in *Early English Stages,* 1.54–55. It is possible in both descriptions that some individuals other than the maidens offered the cups of wine; but this does not seem likely. *The Anonimalle Chronicle 1333–1381,* ed. V. H. Galbraith (Manchester: Manchester University Press, 1927), tells us (108) that the tower ("tour") was made of wood and painted canvas.

7. Goldsmiths' MS 1519, p. 21, col. b. The MSS of the Worshipful Company of Goldsmiths are located at Goldsmiths' Hall, and I am grateful to the Company and especially to its former and present librarians, Susan Hare and David Beasley, for generous provision of access. William Herbert, *The History of the Twelve Great Livery Companies of London,* 2 vols. (London: privately printed, 1834–37; rpt. Newton Abbot/New York: David & Charles/Augustus M. Kelley, 1968), 2.216–17, wrongly states that the Goldsmiths' MS accounts do not include the 1377 pageant.

8. Goldsmiths' MS 1518, p. 57, col. b. (Herbert's description, *History,* 2.218 contains some errors and omissions.)

9. See Herbert, *History,* 2.218.

10. See, for example, Mary-Rose McLaren, "The Aims and Interests of the London Chroniclers of the Fifteenth Century," in *Trade, Devotion and Governance: Papers in Later Medieval History,* ed. Dorothy J. Clayton, Richard G. Davies, and Peter McNiven (Stroud, Gloucestershire, and Dover, NH: Alan Sutton, 1994), 158–76. McLaren deals with fifteenth-century London chroniclers, but the same argu-

ments can largely be made about earlier and later chroniclers, both general and specific, as well.

11. See Richard H. Osberg, "The Goldsmiths' 'Chastell' of 1377," *Theatre Survey* 27, nos. 1–2 (May and November 1986):1–15.

12. For thirteenth-century royal entries, see Robert Withington, "The Early 'Royal-Entry'," *PMLA* 32 (1917): 616–23; Ian Lancashire, *Dramatic Texts and Records of Britain: A Chronological Topography to 1558* (Cambridge/Toronto: Cambridge University Press/University of Toronto Press, 1984), lists two of these entries as possibly involving pageants, #880 (1207) and 881 (1236). For the 1313 portable pageant, see Withington's *English Pageantry*, 1.126 (portable pageants in 1298, noted at 1.124, were not for a royal entry). For London-area tournaments with role-playing before 1377, see *Dramatic Texts and Records*, #887 (1331), 889 (1343), 892 (1359), 893 (1362), and 896 (1375).

13. Holinshed, *Chronicles*, 2.669; Grafton, *Chronicle*, 1.395; Fabyan, *New Chronicles*, 467; Stow, *Annales*, 409. (The first three similarly comment, for 1382, only that Anne was met and conveyed with great triumph to Westminster: see Holinshed, 2.753, Grafton, 1.429, and Fabyan, 531; and Stow says nothing about a London entry for Anne.)

14. See *Knighton's Chronicle 1337–1396*, ed. and trans. G. H. Martin (Oxford: Clarendon Press, 1995), 150 (Latin text) and 151 (English text: "And what quantities of bows and arrows, and of every kind of arms, there were on display . . .").

15. See the *Chronicon Anonymi Cantuariensis* in *Chronica Johannis de Reading et Anonymi Cantuariensis 1346–1367*, ed. James Tait (Manchester: Manchester University Press, 1914), 205, and the *Anonimalle Chronicle*, 41. In the *Anonimalle Chronicle* the maidens are described as "seaunt ou esteaunt sur cordes de say sotilement et mervaillousement;" and cords are also mentioned in the *Chronicon Anonymi Cantuariensis*. *Dramatic Texts and Records*, #891, suggests (with a query mark) that the maidens were suspended in a cage ("in quadam catasta"); but the word "catasta" normally ("catesta") meant a platform or scaffold.

16. For the specific Cheapside location of the 1357 pageant, extending from the area of the Goldsmiths to that of the Saddlers (or between the two areas), see the *Chronicon Anonymi Cantuariensis*, 205, and the map in George Unwin's *The Gilds and Companies of London* (London: Methuen, 1908), 34; for 1377, see Holinshed, *Chronicles*, 2.713 ("the vpper end of Cheape"), and Walsingham, *Historia Anglicana*, 1.332 (although Wickham in *Early English Stages*, 1.55, believes—seemingly wrongly—that the 1377 castle was at the Great Conduit). For 1392's castle as located at Cheapside's Standard, see above, n. 2. (The modern English translation in *The Westminster Chronicle 1381–1394*, ed. and trans. L. C. Hector and Barbara F. Harvey [Oxford: Clarendon Press, 1982], places [505] the 1392 castle in East [not West] Cheap, but the original Latin [504] has merely "Chepe".) Bodleian MS Ashmole 793, as quoted in Withington's *English Pageantry*, 1.130, places the 1392 castle ("stage") between the Cheapside Cross (just west of the Standard) and St. Paul's, as does the letter ("parentre lez deux croys"—presumably the Cheapside Cross and St. Paul's Cross) to which Suggett (see above, n. 2) drew attention in 1947. For all of these locations, see the excellent Map #3, c. 1520, in Mary D. Lobel, gen. ed., *The British Atlas of Historic Towns*, vol. 3, *The City of London: From Prehistoric Times to c. 1520* (Oxford: Oxford University Press in conjunction with the Historic Towns Trust, 1989).

17. See, for example, Kipling, "Richard II's 'Sumptuous Pageants,'" 88–89.

(Much of his interpretative work reappears—and is extended for other entries—in his recent *Enter the King: Theatre, Liturgy, and Ritual in the Medieval Civic Triumph* [Oxford: Clarendon Press, 1998].)

18. Kipling, "Richard II's 'Sumptuous Pageants,'" 88, interprets the maidens of 1377's castle as angels.

19. See the *Westminster Chronicle*, 504–5.

20. Janet S. Loengard, "An Elizabethan Lawsuit: John Brayne, his Carpenter, and the Building of the Red Lion Theatre," *Shakespeare Quarterly* 34, no. 3 (Autumn 1983): 298–310.

John Brayne and His Other Brother-in-Law

Herbert Berry

WHEN IN 1579 John Brayne and his brother-in-law, James Burbage, mortgaged their playhouse in Shoreditch, the Theatre, Bayne had just resolved a quarrel with another brother-in-law over another mortgage. He was Edward Stowers, a blacksmith, who explained his side of the quarrel in a lawsuit against Brayne in the Star Chamber.[1] The events at issue began in or before 1562 and ended in 1578. Brayne, a grocer, built the Red Lion playhouse in 1567, and he and Burbage built the Theatre in 1576. Brayne's wife was Stowers's sister, and Burbage's wife was Brayne's sister.

In the lawsuit, which consists only of Stowers's bill of complaint, Stowers says he is of "Averstone," Essex, yeoman—rather than blacksmith, presumably, because he wanted to appear as a property owner, not a rude mechanical. "Averstone" is Alphamstone, then also called Alverston. He explains that he owned "one messuage or tenemente wth thappurten*a*nces theare vnto belonginge" together with two parcels of land containing six acres in Bures St. Mary, Essex. That parish extends across the Stour into Suffolk, where the church is. The part in Essex was and is often called Bures Hamlet, and it adjoins Alphamstone.[2]

Stowers mortgaged the property to William Sparkes for £15. Then William Warrison, citizen and pewterer of London, paid off the mortgage and took a new one. When Warrison died, he left the new mortgage to his uncle and next heir, Peter Warrison, clerk, parson of Brown Candover in Hampshire, who conveyed it to Alice Abell, widow of St. Andrew Holborn in London. In her hands it became forfeit so that she owned the property. She would not, however, take advantage but (like John Hyde, the mortgagee at the Theatre) allow Stowers to redeem the property when he could pay off the debt, because the value of the property was great, the amount still owing was small, and she cared for Stowers's welfare.

Now Brayne, "a verry dangerous sobtell and craftie mane," secretly "intreated" the widow to convey the property to him. Brayne alleged "vnto her by greate and sollem vowes . . . that he did it only for the love he bore vnto" Stowers, to whom "he was tied in concience as well as in respecte of marriadge of his sister to doe what good he coulde for" Stowers. The idea, Stowers thought, was to enable him more easily to redeem the property. Brayne would control it and the widow would continue to hold the mortgage so that Stowers could "wth better and greater ease . . . and lese grefe of mynd" make small payments that Brayne would give to the widow. Brayne often solicited Stowers "to the said purpose," alleging that he would "franckly and frely wthout any recompence at all" allow Stowers to redeem the property and speaking of "betteringe and p*re*searvinge" Stowers's "estate and welfare." Supposing that Brayne "ment honestly and faythefully as he did speke and swere," the widow "willed" Brayne to send Stowers to her, and she, too, urged Stowers to consent to the arrangement. So "vpon thes and many other solleme othes and professiones," Stowers consented, and in two indentures dated in the fourteenth year of Elizabeth (which began on 17 November 1571) the widow assigned the property to Brayne.

Stowers then spent great sums on the place, on traveling to it, and "for the lone of the saide money." Eventually he repaid Brayne and demanded that Brayne convey the property to him along with the evidences by which he controlled it. Brayne complied. He had a lawyer draw up "an ample and sufficient reassueravnce of the messuage & lands" to Stowers and "Vppon the sodden broughte fourthe & deliu*er*yd vnto" him "a great many of owld wrightinges" about it. Stowers could not read and "neuer trobled" anybody "wth the sighte of" the documents, but "beleued faythefully" everything Brayne had said about them. Then "for the p*re*servacione of him selfe his wife and famelly," he "was constrayned to once more morgadge the saide messuage or tenement wth the twoe peces of land therevnto belonginge vnto one of his trustie frendes who did not refuse to pleasure" him. The trusty friend could read and found that the documents were not what Stowers thought. Worse, they included "Indentures of bargayne and sale" by which Brayne had conveyed "vnto diu*er*s other p*er*sones . . . the saide landes and messuage."

With "falshode and cosseninge" Brayne meant "to gayne vnto him selfe and his heires the Inherritavnce of the saide messuage and land." He did not have "the feare of god before his eyes or any remorse or sparke of grace to thinke of his depe and great vowes sworne vnto" Stowers, "but [was] seduced and lede by the devell who hathe drawen him in to a great many of suche like fowle and bade acciones." Brayne had "committed moste horrable and vilde decayte and cossenadge, by reason of wch cossenadge and decayte" Stowers could not borrow money on the property—"could not nor cannot eny waye performe relefe vnto him selfe and charge, wch vilde and horrable parte is most odious before the almightie god, contrary to the dewtie of a good and faythefull subiecte[,] the evell example of others[,] The vtter vndoinge and ouerthrowghe of" Stowers, "his pore wife children and famelly, and to the viollatinge of his [Brayne's] owne depe . . . vowes [and] othes." Stowers then ended the bill as customary, by asking the court to subpoena Brayne.

Stowers's bill is an untidy and unconvincing piece of legal writing. Not only is it undated, but Stowers left the date of the original mortgage blank (twice), ignored the dates of other events, and gave that of the two indentures only as the fourteenth year of Elizabeth. Major assertions should be wrong: that Stowers's welfare was the whole point of the widow's and Brayne's negotiations, and that Brayne's documents included both an ample and sufficient conveyance to Stowers and an indenture of sale to somebody else. He was also wrong, as we shall see, to think that in Elizabeth's fourteenth year the widow's name was Abell. Moreover, Stowers's remarks about Brayne and his dealings seem excessive, to justify, probably, filing the lawsuit in the Star Chamber rather than a more mundane court. Luckily, documents survive explaining much of what really happened and when.

Mortgages looked like outright sales, but at the end or in a separate contract the mortgagee conceded that the sale would be void if the mortgagor paid a sum or series of sums by a time or times specified. The pewterer, William Warrison, acquired Stowers's mortgage on 10 October 1562. He died in 1563, leaving it to his uncle, Peter Warrison—who, as the nominee of the abbot of Hyde, had become rector of Brown Candover on 2 March 1558. In a deed that does not say Stowers could redeem the property, Peter Warrison gave the mortgage to Alice Abell, the widow of Henry Abell, on 14 February 1565. He wrote his will on 7 October following, and it was proved on 16 November.[3] Alice Abell was his main beneficiary, one of his overseers, and a witness to a codicil in which he left clothing to "his freindes," who included Brayne and his wife. He also left in her keeping two pieces of jewellery for her granddaughter, Katherine Wolveridge[4]—one a "chaine of golde with a crucifixe with thre perlls at it." Alice Abell ceased to be either a widow or Abell on 13 May 1566, when she married Roger Rapper of St. Andrew Holborn at her parish church, St. Dionis Backchurch, recently the parish church also of Brayne's wife. Late in 1568, however, she became a widow again.[5]

She sold Stowers's property to Brayne in three (not two) contracts on January 28, 1572, earnestly making the sale seem outright and giving him a bond of £100 that would be forfeit if it was not. The property is a "messuage" with "twoe parcelles of lande . . . whereof the one is called lytle Mayefelde and the other Robertes Crofte . . . conteyninge together . . . sixe acres more or lesse."[6] The main contract does not specify the price, but on the same day Brayne gave her a bond of £80, forfeit if he did not pay her an annuity of £3 for two years and £4 for fourteen more. On 19 June 1578, she said that she was "a poore aged and impotent widowe" sixty years old "and vpwardes," and in 1590 she died as Alice Rapier, widow, of St. Andrew Holborn.[7]

If Brayne did not reply to Stowers in the Star Chamber, he did reply in his will, which "syck in bodey," he wrote on 1 July 1578.[8] He described the property as "my howse mesuage or Tenemen*t*e with all landes howses yardes and appurtenaunces whatsoever to the same belonging," which he had "purchased and bought of Alice Rapers of London widdow." The property was now occupied by Brayne's tenant, John Claye, bricklayer. Brayne, therefore, had neither conveyed it to Stowers nor sold it to others. The documents he gave to Stowers, however, could have included a copy of a lease to Claye that made the place unmortgageable.

Brayne did not go on to deny Stowers's claim to the property or say that Stowers had not paid off the mortgage. Instead, he bequeathed the place "to my brother Edwarde Stowers of Averstow in the Countie of Essex Smith" on condition that Stowers pay Brayne's widow £10 "for such Costes Chardges and expences w[ch] I haue laide owte . . . in sutes of lawe towchinge the said howse or messuage." The lawsuit, no doubt, was that in the Star Chamber, and Stowers, having paid for the bill, would also pay for the responnse to it.

Stowers soon died. He was buried on 21 August 1578, in the parish of St. Leonard Shoreditch, where Brayne and the Burbages lived and the Theatre was.[9] His death, and Brayne's will, may have caused the lawsuit to collapse before the Star Chamber could do much about it. Brayne would quarrel bitterly, even violently, with Burbage and another associate, Robert Miles, and die bankrupt in 1586.[10]

If Stowers did not redeem his property, a relative probably did. For Edward Stower, blacksmith, owned much land and three houses in Bures Hamlet, Essex, when he wrote his will on 4 February 1604.[11] Two houses were in a "crofte of land": a new "messuage" where he lived and a "howse thirvnto belonginge." The third was a "messuage" called Lowis with "yerds Orcherds & gardyns." He could have been of the right age to be the son of Brayne's brother-in-law, for his eldest son lived separately in Lowis, his second son and eldest daughter were married and each had one child, his second daughter had just married, and his third and fourth daughters were unmarried. The will was proved on 30 September 1606.

In the transactions of 1572, Alice Rapier would capitalize her stake and Brayne would have Claye's rent and either Stowers' payments or the place outright if Stowers did not make them—the more likely if Stowers could not remortgage the place. Were these dealings horrible, vile, dishonest, and odious before almighty God? By the standard of the ways in which Miles squeezed Brayne out of the George Inn in Whitechapel and (thanks to the mortgage of 1579), Burbage squeezed Brayne's widow out of the theatre, the answer is no.

Notes

1. Public Record Office (hereafter PRO), STAC.5/S.31/37.
2. English Place-Name Society, *Essex.* 405, 420.
3. PRO, PROB.6/1, f. 67ᵛ (William Warrison's probate act); C.54/675, no. 4 (the deed of gift); PROB. 11/48, ff. 234ᵛ–235ᵛ, 362ᵛ–363ᵛ (Peter Warrison's will); and Hampshire Record Office, Winchester, 21M65/A.1/25,f. 10ᵛ (his appointment). The abbot of Hyde was John Capon (alias Salcot), who was also bishop of Salisbury. He cooperated with the reformers in the 1530s, reconciled to Rome when Mary became queen, and died in October 1557. See William Dugdale, *Monasticon Anglicanum* (London, 1846), 2.432, and *DNB*.
4. The Abells' only child, Fortune, married Thomas Hychcok and had three

children; she then married James Wolveridge, gentleman, of Odiham, Hampshire, and had Katherine (PRO, Req.2/261/8, the bill).

5. Guildhall Library (hereafter GL), Mss. 17602, and 9050/1, f. 53^v. Margaret Stowers belonged to St. Dionis Backchurch when she married Brayne there on 14 January 1565.

6. PRO, C.54/873, mm.22 (Alice Raper's bond), 23 (Brayne's bond), 29–30 (the indenture of sale). This description of the property virtually translates that in Latin in the deed of gift).

7. PRO, Req.2/261/8, the bill; and GL, 9050/2, f.46.

8. GL, Ms. 9171/17, ff. 29^v–30. The London Commissary Court accepted the will without demur, but in 1588 James Burbage apparently suspected that Brayne' widow had forged it (PRO, C.3/222/83).

9. GL, Ms. 74991/1, f.21.

10. See my "Shylock, Robert Miles, and Events at the Theatre," *Shakespeare Quarterly* 44 (Summer 1993): 183–97.

11. Suffolk Record Office, Bury St. Edmunds, IC 500/1/64/77.

Domestical Matters

R. A. FOAKES

A PROPOSED REISSUE of my edition of *Henslowe's Diary* (1961)[1] by Cambridge University Press led me to work through it again, recalling the bad press Henslowe has continued to suffer. W. W. Greg thought of Henslowe as "an illiterate moneyed man . . . who regarded art as a subject for exploitation,"[2] and he therefore assumed that the dealings recorded in the diary were untypical of the Elizabethan companies. Scholars have been the more willing to accept such a notion because it enabled a comforting contrast with Shakespeare and the Lord Chamberlain's Men for whom he wrote. The sweet and gentle Shakespeare could be thought of as belonging to a better class of people, while Henslowe might be imaged as an "unscrupulous mismanager" who "employed" a bunch of "hack-writers" to patch up plays or scribble new ones in collaboration for quick consumption at his theater, the Rose, and who imposed an "autocratic rule" on the players.[3] Has he been demonized largely in order to substantiate a belief that Shakespeare belonged to a morally superior company that somehow escaped the stigma of profit-making?

In 1961 I argued that there were no grounds for seeing Henslowe as untypical, or for regarding his arrangements with the company and the dramatists in the 1590s as unscrupulous and designed to keep them in subservience. Others have gone much further in rejecting the notion of Henslowe as exceptional. Carol Rutter, indeed, says bluntly that "from top to bottom the Elizabethan playhouse was organized for profit,"[4] and points out that James Burbage, whose example may have prompted Henslowe to invest in a theater, was more pugnacious and more absolute in control of his theater than Henslowe. She also corrects what remains a misleading impression that Henslowe somehow controlled the players and writers at the Rose. She notes that he did not employ them, commission them, or manage them. He owned the theater, and so was landlord, and provided a service as banker to the company, without (it appears) charging the group the interest he expected for personal loans and loans on pawn. Hardly the method of an unscrupulous profiteer.

Interpretation of the accounts is bound to be affected by what we think of Henslowe himself, and it is difficult to see him plain if only because of lingering prejudices against linking art and business; we have only to think of some recent biographies of Shakespeare that register with a sense of disappointment his financial dealings, concern for property, and ambitions for status, as though it is somehow improper for a great artist to mess with such things. Henslowe is much more difficult to see clearly because he was a facilitator and no artist. But in revisiting the diary I am struck by what one might call its human aspects. What, after all, were Henslowe's own ambitions? He would today have been a good Rotarian as he became richer, and he served his community in various capacities: collector of tax subsidies, vestryman, churchwarden, collector of poor relief, governor of the grammar school in his parish of the Clink. It was no doubt useful for him to be a Groom of the Chamber to Queen Elizabeth, and then Gentleman Sewer to King James in connection with performances by the Rose and Fortune players at court. But as late as 1603, Francis Woodward acknowledges a debt to Philip Henslowe, who still called himself "Citizen and Dyer" of London (*HD* 262), so he does not seem to have been too concerned about his social standing. The players address him as "Mr," the same title used for the sharers in the company. "When I lent I was a friend, & when I asked I was unkind" was scrawled by Henslowe on the first page of the diary, words that perhaps we should take seriously.

Henslowe was not consistent or fussy about titles. Playwrights often are recorded as "m^r dickers" or "Mr Chapmane," but also casually as "Cheatell" (45^v, 89), or "m^r drayton, willsone & dickers" (f49, 96). My impression is not that Henslowe was careless, but that he was casual in making the entries in his account book. When he began to list receipts from performances in 1592, his first entry is for 17s. 3d. at *Friar Bacon* in February. In March *Henry VI* brought in £3. 16s. 8d., but from then on he rounds his sums to shillings or shillings and sixpence. The last entry that includes sixpence is for 26 May 1592; thereafter Henslowe lists sums in shillings or pounds and shillings only until 2 July 1594, when sixpence again begins to figure in the receipts. From 24 September 1594 until 21 November

1595 no sixpences are recorded, but twice, on 22 November and 12 December 1595, a sixpence again appears. After this date there are no more until January 1597, when the form of entries changes into the still puzzling five-column style, marked "tt" (= total?) instead of the usual "Rd" (= received). The first two columns of these entries seem to continue to represent half the gallery receipts rounded to pounds and shillings. The last three columns appear to signify pounds shillings and pence, for though the last column understandably once has 13, and once 14 in entries of £2 and 13 pence, £3 and 14 pence, the remaining figures are all less than twelve. So what is going on here? It seems likely, as Carol Rutter suggested, that the last three columns represent amounts passed on to Henslowe in partial repayment of the company's debt to him, after they borrowed heavily from him. The amounts listed vary from nothing to £9 or more, with one later sum of £30 (unless Henslowe accidentally reversed the figure and meant to write 03). These entries began in January 1597 and run to July, by which time Henslowe seems to have grown bored, as they stutter with days missed and peter out on 28 July. In October he briefly tried again, but abandoned the method on November 5 after failing to make entries for a number of days.

If Henslowe was casual in his social relations, he seems also to have been somewhat casual here in his accounting procedures. The gallery moneys must daily have included odd pence, as the first entry for 17s. 3d. shows, but almost at once he recorded only sixpence from time to time, and phased these out to list only pounds and shillings. He rounded his figures up or down, and either kept the odd pence or passed them to the players for their half of the gallery takings. After losing interest in his detailed five-figure entries, he started a new set of entries recording the money he received from the company by the week instead of by the day; and, presumably because he was noting the company's payments rather than his own receipts, he is careful to record pence—so the listing begins (f36v, 71): "Rd the 21 of October 1597 . . . £5 1s 11d." He bankrolled the company for years, paying out for plays, costumes, properties, licensing fees to the Master of the Revels, and so on, and the company was almost always in debt to him for quite large sums. At various periods he took the whole of the gallery receipts, not just the half he was entitled to as owner, but the players' half as well, by which means debts were reduced or, more rarely, paid off. Periodically Henslowe totalled up his accounts against the company's borrowings, and the penultimate one, dated May 1603, is characteristic: it marks the arrival of James I in London, when they left off playing at the King's coming: "all reckonings abated" the company owed him "197^{li}—13^s—4^d, the fyftye pownds which Jonnes & shawe had at ther goinge a way not Reconed." It is followed immediately by another loan of 9s. for "facynge of A blacke grogren Clocke wth taffytye" (f.109^v, 209). Once more Henslowe tallied his state of affairs in March 1604:

> Caste vp all the acowntes frome the begininge of the world untell this daye beinge the 14 daye of marche 1604 by Thomas Dowghton & edward Jube for the company of the princes men & I Phillipe henslow so th^r Reastethe dewe unto me P henslow the sum of xxiiij^{li} all Reconynges consernynge the company in stocke generall descarged & my sealfe descarged to them of al deats. (f.110, 209–10)

There seems a touch of weariness about this entry—was he ever repaid all that he had lent?

Henslowe was not a sharer, but (like Thomas Greene, leader of the Red Bull company) he seems to have paid for necessary provisions for the company out of his own pocket, and to have been a "full adventurer and storer."[5] The playhouse inventories of 1598—first printed by Malone from originals now lost—show Henslowe's spellings, and some of the apparel listed was "Leaft above in the tier-house in the cheast" (319), so a reasonable inference is that Henslowe was the storer of clothes and properties, which were kept in or near the Rose. The properties famously seem listed at random as they came to hand, and include a hell mouth, two steeples, the city of Rome, two moss banks, a tree of golden apples, a lion and a "great horse," and Phaeton's chariot. Henslowe must have had quite a time of it dusting off all this miscellaneous collection. The itemization in March 1598 may have had something to do with sorting out company finances, but reflects also Henslowe's concern to have a written notation of everything, though it is questionable whether he ever looked again at most of the entries in his account book.

The diary includes other personal and family accounts. Henslowe evidently made a habit of recording such business, perhaps just to clarify for himself how matters stood. So, in between notes of loans to actors, he details what his brother Edmund owed him in 1593—debts not discharged, since Edmond died that year. Henslowe notes a little later his expenses on behalf of his children, and then, in between a loan to his attorney and one to the actor Thomas Downton, is the laconic entry, "The ij chelldren of edmond hensley mary & nan came up to london to me to keppe the 27 of febreary & in the yeare of o^r Lord 1595" (f.40^v, 79). Their mother Margery died that year, and as Henslowe had paid for their board to their mother, he looked "a cordynge to the will to be a lowed yt agayne" (f124, 230). In 1604 he was laying out money to defend one of these children, John, in some suit involving his father's will, and on another occasion he bought the other, Nan, a gown "when her syster turned her awaye" (123^v, 228). All these notations appear to be memoranda by someone who liked to note things down.

The articles of grievance brought against him and his partner Jacob Meade much later in 1615 by the Prince's Men have too often been taken as prime evidence about Henslowe's character. This document contains a long miscellaneous list of complaints put together as if at a gathering in some inn, where every member of the company put his oar in—one can almost hear an actor whose anger has been enhanced by drink shouting, "Hey, don't forget he diddled us that time too." The list is incoherent, and it is not clear whether the sums mentioned have any validity. The company accused Henslowe of withholding their stock of apparel and plays, and of cheating the players over a period of three years since 1612, saying "should these fellowes Come out of my debt I should have noe rule wth: them." The next article relates to the new situation brought about by Henslowe's death in January 1616 some months later. In this the players acknowledged that they owed Henslowe and his partner Jacob Meade £400 for loans and costumes, and Alleyn discharged their debt for £200.[6] It is not clear what the connection is between this document and the complaint, but it is apparent that they had been substantially in debt to Henslowe, and some time later they lamented the "intemperate weather and still more intemperate Mr Meade," so the resentment they had built up since 1612 may have been provoked by him.[7] There seems to me little reason to take this muddled affair at the very end of his life, which only confirmed that the players owed Henslowe a lot of money, as having much to do with his character as shown more or less throughout the diary.

I see little in Henslowe's 1590s accounts that conflicts with the impression given by the few remaining letters exchanged between him and Edward Alleyn, when he was touring with the company during the plague year of 1593. These include much attention to what Alleyn called "domestycall matters." Henslowe looked after Alleyn's horse, his clothes ("your whitte wascote & you^r lute bockes & other thinges"), his "mouse" (as he called his wife), and his garden: "you^r beanes are growen to hey headge & well coded & all other thinges doth very well." He also took Alleyn's advice about keeping the house clean and strewing his doors and windows with wormwood and rue against the plague that was killing off his neighbours. He ends "I praye ye sonne comend me harteley to all the Reast of you^r fealowes in generall for I growe poore for lacke of them therfor have no geaftes to sende but as good & faythfull a harte as they shall desyer to have comen a mongeste them" (Article 13, 279). I think the diary shows Henslowe had in general a good and faithful heart towards his family, friends, and companies of players. He lent freely and tried to keep the company together, and even when getting the players to acknowledge their debts to him in 1600 he at once lends another £22 (f.70 136). The book was not used to threaten or cajole, but to provide notes. When reconstituting the company in 1597–98 Henslowe notes specifically in each case as a "memorandum" the bonds entered into by sharers and players to perform at the Rose for two or three years. The bonds are carefully set out (ff. 229^v–233, 238–42) with the names of witnesses, but these names are in Henslowe's own hand, so as bonds they had no legal standing. Maybe Henslowe liked when necessary to be able to say "It's in the book, you know," but the indications are that he did well out of his theaters and that it was not in his interest to make things difficult for the players. Fussy he may have been, and keen to put things in writing, but mainly for his private satisfaction or as a record for the company, and it is not inappropriate that the book has become generally known as Henslowe's diary.

Notes

1. *Henslowe's Diary,* Edited for Cambridge University Press by R. A. Foakes and R. T. Rickert. My collaborator sadly is no longer alive.
2. See *Henslowe's Diary,* xxv.
3. Andrew Gurr, *The Shakespearean Stage,* 3rd edition (Cambridge: Cambridge University Press, 1992), 58–59; *The Shakespearean Playing Companies* (Oxford: Oxford University Press, 1996), 9.
4. Carol Chillington Rutter, *Documents of the Rose Playhouse* (Manchester: Manchester University Press, 1984; revised 1999), 7.

5. See C. J. Sisson, "The Red Bull Company and the Importunate Widow, *Shakespeare Survey* 7 (1954): 57–68.

6. The articles were printed in *Henslowe Papers: Being Documents Supplementary to the Diary,* ed. W. W. Greg (London: A. H. Bullen, 1907), 86–91.

7. *Henslowe Papers,* 93.

Sir John Astley and Court Culture

John H. Astington

SIR JOHN ASTLEY, the man who became Master of the Revels in 1622, and (for reasons we do not fully understand) deputized the post to Sir Henry Herbert soon thereafter, has not left many traces of his career that have so far been discovered. His father, Master of the Jewel House to Queen Elizabeth, was a moderately important court figure, and received attention in the *DNB,* while his son did not. Richard Dutton clarified the confusion that is sometimes made over Astley *père et fils,* and pointed out that the younger Astley is the only Master of the Revels we know of who participated in court revels as a performer: he danced as a costumed masquer in both *Hymenaei* in January 1606 and *Lord Hay's Masque* in January 1607.[1] On the first occasion he was the most lowly male dancer of a very distinguished group of aristocratic performers; on the second he is listed fifth of nine in the printed text of the show, or jointly fourth with Sir Richard Preston as "Gent[lemen] of the K[ing's] privie Chamber."[2] His appointment to the Privy Chamber, made when he was knighted in 1603, must have been an important step in his rise, and have facilitated his access to the kind of post to which he acquired the reversion in 1612, and took up ten years later; his predecessor as Master of the Revels, Sir George Buc, received the same advancements as Astley at precisely the same time. Dutton raises the questions of who Astley's patrons may have been, and whether they were too weak or marginal to have supported him when he eventually became master of the Revels.[3] The signs from the early Jacobean years, at least, are that this seems unlikely. Younger masquers were sometimes given their roles on the strength of their legs or good looks, but Astley can hardly have been in his first youth by 1606–7—probably he was about fifty. That he was chosen to celebrate James Hay's marriage in the year following, having danced with Hay at the Essex wedding, suggests that Astley may have connected himself with Hay's circle. Having come from Scotland with the new king, Hay was to be a prominent member of the court, and a loyal servant of the realm: Viscount Doncaster, first earl of Carlisle, Master of the Wardrobe, special ambassador to France and Germany, chief negotiator in the marriage of Prince Charles to princess Henrietta Maria of France, patron of Ben Jonson among others, and sponsor of entertainments at his London residence, Essex House.[4] Any connection Astley may have made with Hay is likely to have been to his advantage in those aspects of the Mastership that involved the ceremonial and political functions of court entertainments, for example.

If, like Buckingham, Astley partly danced his way to favor, however, there are signs that he was also a man of some literary accomplishment, as were other Masters of the Revels before and after him: the tradition of skill in the liberal arts had persisted since the days of Sir Thomas Cawarden.[5] Only one example of his work as a court poet was ever published, though other pieces may yet await discovery in manuscript. His dedicatory sonnet to Lewis Lewkenor's translation of Gasparo Contarini's *Commonwealth and Government of Venice* (London, 1599; *STC* 5642) appears between two others, the first by *"Edw. Spencer"* (that is, Edmund Spenser) and the last by Maurice Kyffin. The second poem is followed by the name *"I. Ashley,"* a common variant of Astley's surname that appears in both the masque texts in which he is mentioned.[6] The poems follow Lewkenor's dedication of the book to Lady Anne Dudley, countess of Warwick (1548–1604). Since the poem has never been noticed, as far as I am aware, in the context of Astley's life and work, I reproduce it here with modernized spelling and punctuation. It has no title, but might be called "On Venice."

> Fair maiden town, that in rich Thetis' arms
> Hast still been fostered since thy first foundation,
> Whose glorious beauty calls unnumbered swarms
> Of rarest spirits from each foreign nation,
> And yet (sole wonder to all Europe's ears,
> Most lovely nymph that ever Neptune got)
> In all this space of thirteen hundred years
> Thy virgin's state ambition ne'er could blot;
> Now I prognosticate thy ruinous case,
> When thou shalt from thy Adriatic seas
> View in this ocean isle thy painted face
> In these pure colours, coyest eyes to please.

Then gazing in thy shadow's peerless eye,
Enamoured like Narcissus thou shalt die.

Astley's sonnet stands up well when compared with Spenser's, which precedes it ("The antique *Babel,* empress of the east"), and it is considerably superior to the following poem by Kyffin. It is in English form, with three alternately rhymed quatrains and a final couplet, and its central conceit, of an exotic water-nymph drawn to "this ocean isle" by the power of native genius, is interestingly close to that used by Jonson for the masques of *Blackness* and *Beauty* some years later, save that in Astley's poem *tradotta* proves to be *tradita.* In addition to Henry "Elmes," whose eight lines of verses follow the sonnets,[7] a fifth poet also contributed to Lewkenor's prefatory material: Sir John Harington (1560–1612), whose twelve-line poem "Lo, here's described, though but in little room" is placed after Lewkenor's address to the reader. Harington and Astley undoubtedly knew each other: their fathers had been close friends and associates in the Marian years, and remained so in the Elizabethan court.[8] In the later collection of Harington's verse, *The Most Elegant and Witty Epigrams* (1618), the poem is dated 1595, which seems a more likely date for the other material also. Spenser died early in 1599, very soon after having arrived in London from Ireland; his prior residence in London had been in 1595–96, and in the later year he had dedicated *Four Hymns* to Anne Dudley and her sister. The prefatory material to Lewkenor's book was probably assembled some time before the author completed his dedicatory epistle, which is dated 13 August 1598; the book was entered in the Stationers' Register in December of that year.

Thus we are presented with three coordinates for Astley's activities in the final decade of the Elizabethan court. It is of considerable interest that the first Master of Ceremonies, Lewkenor, and the fourth Master of the Revels had known each other for a long time before their official duties at the Jacobean court brought them together in the 1620s, however briefly. Of the four other writers contributing to Lewkenor's book, only two, Spenser and Harington, had particular knowledge of Italian poetry; perhaps Astley, like Lewkenor himself, and like the Masters of the Revels Tilney, Buc, and Herbert, was a linguist and a traveler. Lewkenor's contact with Kyffin was probably through military experience in the Low Countries, perhaps under Leicester and Sir Robert Sidney; Astley, who was a Gentleman Pensioner, may also have had some knowledge of war service. Lewkenor's patroness, the countess of Warwick, suggests a further circle in which Astley may have had a place. A surviving Dudley, she provided a focus for those formerly patronized by her brother-in-law Robert (d. 1588) and her husband Ambrose (d. 1590), including the latter's troupe of players.[9] In her own right she was a trusted intimate of the queen, and was, according to her niece Lady Ann Clifford, no less valued "in the whole Court and the Queen's dominions."[10] She survived to see and to participate in the transition from the old reign to the new, and was in a position to advance the careers of those who looked to her for support. Lewkenor was certainly one of these, and Astley may have been another, as Spenser had been. The first had already been appointed to his new post by the time of her death early in 1604,[11] whereas Astley would have had to cultivate new supporters of his court ambitions, James Hay apparently among them. Both Astley's literary skill and his experience in "kickshawses" are likely to have recommended him to a leading Jacobean courtier who sponsored revels in his own household.

Notes

1. Richard Dutton, *Mastering the Revels* (Iowa City: University of Iowa Press), 218–20.

2. Walter R. Davis, ed., *The Works of Thomas Campion* (London: Faber and Faber, 1969), 212–13. Dutton points out Davis's error in his note on Astley.

3. Dutton, *Mastering the Revels,* 220–30. His account of the change in mastership is contested by N. W. Bawcutt in "Evidence and Conjecture in Literary Scholarship: The Case of Sir John Astley Reconsidered," *English Literary Renaissance* 22 (1992): 333–46.

4. See Timothy Raylor, "The Lost Essex House Masque (1621): A Manuscript Text Recovered," *English Manuscript Studies 1100–1700* 7 (1998): 86–130; "The Design and Authorship of *The Essex House Masque* (1621)," *Medieval and Renaissance Drama in England* 10 (1998): 218–37; *The Essex House Masque of 1621* (Pittsburgh: Duquesne University Press, 2000).

5. See W. R. Streitberger, *Court Revels 1485–1559* (Toronto: University of Toronto Press, 1994); "On Edmond Tyllney's Biography," *Review of English Studies* n.s. 29 (1978): 11–35; *Edmond Tyllney, Master of the Revels and Censor of Plays* (New York: AMS Press, 1986); Mark Eccles, "Sir George Buc, Master of the Revels," *Sir Thomas Lodge and other Elizabethans,* ed. C. J. Sisson (Cambridge: Harvard University Press, 1933), 409–506; Amy P. Charles, "Sir Henry Herbert as a Man of Letters," *Modern Philology* 80 (1982): 1–12.

6. Franklin B. Williams, Jr., *Index of Dedications and Commendatory Verses in English Books before 1641* (London: Oxford University Press, 1962).

7. According to Williams, Sir Henry Helmes of Gray's Inn.

8. See Ruth Hughey, *John Harington of Stepney* (Columbus: Ohio State University Press, 1971), 34, 51, 57, 70.

9. E. K. Chambers, *The Elizabethan Stage,* 4 vols. (Oxford: Clarendon, 1923); vol. 2, 99.

10. As quoted in George C. Williamson, *Lady Anne Clifford* (Kendall: T. Wilson & Son, 1922), 37.

11. See Susan Cerasano, "The Patronage Network of Philip Henslowe and Edward Alleyn," *Medieval and Renaissance Drama in England* 13 (2001): 82–92: 84 and n.

Two Playhouses, Both Alike in Dignity

Roslyn L. Knutson

JAMES WRIGHT, in *Historia Histrionica* (1699), invents a dialogue between two gentlemen, Lovewit and Truman, who reminisce about the good old days at the playhouse.[1] Truman answers Lovewit's query about the number of playing companies in former times by saying:

> Before the Wars, there were in being all these Play-houses at the same time. The *Black-friers,* and *Globe* on the *Bankside,* a Winter and Summer House, belonging to the same Company called the King's Servants; the *Cockpit* or *Phœnix,* in *Drury-lane,* called the Queen's Servants; the private House in *Salisbury-court,* called the prince's Servants; the *Fortune* near *White-cross-street,* and the *Red Bull* at the upper end of St. *John's-street:* The two last were mostly frequented by Citizens, and the meaner sort of People. All these Companies got Money, and Liv'd in Reputation, especially those of the *Blackfriers,* who were Men of grave and sober Behaviour. (B3)

This passage is the primary authority for the belief that the King's Men, after they acquired the lease of Blackfriars in August 1608, alternated between their two playhouses, playing at the Blackfriars in winter and the Globe in summer. Edmond Malone believed so, and he found evidence in the now-lost accounts of Henry Herbert, Master of the Revels from 1623 to 1673, that the King's Men as a rule moved to the Globe from Blackfriars in May. G. E. Bentley suggests that the move was coordinated with term time: to Blackfriars "on or about the sixth of October," at the opening of Michaelmas term; and to the Globe, "between 3 May and 4 June," at the close of Easter term.[2] Although acknowledging that Wright was referring to the Caroline playhouses (*JCS,* 6.15), Bentley explores the influence of the acquisition of Blackfriars on the repertory of the King's Men as though the company divided their labors between the two playhouses from the start.³ Andrew Gurr explicitly declares that "from 1609 onwards" the King's Men used the Globe "for the months from May to September" and the Blackfriars for the rest of the year.⁴ The effect of these opinions has been to subordinate the Globe to the Blackfriars in revenue, repertory, and clientele. However, there is evidence on the use and value of the two playhouses to suggest that from 1609 to 1619, and even into 1625, the Globe playhouse was more important to the business of the King's Men than is generally believed.

While accepting in principle the theory that the King's Men played at Blackfriars from October to May, scholars have recognized that some evidence undermines its literal application. For example, the Globe was open on April 30, 1619, when Prince Lewis Frederick of Württemburg saw *Othello,* and on April 20 and 30, 1611, when Simon Forman saw *Macbeth* and "Richard the 2," respectively.⁵ Also, there is a question about just how frequently the King's Men could have played at any house in the decade following their acquisition of the Blackfriars lease. Leeds Barroll, studying the monthly number of reported plague deaths from 1603 to 1613, argues against the optimistic view of playing "every afternoon for year after sunny year" from 1609 onwards.⁶ He calculates that the London playhouses (public and private) were closed more often than open from 1610 through 1613, if the rule of thirty deaths per week was observed.⁷ Barroll's open months, coordinated with Gurr's calendar of playhouse use (May to September at the Globe), coordinated with the Prince Lewis Frederick and Forman records, mean that the King's Men played at their two playhouses as shown in Table 1.

Another wrinkle in the use of the two playhouses is touring. Records of provincial performance locate the King's Men in Dover (Kent) on July 6, 1610; in Oxford sometime in 1609–10; in Dunwich (Suffolk) sometime between October 19 and 26, in 1610; in New Romney (Kent) on April 21, 1612; and Folkestone (Kent) and Oxford sometime in 1612–13.⁸ These records are doubtless incomplete; also, only three of the 1610–13 visits can be dated precisely. Nonetheless, it is reasonable to suppose that the visit to Dover in July 1610 represents a tour of some length in the southwest circuit; that the visit to Dunwich in October 1610 represents a return to the circuit of towns in the southwest.⁹ It may be coincidence that these visits occur in months when Barroll theorizes playhouse closures; but at the least they suggest that in two instances (October 1610,

Table 1. The King's Men at the Blackfriars and the Globe

	Blackfriars	Globe
1610	February	April (Prince Lewis Frederick), June
1610–11	December, January	
1611	October, November, December	April (Forman), May, June, July, August, September
1611–12	January, February	
1612	October	May, June, July, August, September
1612–13	January	
1613	April	May, June (Globe burned June 29)

April 1612) when the King's Men supposedly would have been playing at the Blackfriars (by Gurr's calendar), the players were on the road for part of the month.

According to F. P. Wilson, "from 1613 to 1624 the City was extraordinarily free" of plague.[10] Presumably, then, the King's Men were able to play at the Blackfriars from October through April and at the Globe from May through September. Yet the touring records for these years indicate that on many occasions the players interrupted their run of London performances in order to play in the provinces. The records that may be dated with some accuracy between January 1614 and the onset of plague in 1625 indicate the following trips during the months when the company was supposedly at the Blackfriars:

- **1614:** Coventry in November
- **1617:** Marlborough in November
- **1620:** Coventry in January, Londesborough (Derbyshire) in February, Kendal (Westmorland) in October, and Dunkenhalgh (Lancashire) in December
- **1621:** Nottingham (Nottinghamshire) in April, and Lydd (Kent) in October
- **1622:** Dover and Lydd (Kent) in April
- **1623:** Kendal (Westmorland) in February, and Canterbury and New Romney (Kent) in April
- **1624:** Dunkenhalgh (Lancashire) in December

- **1624:** Bridport (Dorset) in December
- **1625:** Londesborough and Doncaster (Derbyshire) in January

Another interruption in the playing schedule at the Blackfriars was Lent. Officially, playing was suspended, though no doubt there were performances on some days. In fact, on 29 March 1615, four weeks into the Lenten season that had begun on 22 February and would end on 9 April, the Privy Council admonished the King's Men for having played during Lent, decreeing "that neither they, nor the rest of their Company [should] presume to present any Playes or interludes, as they will answere the contrary at their perills."[11] This transgression notwithstanding, if the company did normally obey the Lenten suspension in the years represented by the chart above, their performances at the Blackfriars would have been further reduced from 21 February 1610 (Ash Wednesday), from 26 February 1612 (Ash Wednesday), and in April 1613, for the days preceding Easter on the 4th. For the years from 1614 to 1625, the King's Men would have lost the following playing periods at Blackfriars from Ash Wednesday to Easter: 1614, 9 March to 24 April; 1615, 22 February to 9 April; 1616, 14 February to 31 March; 1617, 5 March to 20 April; 1618, 18 February to 5 April; 1619, 10 February to 28 March; 1620, 1 March to 16 April; 1621, 14 February to 1 April; 1622, 6 March to 21 April; 1623, 26 February to 13 April; 1624, 11 February to 28 March; and 1625, 2 March to 17 April.

Bentley justifies the claim that "the Blackfriars was the premier theatre of England" from 1616 onwards and the Globe its "second" house by citing comparative profits, audiences, and repertory (*JCS*, 6.4, 179). Prominent in the evidence of income are the figures received by Henry Herbert, Master of the Revels, for two benefit performances, 1628–33; invariably, the receipts for the winter benefit are higher than those for the summer. In addition, Edward Kirkham testified in 1612 that the King's Men received "more in one winter in the said great hall [Blackfriars], by a thousand pounds, than they were used to get in the Bankside."[12] Furthermore, the profits at Blackfriars were supposedly elevated because the admission fees were higher than at the Globe, the seasons longer (seven months), the performances offered daily, and playgoers charged an extra 6d. to sit onstage. As evidence of a higher class of playgoer at Blackfriars, Bentley cites a letter from John Chamberlain (1625), a letter from Viscount Conway (1635), an argument between two playgoers (1632), and the visits of Sir Humphrey Mildmay (1635 ff.) (*JCS*, 6.4,

6, 16).[13] Bentley conjectures that the King's Men began as early as 1608 to adjust their repertory to the taste of a sophisticated audience at the Blackfriars.[14] Andrew Gurr sees that adjustment as taking place in 1611 with *The Tempest*.[15]

But there are problems with the solidity of this evidence as proof of the early superiority of the Blackfriars. Kirkham was comparing the revenue at the Blackfriars not with the Globe in that same year but with the Globe in winter in former years. The agreement between Herbert and the King's Men was not made until 1628, and the document does not specify the playhouses from which each benefit will come. The admission charges were undeniably higher at Blackfriars, and playgoers did pay extra to sit on the stage. However, the season was shortened by plague, touring, and Lent. Also, the evidence of daily performances may be more special pleading or advertising than fact. One piece of evidence circa 1619 is the petition by officers of the Blackfriars precinct, which complains about the congestion and uproar around the playhouse "almost everie daie in the winter tyme (not forbearinge the tyme of Lent)."[16] Another is the comment by John Heminges and Henry Condell in the preface, "To the Readers," in the 1623 Folio that playgoers sit on the stage at the Blackfriars and Cockpit "to arraigne Playes dailie." As to the class of playgoer at the Globe and Blackfriars, Andrew Gurr points out that there are more records of privileged playgoers at any playhouse any time than of citizen or commoner playgoers; he finds it telling that "in the decade 1590–99 . . . [when only public theaters were open] there is barely more than a single reference to citizens as playgoers."[17] Thus the evidence of upper-class playgoers at the Blackfriars is not in itself particularly significant. The two playgoers who undeniably attended performances by the King's Men, 1609–1625, were Prince Lewis Frederick and Simon Forman, and both men attended the Globe. The question of a "Blackfriars repertory" is too complicated to be answered here; suffice it to say that the first play printed with an exclusive advertisement of the King's Men at Blackfriars was in 1619 *(The Maid's Tragedy)*, whereas *A King and No King* in 1619 and *Philaster* in 1620 advertised the Globe. Even *The Duchess of Malfi*, which Gurr asserts was "first staged at Blackfriars in 1614,"[18] advertised the Globe as well as Blackfriars when it was printed in 1623.

Truman, James Wright's spokesman in *Historia Histrionica*, gave theater historians information about the playhouses in former times that has been somewhat carelessly applied, to the detriment of the reputation of the Globe. Truman's observation that the Blackfriars and Globe were winter and summer houses "before the Wars" has been backdated to 1610 and taken as a description of the King's Men's practice immediately on the acquisition of the Blackfriars lease. Truman's observation that "Citizens, and the meaner sort of people" attended the Fortune and Red Bull has been expanded to include the Globe. The hypothesis offered by Bentley in 1948—that a smart company would save its best new plays for the elite audience at its private house—has contributed to a belief that the Globe quickly lost standing in relation to the Blackfriars. But such a perspective distorts the evidence. The season at the Blackfriars was probably not as lengthy or continuous as many scholars would like to believe. The Globe burned in June 1613, and the King's Men rebuilt it immediately. Gurr sees an arrogance toward other playing companies in that choice, claiming that the King's Men "even rubbed their superiority in by rebuilding the Globe as their spare playhouse in 1614,"[19] but contemporaries of the event saw something else. John Chamberlain, writing to the Lady Alice Carleton on 30 June 1614, passed on the talk of the town that the rebuilt Globe was "the fayrest that ever was in England" (quoted in *JCS*, 6.182). One group of men in the best possible position to know the value of the King's Men's two playhouses was the company sharers. The fact that three player-petitioners in 1635—Robert Benfield, Eliard Swanston, and Thomas Pollard—wanted shares in the Globe playhouse as well as the Blackfriars indicates that they believed those shares to be more valuable than a portion of a "second" or "spare" playhouse would have been if it were used only in the summer when plague and touring permitted. The petitioners were awarded shares, even though the current owners such as Cuthbert Burbage and John Shank fiercely refused to give any of theirs up. A view of the evidence *sans* a bias in favor of the Blackfriars suggests that in the years immediately subsequent to their acquiring the Blackfriars lease, the King's Men had two playhouses, both alike in quality. The status of the Blackfriars as the company's premier playhouse came later than 1619, perhaps later than 1625.

Notes

1. Peter Davison, ed., *Historica Histrionica* (New York: Johnson Reprint Corp., 1972), B2v.
2. G. E. Bentley, *The Jacobean and Caroline Stage,* 8 vols. (Oxford: Clarendon

Press, 1941–68), 6.15; subsequent quotations from this source are cited in the text and abbreviated *JCS*.

3. Bentley admits that no one knows "how the King's Men divided their time between the two houses from 1608 to 1616," but he assumes "the company had settled down to its Caroline programme within a year or two after taking over Blackfriars" (*JCS*, 6.16 n.1). For Bentley's fullest discussion of the Blackfriars repertory, see "Shakespeare and the Blackfriars Theatre," *Shakespeare Survey 1* (1948): 38–50.

4. Andrew Gurr, *The Shakespearian Playing Companies* (Oxford: Clarendon Press, 1996), 296.

5. Forman also saw *The Winter's Tale* at the Globe on May 15 and *Cymbeline* (entry undated). Titles of lost plays are indicated by quotation marks; titles of surviving plays are in italics.

6. Leeds Barroll, *Politics, Plague and Shakespeare's Theater* (Ithaca: Cornell University Press, 1991), 172. I do not address the issue of playing at Court in this essay because companies apparently did not cancel a scheduled commercial performance in order to play on that same date at Court.

7. Barroll's measure of thirty plague deaths per week (100) reflects the standard set by the Privy Council under James I (99).

8. Of course, the dates of payments are not necessarily the dates of the performances. Transcriptions of the touring records cited throughout this essay are in the following works: Malone Society *Collections*, vol. 7 (Kent, ed. Giles Dawson), vol. 9 (Norfolk & Suffolk, ed. David Galloway and John M. Wasson); REED volumes published: *Coventry*, ed. R. W. Ingram, 1981; *Cumberland / Westmorland / Gloucestershire*, ed. Audrey Douglas and Peter Greenfield, 1986; *Lancashire*, ed. David George, 1991; *Dorset*, ed. Rosaline Conklin Hays and C. E. McGee, 1999; REED volumes unpublished: *Derbyshire*, ed. Barbara Palmer and John M. Wasson; for records from Marlborough, Nottingham, and Oxford, see Gurr, *The Shakespearian Playing Companies*, 390–91.

9. For an identification of touring circuits by region, see Scott McMillin and Sally-Beth MacLean, *The Queen's Men and their Plays* (Cambridge: Cambridge University Press, 1998), 39–40 and 55–60.

10. F. P. Wilson, *Plague in Shakespeare's London* (Oxford: Clarendon, 1927), 122.

11. Malone Society *Collections*, 1.4/5, 372.

12. Irwin Smith, *Shakespeare's Blackfriars Playhouse* (New York: New York University Press, 1964), document 43, 545.

13. Andrew Gurr claims that the "strongest material basis for assuming" a higher class of playgoer at the Blackfriars is "the price of admission" (*Playgoing in Shakespeare's London* [Cambridge: Cambridge University Press, 1987]), 75.

14. Bentley, "Shakespeare and the Blackfriars Theatre," 43.

15. Gurr, *The Shakespearian Playing Companies*, 367.

16. Malone Society *Collections*, 1.1.92. Two other complaints—that the performances continue in Lent and last "from one or twoe of the clock till sixe att night"—also like self-serving hyperbole.

17. Gurr, *Playgoing in Shakespeare's London*, 59.

18. Gurr, *The Shakespearian Playing Companies*, 130.

19. Ibid., 121.

Playhouses Make Strange Bedfellows: The Case of Aaron and Martin

William Ingram

>They tooke from me the vse of mine owne house
>—*King Lear*

>Why then ile [retro]fit you
>—*The Refurbisher's Tragedy*

THE DOCUMENT I WANT to consider dates from 1605 or 1606. At some point during those years an order was apparently issued by the privy Council to halt work on a playhouse then being built in an innyard somewhere by Aaron Holland and Martin Slater. We know of these two men from other sources: Slater as a stage player and manager, Holland as the owner of the Red Bull playhouse in Clerkenwell. But we know of this particular incident, and about their partnership, only because of the survival of a petition addressed to the Privy Council, written apparently by Slater, asking for relief from the council's decree. The petition, in a fair hand, bears no date or signature. The records of the Privy Council for this period having perished, there is no way to confirm any such decree, either for the order to stay or—if such there was—for regranting of permission to build. As documentation for the event in question, then, Slater's petition is all there is. Here follows a transcription of this petition.[1]

To the right honorable the Lordes
of his Ma[tes] most honorable Priuie counsell

The humble petic*i*on of Martyn Slatiar
one of her Ma[tes] servaunt*es*

Most humbly shewinge that whereas it pleased the right gratious the Duke of Holstein to make choice of yo[r] sup*pli*an*t*, as by his Graces warrant appeareth, to selecte and gather a company of Comedians to attend his Grace here or elswhere at his Comaundment, and having made choice of them beinge vnprouided of a howse to play in, as others of their profession haue:

Your sup*pli*an*t* very willing to shew himself in the best manner he could for his Graces service, together wth one Aaron Holland servaunt to the right Honorable the Earle of Devonshire, having ioyntly the lease of the howse betwixt them for Thirty yeeres hath alterd some stables and other roomes, beinge before a square Court in an Inne to turne them into galleries, first having in gen*e*r*a*ll the parishes consent, whoe haue subscribed their names to a petic*i*on alredy exhibited to yo[r] hono[rs] at the Counsell table wth due consideraci*o*n for diuers causes, and especially towardes the poore of the parish whoe hath allowed them Twenty shilling*es* a moneth towardes their maintenaunce And likewise for the amendinge and maintayninge of the pavement*es* and highe waies thereabout*es* And yo[r] sup*pli*an*tes* haue bestowed vpon the same the sum*m*e of 500[li].

Since w[ch] tyme there is a le*tt*re come from yo[r] honoreble Lo[pes] to staie the finishinge of the same being all framed and almost sett vp to your sup*pli*an*tes* vtter vndoeinge foreuer w[th]out it shall please God to move yo[r] Hono[rs] hart*es* to pittie vs.

May it therefore please yo[r] Hono[rs] the premisses considered to graunt vnto yo[r] poore sup*pli*an*tes* yo[r] lawfull favours and allowaunc*es* to finish the same, and to haue such priuieleige as others of their qualitie haue. And the rather that many poore men are left destitute of lyveinge and are vtterly ouerthrowne foreuer.

And yo[r] sup*pli*an*tes* with the rest of the Company shall continually praie for your Hono[rs] health and hapines long to continew.

Slater identified himself as "one of her Ma[tes] servaunt*es*" and Holland as "servaunt to the right Honorable the Earle of Devonshire." The subject of this petition, the inn being converted to a playing space, is less easy to pin down. In his petition Slater said only that he and Holland had "ioyntly the lease of the howse betwixt them" without saying what house or where it was located. The easiest assumption is that the building in question was the Red Bull in Clerkenwell, a former inn converted in about 1605 into the Red Bull playhouse. But such an assumption is nowhere made requisite by the document itself. The Red Bull is the only playing structure in London associated with Holland's name. But it has never been associated with Slater's except in the most general sense.[2]

As documents go, Slater's petition is a relative newcomer. Theater historians have known for centuries about the Red Bull playhouse, but not until near the middle of the last century did they learn abut this particular document. Chambers didn't know about it in 1923, nor did Edwin Nungezer in 1928. It came to general attention in 1938 with the publication of volume 17 of the ongoing *Calendar* of Cecil manuscripts. From then on it was presumably known, though what to make of it was less well known. It was easier to ignore it, as most post-1938 studies did. C. J. Sisson, in his oft-cited "The Red Bull Company and the Importunate Widow" (1958), preferred to leave it aside, perhaps out of a sense that it didn't belong with his other materials on the early history of the playhouse. G. E. Bentley noticed it in volume 6 of his *Jacobean and Caroline Stage* (1968), to the extent of reproducing the flawed synopsis from the *Calendar* and speculating briefly about its import (he assumed it referred to the Red Bull); but he hadn't learned about it in time to include a mention of it in his biography of Slater in volume 2 (1941), and even in volume 6 he devoted only a few sentences to it, scanting the duke of Holstein's proposed company, a potentially fascinating topic, in similar fashion.

Without question, Slater's petition is puzzling. In the other known documents about the Red Bull—the famous lawsuits *Woodford v. Holland* of 1613, or *Smith v. Beeston* of 1619 (both published by Wallace in 1909) or *Worth v. Baskerville* of 1623 (published by Greenstreet in 1885, with its supplement by Sisson mentioned above), in each of which the early history of the Red Bull playhouse is rehearsed—one looks in vain for any mention of Martin Slater. In the collective memory of all the litigants in all these lawsuits, as they recalled the history of the house and its occupants, Slater's name never came up. So it is perhaps understandable that this petition has had some difficulty finding its place in our ongoing account of London theatre. The document's import is predicated upon our knowing what inn, and where; but we don't know that. We can, however, ask some other questions. Here are some of the first ones that come to mind.

Who was the duke of Holstein, and why did he want a company of players? The first part is easy. Holstein was brother to James's queen, Anne of Denmark. He had come to London in November 1604, perhaps intending to visit the English court over the Christmas season; he ended up staying until the end of May 1605.[3] He was active in the court's Christmastime festivities, attending a wedding and participating in a masque.[4] Possibly the example of his sister's company of players aroused his interest in having a company of players of his own. An early act of James's Privy Council had been to consolidate theatrical patronage in the royal family; only three companies of stage players had been authorized by them, those belonging to the king, the queen, and the prince. Slater's petition speaks of a "warrant" issued to him "to selecte and gather a company of Comedians" for the duke, but does not say who issued the warrant or whether it carried royal approval. If it did not—if the duke of Holstein had been simply acting upon a wish of his own, on the assumption that he too was a member of the royal family, without first clearing matters with his host—then the council's unhappiness with it may be understandable.

Why and when did the duke of Holstein settle upon Slater as the person to fit him out? The "when" part is easy to ascertain from the foregoing; it must have been between November 1604 and the end of May 1605. Slater's petition says the duke wanted a company "to attend his Grace here or elswhere at his Comaundment." Assuming that "here" meant London, the implication was either that the duke's visit still had some days or weeks to run, or else that he was about to depart but intended to return. The former strikes me as more likely, and suggests a possible date of late winter or early spring 1605 for the duke's arrangement with Slater.

As for the "why Slater?" part of the question, Bentley's view (*JCS* 6.217, n.1) was that "Slater's association with the Queen's men is probably the grounds for the Duke of Holstein's selection of him." This is plausible, but perhaps only a partial explanation. As the queen's brother, the duke could have approached any of the players in any of the three companies with his proposal; his preference for his sister's company is understandable, but the most prominent member of that company was Thomas Greene, not Martin Slater. My own sense is that Slater's ever-proliferating entrepreneurial activities, in London and the provinces, with companies of adults and children, as player and manager, marked him as a person perhaps more than usually alert to potential business opportunities.[5] Indeed, my sense of Slater's opportunism leads me to imagine that the idea for "a company of Comedians to attend his Grace" was originally not the duke's idea at all, but was Slater's.

Who was "the right Honorable the Earle of Devonshire," and in what sense was Aaron Holland his "servaunt"? One can do little more than speculate about the second part, which I will do in a moment; but again, the first part is easy. The title "Earle of Devonshire" had only a brief life; it was created and bestowed by James I in the summer of 1603, and became extinct in 1606 when its occupant died without legitimate heirs. The holder of the honor was Charles Blount, by inheritance the 8th baron Mountjoy, and perhaps best known to literary scholars as Penelope Rich's lover.[6] In 1604, following the Irish debacle of Penelope's brother the earl of Essex, the queen sent Blount there as lord deputy, and Blount succeeded where Essex had failed; Tyrone surrendered to him just at the queen's reign came to an end. When Blount returned to London, the new king conferred an earldom upon him, and made him master of ordnance and a member of the Privy Council. By the time of Slater's petition, then, Blount was a newly eminent part of the establishment; Slater may have thought it advantageous to mention Holland's connection with Blount.

I haven't yet been able to learn where in London Blount lived (and therefore where Holland might have performed his duties), though certainly by 1603 he must have had a London residence. His liaison with Penelope Rich had begun about 1590, and over the years she bore him six children, though no one knows where the encounters that produced those children took place. The efforts of the two principals to legitimate the relationship (and the offspring) by a spurious marriage in 1605 were unsuccessful, and Blount's peerage became extinct a year later, with his death on April 3, 1606 of a respiratory inflammation. He died in Savoy House, in the Strand, a place I've been so far unable to identify, but which may have been where he lived.[7] If Blount did live in the Strand, another link is made possible with Aaron Holland, who lived there himself for some years before moving to Clerkenwell. Holland's position as "servaunt" in the Devonshire household might thus have involved his being domiciled there; but whatever it may have consisted in, the Blount connection would have ended with the earl's death on 3 April; the date is thus a convenient *terminus ad quem* for Slater's petition.

There's more to notice about Holland. His first venture as an innholder seems to have been not with the Red Bull in Clerkenwell but with an inn in the Strand. He was "Aaron Holland of the parish of the Savoy, innholder" by 6 June 1598, when he bound himself in

£100 for his good appearance at the jail delivery scheduled for 7 July.[8] Holland also appears in the records of the "parish of the Savoy," a common if not wholly accurate synonym for the parish of St. Mary le Strand, whose records have survived from 1600. The churchwardens yearly assessed the hundred or so rateable households in the parish for the maintenance of the church and the wages of the clerk and other officers. The first year for which these assessments have survived is 1600, and they range from a low of 16d. to a high of 15s. 4d., the latter being the assessment for Edward Kirkham, the yeoman in the Revels office. Aaron Holland the innholder was assessed nearer the median, at 6s. 8d., and is marked as having paid.[9]

Did Slater and Holland really have "ioyntly the lease of the howse betwixt them"? Not an easy question, especially as we don't know what house is being talked about. Was it Holland's inn in the Strand, abandoned by the two men when the Privy Council halted their construction? If one is to believe the claims in Slater's petition, the conversion of what was "before a square Court in an Inne" into a playing space with "galleries" was taking place in 1605 or 1606. There is no documentary evidence linking Holland with the Strand as late as 1605, but equally there is none before 1608 linking him with Clerkenwell;[10] so certitude is slippery here. It's conceivable that Holland took Slater in as a joint leaseholder for the inn in the Strand, and that they both decamped when its prospects failed, Holland to Clerkenwell and Slater ultimately to Whitefriars. The best available alternative scenario is that the inn in question was indeed the Red Bull, but in that case one needs to understand not only how construction was allowed to continue after the council's order to stop, but also how Slater first became, then disappeared as, a joint leaseholder. The person most commonly partnered with Holland at the Red Bull in the surviving documents is not Slater but the stage player Thomas Swinnerton.

How did Holland and Slater intend to furnish "Twenty shillinges a moneth" towards the parish poor? This shouldn't pose any difficulty; even a modestly successful playhouse would have been able, in 1605, to set aside that much of its profits for social insurance. Had Slater and Holland really concluded such a negotiation with their parish, or was this merely rhetoric? And which parish? St. Mary le Strand, or St. James Clerkenwell?

Had they really spent £500 for the "amendinge and maintayninge of the pavementes and highe waies" by their intended play-

house? Unlike the twenty shillings a month for the poor, this is a quite breathtakingly large sum, far more than one can imagine spending upon walkways. But the syntax of the claim is a bit tangled, and also perhaps disingenuously phrased, in the petition: Slater speaks, in a single paragraph of the inn being altered to a playing place, of the approval secured from the parish, of money to be spent on the poor, "And likewise for the amendinge and maintayninge of the pavement*es* and highe waies thereabout*es* And yo*r* sup*p*liant*es* haue bestowed vpon the same the sum*m*e of 500[li]." It's quite likely that "the same" refers not at all to the proximate topic of the pavements but rather to the initial subject, the inn, and the money spent remodeling it (perhaps even the cost of purchasing it).

If the claim is true—if Slater and Holland had indeed already spent that much on the inn by the time the Privy Council stayed their activity—then the two men would have found themselves considerably in debt.[11] If the stay was permanent—and we have no evidence that it wasn't—then their inn would have needed to have a great deal of unfinished remodeling removed. If the inn was in the Strand, some nearby residents may have been pleased to learn that they would not, after all, be having a playhouse in their midst. Perhaps the most directly involved of those residents would have been Sir Robert Cecil himself, the recipient and preserver of Slater's petition (and perhaps the impetus behind the stay), whose new residence at the western end of the Strand, Cecil House, had just been completed in 1602.[12]

On the other hand, if the inn was in Clerkenwell, then we still need to understand how it was that construction continued despite the stay, that the playhouse opened and made money, and that Slater, so prominent in this petition, was never again named in connection with its activity. Like the Privy Council order of 28 July 1597 for the pulling down of all London's playhouses, the present stay—if targeted at the Red Bull—seems also to have been quietly ignored by all concerned. Any coherent narrative of these events needs to make an accounting of these discrepancies and to offer some guess at what these strange behaviors might imply.

Chambers noticed that the draft patent for Queen Anne's company permitted them to play not only in the Boar's Head and the Curtain theaters but "Aswell . . . as in any other play howse not vsed by others, by the said Thomas Greene, elected, or by him hereafter to be builte" (*ES* 2.229–30). Bentley thought the final six words of this extracted phrase were significant. He noted C. J. Sisson's speculation that "Aaron Holland designed the Red Bull for the use of Queen Anne's men under a bargain with them, and that this conjectured agreement is the reason for the odd provision in the draft patent for a playhouse 'hereafter to be builte' by Greene, the most prominent member of Queen Anne's company." Bentley found Sisson's line of reasoning "very persuasive, if not yet demonstrable" (*JCS* 6.217–18).

But if Holland had had such an arrangement with the queen's players, his logical partner would have been Greene, and the petition to the Privy Council ought to have come from Greene, or from both of them. Thomas Swinnerton, Holland's partner in the Red Bull, was also a queen's player; so if not Greene, then Swinnerton should have sent the petition. If the inn in question was the Red Bull, then Slater's sudden precedence over those other two men, and his equally sudden disappearance, remain to be accounted for.

As for the duke of Holstein's company of comedians, there is no evidence that they ever performed anywhere, either in London or in the provinces.[13] It's likely that the members of the company were never actually called together; though Slater's petition implies that he had already "made choice of them" and now needed "a howse to play in," the true sequence may have been the reverse. It's possible that Slater, having somehow persuaded Holland to turn his inn into a playhouse on speculation, may have heard rumblings of Privy Council discontent, may quickly have talked the duke of Holstein into commissioning him to form a company of comedians, and may then have been prepared, when Cecil's stay was communicated to him, to present himself in his petition as being in need.

On the other hand, that may not be what happened at all. But until we can resolve the identity and location of the inn in question, our musings are not likely to carry us much further. If the inn in question is *not* the Red Bull, then Aaron Holland must have been the lessee of not one but two inns in 1605, and must have been in the process of converting both of them to playhouses, succeeding with one and failing with the other. I don't know of anyone, myself included, who is ready to make such a proposal, for it runs well beyond any currently available evidence; such a narrative would require an Aaron Holland of astonishing entrepreneurial skills, or at least with a degree of financial backing hitherto unsuspected. But before such a claim can be thrown out of court, one needs to demonstrate that the inn mentioned in the Slater petition is really the Red Bull; and the path to that demonstration—as I have tried to show—is strewn with problems. One can perhaps be forgiven for wishing that this document would simply go away.

Notes

1. The original is at Hatfield House, among the manuscripts of the Marquess of Salisbury, where it is Petitions 197.91(e). It is summarized, with errors, in the printed *Calendar of the Manuscripts of the Most Honourable the Marquess of Salisbury . . . preserved at Hatfield House . . .* , London, vol. 17, p. 234, where the reference to the ms volume is erroneously given as 199.91(2). I am indebted to Leeds Barroll for communicating this correction to me (the correction is also published in his *Politics, Plague, and Shakespeare's Theater* [Ithaca: Cornell University Press, 1991], 188 n. 25); and as well for furnishing me with a photocopy of the document itself, from which the present transcription is made.

2. Bentley says "the earliest occupants known for the Red Bull were the members of Queen Anne's company, which was there until 1617. Swinnerton was a member of this troupe, and Slater seems to have been, though he generally appears in provincial records rather than London ones" (*JCS* 6.217).

3. A document of the time, dated 15 June new style 1605 (*Cal S P Venetian 1603–7*, 248), states that the duke had left England to return home on the previous Friday. June 15th n.s. was June 5th o.s., and was a Wednesday, so the Duke's departure would have been on Friday 31 May English style.

4. For some reason he appears in E. K. Chambers's narrative of these events as the duke of Holst, an otherwise unknown title that, uncharacteristically, Chambers did not pause to question.

5. By the autumn of 1607 Slater was already negotiating for a share in a syndicate aiming to install a children's troupe at Whitefriars, with Slater as the manager of the company, a project that was to culminate in a lawsuit against him in 1609; see *Medieval and Renaissance Drama in England* 2 (1985): 209–31 for more on this venture.

6. As a young man, Blount had attracted the interest of the queen, thereby exciting the jealousy of the earl of Essex. Defeated by Blount at a tilt, Essex was defeated by him yet again in a famous duel that resulted in the banishment of both young men from court (though soon after they became fast friends). Blount seemed to enjoy the combative life; he served in the Low Countries, where Leicester knighted him; he commanded a ship in the fight against the armada; he was with Essex and Ralegh in the capture of Cadiz, and in their expedition to the Azores.

7. G. E. Cokayne (*The Complete Peerage*, 9.346), who cites no reference for this claim. Savoy House might have been an alternative name for the chapter house attached to the Savoy hospital, though a man of Blount's stature is unlikely to have passed his final breath in so disreputable a place as the Savoy hospital had become by 1606. Or it might have been another name for the old duke of Lancaster's palace, hard by. Further searching in the records of the Duchy of Lancaster might reveal more. Blount was buried in Westminster Abbey.

8. See J. C. Jeaffreson, *Middlesex County Records*, 1.245. There is nothing further on this matter in the documents, either about the alleged offense or its resolution.

9. Westminster Public Library: churchwardens' accounts of St. Mary le Strand.

10. He may have relocated from the Strand to Clerkenwell in 1606 when his connection with the Devonshire household terminated. Surviving records suggest that the Red Bull playhouse was already in operation by that time, but the commencement of its activity is not contingent upon Holland's place of residence.

11. Where could Holland have gotten so much money? The freely fantasizing mind will know at once which questions to ask next: was Blount interested in maintaining an inn near his house in the Strand? Did it figure in his liaison with Penelope Rich? Was Holland his front man? And was Holland stuck with the inn after Blount's death? [This footnote was written by Barbara Cartland.]

12. Robert Somerville, *The Savoy* (London: n.p.,1960), 152. It has lately become fashionable to speak of the "ambivalent terrain" of London's "marginalized" extramural Liberties as appropriately destabilizing sites for the radical activity of playmaking. Sir Robert Cecil and his neighbors in the extramural Liberty of the Savoy might well have been surprised at the use of such terms to describe the fashionably upscale area where they preferred to live (and perhaps where they preferred not to have a playhouse).

13. I'm grateful to Dr. Abigail Young of the REED office for searching the REED database for me in order to verify the latter half of this negative claim.

Some Recent Dramatic Manuscript Studies

Grace Ioppolo

THE STUDY OF EXTANT English Renaissance poetry, prose, and dramatic manuscripts is once again flourishing. Spurred on by the frequent reluctance of "history of the book" scholars to grapple with the role of manuscripts in the transmission, and history, of a text, manuscript scholars are again insisting on the primacy of manuscripts in textual and authorial production. This resurgence, especially in dramatic manuscript studies, can be seen in recent publications as well as in the inauguration of annual conferences on Manuscript and their Makers in the English Renaissance at the University of Reading in the last two years.

Publications

The mysteries of the collaborative manuscript "Book" of *Sir Thomas More* continue to attract scholarly attention. In *The Review of English Studies* 51 (2000), Thomas Merriam argues that Anthony Munday has been "misunderstood" as the original author of the play. Merriam extends an earlier argument of E. A. J. Honigmann's that Munday was predominantly a copyist rather than the composer of the play. In a series of not always persuasive conjectures about stylistics, Merriam argues that Munday's portions of the manuscript suggest he was fair-copying another author's text to pass it off as his own, rather than composing or fair-copying his own text. Merriam claims Munday did so "to create a provocation in order to injure a theatre company under suspicion because of its patron, its playwrights, and its daring and popular presentations on the public stage." Merriam's failure to compare Munday's paleographic characteristics with those of authors and scribes, as foul and fair copyists, in the numerous other extant manuscripts of the period (relying instead evidently on Malone Society reprints of the play-texts) provides a weak foundation on which to build his case. Only by surveying all extant authorial fair copies could Merriam command as much information as necessary to promote Munday's work as copyist rather than composer in the *More* manuscript. Thomas Middleton, for example, fair-copied all of one manuscript of his notorious, banned, and highly provocative play *A Game at Chess* and part of another (in total, six manuscripts of the play survive); his copying habits vary between manuscripts. This case alone suggests that conjectures about the conditions under which a copyist or composer wrote at any given time (even under stress, as Middleton apparently was) and about the way such conditions are reflected in the handwriting are too difficult to sustain. Nonetheless, Merriam offers enough energetic arguments to convince others to re-examine possible evidence hidden or readily available in the unique manuscript of *Sir Thomas More*.

N. W. Bawcutt similarly admonishes scholars to return to manuscripts, rather than invent theory, in order to make persuasive arguments about the practices of Renaissance authors in his essay "Renaissance Dramatists and the Texts of Their Plays" in *Research Opportunities in Renaissance Drama* 40 (2001). Bawcutt especially attacks Stephen Orgel, David Scott Kastan, W. Speed Hill, and Paul Werstine for ignoring documentary and archival evidence, particularly manuscripts, in formulating editorial theories designed to attack the work of traditional editors (and manuscript scholars) such as W. W. Greg. In his essay, Bawcutt, an impressive editor and manuscript scholar himself, offers a much-needed corrective to the stream of garbled theory that has recently popularized the notion that dramatic manuscripts are "figments of the imagination" and are negligible in the process of textual transmission.

As usual, the annual journal *English Manuscript Studies* (published by the British Library) continues to be a rich resource for manuscript scholars, especially in offering a number of recent essays on dramatic authors and on newly discovered manuscripts or manuscript fragments of plays and masques. In *English Manuscript Studies* 6 (1997), Arthur Freeman discusses a manuscript leaf from an unidentified play found in 1988 as binder's waste in a 1586 edition of Homer's *Odyssey* printed in Geneva and bound in England between 1586 and 1620. Freeman names the leaf—which offers a portion of a scene involving a Tapster and two thieves who seal their pact to rob a rich lodger by drinking and smoking tobacco—"The Tapster Manuscript," and argues that it is a close analogue to the scene of the Gadshill robbery plot in act 2, scene 1 of Shakespeare's *Henry IV, Part 1*. The scribal(?) quarto-sized leaf, with marginal and interlinear revisions and additions, is written in a fluent secretary hand. It resembles other extant dramatic authorial and scribal manuscripts in its use of flush-left speech prefixes, mostly centered stage directions (unusually boxed here, however), flush-right exit directions, and ruled margins. Freeman argues that the scene does not predate Shakespeare's but is an adaptation of it for a play performed for a university or London audience, perhaps in the late 1590s. Whatever its source, the scene adds to the relatively sparse body of manuscripts of play-texts of this period, offering exciting new material evidence for theater historians and drama specialists as well as for textual scholars.

In *English Manuscript Studies* 8 (2000) Hilton Kelliher, in a tour-de-force of archival investigation, offers important new manuscript evidence from the Cambridge University Archives (housed in the University Library) about the early lives of Francis Beaumont and Nathan Field, which confirms that these authors were in residence in Cambridge in 1604. Kelliher, a Western manuscripts curator at the British Library, closely examines documents, including a copy of Beaumont's baptismal record, from a series of Cambridge court cases to which Beaumont was a party, echoes of which may appear in Beaumont's plays. Kelliher also finds allusions in Field's plays to his life in Cambridge, and further suggests that Field and Beaumont first encountered John Fletcher at Cambridge. The records that Kelliher handles so superbly in this essay show us that Beaumont indulged in slander, dicing, gaming, and other unsavory adventures. They offer exciting new information about the nature of Beaumont's character and work, records of which were previously scant, and of his collaborators and friends.

English Manuscript Studies has also been generous in publishing lengthy essays on, and complete texts of, rediscovered Jacobean and Caroline masques. In volume 7 (1998), Tim Raylor discusses his rediscovery of the 1621 "Lost" *Essex House Masque,* written to celebrate the visit of the French Ambassador to London, which is among the University of Nottingham Library's Portland Papers (containing documents from the Holles family). Raylor dates the fair copy from the second two decades of the seventeenth century, and discusses its four mixed hands, none of which can be matched to the hands of the Holles' family members or servants found in other Holles documents. James Knowles had also located the 1619 anonymous "The Running Masque" in the British Library, among Conway papers, in 1990. In *English Manuscript Studies* 8 (2000) he describes the 1619–20 Christmas season, for which this latter masque was written, "as one of the most extensive periods of Jacobean court entertainments." Knowles does not attribute "The Running Masque," performed by the marquess of Buckingham, the earl of Oxford, Lord Hunsdon, and other courtiers, to any single author and argues instead for its being collaborative and "improvisational." The regularity and neatness of this scribal fair-copy manuscript suggest that it was made as a presentation or commissioned copy. Knowles had also found a manuscript in three hands of Jonson's 1609 "Entertainment at Britain's Burse" (which Knowles renamed "The Key Keeper"; see *Times Literary Supplement*, 7 February 1997) also among Conway papers in the Public Record Office in Kew in 1997. He presents an edition of *The Entertainment* and discusses its occasion and performance before King James in *Re-Presenting Ben Jonson: Text History, Performance* (London: Macmillan, 1999). These various studies by Raylor and Knowles offer us much new information about the Stuart masque and its impact on court and culture.

Two editions of prose and poetry works published recently that raise important issues about the modern editing of variant, revised authorial or nonauthorial manuscripts, and may thus be of interest to the modern editors of dramatic texts dealing with the same issues, were published recently. Michael Rudick subtitles his volume of *The Poems of Sir Walter Ralegh* (Renaissance English Text Society, 1999) "a historical edition" because he offers variant texts as they have been "preserved in some historical source," without attempting to reconstruct the lost original (as Greg's rationale of copy-text suggested) from which they supposedly descended. Due to the sheer volume of extant variant texts, chiefly manuscript, of particular works, Rudick has been "selective" in his collations and textual notes. While such selections may not please manuscript scholars, they are more than reasonable for the general academic audience, who will be grateful for a modern edition of Ralegh. Similar compromises, to more questionable effect, have been made by the three editors of the equally long-awaited *Elizabeth I: Collected Works* (Chicago: University of Chicago Press, 2000). Like Rudick,

Leah S. Marcus, Janel Mueller, and Mary Beth Rose refuse to present "ideal" composite versions of the texts and are as selective in listing textual variants. They make no apology in arguing that they "list manuscript copies and offer variants only for texts that [they] judge to be early or significant for some other specified reason. To list all of the extant copies of a given speech or letter would be unnecessarily cumbersome." This last statement would appear to defeat the purpose of manuscript study, if not of editing, especially in the case of such a prominent figure as Elizabeth, whose literary works reflect and influence those of other Renaissance authors. The purposes, aims, and methods of manuscript study, and those of editors in general, are impressively argued in G. Thomas Tanselle's *Literature and Artifacts* (Charlottesville: Bibliographical Society at the University of Virginia, 1998). His collection of previously published essays in this volume could have offered the *Elizabeth I* editors some useful instruction in the cultural use and scholarly treatment of manuscripts, particularly in listing extant copies of a given work. In several of the essays, Tanselle manages to convince readers that the commercial concerns of publishers can be reconciled to the needs of an academic audience.

Lastly, in terms of improbable publications, there continue to be false alarms raised about the "discovery" of lost English renaissance manuscripts, the most prominent of which was British newspaper reports in 2000 that a new manuscript of two Jonson masques had surfaced at Wilton House, seat of the earl of Pembroke, in Wiltshire. The experts in charge of the investigation later quietly withdrew their claims, implying that they (or the newspapers) had mistaken printed pages from a Jonson Folio for manuscript pages.

Conferences

In the first of the Reading conferences (the proceedings of which will be published in the forthcoming Volume 11 of *English Manuscript Studies*) held in June 2000, speakers Peter Beal, Cedric Brown, Katherine Duncan-Jones, Harold Love, Steven May, and H. R. Woudhuysen used the cases of particular poetry and prose manuscripts to discuss at length numerous topics, including: manuscript circulation as a form of publication; authorial collaboration and revision; authorial versus scribal treatment of manuscripts; the manuscript and the printer; the use of sigla; social editing and manuscript miscellanies; and modern access to manuscripts.

In the second conference, held in June 2001 and focused on Philip Henslowe and his Dramatists, speakers debated many of the same issues. However, they emphasized the unique concerns of dealing with dramatic manuscripts, particularly insisting on the importance of classifying and categorizing them, whether foul papers, fair copies, prompt-copies (properly termed "books") or other playhouse copies, printer's copy, or presentation or commissioned copies. Unlike poetry and prose works primarily or ultimately designed for publication, plays were produced primarily for performance, and only incidentally for print. Dramatic manuscripts therefore entered an extra stage of private transmission—circulation in the playhouse—and acquired an extra layer of censorship (two factors that have been underemphasized in recent theoretical studies of Renaissance drama and in manuscript studies in general).

This conference began with a session reconsidering Philip Henslowe's rich manuscript archive, including his famous *Diary,* and what it tells us about his relationships with the companies for which he commissioned or purchased play-texts. R. A. Foakes, coeditor with the late R. T. Rickert of the now classic 1960/1961 edition of the *Diary* (soon to be reprinted by Cambridge University Press), began the session by discussing how Henslowe's archive has been interpreted and misinterpreted since 1960 in defending his reputation. S. P. Cerasano placed Henslowe's *Diary* in context by examining other extant account books and what they suggest about contemporary economic and financial record-keeping, methods, and concerns. Andrew Gurr then reevaluated Henslowe's repertory of play-texts, analyzing how, when, and why some were sold off to other companies or printers.

The second and third sessions took up manuscripts and their makers and users, rather than just their commissioners. In the second session, the speakers debated authorial versus scribal treatment of play-texts, considering the transmission of the play from author to playhouse. First, Grace Ioppolo made a case for the extant authorial manuscript of Heywood's *Captives* being a foul paper, rather than a fair copy, manuscript, drawing on correspondence between Robert Daborne and Henslowe about the nature of authorial copies. William B. Long reassessed the extant manuscript of *The Telltale,* the only complete manuscript play-text surviving in Henslowe and Alleyn's papers at Dulwich College, in order to catalogue the characteristics of scribal copy based, probably, on the playhouse "book." In the final session, Richard Proudfoot offered some ground rules for and against the editorial reconstruction of lost manuscripts behind extant play quartos by correlating examples from extant manuscripts and their printed counterparts. Finally, Alan H. Nelson outlined his inventory of play quartos owned by the scrivener Humphrey Dyson, whose seventeenth-century collecting habits, and those of other bibliophiles like George Buc, a Master of the Revels, can tell us a great deal more about the cultural reputations of particular dramatists and of the "material" value of such texts.

Once the sole preserve of a handful of early twentieth-century "new bibliographers," dramatic manuscripts are now serving as the fundamental, rather than just preliminary, witnesses to the history of the text, and of the book, for increasing numbers of scholars, as evidenced by the very enthusiastic and knowledgeable audiences at the Reading conferences. Such audiences have also greeted the continuing seminar series of the Perdita Project (based at Nottingham-Trent University), designed to create a database of women's writing (particularly as found in literary and domestic manuscripts) in the English Renaissance. Thus the training and support of postgraduates in paleography, manuscript studies, and bibliography continue to be a wise and worthwhile investment.

On this subject, congratulations and thanks are also due to Laetitia Yeandle (formerly Laetitia Kennedy-Skipton), who retired in early 2001 from her position as curator of manuscripts at the Folger Shakespeare Library, Washington, DC. Laetitia is one of the truly foundational figures in manuscript studies, whose publications (including two handbooks on Renaissance handwriting), Folger paleography seminars, and always gracious and generous support to inquisitive Folger readers and correspondents over many years have offered current and future manuscript scholars a rich legacy indeed. The number of us who have gratefully benefited from her expertise and advice is legion.

ARTICLES

"Crack'd Crowns" and Counterfeit Sovereigns: The Crisis of Value in *1 Henry IV*

JESSE M. LANDER

> Money has the advantage of presenting me immediately the lurid face of the social relation of value; it shows me value right away as exchange, commanded and organized for exploitation . . . money has only one face, that of the boss.
> —Antonio Negri

A PERVASIVE ATMOSPHERE of venality has often been noted in *1 Henry IV*. The denizens of Eastcheap are not exceptional in their focus on pecuniary matters: the play opens with a dispute between the King and Hotspur over the payment of ransom that soon blossoms into rebellion. King Henry, as Hotspur reminds Blunt, "Knows at what time to promise, when to pay" (4.3.53), and Prince Hal uses the same language when he plans to "pay the debt I never promised" (1.2.204).[1] Worcester argues that the king's strict accounting makes reconciliation an impossibility: "The King will always think him in our debt . . . Till he hath found a time to pay us home" (1.3.280–83). This language does more than suggest that certain characters are adept at calculating their debts—it connects the language of economic value to the question of disputed sovereignty.

Rather than consider the admittedly obtrusive language of credit and debt, I want to examine a set of specifically numismatic images that serve to focus attention on the relationship between the monarch and economic value in a particularly acute manner. The language of coins and coinage, informed by the history of the English currency with its debasements, enhancements, and reforms as well as the daily practices associated with the circulation of coin, is animated by the peculiar and shifting nexus of sovereign power and economic value found in a coin.[2] As Posthumus remarks in *Cymbeline:* " 'Tween man and man they weigh not every stamp; / Though light, take pieces for the figure's sake" (5.4.24–25).[3] Though David Scott Kastan has observed, with some justice, that the play is "about the production of power," it is also about the production of value.[4] While the discourse of sovereignty and the proliferation of power are now familiar themes (especially in readings of the history plays), questions of value, particularly economic value, have been given less attention.[5] However, an examination of the relationship between power and value made visible by the language of coinage reveals *1 Henry IV,* and the history play more generally, to be an aesthetic response to the crisis of value that roiled the world of late sixteenth-century England.

The principal element in this crisis was an acceleration in inflation, an economic fact that had real consequences for all those who participated in monetary transactions. But to this mysterious and disorienting price spiral, one must add the dislocations caused by three changes in official religion all in the course of a single generation, an increasing awareness of what was called the New World, the early stirrings of modern science, and the advent of novel technologies. The playhouses themselves, where Shakespeare made his living by entertaining a paying audience, were both a product of this ferment and a contributor to it. "A collective Stock Exchange of ideas," as well as, "a laboratory of and for the new social relations of agricultural and commercial capitalism," the new professional theater was able to profit from make-believe.[6] It is not surprising, then, that the crisis in value that might be said to be the enabling condition of the theatrical enterprise became, at times, its subject.[7]

Lacking a philosophical concept of value, never mind a fully formed theory of value, the culture of early modern England deployed the term *value* in a range of religious, ethical, economic, and political contexts.[8] The complexity of this situation is well illustrated by an example from the Geneva Bible. The Gospel of Matthew, which sets out to establish the transcendent value of the kingdom of heaven, the "perl of great price," consistently supplies marginal notes giving the English values of the coins mentioned. "A piece of twentie pence" mentioned at 17.27 is glossed: "The worde is (Statera) w[hi]c[h] co[n]teineth two didrachmas, & is valued about 5 grotes of olde sterling."[9] Strictly speaking, one does not need to know the contemporary value of a talent in order to understand the parable, nor presumably does it greatly clarify matters to know the present-day value of the silver paid to Judas. A rigorous account of the absolute gap between earthly and heavenly value might well render such attempts at translation otiose, and yet the producers of the Geneva Bible clearly thought this information important.

This is in large part because the Geneva translators do not recognize a conceptual divide between economics and religion (a distinction that serves to organize knowledge in the modern world): they treat value as an attribute that operates continuously and extensively across the universe. According to such a theological vision, values are commensurate and therefore translatable. A classic statement of this vision, the subject of Tillyard's much derided *Elizabethan World picture,* is provided by Raleigh in the preface to *The History of the World;* having asserted the transcendent value of things heavenly, he asks rhetorically, "Shall we therefore value honour and riches at nothing?" (C4r). His emphatic defense of honor and riches depends upon a description of the universe as arranged into divinely ordained hierarchies, a place in which avidity, the pursuit of the best things, can be redescribed as a form of worship. A similar commitment to a total structure of divinely established value leads the Geneva translators to set up a textual apparatus insisting on the proper rate of exchange between biblical and English currency. They become, in effect, moneychangers on the page if not in the temple. Though this is most obviously a comprehensive act of translation, an effort to transpose the ancient truths of the Bible into a modern, vernacular idiom, the reference to "olde sterling" suggests that the conversion is belated, if not impossible—the contemporary standard has itself already been superseded. The attempt to establish commensurate value only succeeds in revealing that present-day sterling is an uncertain standard.

This editorial attention to currency also reveals a more narrow scholarly and archaeological interest in the specificities of coin, for the discovery of ancient coins had contributed greatly to the development of Renaissance antiquarianism, a development that in turn influence the philological work of the humanists.[10] The first two papers offered to the Elizabethan Society of Antiquaries, treating the "antiquity of sterling money and of noble titles," indicate the importance placed on coins by the emerging historiography.[11] An interest in the material and mechanics of coinage produces a numismatic language that constantly invokes value as a contested attribute, juxtaposing a natural economy of rare metals against a political economy of monarchical prerogative. As Foucault observes: "In the sixteenth century, economic thought is restricted, or almost so, to the problem of prices and that of the best monetary substance."[12] These two concerns are intimately bound together: fluctuations in price provoke attention to coinage, changes in coin and the supply of precious metals are adduced as explanations for rising prices. Arguing that a Renaissance understanding of money as precious substance is decisively eclipsed in the Classical age by an account of the money form that focuses on its representative quality, Foucault somewhat overstates the case for discontinuity between the two periods, and, although his description of the powerful role of analogy in Renaissance thinking remains instructive, it exaggerates the degree of cohesiveness characteristic of the age.[13] Even the solid, imposing structure of a monolithic and monotheistic value system admits the possibility of conflict between God and king, king and gold. In other words, the harmonious ideal established by analogical thinking creates a standard that can then be used to criticize the inadequacies of actuality, serving, under certain conditions, to delegitimate rather than to legitimate the status quo. The language of coinage, attuned to the potential contradiction between the sovereign's stamp and the coin's alloy, conveys the complex intertwining of value and legitimacy.

Hotspur's contention that Douglas deserves such recognition that "not a soldier of this season's stamp / Should go so general current through the world" (4.1.4–5) employs the imagery of coinage to suggest an analogy between the chivalric realm and the economic sphere. Hotspur's commendation invokes the coin's stamp as certain accreditation, a guarantee of value. But where the stamp ordinarily functions to guarantee the equivalence of a particular group of coins, here Douglas is identified as superior to his fellow soldiers. More intriguing is Hotspur's assertion to Kate that "We must have bloody noses and crack'd crowns, / And pass them current too" (2.3.94–95). Crown as head, as monarchy, and as coin all coalesce in a fantastic boast that points to a connection between violence and both economic and political systems of value. The usually surreptitious act of passing cracked or deficient coin is here presented as an act of coercive, masculine force: Hotspur imagines himself imposing a new currency of wounds. This recurrent use of numismatic language articulates, in the aesthetic terms of the history play, a crisis of value that impinges upon both the economic world and the political realm. However, the complexities of value registered by the play are ultimately resolved by a return to an aristocratic dispensation that grounds itself on the possibility of violence. By returning to an earlier historical moment in which value and sovereignty were contested, the play attempts to manage the crisis of inflation as well as the unsettling history of the Tudor coinage.

Henry VII, who acceded to the throne after dispatching his rival Richard III at Bosworth Field, was responsible for the introduction of the heaviest gold coin ever minted by an English monarch: the sovereign, as it came to be called, was a magnificent piece of royal propaganda.[14] Painfully aware of the need to legitimate his reign, the king saw the coinage as a way in which to accumulate the symbolic wealth of prestige. Henry VII was also responsible for another change in the English coinage: the introduction of profile portraiture. Inspired by ancient Roman examples, profile coins celebrated the monarch as a recognizable individual with a distinctive physiognomy, a possibility that may have held special attractions for a king who was plagued by pretenders. In contrast, earlier English coins had rendered the monarch from the front as an iconic image of royalty. It was not clear that such a change would be welcomed, and it has been argued that Henry VII produced a number of experimental coins to test public reaction.[15] Though profile coins proved a success and were used by later English monarchs, subsequent linguistic developments suggest that Henry VII was well advised to proceed with caution.

The negative associations surrounding the profile coin are registered at the conclusion of Hotspur's speech extolling the heroic and solitary quest for honor: "But out upon this half-fac'd fellowship!" (1.3.206). Principally Hotspur is rejecting the "corrival" who would demand a share of honor's "dignities," but the expression "half-fac'd fellowship" suggests something more than disdain for collaborative action. "Half-fac'd" refers to the profile stamped on a coin. In *King John,* the Bastard rails against his brother:

> Because he hath a half-face, like my father.
> With half that face would he have all my land.
> A half-faced groat five hundred pounds a year!
> (1.1.92–94)

In both cases the expression connotes the puny and the petty, that which is not to be relied upon, the untrustworthy. The switch from a full-face to a profile portrait involved a trade-off: the king was able to personalize his image, but only by halving it. The profile coin presents the king's image as something to be recognized and worshiped; the monarch does not return the subject's gaze. In contrast, the full-face, iconic image of the king meets gaze with gaze. This change is emblematic of the transition from a feudal kingship, with its emphasis on reciprocity between king and subject, to a new form of monarchy with imperial ambitions (Henry VII also substituted a closed imperial crown for the open English crown that had appeared on earlier coins). However, the phrase "half-faced" suggests that the depiction of such ambition was subject to aesthetic, as well as political, criticism. Though Sydney Anglo admits that "the coinage was, beyond comparison, the most far-reaching medium for the display of royal portraiture, dynastic badges and political epigraphy," he concludes that "it remains the most striking example of its limited efficacy."[16] Nonetheless, Henry VII clearly attempted, as Elizabeth would during her reign, to use the coinage to bolster the prestige and legitimacy of his reign.

Henry VIII shared his father's imperial ambitions but, emboldened by a smooth succession, he was notoriously opportunistic in his search for revenue. Neglecting his father's strategic use of the coinage to increase the monarchy's symbolic wealth, Henry VIII exploited it as a source of revenue. Not content with the profits yielded by the Mint, Henry VIII debased the coin: the pureness of the alloy used to mint coins was decreased, the actual weight of various coins was decreased, and certain coins were "called up" or given a higher nominal value by royal fiat.[17] This last operation was made possible by the existence of two separate systems of money: money of exchange and money of account. Money of exchange refers to the actual coin in circulation: such as sovereigns, angels, nobles, groats, and testons. Money of account was a standard used for bookkeeping: pounds, shillings, and pence. Though setting the equivalences between money of exchange and money of account as well as the weight and fineness of the coin was a royal prerogative, there is no question that Henry's manipulation of the Mint was subsequently seen as foolish and destructive. Arguing against debasement in 1626, Robert Cotton remarked: "When *Henry 8.* had gained as much of power and glory abroad, of Love and Obedience at home, as ever any; he suffered shipwrack of all on this Rock."[18] Indeed, the effects of Henry's debasement continued to be felt throughout the reigns of Mary and Edward VI.

When Elizabeth came to the throne she was faced with a currency that was still suffering from the consequences of Henry's adulteration. In a letter to the queen dated 1558, Sir Thomas Gresham begins, "Ytt may pleasse your majesty to understande, thatt the firste occasion off the fall of the exchainge did growe by the Kinges majesty, your latte ffather, in abasinge his quoyne."[19] Topping Gresham's list of remedies is a restoration of the coinage. Elizabeth did in fact restore the predebasement standards of purity and weight, returning to the sterling standard of 11 ounces, 2 pennyweights of fine silver in the pound.[20] But before this old standard could be reintroduced it was necessary to take the debased money out of circulation. This was done by "calling down" the base coinage to its "true" value. Obviously such instability has a corrosive effect on the coin's ability to function as a standard of value. When Falstaff jokingly tells Hal, "thou cam'st not of the blood royal, if thou darest not stand for ten shillings" (1.2.136–37), he is punning on the fact that a royal was worth, or stood for, ten shillings. However the joke does more, it reverses the conventional view that the sovereign establishes the relationship between coin and value, suggesting instead that it is this immutable equivalence that determines true royalty. In other words, if Hal refuses to endorse the equation between 10 shillings and a royal, then his own royalty is suspect. Correct monetary policy—the proper equivalence between coin and value—now determines the true king. Of course, the wonderful thing about this pun is that it offers up another and opposite meaning: Falstaff is teasing Hal for his reluctance to engage in robbery. In this case, it is cowardice that calls his royalty into doubt, and somehow we arrive at the disturbing conclusion that to be a courageous robber is to be truly royal, a joke that glances knowingly at the Lancastrians Henry IV and Henry VII.

The orthodox notion in which the monarch stands at the center of the socioeconomic system guaranteeing both equivalence and identity is put under significant pressure when an adjustment is made to the coinage. In a world deeply committed to the normative value of stability, any change is suspect: "Hurlyburly innovation" is, according to Henry IV, rebellion. The only way such orthodoxy can accommodate change is as a return. Consequently, Protestants defended the Reformation as a return to the truth of the primitive church rather than a new departure, just as humanists explained their attack on the scholasticism of the schools as a reversion to the pristine standards of classical antiquity. Thus when, on 27 September 1560, Elizabeth issued a proclamation devaluing base coin,[21] the action was justified as a return to the true, old standard. This recoinage was carefully planned to spare the queen any expense; in fact, she appears to have made a profit because the "called down" value of the base coin was lower than the actual average metallic value of the coins collected by the Mint.[22] Her subjects were given a limited amount of time to exchange their old coins (with a new nominal value) for new coins. At the same time, they were warned that it was a felony to melt down any of the queen's coin. These reminders, along with the secrecy that surrounded the plans for recoinage and the speed with which it was effected, were all intended to keep entrepreneurs from exploiting the differential between nominal and metallic value by buying up "called down" coins and realizing a profit by converting them into bullion.

Shortly after the appearance of this proclamation, the government published *The Summarie of Certain Reasons which have moved the Queenes Maiestie to procede in reformations of here base & corse monies.* At the center of this justification for the recoinage is an articulation of what is now called Gresham's law. The tract explains that base and counterfeit money has driven all the good money out of circulation; for despite the fact that fine coins were minted in the later part of Edward's reign, during Mary's reign, and in the first years of Elizabeth's reign, "yet no part thereof is sene cõmonly currant; but, as it may be thought, some part thereof is caryed hence, and some, percase, by the wyser sort of people, kepte in store, as it were to be wished the whole were" (Sig. A2ᵛ). The rise in prices is described as a direct result of this state of affairs:

> For every man, of the least understanding, by one means or other, knew that a teston was not worth six-pence . . . and therfore no man woulde gyve gladly that thing which was and ever had ben worth six-pence, for a teston, but would rather require two testons. (Sig. A2ᵛ)

This theory is not without support among economic historians, but it is at best a partial explanation of the Tudor inflation. The text assumes that a "thing" has a permanent price and that the problem lies entirely in the coin's failure to be worth six pence. "Every man" is eventually able to see through the imposture and conclude that a teston is no longer worth six pence. If the coin is reformed, prices will return to their prebasement level:

> And, consequently, every man ought to thank Almyghtye God, that he may lyve to see the honour of his countrey thus partely recovered; sylver to come in place of cooper, pryces of thynges amende, all people more able to lyve of theyr wages, every man's purse, or coffer, made free from the privie thefe, which was the counterfaytour. (Sig. A3ᵛ–A4ʳ)

The past tense applied to that insidious figure, the "privie thefe, which was the counterfaytour," reveals the scope of this fantasy of reformation. The counterfeiter is seen as an especially insidious figure, able to penetrate the enclosed spaces of purse and coffer by adulterating the coin. However, the plan offers no compelling reason for supposing that the recoinage will stop the activities of the counterfeiter. Admittedly a wide discrepancy between a coin's nominal and metallic value encourages counterfeiting, since a counterfeiter may manufacture coins that are metallically equivalent to those produced by the Mint and still profit. Nevertheless, even a close correlation between metallic and nominal value will not end counterfeiting. Argument is replaced by assertion: "And fynally, no maner of person in the whole Realme shall have after one or two monethes hurt hereby, except onely the traytour which hath lyved by counterfaictying" (Sig. A3ᵛ). The demonic presence of the "counterfaictour," the traitor responsible for adulterating the monetary system, is a rhetorical device; it diverts attention away from that royal counterfeiter, Elizabeth's father, Henry VIII. It may appear oxymoronic to speak of a royal counterfeiter; counterfeiting was treason precisely because it was an offense against the person of the king, an example of lese-majesty. The coinage was part of the royal prerogative, and consequently the king was deemed incapable of counterfeiting. As Lear says, "No, they cannot touch me for coining. I am the King himself" (4.6.83). However, as early as the mid-fourteenth century, Nicholas Oresme had argued that the coinage is the property of the community and that, therefore, the monarch does not have an absolute right to debase it.[23] Though this line of argument was not prevalent in the sixteenth century, the anxious rhetoric of *The Summarie* reveals that, whatever the legal situation, a change in the coinage needed to be legitimated in terms of the common good.

The most vexing problem facing the queen and her coinage in the

1590s was the persistence of inflation. The rate of inflation did not remain constant: it accelerated in the middle of the sixteenth century, dropped off in the 1560s and 1570s, and sped up again at the close of the century.[24] The recurrence of steep inflation during the 1590s made it clear that Mint reform alone was not enough to guarantee price stability. The social dislocation that attended the inflation of the 1590s, especially in and around London, has often been designated a crisis by historians, though recently scholars have downplayed the disruption caused by high inflation, focusing instead on the effectiveness and elasticity of social institutions. Nonetheless, Ian Archer is surely correct in "asserting the reality of a *perceived* crisis in the 1590s."[25] This perceived crisis, in turn, served to put enormous strain on the language of value in its various forms. The impressive cultural efflorescence of the 1590s—a development not limited to the rarefied world of literary production—was in part a response to the unsettling sense that inherited values no longer had purchase in the world.

1Henry IV was written sometime between 1595 and 1598, a period of especially severe dearth and inflation, yet it reveals none of the anger and confusion so visible in the prose tracts written to address the economic situation.[26] The one important exception is the Carrier's rueful remark that Robin Ostler "never joyed since the price of oats rose, it was the death of him" (2.1.11–12), an observation recalled by the inclusion amongst Falstaff's recruits of "ostlers trade-fallen" (4.2.29). In general, however, the play celebrates those characters adroit enough to thrive in a world of change and uncertainty, a reeling world insistently figured through numismatic language. Though the play's consideration of value is complex, it is unconvincing to describe Shakespeare as a celebrant of the immutable truths of customary practice.[27] Such readings tend to make Shakespeare into an anticapitalist *avant la lettre,* a percipient and conservative write who saw the chaos and pain that would come to a society ruled by the market. For the very same reasons, it would be rash to recruit Shakespeare as a proto-liberal advocate of laissez-faire economics.[28] Both positions anachronistically operate within a framework based on a fully modern economic history.[29] Attending to the language of coinage as it resonates within *1 Henry IV* and late Elizabethan culture reveals a more complex situation.

The language of coinage provides a historically specific conceptual constellation: it is one prominent vocabulary in which a range of problems that we identify as economic get thought out in the early modern period. And yet the language of coinage is also used to articulate the peculiar relationship between authority and value in contexts far removed from the world of money and trade. John Hayward, recounting an episode in which a proposal of his was rejected only to be approved when put forth in the "very same words" by another, remarks: "speech (I perceiued) was oftentimes like vnto coine, which passed for currant, not in regard of the mettal onely, but chiefly in regard of the stampe that was set upon it" (B1^v).[30] The authority of the source or origin of an idea is, according to Hayward, usually more important in determining its acceptance than the substance of the claim. But it is important to remember that the metal also matters; in fact, Hayward gently criticizes the intellectual timidity of the majority who refuse to assess claims on their merits. Intrinsic worth is here opposed to the distortions imposed by deference in a hierarchical social world.

Shakespeare's *1 Henry IV* operates in a similar fashion: it recognizes the overwhelming importance of the social world as a terrain riven by conflicting evaluative claims and yet it does not renounce the notion of intrinsic value. *1 Henry IV* certainly subjects the official discourse of true and false that characterizes *The Summarie* to careful scrutiny, using the terminology of coinage and counterfeiting to depict an England that has become, in Bacon's phrase, "a very labyrinth of cozenages and abuses."[31] But rather than offering a simple return to the true old standard (whether it be the legitimate line or the proper pound sterling), the play imagines an alternative return to aristocratic chivalry. Elaborating on the possibilities and dangers offered by a secular world in which value and authority are revealed to be both provisional and improvisational, *1 Henry IV* suggests that value emerges through a specifically historical process of strife and contention.[32] The play offers an agonistic vision of history that refuses to see victory as merely adventitious: Henry and his sons succeed because they are prepared and fully committed to their cause. The decisiveness, or even ruthlessness, that led Hazlitt to accuse Henry V of having "no idea of any rule of right or wrong, but brute force,"[33] is also evident in Prince Hal, but this ethical deficiency is precisely what allows him to succeed in a time of tumultuous change.

The troubled (and troubling) connection between prince and coin is visible in Hal's first scene when he reminds Falstaff that he has always paid the tab, "so far as my coin would stretch, and where it would not I have used my credit" (1.2.52–53). The metaphor of stretched coin used by the heir apparent suggests a disturbing elasticity that recalls debasement. Despite the availability of financial credit, Hal yearns for a more inclusive credibility, and his soliloquy at the end of the scene outlines his intended strategy: he will allow the "base contagious clouds" to obscure his magnificence only so that he may be "more wonder'd at" when he breaks forth in his full glory (the sort of maneuver the Elizabethans condemned as forestalling). He plans to obscure his true qualities so that

> . . . like bright metal on a sullen ground,
> My reformation, glitt'ring o'er my fault,
> Shall show more goodly, and attract more eyes
> Than that which hath no foil to set it off.
> (1.2.207–10)

This image suggests that value is enhanced through the comparative or "foil," and that this differential must be represented and recognized, attracting "more eyes." Hal here claims that people and precious metals both are evaluated by the appraising gaze of an audience or society and that because context affected evaluative judgments, approbation can be advantageously manipulated. Both Hal and the king make the connection between rarity and value, but the king describes the quality of kingliness as if it were a substance to be conserved and not "swallow'd." Hal sees it as something to be produced. The difference between the two is in part a result of their relative positions. Bolingbroke established his own value by using Richard II as a "foil"; in contrast to Richard's frequent appearances, he appeared rarely, "like a comet," and won men's hearts. Hal first differentiates himself from his father, by playing the prodigal, but plans soon to make manifest the difference between his "old" and "new" selves.

The success of Hal's strategy is first revealed in Vernon's description of the reformed Hal and his troops armed for battle, "Glittering in golden coats like images" (4.1.100). The immediate allusion is to religious icons, saints wrapped in gold leaf, but the collocation of "golden" and "image" also suggests a coin, a line of thought that is reinforced by Vernon's subsequent remark that Hal appeared as "an angel" (4.1.108). This language, at once religious and numismatic, points insistently at the glamorous spectacle of Young Harry armed for battle but also raises the troubling possibility of a merely meretricious appearance—an inefficacious idol, a counterfeit coin, an empty suit of armor. The image of Hal on horseback presents a resplendent emblem of chivalry, but there is no immediate reason to conclude that this is not simply another pose.

The problem of deceptive appearances has, after all, been raised by Hal himself, who rather than accept a static vision of the world that equates a person's worth or dignity with a particular place in a fixed social hierarchy, sees honor, the coin of social capital, as fungible, something that can be both alienated and appropriated.[34] He promises his father: "For the time will come / That I shall make this northern youth exchange / His glorious deeds for my indignities" (3.2.144–46). He speaks of honor as a commodity, describing Hotspur as his "factor" who has been allowed to "engross up glorious deeds" but who will be called to "strict account" and forced to make the proper "reckoning."[35] Falstaff expresses a similar sentiment, suggesting that social capital is convertible, when he remarks, "I would to God thou and I knew where a commodity of good names were to be brought" (1.2.80–81). Hal will do even better, rather than pay, he will seize Hotspur's good name: "O Harry, thou hast robb'd me of my youth! / I better brook the loss of brittle life / Than those proud titles thou hast won of me" (5.4.76–78). *1 Henry IV* displays a world in which honor is seen to be corrupted by economic calculation, and value, whether in Eastcheap or at court, is subject to manipulation.

Falstaff, despite his cynicism, appreciates the way the honor and reputation of the coin confer purchasing power. This sensibility is visible in his insult to Bardolph: "if I did not think thou hadst been . . . a ball of wildfire, there's no purchase in money" (3.3.39). The expression "purchase in money" is used as incontestable fact, supporting the outlandish assertions that precede it; nevertheless, the effect is to suggest that money has a will o' the wisp quality, something in common with the spectacular and pyrotechnical. By drawing attention to the purchasing power of money, Falstaff identifies money as a means of exchange, though it might be more accurate to say that he regards money as a means to consumption. When Bardolph warns Falstaff to prepare, because, "there's money of the King's coming down the hill, 'tis going to the King's exchequer," he immediately responds: "You lie, you rogue, 'tis going to the King's tavern" (2.2.54). Falstaff simply wants to reroute the king's money, inserting himself into a circuit of exchange without making any proprietary claims. As Hal points out, the purse snatched on Monday night is spent by Tuesday morning: "got with swearing 'Lay by!', and spent with crying 'Bring in!' " (1.2.35–36). Falstaff's view is diametrically opposed to that of the king, who asks, "Shall our coffers then / Be empty'd to redeem a traitor home?" (1.3.84). The king considers money to be a stable store of value and speaks in terms of its conservation and retention, while Falstaff, who sees money as a medium of exchange, speaks the language of expenditure and consumption.

Falstaff's seemingly limitless appetite predictably leads to fantasies about limitless coining. Attempting to avoid settling his bill at the tavern, he tells the Hostess to seek payment from Bardolph: "Look upon his face. What call you rich? Let them coin his nose, let them coin his cheeks" (3.3.75–78). All the coin spent on sack has magically been preserved in Bardolph's rubicund flesh, which is now grotesquely figured as proper matter for the Mint. When Bardolph apprises him of his debt—"This bottle makes an angel" (4.2.6)—he answers: "And if it do, take it for thy labour—and if it make twenty, take them all, I'll answer the coinage" (4.2.7–8). Both these jokes revolve around the curious way in which coins combine form and matter, image and metal. Is coinage defined by its substance (Bardolph's nose) or by the authority of the figure (Falstaff) who agrees to "answer" for it? Falstaff's punning take on coinage, as well as his more general skepticism, reveals a lack of confidence in the coin's ability to act as a stable measure of value. Indeed, his very corpulence figures inflation, and his profligate attitude is one perfectly suited to an inflationary economy in which consumption is a sensible strategy.

Falstaff's refusal to grant a stable value to coinage is accompanied by an appreciation for the elasticity of prices. As a result of the rebellion, he claims, "you may buy land now as cheap as stinking mackerel" (2.4.355–56). Certainly the main thrust of this comment is that rebellion has turned the world upside down, but one cannot escape the implication that price, even that of land always depends on expectation. Hal responds, "Why then, it is like if there come a hot June, and this civil buffeting hold, we shall buy maidenheads as they buy hob-nails, by the hundreds" (57–59). This cynical remark anticipates a similar collapse in the price of female bodies, revealing that the means of both sexual and agrarian reproduction are subject to the fluctuations of the market and the contingencies of war. Later Falstaff proves adept at trading in men's bodies: "I have got in exchange of a hundred and fifty soldiers three hundred and odd pounds" (4.2.13–14). This "commodity of warm slaves" quickly buy out of service, leaving Falstaff to pocket the proceeds. Falstaff himself acknowledges that he has "misused the King's press damnably" (4.2.12), and one finds in this episode not only further evidence of the convertibility of various forms of capital, but a recognition that the state is, in the last resort, able to extract value with the threat of violence.

Though Falstaff is an accomplished entrepreneur with a well-developed sense of the market, he is not above using the language of intrinsic value when it suits him. Urging Hal not to turn him over to the sheriff, Falstaff implores: "Never call a true piece of gold a counterfeit. Thou art essentially made without seeming so" (2.4.486–87). The purport of the first sentence seems clear enough: I, Falstaff, am genuine and not to be repudiated, a claim that applies both to Hal's indictment of him as "old white-bearded Satan" and to the immediate threat raised by the sheriff. A piece of gold is a coin, but by ignoring denomination the formulation erases the coin's stamp, focusing instead on its substance, true gold. The difficulty raised by the next sentence concerns the force of the adverb "essentially," which could be read as an intensifier meaning "in fact," a possibility that places an emphasis on Hal's constructed nature, the fact that he is made up. Reading "essentially" as "according to an essence," produces an almost opposite meaning: Hal, like the true piece of gold, has a substantial essence, admittedly unspecified, that has, for whatever reason, been obscured. The unresolved ambivalence of this claim about Hal is in keeping with the play's exploration of the problem of value. What appears to be a nicely ironic reversal—the man who consistently claims that the false is true is forced by circumstance to make a plea for the truth—is simultaneously an acknowledgement that the counterfeiter must uphold the standard of value in order to exploit it.

The rapacious appetite of Falstaff's economic vision is never corrected within the play, which concludes with the battle of Shrewsbury. It is here on the battlefield that the personages of Eastcheap confront the denizens of the court: Falstaff, Hal, and the king are brought together for the first time. Rather than precipitating an immediate and definitive separation of the noble and heroic from the base and venal, the episode reveals a persistent confusion of categories. Though Hal has often been seen as mediating between two "worlds" with Falstaff and King Henry standing at the center of their respective spheres, such a polarization misleadingly suggests that there is an enormous gulf between Falstaff and the king. In fact, the battle of Shewsbury reveals that both characters are counterfeiters. The figure of the royal counterfeiter, repressed by *The Summarie,* returns in the person of Bolingbroke.

That Falstaff resorts to counterfeiting is hardly a surprise. He displays irreverence toward most conventional values, delighting in their insubstantiality. His famous speech on "honour" provides a succinct statement of this skeptical attitude: honor is "A word . . . Air. A trim reckoning!" (5.1.135). The emphasis on language and breath reveals honor to be a social fact, conferred by the recognition of others. However, Falstaff's nominalism does not entirely deny the value of honor. The sarcasm of "trim reckoning" implies a notion of calculable value, and Falstaff's attempt to win honor through subterfuge reveals that he is quite aware that honor may lead to financial reward, that the social capital of honor may be converted into monetary form. And money, of course, can be transformed into sack.

Falstaff's stratagem depends on an act of counterfeiting:

> 'Sblood, 'twas time to counterfeit, or that hot termagant Scot had paid me, scot and lot too. Counterfeit? I lie, I am no counterfeit: to die is to be a counterfeit, for he is but the counterfeit of a man, who hath not the life of a man: but to counterfeit dying, is to be no counterfeit, but the true and perfect image of life indeed. (5.4.112–19)

Falstaff's quibble employs two competing definitions of "counterfeit." It is first used as a verb meaning "to imitate," and then as a noun signifying an imitation that is superficially similar to but lacks the essential quality of the original, in this case, life. Life is the essence of being human; a body without life is a corpse. This claim allows Falstaff to "counterfeit" without becoming a "counterfeit." Pretending does not make one false. However, Falstaff's logic never escapes from the problem of representation: his final assertion is that pretending to die is to be "the true and perfect image of life." This punning defense of cowardice—which also serves as a defense of theatrical impersonation—expresses the vitality that many critics have found central to his character: no pretence is too craven or humiliating for Falstaff if it preserves life.

Falstaff's voluble cynicism, however, is proclaimed in the midst of battle, as others fight and die. Mistaking Blunt for the king, Douglas tells him, "The Lord Stafford dear today hath bought / thy likeness" (5.3.7–8). Blunt soon pays the same price for wearing the king's garb. Douglas's triumph is short-lived; Hotspur informs him that he has not killed the king, but Blunt, "furnished like the King himself" (5.3.21), explaining that "The King hath many marching in his coats" (5.3.25). In a rage, Douglas swears that he will kill all the king's "coats," murder all his "wardrobe," until he comes to the king himself. What might seem an absurd and comic image is given grim substance by the presence of Blunt's body on the stage; no magic animates these coats, they contain real people. Bolingbroke, in effect, engages in a strategic debasement: he puts a multitude of false sovereigns into circulation. Reversing his earlier attitude of conservation, Henry IV is now prodigal with his "presence."

When he next encounters a figure dressed as the king, Douglas is incredulous:

> Another King! They grow like Hydra's heads:
> I am the Douglas, fatal to all those
> That wear those colours on them. What art thou
> That counterfeit'st the person of a king?
>
> (5.4.24–27)

The image of the Hydra's many, multiplying heads, a favorite Elizabethan emblem of rebellion, identifies the king's strategy as monstrous. In addition, the accusation of counterfeiting, with its true/false binary, is particularly troubling when leveled against Bolingbroke. He *is* the king Douglas seeks, and yet the rebellion is itself motivated by the claim that he is *not* the legitimate king. Despite Bolingbroke's assertions of majesty, Douglas remains skeptical, though he does remark, "thou bearest thee like a king" (5.4.35). This variation on a familiar romance motif (nobility, however disguised, will shine forth) hints at continued uncertainty; Douglas seems unable to decide whether he is in the presence of majesty or merely its imitation.[36]

The word *counterfeit* that circulates through act 5, scene 4 is not the same *counterfeit* that appears in Elizabeth's *The Summary of Certain Reasons*. It is not primarily concerned with the problem of false coin, nor does it consistently operate as a moral term onto which a whole host of economic difficulties are displaced. The play reveals the counterfeit to be both more problematic and more productive. The king, like Falstaff, authorizes "counterfeiting" but claims not to be a counterfeit himself. The ubiquity of counterfeiting presents the vertiginous possibility that value is merely an effect of representation. In such a world, the remark attributed to Marlowe in the infamous Baine's libel—that he had "as good Right to coin as the Queene of England"—sounds less like an outrageous assault on the very idea of sovereignty, and more like an astute recognition that all coins are counterfeit.[37]

The play does not, however, completely confound the idea of value. Value is recuperated in the form of martial action by Hal. By cultivating an image of inadequacy, Hal, who begins the play as the "shadow of succession," is able to stage a transformation that obscures the problem of usurpation with a triumphal assumption of the role of prince and heir apparent. An exclusive focus on the power of representation obscures the degree to which Hal's performance includes heroic deeds. The violent overthrow of Hotspur is fundamental to the play's account of value: a decisive action in a world of uncertainties that establishes Hal's value and valor in the eyes of the audience. Hal may be a master manipulator, able to "drink with any tinker in his own language," but this facility is accompanied by a ready ability with the sword. Arguably the play's careful attention to the elaboration and manipulation of value, in the end, concludes with an atavistic scheme according to which a fundamental act of violence secures the standard of value. However, this possibility is immediately tempered by Hal's subsequent behavior.

Having long planned to seize Hotspur's honor, Hal instead goes along with Falstaff's mendacious attempt to take credit for the killing. Hal's willingness to "gild" Falstaff's actions with a lie reveals a degree of magnaminity that appears to be beyond calculation; indeed, this episode serves to distance Hal from the calculative rationality that informs his thinking throughout the play. By repudiating his interest in Hotspur's death, Hal, who has "a truant been to chivalry," effectively restores the tarnished image of heroism.[38] Hal's aristocratic pose of indifference in the face of Falstaff's fabrication solidifies his claim to magnanimity: having achieved victory, to argue over credit would betray a petty mind.

A similar dynamic is visible in his treatment of his prisoner Douglas. In an episode that contrasts with the squabble over ransom that opens the play, Hal, after receiving the king's permission to dispose of the prisoner, gives to his younger brother the privilege of delivering Douglas, "ransomless and free" (5.5.28). This refusal of calculation and exchange asserts the transcendent value of the "high deeds" (5.5.30) for which Douglas deserves his freedom, while establishing Hal as a giver of gifts that cannot be reciprocated. The release of Douglas pointedly contrasts with the killing of Hotspur, the third and last in a series of three coercive exchanges, which includes the robbery at Gadshill and Falstaff's abuse of the press-gang. The final two scenes of the play, depicting Hal as willing to give Falstaff credit for killing Hotspur and ready to recognize the "valours" of Douglas, introduces a new dynamic, a form of exchange that appears to repudiate exchange itself, the gift. Between coercion and gift, what Natalie Zemon Davis refers to as the "mode of sales," which features so largely in the play and contributes so much to the impression that value in this world has become unfixed, fades into obscurity.[39]

The metaphysics of blood that would equate social value and status with genealogy, making royal or noble blood the irrefutable standard, is not replaced by a happy celebration of the market as a mechanism for the production of consensus; rather, an ancient aristocratic commitment to the value of violence stages a return in the form of a smiling and benevolent Prince Hal. A man's worth, according to this masculine understanding, is commensurate with his ability to fight, a vision neatly epitomized by the Archbishop, who, anticipating the coming battle, remarks that "ten thousand men / Must bide the touch" (4.4.9–10). Similarly, Hal is able to overcome his lineal deficiency and the taint of his father's usurpation by proving himself to be a "true piece of gold" on the field at Shrewsbury.

The same questions of royal lineage troubled Elizabeth's accession, and, because she was without an immediate heir, threatened her succession. Shakespeare's *1 Henry IV* responds to this moment of economic and political instability, and yet the history it depicts only succeeds in rearticulating the crisis of legitimacy precipitated by continuing economic difficulties and uncertain dynastic politics. As I have claimed, the coinage, both as a material practice and a fertile set of metaphors, is one place where political and economic concerns meet: a new monarch inevitably meant new coinage. Elizabeth was after all remembered for her recoinage—the epitaph on her tomb declares it her third greatest accomplishment—but even before her death Thomas Tymme noted, in his account of the English monarchs: "Amongst all other her most rare vertues, she hath reformed religion, she hath reduced all base coines (which were currant here before her dayes) into perfect gold and siluer, so that there is no other mony lesse or more curra[n]t within her dominions: which is not to be seene at this day else where vnder any Prince Christian or Ethnicke."[40] Designed to warn against the dangers of debasement, such declarations are as much admonitory as they are epideictic. Evidence that there was concern about the possibility of future debasement appears in the section of Fulbecke's *A Parallele* (1601) that treats borrowing and lending. Here the host, Nomomathes, asks whether a debt can be repaid in debased coin and is told that "if the debasement were before the day of paime[n]t the debtor may pay the det in the coine embased" (54ʳ–54ᵛ). In strictly legal terms this point is beyond dispute, and yet the very question betrays a fundamental uncertainty about the fairness of such an outcome. Indeed, the word *debasement,* used to describe an act that is at once legal and illegitimate, indicates that the extensive royal prerogative concerning coinage provoked fundamental questions about the establishment of value.

It is not surprising, then, that the language of numismatics in *1 Henry IV* reveals an insistent preoccupation with the way in which value is established and maintained. The play refuses to settle into the easy binaries of true and false, stable and changing, legitimate and illegitimate, and yet this does not mean that it depicts "a world drained of intrinsic value."[41] Instead, the play insists that value is complex, a source of conflict and struggle, but not therefore illusory. The tension between the monarch and the market that appears in the Tudor coinage is obviously not a conflict between divine right and liberal democracy; it is, rather, the exposure of the possibility of contradiction within a seemingly coherent and hierarchical universe, a possibility recognized by Sir Robert Cotton, who remarks that monies of gold and silver have two values: "The one, the Extrinsick quality, which is at the King's pleasure. . . . The other the Intrinsick quantity of pure mettal, which is in the *Merchant* to value."[42] The point to be made here is that intrinsic value is based on the market price of the quantity of bullion contained in the coin. For Cotton, the coin is a perfect instance of the uneasy alliance between the Crown and its merchants, a fitting emblem of what would come to be called mercantilism. It is, therefore, precipitous to hear in this, and similar claims, an anticipation of the amoral, rationalized market of nineteenth-century economic theory. However, the simultaneous recognition of market forces or general estimation and intrinsic value entails complicated and conflicted thinking, a problem brilliantly exemplified by Gerard de Malynes:

And concerning pearles and precious stones, is it not straunge, that some men do despise and account them as glistering toyes & trifles, considering the diuersitie of mens opinions, which made the aunceint Philosophers to say: That the world was gouerned by opinions. But if these men should wel consider the pure creation and vertue of the stones, they would iudge otherwise; and their owne opinion (opposite to most men) would condemne their errour: seeing that a generall estimation doth approue the value of things.[43]

De Malynes initially acknowledges the diversity of opinion concerning value, a circumstance that led the ancient philosophers to assert that the world is governed by opinion. However, his invocation of "the pure creation and vertue of the stones" is an affirmation of a divine order that entails a hierarchy of values in the face of classical skepticism. If the doubters would only consider the virtue, or intrinsic qualities, of the stones, they would revise their opinion. Furthermore, even granting that the world is "governed by opinions," those who despise "precious stones" are guilty of rejecting common wisdom for individual idiosyncrasy since "a generall estimation doth approue the value of things." Deploying common sense to rebut skepticism and the possibility of pluralism, de Malynes provides a typical early modern account of value in which disagreement over value is acknowledged while the idea of intrinsic value is maintained. He is untroubled by the potential contradiction between "vertue" or intrinsic value and "generall estimation" because he is confident that the two will inevitably coincide.

In Troilus's question, "What's aught but as 'tis valued?" (2.2.51), one hears a clear echo of Falstaff. But while Falstaff's soliloquy goes unanswered, Troilus is given a reply by Hector: "But value dwells not in particular will; / It holds his estimate and dignity / As well wherein 'tis precious of itself / As in the prizer" (52). Hector sees that Troilus's skepticism may be used to support an autocratic or idiosyncratic theory of value, he denies this possibility by asserting that value is a combination of intrinsic and extrinsic value. However, the only way in which the intrinsic ("wherein 'tis precious in itself") can act as a curb on the wayward individual is when it eventuates in a collective judgment. Like *Troilus and Cressida, 1 Henry IV* is intensely concerned with the establishment of value in a diminished world. The play is neither an embrace of the burgeoning market nor is it a ratification of the existing order; rather, it asks a diverse audience that has paid "good" money to see a counterfeit king to consider the manner in which both coin and king are valued.[44]

Notes

1. William Shakespeare, *The First Part of King Henry IV,* ed. A. R. Humphreys (New York: Methuen, 1960), 174. All references are to this edition. An account of the play's economic language, focusing on the figure of contract, is provided by Sandra K. Fischer, " 'He means to pay': Value and Metaphor in the Lancastrian Tetralogy," *Shakespeare Quarterly* 40 (1989): 149–64. More recently, Nina Levine, "Extending Credit in the *Henry IV* Plays," *Shakespeare Quarterly* 51 (2000): 403–31, reads credit relations within the play as providing a benign vision of mutual reciprocity that competes with the high discourse of politics. For a broad survey of Shakespeare's economic language, see Sandra K. Fischer, *Econolingua* (Newark: University of Delaware Press,1985).

2. For a related account of the way in which the language of coinage operates in *Troilus and Cressida,* see Stephen X. Mead, " 'Thou art chang'd': Public Value and Personal Identity in *Troilus and Cressida,*" *Journal of Medieval and Renaissance Studies* 22 (1992): 237–59. Mead persuasively demonstrates the way in which the language of coinage registers "contemporary anxieties concerning the very substance of wealth and value" (237). However, Mead's conclusion— "*Troilus and Cressida* asserts that when a value system becomes corrupt or ceases to be meaningful, it falls upon the individual—in the face of the general will—to determine worth as well as he or she can" (258)—credits the play with an unconvincing individualism.

3. For plays other than *1 Henry IV,* I cite from *The Complete Works of Shakespeare,* ed. David Bevington, 4th ed. (New York: Longman, 1997).

4. David Scott Kastan, *Shakespeare After Theory* (New York: Routledge, 1999), 129.

5. For an important exception arguing that "the contingency of evaluation served as a recurrent enabling irritant for Shakespeare's creativity," see Lars Engle, *Shakespearean Pragmatism: Market of His Time* (Chicago: University of Chicago Press, 1993). Engle's book, as he is aware, courts the charge of anachronism by attempting to identify Shakespeare's work as an antecedent of philosophical pragmatism. As he points out, this claim could work itself out in at least two ways. First, an argument could be made that Shakespeare is an unacknowledged source for modern pragmatism. Engle, however, chooses a second route, one that involves taking seriously William James's description of pragmatism as "a new name for some old ways of thinking" (7).

6. Victor Kiernan, *Eight Tragedies of Shakespeare: A Marxist Study* (London: Verso, 1996), 25; Jean-Christophe Agnew, *Worlds Apart: The Market and the Theater in Anglo-American Thought, 1550–1750* (Cambridge: Cambridge University Press, 1986), xi.

7. The relationship between the theatrical enterprise and the new economic order has recently been examined, from very different perspectives, by Douglas Bruster, *Drama and the market in the age of Shakespeare* (Cambridge: Cambridge

University Press, 1992) and Theodore B. Leinwand, *Theatre, finance and society in early modern England* (Cambridge: Cambridge University Press, 1999).

8. On this claim, see Claude Lefort, *Writing: the Political Text,* trans. David Ames Curtis (Durham, NC: Duke University Press, 2000). Lefort points out that "taken in its philosophical acceptation, the concept of *value* pertains to a modern way of thinking . . . so long as the idea of a standard of human conduct is affirmed in reference to nature, reason, or God, the notion of value couldn't take on any meaning" (142).

9. *The Geneva Bible: A Facsimile of the 1560 Edition,* ed. Lloyd E. Berry (Madison: University of Wisconsin Press,1969), sig. 2C2^v.

10. The proliferation of publications treating coins and their history is impressive. For a comprehensive bibliography, see C. E. Dekesel, *Bibliotheca Nummaria: Bibliography of 16th Century Numismatic Books* (London: Spink, 1997).

11. Kevin Sharpe, *Sir Robert Cotton, 1586–1631: History and Politics in Early Modern England* (Oxford: Oxford University Press, 1979), p. 18. This coincidence of interest in both coinage and lineage suggests the degree to which the antiquaries were attempting to ground value.

12. Michel Foucault, *The Order of Things: An Archaeology of the Human Sciences* (New York: Vintage, 1973), 168. Foucault goes on to argue that sixteenth-century reforms that demanded equivalence between nominal and metallic value were intent on fixing the two functions of the coin as common measure of commodities and as means of exchange. In his narrative, this metallist theory is disrupted by the recognition that money is a commodity. As a consequence, the earlier understanding according to which money has an intrinsic character (metal is precious) that underwrites its function as measure and means of exchange is reversed so that the exchanging function is seen as the basis for the other two (measure and capacity to receive a price). No longer does the coin's value derive from its metal; instead the stamp or form is seen as guaranteeing the value.

13. For instance, the suggestion that money signifies wealth because it is a real mark (i.e., is itself a precious substance), while common enough during the Renaissance, was contested by the Aristotelian idea that money takes its value from its issuing authority. For an argument that Foucault's Renaissance *episteme* relies too heavily on Platonist writers, see Ian Maclean, "Foucault's Renaissance Episteme Reassessed: An Aristotelian Counterblast," *Journal of the History of Ideas* 59 (1998): 149–66.

14. C. H. V. Sutherland, *English Coinage: 600–1900* (London: B.T. Batsford, 1973), 117.

15. W. J. W. Potter and E. J. Winstanley, "The Coinage of Henry VII," *British Numismatic Journal* 31 (1962): 109.

16. Sydney Anglo, *Images of Tudor Kingship* (London: Seaby, 1992), 118.

17. For a recent and helpful account of the debasement that situates it within the long institutional history of Mint, see *A New History of the Royal Mint,* ed. C. E. Challis (Cambridge: Cambridge University Press, 1992), 228–44. See also J. D. Gould, *the Great Debasement* (Oxford: Oxford University Press, 1970).

18. Robert Cotton, *Cottoni posthuma: divers choice pieces of that renovvned antiquary Sir Robert Cotton, Knight and Baronet, preserved from the injury of time, and expos'd to public light, for the benefit of posterity, by J.H. Esq* (London, 1651), sig. T8^r.

19. John William Burgon, *The Life and Times of Sir Thomas Gresham* (London, 1839), 1:484.

20. Sir Albert Feavearyear, *The Pound Sterling: A History of English Money* (Oxford: Oxford University Press, 1963), 79.

21. *Tudor Royal Proclamations*, ed. Paul L. Hughes and James F. Larkin (New Haven: Yale University Press, 1969) vol. 2, #471.

22. Feavearyear, *Pound Sterling*, 83.

23. Peter Spufford, *Money and Its Use in Medieval Europe* (Cambridge: Cambridge University Press, 1988), 301. See also, André Lapidus, "Metal, Money, and the Prince: John Buridan and Nicholas Oresme after Thomas Aquinas," *History of Political Economy* 29 (1997): 21–53.

24. D. M. Palliser, *The Age of Elizabeth* (New York: Longman, 1983), 142.

25. Ian W. Archer, *The Pursuit of Stability: Social Relations in Elizabethan London* (Cambridge: Cambridge University Press, 1991), 14.

26. See Mark Thornton Burnett, " 'Fill Gut and Pinch Belly': Writing Famine in the English Renaissance," *Explorations in Renaissance Culture* 21 (1995): 21–44.

27. See, for example, the argument made by Fischer, *Econolingua:* "While Shakespeare depicts a dramatic world in which values are changing from medieval to mercantilist economic ethics, his sympathetic characters do not find the new system satisfying. His plays reaffirm the operation of 'natural' economics established in the sonnets: bounty, reciprocal obligations defined by service and tradition, and benevolent social use of material increase" (30). Without denying that Shakespeare privileges such virtues, I belief that Fischer has framed the position in a misleading fashion by suggesting that it is possible to choose between two systems.

28. See, for example, Frederick Turner, *Shakespeare's Twenty-First-Century Economics: The Morality of Love and Money* (Oxford: Oxford University Press, 1999). Turner makes the rather astounding claim that Shakespeare provides a blueprint for the modern global economic system: "Shakespeare was a key figure, perhaps *the* key figure in creating that Renaissance system of meanings, values, and implicit rules that eventually gave rise to the modern world market and that still underpin it" (11).

29. It is the result of a long historiographical tradition that pits the acquisitive individual pursuing profit in the market against the community and its customs. For a helpful account, see Craig Muldrew, "Interpreting the Market: The Ethics of Credit and Community Relations in Early Modern England," *Social History* 18; no. 2 (1993): 163–83.

30. John Hayward, *A reporte of a discourse concerning supreme power in affaires of religion* (London, 1606), sig. B1^v.

31. In a dialogue written around 1592, Bacon makes the following observation: "For who knoweth not (that knoweth anything in matter of state) of the great absurdities and frauds that arise of the divorcing of legal estimation of monies from the general and (as I may term it) natural estimation of metals; and again, the uncertain and wavering values of coins, a very labyrinth of cozenages and abuses, and yet such as great princes have made their profit of towards their own people?" *Francis Bacon,* ed. Brian Vickers (Oxford: Oxford University Press, 1996), 40.

32. Stephen Greenblatt, "Invisible Bullets: Renaissance Authority and Its Subversion, *Henry IV* and *Henry V*," *Glyph* 8 (1981): 40–61, is the most influential account of "improvisational power" in the play. The subtlety and insight of Green-

blatt's reading is undeniable; however, his emphasis on a labile yet constraining conglomeration of power, representation and theatricality tends to downplay the possibility of ideological contradiction.

33. William Hazlitt, *Lectures on the Literature of the Age of Elizabeth and Characters of Shakespeare's Plays* (London: George Bell and Sons, 1899), 144.

34. The concept of social capital is elaborated by Pierre Bourdieu. A succinct account is provided by Pierre Bourdieu, "The Forms of Capital," *Handbook of Theory and Research for the Sociology of Education,* ed. John G. Richardson (New York: Greenwood Press, 1986), 241–58, which defines social capital as "the aggregate of the actual or potential resources which are linked to possession of a durable network of more or less institutionalized relationships of mutual acquaintance and recognition," adding that "the title of nobility is the form *par excellence* of the institutionalized social capital which guarantees a particular form of social relationship in a lasting way" (248, 251). Though Bourdieu emphasizes the durability of social capital and its arbitrary distribution, his account also suggests that social capital can be gained, maintained, or lost. However, it is certainly worth noting that the title of nobility, which Bourdieu sees as the quintessence of social capital, appears, in *1 Henry IV*, to be extremely fragile.

35. This point is made by Michèle Willems, "Misconstruction in *1 Henry IV*," *Cahiers Elisabethains* 37 (1990): 48.

36. My reading of this encounter is indebted to the analysis of David Kastan, who concludes that "even Henry can only bear himself '*like* the king'; he has no authentic royal identity prior to and untouched by representation" (142).

37. A. D. Wraight, *In Search of Christopher Marlowe* (New York: Vanguard Press, 1965), 309.

38. In this regard, I agree with Tillyard, who sees the play as an affirmation of chivalry. However, Tillyard reads Hal's willingness to credit Falstaff's lie as a farewell to arms, an indicator that he is already turning to what Tillyard considers to be the subject of *2 Henry IV:* civil virtues. See E. M. W. Tillyard, *Shakespeare's History Plays* (New York: Macmillan, 1947), 265.

39. Natalie Zemon Davis, *The Gift in Sixteenth-Century France* (Madison: University of Wisconsin Press, 2000), 9. Davis begins her discussion by distinguishing between three "relational modes": the gift mode, the mode of coercion, and the mode of sales.

40. Palliser, 139; Thomas Tymme, *A Booke Containing The True Portraiture of The Countenances ad attires of the kings of England* (London, 1597).

41. H. R. Coursen, *The Leasing Out of England: Shakespeare's Second Henriad* (Washington, DC: University Press of America, 1982), 3.

42. Robert Cotton, *Cottoni posthuma: divers choice pieces of that renovvned antiquary Sir Robert Cotton, Knight and Baronet, preserved from the injury of time, and expos'd to public light, for the benefit of posterity, by J.H. Esq* (London, 1651), sig. V1^v.

43. Gerard de Malynes, *Englands vievv, in the vnmasking of two paradoxes: with a replication vnto the answer of Maister John Bodine* (London: 1603), sig. G3^v–G4^r.

44. I would like to record my thanks to the friends and colleagues whose comments helped in the preparation of this paper, especially David Kastan, Alan Nelson, Dan Vitkus, and Graham Hammill; and thank Linda Woodbridge and the seminar of the Shakespeare Association for whom an early version of this essay was prepared.

"Awake Remembrance of these Valiant Dead": *Henry V* and the Politics of the English History Play

ALISON THORNE

"A PROPAGANDA-PLAY on National Unity: heavily orchestrated for the brass" was how A. P. Rossiter summed up *Henry V* in 1954.[1] The assumption that this play is complicit with the promonarchical, nationalist rhetoric of the Chorus, and with the particular myth of Englishness it propounds, has persisted. In recent years the most cogent articulation of this view has come from Richard Helgerson, who sees the play as the culmination of Shakespeare's gradual tightening of his "obsessive and compelling focus on the ruler" during the writing of his English history cycle, at the cost of occluding the interests of the ruled. In contrast to the historical dramas staged by the rival Henslowe companies, which, he argues, were less concerned with the "consolidation and maintenance of royal power" than with the plight of the socially inferior "victims of such power," Shakespeare's chronicle plays exorcised the common people from their vision of the nation with increasing ruthlessness:

> It is as though Shakespeare set out to cancel the popular ideology with which his cycle of English history plays began, as though he wanted to efface, alienate, even demonize all signs of commoner participation in the political nation. The less privileged classes may still have had a place in his audience, but they had lost their place in his representation of England.[2]

Helgerson explains this exclusionary process as part of a policy of self-gentrification pursued by Shakespeare and the Lord Chamberlain's Men—a determination to remove themselves as far as possible from the humble, "folk" origins of the theater they served.

According to his reading, the banishment of Falstaff at the end of *2 Henry IV,* along with the popular carnivalesque values he stands for, symbolically enacts this desire to be cleansed of the taint of vulgarity associated with the public stage. And in *Henry V* the purgation is completed. Despite the monarch's populist credentials earned in the Eastcheap tavern, the last play in the cycle confirms the "radical divorce . . . between the King and his people," riding roughshod over the "dream of commonality, of common interests and common humanity, between the ruler and the ruled" that had figured so prominently in the popular imagination.[3]

On the face of it, *Henry V* offers ample evidence to validate the proposition that, of all Shakespeare's chronicle plays, this one is "closest to state propaganda," and that such proximity denies the "less privileged classes" a significant place in the nation. One need only cite the near-unanimous commitment to Henry's cause expressed by nobility and commoners alike (in a striking departure from the aristocratic factionalism and popular insurgence that had dominated the preceding plays in the cycle); the curiously muted treatment of those few dissenting voices that do make themselves heard; the play's protective attitude to its royal protagonist, whom it shields from overt inquiry into the legitimacy of his claim to the English as well as the French throne; and, last but not least, the decision to excise Falstaff, whose iconoclastic wit could, on past form, be trusted to play havoc with the nationalistic pieties and chivalric ideals promulgated in *Henry V.* In each of these respects, the play appears to be fully implicated in the Chorus's campaign to "coerc[e] the audience into an emotionally undivided response" in favor of the English monarch.[4] As the play's critical history attests, however, the pressures exerted by its patriotic rhetoric have not precluded more sceptical responses. What might be called the "Machiavellian" reading, first formulated by Hazlitt in 1817, has tended to focus on the gaps between Henry's laboriously constructed public image as "the mirror of all Christian Kings" and his manifest brutality and political opportunism, between the aggrandizing rhetoric of king and Chorus and what is actually shown on stage.[5] Latterly, cultural materialists have argued that, in the act of rehearsing various discourses of national unity, the play unconsciously discloses the faultlines inherent in them.[6]

This essay concurs with such readings in arguing that *Henry V* distances itself from the Chorus's brand of patriotism, but it contends that the play does this not so much by incorporating vocal dissent or through inadvertent self-exposure, as by means of the ironic self-referentiality of its dramatic form.[7] As he reached the end of a period of working intensively within a given genre, Shakespeare habitually turned a searching eye on the structural conventions governing that genre. The last play in his second tetralogy is no exception. From beginning to end, *Henry V* is informed by an acute "metadramatic self-consciousness," which entails a close scrutiny of the discursive modes and conventions associated with the English chronicle play.[8] Through a process of internal mirroring, the ideology of this particular form is opened up to critical inspection in ways that expose both the latent ambiguities and the coerciveness implicit in its discourse of native heroism. The play also invites scrutiny of the rhetorical usage of history ascribed to the genre, by showing how the past is deployed to manipulate audiences (both on- and offstage) into identifying with a political enterprise founded upon a value system and material interests that must, in many cases, have been fundamentally at odds with their own. It is this provocative mixture of reflexivity and self-contradictoriness in the play's modes of address, I argue, which allows scope for a more complex, more divided affective response than that solicited by the Chorus. Indeed it is here that we should perhaps locate the primary source of the play's ideologically ambivalent effects.[9]

As it has become customary to note, the rhetorical energies of King Henry and the Chorus are ultimately directed at producing a collective sense of national identity. The linguistic ploys used in seeking to achieve this will be examined more closely in the second half of this essay. First, though, we need to consider what sorts of problems would have to be imaginatively negotiated when evoking the effects of nationhood on the public stage. It has long been accepted that the outpouring of historiographic texts, including chronicles and plays dealing with English history, in the closing decades of Elizabeth's reign played a crucial part in fostering national self-awareness. The late sixteenth-century vogue for historical drama is said to have "incited patriotic interest in England's past and participated in the process by which the English forged a sense of themselves as a nation"; more specifically, it "provided a 'myth of origin' for the emerging nation," whose people "learned to know who they were by seeing what they had been."[10] In *Henry V* the appeal to history as a means of exciting jingoistic fervor is made unusually explicit. But which version of the nation does the play invite us to endorse? And should we assume the efficacy of its patriotic appeal as given in advance, bearing in mind that the play's success depended on its capacity to engage *all* sections of the socially heterogeneous audiences that patronized the public playhouses of the period, not merely a privileged minority?[11] For what must be emphasized at the outset is the integral involvement of the lower orders in the "cultural project of imagining an English nation." So far from being effaced, demonized, or even confined to mere tokenism (as Helgerson and others claim), popular participation is shown by Shakespeare's English history cycle to be an essential component in the making of the modern political nation. *Henry V*, in particular, vividly discloses the extent to which the monarchy's imperialistic exercise in nation-building depends upon the active collaboration of the common populace—in the context not only of the dramatic fiction itself but of the theater in which that fiction was staged and consumed.

Twentieth-century political theorists and historians of nationalism are generally agreed that the emergence of the modern nation-state presupposed the existence of a broad popular mandate, though they differ sharply in their dating of this event.[12] Expanding on his influential definition of the nation-state as an "imagined community," Benedict Anderson relates the rise of this sociopolitical formation to the decline of the "divinely-ordained, hierarchical dynastic realm" and its displacement by a horizontal sense of community strong enough to engender feelings of kinship between complete strangers and across existing social divisions. The nation is thus

> imagined as a *community,* because, regardless of the actual inequality and exploitation that may prevail in each, the nation is always conceived as a deep, horizontal comradeship. Ultimately it is this fraternity that makes it possible . . . for so many millions of people, not so much to kill, as willingly to die for such limited imaginings.[13]

Others have echoed Anderson's insistence that the mere fact of social stratification need be no hinderance to conceiving of the nation as a community of free and essentially equal individuals with the right, in principle at least, to participate in political decision-making. Arguing specifically for the sixteenth-century origins of English nationhood and nationalism in general, Liah Greenfeld finds that this grew out of an alliance of interests between the monarchy and the common people—the very alliance that, in the civil upheavals of the next century, it would help to destroy. As "an important symbol of England's distinctiveness and sovereignty," the crown provided an initial focus for nationalist sentiment; conversely, the Tudor monarchs, who "were time and again placed in a position of dependence on the good will of their subjects," found it expedient to support this burgeoning national consciousness.[14] Claire MacEachern similarly holds that the Tudor system of monarchical government was not incommensurable with a genuine belief in a "corporate political identity." Existing as an affective utopian structure, this belief, she suggests, was rooted in a sense of intimacy or fellow-feeling between the populace and the personified institutions of the state, concentrated in the person of the monarch himself.[15]

Yet we scarcely need press the point that nations are never as integrated in reality as our myths of national identity would have us believe. The meaning of the nation is continually being contested by different social and ethnic groupings in ways that are liable to expose the fractures within its ideal unity. As Anthony D. Smith remarks, "deep within what appears to the outside as a unifying myth, are hidden many tensions and contradictions, which parallel and illuminate the social contradictions within most communities." Moreover, although as a general rule national loyalties, once established, tend to override local allegiances and sectional interests, this is not always the case.[16] In *Henry V* the contradictions embedded in the myth of corporate identity are registered primarily through the fluctuating boundaries (both geographic and demographic) of the nation, which are constantly being redrawn. As recent investigations of the play's colonial context have reminded us, the question of whether England's Celtic neighbors should be excluded from, or absorbed within, the "pale" of an expanded English or proto-British polity was never wholly resolved under successive Tudor and Stuart administrations.[17] Hence the Irish and the Scots are sometimes stigmatized in this play as inveterate enemies of the English state to be kept at a distance (1.2.166–73; 5.0.30–34). At other times—notably in the scene (3.3) bringing together the four captains from each of the constituent countries of the British isles—they are figured as loyal servants of the Lancastrian crown. A similar prevarication can be traced in the play, as I shall try to show, over the entitlement of the common people (and of other subordinate groups, including women) to be counted as members of the nation's imagined community. How far the king and Chorus choose to recognise the people's contribution in bringing that community into being varies sharply according to the political exigencies of the moment. The likelihood of the tussle between class-based and broader national identities enacted in *Henry V* being replicated in the experience of the play's first audiences is also considered in the conclusion to this essay. Owing to its ideological multivalency and the social inclusiveness of its clientele, the popular theater of the Elizabethan and early Jacobean era has been widely regarded as an authentically national institution, one of the key sites where a sense of collective identity was forged.[18] Yet insofar as they represented a "heterocosm" of the nation, the public playhouses were also bound to reflect its underlying social divisions, and such deep-seated differences among those present at performances (whether as players or spectators) may well have proved easier to activate than appease.

Shakespeare's second tetralogy charts a shift in political *episteme* remarkably like that described by Anderson. That is, it stages a process of transition from the feudal, hierarchically organised realm of *Richard II,* putatively authorized by the principle of divine right, to a recognizably more modern prototype of the nation-state under Bolingbroke and his heir, which, though still centred on the monarchy, acknowledges the need for popular legitimation. Like his father, Henry V is acutely mindful of the necessity of compensating for the loss of sanctified authority, consequent upon the usurpation and murder of the annointed king, by winning popular approval. His adroit manipulation of the royal image to make it "show more goodly and attract more eyes" (*1 Henry IV,* 1.2.214) is wholly directed to that end. Contrary to Helgerson's suggestion, the demotic touch Henry learns in the tavern is not discarded on entering political adulthood; rather, as Joel Altman remarks, such "vile participation" is consistently the "distinguishing feature of Harry's princely career as Shakespeare represents it."[19] No mere short-term "fix" imposed on him by a perilous situation, the rhetoric of cross-class fraternity he invokes on the battlefield of Agincourt is central to his fashioning of the nation's self-image. Hence he figures his army (in whom that nation is synecdochically represented) as "warriors for the working day" (4.3.110), who draw their strength from their broad social origins in contrast to the aristocratic *hauteur* and effeteness of the French. But even among those who fully appreciate the political capital to be made from such "vile participation," the social interdependency it implies may well inspire ambivalent feelings as a potential source of shame and inevitable dilution of royal sovereignty. Equally, the appearance of new forms of national consciousness did not signal the instantaneous demise of the dynastic realm, whose modes of thought and social organization retained a hold on men's minds long after they had lost their absolute political hegemony. Henry's oratory testifies to the ideological fluidity that characterized ideas of the commonwealth at the turn of the sixteenth century. In his speeches, the embryonic discourse of national solidarity collides repeatedly with older self-definitions based on aristocratic codes of behavior, the desire to "pluck allegiance from men's hearts" with the desire to withdraw his royalty from the defiling contacts this entails. And similar tensions, as we shall find, shape the Chorus's dealings with the theater audience.

The compromises demanded by this redefining and opening up of the monarchically governed state to allow for greater popular participation are inscribed in the two best-known contemporary accounts of the English chronicle play. In Thomas Nashe's *Pierce Penniless* (1592) and Thomas Heywood's *Apology for Actors* (printed in 1612, but probably also written during the 1590s), a shared ideological agenda is sketched out for this dramatic genre. For both these writers, the chief function of the history play was to resurrect "our forefathers valiant actes" by reenacting their "memorable exployts" with such "lively and well-spirited action" that the spectator would be induced to emulate their example.[20] One reason for emphasising the exemplary nature of historical drama, we may surmise, was to sustain a sense of continuity between the present and England's glorious past in ways that appealed to, and helped to bolster, the nation's growing self-confidence.[21] Yet in his legendary account of the origins of the genre, Heywood dwells on the exclusively "noble," even quasi-divine, derivation of this historical tradition:

> In the first of the *Olimpiads,* amongst many other active exercises in which *Hercules* ever triumph'd as victor, there was in his nonage presented unto him by his Tutor in the fashion of a History, acted by the choyse of the nobility of Greece, the worthy and memorable acts of his father *Jupiter.* Which being personated with lively and well-spirited ac-

tion, wrought such impression in his noble thoughts that in meere emulation of his fathers valor . . . he perform'd his twelve labours: Him valiant *Theseus* followed, and *Achilles, Theseus.* Which bred in them such hawty and magnanimous attempts, that every succeeding age hath recorded their worths, unto fresh admiration.[22]

And so it goes on: a dramatic reconstruction of Achilles' part in the fall of Troy made so great an impression on Alexander the Great that "all his succeeding actions were meerly shaped after that patterne," just as Julius Caesar's actions were patterned on those of Alexander. Heywood imagines the principle of dramatic imitation engendering its own eminent genealogy of valor, as each performance begets a new generation of royal heroes, from Hercules down to the present: "Why should not the lives of these worthyes, presented in these our dayes," he inquires, "effect the like wonders in the Princes of our times . . . ?"

When he turns to "our domesticke hystories," however, Heywood is forced to modify this discourse of aristocratic heroism in order to accommodate the socially mixed clientele of the public playhouses. That the Elizabethan history play was targeted primarily at the ordinary citizens in its audience is strongly implied by Heywood's citing, among his justifications for the theater, that it "hath taught the unlearned the knowledge of many famous histories, [and] instructed such as cannot read in the discovery of all our *English* Chronicles."[23] It is presumably this plebeian presence that dictates the insinuation of a calculated imprecision, a politic ambiguity, into Heywood's language: "To turne to our domesticke hystories, what *English blood* seeing the person of *any bold English man* presented and doth not hugge his fame, and hunnye at his valor. . . . What coward to see his *contryman* valiant would not bee shamed of his owne cowardise?" (my emphasis). By refusing to locate the grammatical subject in terms of the social categories insisted upon earlier in the *Apology*, Heywood manages to create the impression that any Englishman, whatever his class origins, is capable of being "inflam'd" by the spectacle of native valor, and so "may be made apt and fit for the like atchievement."[24] Nationality, coming of "English blood," has replaced narrower status definitions as the criterion for participating in this heroic tradition. Comparable efforts to broaden the appeal of the English chronicle play, to render its elitest discourse more flexibly inclusive, are made on Nashe's side. In return for the patriotic sentiments it would elicit, he hints, this type of historical drama offers its audiences a stake in the "right of fame that is due to true nobilitie deceased." Hence the chief bait it "propose[s] to adventurous minds, to encourage them forward" is the prospect of sharing, at some unspecified level, in the "immortalitie" normally bestowed by the chronicle play on such dead English heroes as "brave Talbot," Edward III, or Henry V.[25] Underlying both texts is a suggestion that the malleable spectator, who allows images of the past to act upon him in this way and "fashion [him] to the shape of any noble or notable attempt," will be rewarded by being joined with the valiant dead in what Nashe calls "one Gallimafry of glory" that transcends class differences.

If the heroic vision of Englishness projected by the chronicle play is seen here as dependent for its very force and validation on the involvement of the common spectators, what precisely was expected of them? It is clear from Nashe and Heywood's vivid descriptions of the reception given to such plays that the contribution sought was primarily of an imaginative kind. Both writers ascribe a "bewitching" power to the genre that derives, firstly, from its ability to impart a living presence to the dead (who are "raysed from the Grave of Oblivion, and brought to pleade their aged Honours in open presence") and, secondly, from the power of dramatic impersonation to make audiences experience in themselves the full immediacy of the emotions enacted on stage (known in rhetoric as *ethopeia*). Indeed, it is the unmatchable reality effects made possible by the theatrical medium, according to Nashe, that renders the history play a far more effective instrument for inculcating patriotic values than "worme-eaten bookes" of chronicles. At one point he asks:

> How would it have joyd brave Talbot (the terror of the French) to thinke that after he had lyne two hundred yeare in his toomb, he should triumph againe on the Stage, and have his bones new embalmed with the teares of ten thousand spectators at least . . . who in the Tragedian that represents his person, imagine they behold him fresh bleeding.[26]

This illusion of presence, combined with the powerful affects it stirs in the spectators, solicits an imaginative identification with what is witnessed on stage so complete that the distinction between dramatic fiction and historical reality, between the actor and the part he plays, is temporarily erased.[27] In much the same vein, Heywood asserts that audiences, "seeing the person of any bold English man presented," will be irresistibly impelled to "hugge his fame, and hunnye at his valor, pursuing him in his enterprise with [their] best wishes . . . as if the Personator were the man Personated."[28] In the context of the popular commercial theater, then, it would appear that the mimetic desires aroused by a dramatic reenactment of the past are no longer regarded chiefly as a means of calling forth heroic deeds. Instead their function is to secure the spectator's acquiescence in, and identification with, the nationalist ideologies staged by the play.

Benedict Anderson repeatedly poses the question of why the imagined community of the nation should command such deep emotional attachments that even its most oppressed or disenfranchised members are prepared to sacrifice their lives for this idea. For an explanation of how such identifications are produced, however, we may find it more useful to turn to Louis Althusser's now-classic account of interpellation: that is, the procedures whereby ideology addresses the individual subject in a manner that ensures his or her cooperation with the existing sociopolitical formation.[29] Echoing Jacques Lacan's emphasis on the importance of the "mirror phase" in the psychic construction of identity, Althusser argues that interpellation always takes a specular form. Individuals are invited to recognize themselves in the image of authority in whose name a given ideology exists, and to identify with the roles, or subject positions, designated for them within that ideology. Crucially, interpellative techniques operate through rhetorical manipulation, not force. By persuading us to accede to the fictive representation of actual social relationships it reflects back at us, ideology masks our subjection to the dominant order and ensures that we will freely give of our own labor—or, as Althusser puts it, that we work by ourselves. Theatrical experience, because of the ways it is structured, is peculiarly well adapted to producing such specular effects. In its exemplarity the chronicle play capitalizes on that potential by urging spectators to discover their own image in—and transform themselves into—the heroic models it sets before them. Its success in fostering such identifications may partly explain why Nashe and Heywood chose to focus on this particular dramatic genre when defending the theatre against the endlessly reiterated charge that it promoted sedition and civil unrest.[30] The use of historical exemplars as an incitement to patriotic behavior, they believe, offers the strongest proof that "stage-plaies" are, in fact, a "rare exercise of vertue," instrumental in deflecting rebellious impulses and fashioning compliant subjects who willingly defer to the rule of constituted authority.

Henry V, I would argue, stands in a profoundly ambivalent relationship to these sixteenth-century definitions of the English chronicle play and its politico-moral functions. On the one hand, it cannot be denied that Shakespeare's play exploits the strong affective charge generated by identification with dead English heroes—as the regularity with which it has been either performed or invoked at times of national crisis confirms.[31] Yet it does so in ways that seem to discourage, rather than invite, an uncritical acceptance of the imaginary versions of the nation articulated within the play. This paradoxical effect, I suggest, is achieved largely by self-reflexive means. In particular, the play insistently foregrounds the interpellative techniques used with fearsome efficiency by various characters, laying open its own ideological stratagems in the process. Thus Henry is shown addressing his common soldiers as "so many Alexanders" in the making as he endeavors to mould them into a redoubtable fighting force in 2.1 and 4.3, while the Chorus's appeals to the theater audience position them as the king's loyal camp followers who embrace his trials and tribulations as their own (cf. 3.0.17–24). Concomitantly, the normally dissembled purposes for which such techniques are deployed are also made visible. Summoning up the *idea* of a harmoniously integrated commonwealth in 1.2, the Archbishop of Canterbury reflects knowingly on its effectiveness in "setting endeavour in continual motion; / To which is fixed, as an aim or butt, / Obedience" (lines 186–88). A similar observation is made by Henry as, preparing to set himself up as an inspirational model to his troops, he extols the power of "example" to "quicken" the mind and cause the bodily organs to "move with casted slough and fresh legerity" (4.1.18–23).[32] Whether the king is demanding extraordinary physical efforts from his soldiers, or the Chorus is urging the audience to "work, work [their] thoughts," their characteristic modes of address are quite blatantly directed at getting others (mostly representatives of the lower orders) to labor on behalf of the king's cause.

Superficially, *Henry V* also appears to reaffirm the populist agenda ascribed to the English chronicle play to the extent that both Henry and the Chorus strive to invoke a socially inclusive model of history. Replicating Nashe and Heywood's tactics, they manage this by putting a more egalitarian "spin" on the patrician ideals of martial heroism associated with the genre. But even as the play celebrates the king's ability to enlist every stratum of society in his imperialist enterprise, uniting them in "one purpose" through a charismatic appeal to "mean and gentle all" (cf. 4.0.28–47), it discloses the anxieties, strains, and contradictions attendant on this project. All Henry's rhetorical dexterity cannot smooth away the class tensions inherent in the goal of national unification that, ironically, are thrown into greater prominence by his attempts to reconfigure aristocratic idioms for popular consumption. Cumulatively, these reflexive devices seem designed to provoke us into questioning the fundamental, if tacit, claim underpinning contemporary defences of the genre: that the common subject can participate on an equal footing in the creation of a national community that continues to be defined in the interests of a ruling elite.

Within the play, the coercive use of historical *exempla* as a means of "setting endeavour in continual motion" is reflected on three different levels: in the analogous modes of address employed by the king's counselors towards him, by the king to his troops, and by the Chorus to the audience. The Archbishop of Canterbury sets the tone in 1.2 with his convoluted exposition of the Salic law, which shamelessly manipulates historical precedent in the hope of inciting Henry to pursue his hereditary claim to the French throne and so divert him from implementing a bill that would strip the Church of the "better half of [its] possession." With the same end in view, the archbishop proceeds to invoke the "tragedy" enacted on French soil by Henry's "mighty ancestors" at the battle of Crécy nearly seventy years before:

> Look back into your mighty ancestors.
> Go, my dread lord, to your great grand-sire's tomb,
> From whom you claim; invoke his warlike spirit,
> And your great-uncle's, Edward the Black Prince,
> Who on the French ground played a tragedy,
> Making defeat on the full power of France,
> Whiles his most mighty father on a hill
> Stood smiling to behold his lion's whelp
> Forage in blood of French nobility.
>
> (1.2.100)

Other counselors take up this exhortation to emulate past greatness, urging the king to "awake remembrance of those valiant dead, / And with [his] puissant arm renew their feats" (1.2.115).

Conscious of the obligations this heroic lineage imposes, Henry accepts their challenge, and the terms of his acceptance reveal what is personally at stake for *him:*

> Or there we'll sit,
> Ruling in large and ample empery
> O'er France and all her almost kingly dukedoms,
> Or lay these bones in an unworthy urn,
> Tombless, with no rememberance over them.
> Either our history shall with full mouth
> Speak freely of our acts, or else our grave
> Like Turkish mute, shall have a tongueless mouth,
> Not worshipped with a waxen epitaph.
>
> (1.2.225)

The dialectical structure of this speech implicitly equates military victory with fame; for Henry occupying France is, first and foremost, a route to securing his place in history. By reenacting the drama of imperial conquest performed by his ancestors in this land, he will ensure that his exploits too are preserved from oblivion in their turn, and that "history" will "speak freely of [his] acts" to future generations.[33] Without such forms of official "remembrance," Henry admits, he would be reduced to the impotent condition of a "Turkish mute," lacking any influence in shaping the national destiny.

In staging the council scene as a contest in deliberative oratory, Shakespeare takes his cue from Holinshed, who narrates the "earnest and pithie persuasions" employed by Henry's advisors to "induce" him to adopt the course of action they prescribe.[34] But Shakespeare infuses this rhetorical occasion with an ironic self-consciousness largely absent from his source, and thereby makes provision for a more skeptical appraisal of the practice of resorting to an exemplary past. The archbishop's figuration of the Black Prince's victory at Crécy in 1346 in terms of a dramatic mise-en-scène (cf. 2.4.53–62) pointedly calls attention to the role of the theater as a site where such national traditions are not simply commemorated but actively manufactured. Phyllis Rackin has argued that such metadramatic allusions can produce "a kind of alienation effect," pushing the audience into adopting a critically detached position relative to the action, especially when combined (as they are here) with anachronism.[35] For it should not be forgotten that the idealized chivalric past evoked by the name of Crécy existed at a double historical remove from the audiences who first saw *Henry V* in 1599. As we noted earlier, the ethos of the English chronicle play was epitomized for Nashe by the figure of "brave Talbot," whose death wrung tears from "ten thousand spectators at least." Nashe's remark has been taken as an allusion to Shakespeare's *1 Henry VI* (which is usually, though not conclusively, dated to 1590–91), where the discourse of ancestral valor, kept alive by funerary monuments to the "valiant dead" and by the aristocracy's self-sacrificing feats of bravery, is firmly centred on Talbot and his son. But even in the earlier play the values upheld almost single-handedly by the Talbots are represented as a throwback to a vanishing chivalric world (associated ironically with the memory of Henry V's French conquests), whose passing leaves them vulnerable to the machinations of a more secular, pragmatic age. And by the time *Henry V* was staged roughly a decade later, this discourse had become still more conspicuously outmoded, more jarringly at odds with the context of realpolitik in which it is invoked.[36] In such circumstances, it would have been hard for an audience not to register the competing political interests that motivate the characters' appeals to "bygone valour," or to overlook the way that past is being manipulated as a means of mobilizing and channeling activity in the present.[37]

In the following acts Henry redirects the rhetorical strategies used so effectively on him at the plebeian subject, with the aim of eliciting superhuman exertions from his troops. For that purpose he seeks to assimilate the rank-and-file to the loftily aristocratic vision of English heroism conjured up in 1.2 by giving this a more demotic inflection. His celebrated oration before the walls of Harfleur, which first holds out the possibility of an egalitarian partnership that suspends class differences, is deeply and ineluctably ambiguous. Henry prefaces the speech with an oblique acknowledgment that wartime situations such as this license the violation of normal social decorums, according to which "there's nothing so becomes a man [especially, it is implied, the low-born man] / As modest stillness and humility" (3.1.3). The self-transformative action Henry calls for in exhorting his soldiers to "bend up every spirit / To his full height" (line 16) is nevertheless accompanied (as Michael Goldman has shown) by a terrible sense of strain, as though betraying his belief in the grotesque unnaturalness of aspiring to transcend one's allotted place in the social hierarchy.[38] The troops are then urged to authenticate their mythologized ancestry by fighting bravely:

> On, on you noblest English,
> Whose blood is fet from fathers of war-proof,
> Fathers that like so many Alexanders
> Have in these parts from morn till even fought,
> And sheathed their swords for lack of argument.
> Dishonour not your mothers; now attest
> That those whom you called fathers did beget you.
> Be copy now to men of grosser blood,
> And teach them how to war. And you good yeomen,
> Whose limbs were made in England, show us here
> The mettle of your pasture; let us swear
> That you are worth your breeding—which I doubt not,
> For there is none of you so mean and base
> That hath not noble lustre in your eyes.
>
> 3.1.17)

Essentially Henry faces the same problem here as Heywood did in the *Apology:* he has to find a way of negotiating the uncomfortable gap between an elitest tradition of martial valor and its popular reenactments. Not surprisingly, he too hits upon the solution of subsuming social demarcations in an ambiguously inclusive discourse of nationhood. Henry's speech is addressed first to "you noblest English," the nobility whose duty is to "by copy [i.e., an example] to men of grosser blood / And teach them how to war," before turning to the "good yeomen," who are admonished to model their behavior on that of their military leaders. But these sharply differentiated designations are offset by his skillful playing upon the indeterminacy of words such as "noble," "base," and "mean," which, though they originated as status terms, were increasingly used in this period to denote relative moral worth. A similar slippage occurs in his references to "blood" and "breeding"; initially defined in a hereditary context as coming of noble parentage or blood, having the required breeding is later broadened to include anyone born and raised on English soil. Through such rhetorical sleights-of-hand, Henry contrives to suggest that all Englishmen, irrespective of class origins, are eligible to participate in his exalted "fellowship," provided their actions prove them worthy of it.

The incipient contradictions in Henry's interpellation of the soldiers make his vision of a socially inclusive partnership highly vulnerable to contestation.[39] And in 4.1 the implication (reinforced by the Chorus at the beginning of the act) that "mean and gentle all" can become equal participants in this imagined community is duly challenged. As has often been observed, Henry's disguised encounter with three of his common foot soldiers, in which he tries unsuccessfully to convince them that "the King is but a man" of their sort, serves only to expose the "complete lack of rapport," the ineradicable differences of perspective, separating him from them.[40] In disputing Henry's claims to ordinariness, Soldier Williams and his companions drive a wedge into the self-serving myth that the monarch and his common subjects are bound together not so much by political expediency as by their shared humanity and commonality of interests. The humiliation inflicted on the king in this debate provokes a backlash in his ensuing soliloquy. Where once he courted the approval and loyal cooperation of his subjects, he now laments the "hard condition" that subjects his own "greatness" to "the breath / Of every fool, whose sense no more can feel / But his own wringing" (4.1.221–3). His rhetorical energies also undergo a radical reorientation, as he seeks to reestablish his distance from the multitude; no longer addressed as "brothers, friends, countrymen," the common soldiers are now reclassified in terms of aristocratic contempt as "lackey[s]," "wretched slave[s]," and ignorant "peasants" (lines 255–72). But with his army teetering on the brink of a catastrophic defeat, Henry is again compelled by circumstances to seek assistance from those whose social consequence he dismissed a short while before.

Accordingly, his prebattle address to the troops resorts once more to the rhetoric of brotherhood. Previous hints that the ordinary conscript, "be he ne'er so vile," will "gentle his condition" by his valiant deeds and earn the right to partake of the fame normally reserved for patrician warriors, are restated more baldly in an attempt to bribe him into action. With this we see a return to the same fudging tactics, the same ambiguities and inconsistencies, that allow Henry to construct the image of an egalitarian national community, but that simultaneously threaten to unravel that fantasy. His reiterative use of the first-person plural hovers between the royal and the collective "we," between the exclusive and inclusive senses of that pronoun. (Cf. "If we are marked to die, we are enough / To do our country loss" [4.3.20]; or "We would not die in that man's company / That fears his fellowship to die with us" [line 38]). Yet, in one sense, there is no contradiction here, since the community envisaged turns out to be little more than an expansion of the regal persona. For as Henry's rallying cry—"the fewer men, the greater share of honour"—should remind us, the fame promised the soldiers is predicated on a feudal cult of honour and ancestral pride that is, by definition, jealously individualistic. The nearest approximation to genuine fellowship this aristocratic code of honor admits is the *blut-bruderschaft* of Suffolk and York, whose deaths in battle are invested, in Exeter's elegaic narrative (4.6.6–27), with the full panoply of chivalric values once bestowed on Talbot or Hotspur. To attempt to found a modern nation-state on such an inherently elitest and anachronistic code is self-evidently untenable. That Henry winds up the speech by drawing the parameters of his imagined brotherhood in relation not to the foreign enemy but to the significant proportion of his subjects it excludes—among whom are numbered not only "grandsires, babies, and old women" (3.0.20) but all "those men in England that do no work today" (4.3.64–67)—merely underscores the problem.

The second half of the speech leaps forward to a hypothetical future perfect where the "Feast of Crispian" has become a day of national commemoration honoring the English triumph at Agincourt. Henry's ingenious manipulation of his audience's temporal perspective fulfils various purposes. On one level, it mimics the peculiar motivational logic of the chronicle play; treating a yet-to-be-accomplished victory as something long since achieved and sanctified by memory enables the soldiers to be inspired by their own historical example and, by spurring them into action, ensures that the day will indeed be won. But it also offers assurance that the fraternal cross-class community forged on the battlefield will be maintained into futurity through the observance of collective forms of remembrance. Imaginatively projecting this annual event as a popular domestic scene, combining the functions of an aural history lesson with a convivial feasting of the neighborhood, is another brilliant touch, in that it presents an image, at once homely and heroic, with which the common soldier can hardly fail to identify. Yet this carefully crafted vision of shared national rituals cannot entirely dispel the social tensions latent within it. In a recent essay highlighting the importance of memory in the play, Jonathan Baldo notes that, although the Elizabethan establishment was no less intent on orchestrating the collective memory in the pursuit of national unity than Shakespeare's Henry V, the act of remembering continued to be a potential site of division and resistance.[41] The same holds true here:

> Old men forget; yet all shall be forgot,
> But he'll remember, with advantages,

> The feats he did that day. Then shall our names,
> Familiar in his mouth as household words—
> Harry the King, Bedford and Exeter,
> Warwick and Talbot, Salisbury and Gloucester—
> Be in their flowing cups freshly remembered.
> This story shall the good man teach his son,
> And Crispin Crispian shall ne'er go by
> From this day to the ending of the world
> But we in it shall be remembered,
> We few, we happy few, we band of brothers.
>
> (4.3.49–60)

At the same time that the personal recollections of the Agincourt veterans are granted a central role in perpetuating the fame of that legendary victory, it is archly insinuated that their memories will play them false, leading them not only to embellish "feats [they] did that day," but (by extension) to exaggerate the degree of intimacy they once enjoyed with the "great commanders," whose names are "familiar in [their] mouths as household words."[42] This nostalgic fantasy of brotherhood will be belied even as they speak by the fact that the names immortalised through their reminiscences are confined to the aristocratic titles of their leaders. (Again, the fluctuating use of the first-person plural at once encodes and masks this shift: "*our* names" are syntactically opposed to "*their* flowing cups" in lines 51–55, the pronoun only recovering its inclusive meaning at line 60.) While Henry thus concedes the need for popular involvement in establishing such national traditions, he cynically anticipates that the ordinary veterans will be denied the honorable place promised them in the official (and unofficial) historical records. This is confirmed after the battle when, reading from the roll call of the English dead, he lists several casualties among the ranks of the nobility and gentry, concluding "none else of name, / And of all other men, / But five-and-twenty" (4.8.103). Significantly, these lines closely paraphrase Holinshed, who rarely bothers to identify individual foot soldiers by name in his chronicling of Henry's French campaigns.[43]

Both Henry's methods of galvanizing his troops into action and the ambiguities inscribed in those methods are paralleled in the Chorus's repeated exhortation of the play's audience. From the outset, the Chorus helps to construct a reflexive, metacritical framework for the dramatic action by foregrounding the difficulties posed by historical representation and the theatrical medium through which the past must be brought back to life. Initially, like Heywood, he fantasizes about an exclusively royal performance, "a kingdom for a stage, princes to act, / And monarchs to behold the swelling scene" (1.0.13), before ruefully conceding that this ideal is unrealizable on the public stage where common players masquerade as kings. Conversely, he displays none of Heywood or Nashe's confidence in the theater's ability to produce a compelling recreation of ancient prowess by means of powerful reality effects. On the contrary, he assumes that this can only be achieved if the playhouse's inadequate technical resources are supplemented by the spectators' cerebral activity. It is *their* "thoughts," he urges them, that "now must deck our kings," *their* laboring imaginations that must give impetus to Henry's campaign. The Chorus's apparent readiness to defer to the "imaginary puissance" of the humbler sections of the audience—as implied by the artisanal metaphor of "the quick forge and working-house of thought" (5.0.23)—making them co-partners in his theatrical enterprise, has led some critics to find an expression therein of the communal ethos of the Elizabethan theater.[44] But while his entreaties to the audience to "eke out our imperfections with your mind" certainly confirm (once again) the indispensability of popular participation, they also reveal this recognition of dependency to be fraught with tension and anxiety. Often accepted at face value as a token of (quasi-authorial) modesty, the Chorus's apologetic references to the "imperfections" of the stage can more plausibly be seen, I suggest, as rehearsing a familiar set of anxieties regarding the subversive potential of the popular commercial theater. As Stephen Orgel (among others) has argued, a recurrent concern of the theater's opponents in this period was that the "great image of Authority" would be undermined and debased by being staged to the common view, a fear that greatness might be demystified in the very act of dramatizing it.[45] It is surely an echo of this social pathology that resonates in the Chorus's claim that "so great an object" as Henry's famous victory cannot be "cramm'd" within the walls of this "wooden O" without travestying its true magnitude (1.0.8–18), or in the apology he tenders in the epilogue for the playwright's "rough and all-unable pen," which has allegedly defaced the reputation of "mighty men," "mangling by starts the full course of their glory." For all his eagerness to recruit the spectator's "imaginary forces" to the service of the royal cause, the Chorus (like the king of whose image he makes himself custodian) betrays considerable nervousness at the thought of allowing a tradition of aristocratic heroism to be adulterated by being performed and intimately witnessed by low-born subjects—in this case, on the "unworthy scaffold" of the Curtain or the newly opened Globe.

Henry's pledge that his soldiers will be ennobled (in the moral if not social sense) by their participation is also echoed in the Chorus's practice of addressing the spectators as "gentles all" (1.0.8, cf. 2.0.35), who are entreated "gently to hear, kindly to judge our play" (1.0.34). The prospect of gentling their condition is itself conditional upon their willingness to collaborate in the construction of the play's heroic vision of Englishness, and is obviously intended to bind them into that vision. But it is, of course, an inescapable fact that a large proportion of the play's original audiences would have been drawn from the "base, common and popular" classes.[46] Exposing the actions of the monarchy to the gaze and judgment of the common multitude congregated around the platform stage was a risky and unpredictable affair—indeed the very fervency of the Chorus's appeals may perhaps indicate that they are designed to head off unsympathetic responses from that quarter. Given their predominantly modest social origins, however, we may reasonably infer that some spectators at least would have been more inclined to follow Soldier Williams's example in resisting the invitation to identify with the royal viewpoint. (It is Williams, after all, who brings home to the king that there are limits to the power of interpellation, that he may command the "beggar's knee," but not necessarily his innermost thoughts [4.1.228–45]). Women, too, formed an important constituency within the theatergoing public of the day, and they are even more emphatically excluded by the chivalric, masculine terms in which Henry's confraternity is defined (cf. 3.0.17–24).[47] Should we assume that the manifold ironies in the exhortations of king and Chorus would have escaped the attention of these playgoers? The less privileged members of the play's audience may well have balked at being asked to overcome through their imaginative exertions deficiencies that are seen as arising directly from their own lowly status and that of the theater they patronised. Female as well as plebeian spectators may equally have resented attempts to coerce them into identifying with an imagined community that, overtly or not, defines itself in opposition to them.

This essay has argued for the need to reappraise Helgerson's generalizing and oversimplified account of the attitude to the common populace expressed by Shakespeare's English history plays. A careful analysis of the rhetoric of class in *Henry V* reveals that those beneath the rank of gentleman are not, as alleged, progressively erased from the play's ideological construction of the nation, but neither are they fully embraced as equal partners in its formation. Instead, a more complicated picture of class relations emerges in which the leveling dynamic inscribed in the newly formed discourse of nationalism interacts with an older status-defined politics of exclusion in complex and unpredictable ways. Similarly, there has been a critical tendency to homogenize the reception that its original audiences gave to Shakespeare's history cycle. Dissenting from the widely accepted premise that the response elicited by these plays was straightforwardly patriotic and must have functioned to soldify the spectators' sense of belonging to a larger national community, I have suggested that in all likelihood audience reactions varied markedly, depending on a number of factors. In the case of *Henry V* it seems probable that differences in social allegiance would have inflected the way each spectator related imaginatively to the ambiguous position assigned to the lower orders in the play's representation of the nation as a heroic fellowship incorporating both "mean and gentle."

Yet while there is every reason to suppose that the political significance of *Henry V* would have been contingent, in part, on the particular social make-up of its audiences along with other extra-textual circumstances affecting its production and reception, we should not therefore deny Shakespeare's text a decisive role in determining its meaning and ideological effect. In the last analysis, as I have tried to show, it is the rhetorical mechanisms of that text which, by acting upon the emotional proclivities and class loyalties of individual spectators, create the conditions for a more complex and diverse response than the characters' patriotic effusions might seem to call for. For if, on the one hand, the play's modes of address, together with its rhetorical invocation of history, are framed to elicit an unquestioning commitment to the values inculcated by king and Chorus, on the other, its generic self-consciousness, by working to expose the coercive and contradictory aspects of such strategies, enables resistance to the process of interpellation. In adopting this paradoxical stance, *Henry V* makes available to the spectator (or reader) a range of possible subject positions. Like the disaffected conscripts of 4.1 who, despite being suspicious of Henry's fraternal rhetoric, resolve to "fight lustily" for him, we may thus move between—or even experience at one and the same moment—a critical distantiation from, and emotional identification with, the royal myth of Englishness.

Notes

1. A. P. Rossiter, "Ambivalence: The Dialectic of the Histories," rpt. in *Angel with Horns,* ed. Graham Storey (London and New York: 1961), 57.
2. Richard Helgerson, *Forms of Nationhood: The Elizabethan Writing of England* (Chicago and London: University of Chicago Press, 1994), 214.
3. Helgerson, *Forms of Nationhood,* 232.
4. Andrew Gurr ed., *Henry V,* New Cambridge ed. (Cambridge: Cambridge University Press], 1992), 7.
5. See William Hazlitt, *Characters of Shakespear's Plays,* ed. Ernest Rhys (London, 1906), 156–64. For a more recent Machiavellian reading, see H. C. Goddard, *The Meaning of Shakespeare* (Chicago: University of Chicago Press, 1951), 215–68.
6. See, e.g., Alan Sinfield and Jonathan Dollimore, "History and Ideology, Masculinity and Miscegenation: The Instance of *Henry V,*" in Alan Sinfield, *Faultlines: Cultural Materialism and the Politics of Dissident Reading* (Oxford: Oxford University Press), 109–42.
7. All references to the play cited in this text are taken from the Oxford edition (1982), ed. Gary Taylor. The majority of the reflexive features identified below are present only in the Folio version, including all the Chorus's speeches, crucial parts of the council scene (1.2.115–35), 3.1, and the king's soliloquy (4.1.218–72). Critical opinion generally concurs with the view that the omission of these and other passages in the 1600 Quarto, whether theatrically or politically motivated, "simplif[ies] the play in order to make it more uncomplicatedly patriotic" (Oxford edition, 23; cf. Annabel Patterson, *Shakespeare and the Popular Voice* [Oxford: Oxford University Press, 1989)], 76–77).
8. The phrase is borrowed from Phyllis Rackin, *Stages of History: Shakespeare's English Chronicles* (Ithaca and London: Cornell University Press, 1990), 71. Previous critics have seen the dramatic self-reflexivity of *Henry V* as a vehicle for exploring the hazards of imposing dramatic unity on the chaos of history (James L. Calderwood, *Metadrama in Shakespeare's Henriad: "Richard II" to "Henry V"* [Berkeley: University of California Press, 1979], chap. 7), or for highlighting the performative basis of royal power (Rackin, *Stages of History,* 76–85).
9. Norman Rabkin's classic study of this ambivalence of effect invokes the model of a *gestalt* drawing, which can be seen either as a rabbit or a duck but never both at once, to argue that the play lends itself equally to being construed as a celebration of ideal kingship or a disillusioned study of Machiavellian imperialism ("Either/Or: Responding to *Henry V,*" in *Shakespeare and the Problem of Meaning* (Chicago: University of Chicago Press, 1981). Where I part company with Rabkin is (firstly) in positing the play's rhetorical mechanisms and generic self-consciousness as the main source of this ambivalence, rather than characterization, plot, or dramatic sequencing, and (secondly) in arguing for the possibility of experiencing simultaneously conflicting responses to Henry's nationalist project.

10. See Jean Howard and Phyllis Rackin, *Engendering a Nation: A Feminist Account of Shakespeare's English Histories* (London and New York: Routledge, 1997), 18, and Philip Edwards, *Threshold of a Nation: A Study in English and Irish Drama* (Cambridge: Cambridge University Press, 1979), 68. For much of the twentieth century the rise of the English history play was directly attributed to the tide of patriotism and "exuberant national sentiment" that swept England in the wake of the defeat of the Spanish Armada in 1588. (On the history of this critical commonplace, see Lily B. Campbell, *Shakespeare's "Histories": Mirrors of Elizabethan Policy* (San Marino, CA: Huntington Library Press, 1947), chap. 2). Although recent writing on Shakespeare's history plays has tended to reject the more triumphalist and politically naive aspects of this theory, a causal connection between the emergence of the genre and a growing sense of nationhood is still widely postulated.

11. As Larry Champion observes of this patriotic reading, "the essential difficulty with such an approach is that it assumes both an audience basically sympathetic to the monarchy and a universal perspective in plays that, in fact, are designed to appeal to, and engage the emotional interests of, as many spectators as possible" (*The Noise of Threatening Drum": Dramatic Strategy and Political Ideology in Shakespeare and the English Chronicle Plays* (Newark: University of Delaware Press, 1990), 9.

12. Many regard both nations and nationalism as a distinctively modern phenomenon, locating its origins in the revolutionary movements of the late eighteenth century along with the advance of industrialisation and capitalist economics, but this theory (as propounded by Hobsbawm, Gellner, and Anderson) has come under increasing pressure in recent years from those who believe that the antecedents of the modern nation-state are traceable back to the sixteenth century and beyond.

13. Benedict Anderson, *Imagined Communities: Reflections on the Origin and Spread of Nationalism* (1983; rev. ed., London: Verso, 1991), 7.

14. Liah Greenfeld, *Nationalism: Five Roads to Modernity* (Cambridge: Harvard University Press, 1993), chap. 1, esp. 50–51, 65.

15. Claire McEachern, *The Poetics of English Nationhood, 1590–1612* (Cambridge: Cambridge University Press, 1996), chap. 1. McEachern's thesis is extended, and subtly qualified, by her later analysis of *Henry V*, which she rightly considers to be "as vigilant in limiting the scope of common feeling as it is in encouraging it" (108).

16. Anthony D. Smith, *Myths and Memories of the Nation* (Oxford: Oxford University Press, 1999), 71, 86–88.

17. See, e.g., Michael Neill, "Broken English and Broken Irish: Nation, Language and the Optic of Power in Shakespeare's Histories," *Shakespeare Quarterly* 45 (1994): 1–32, and Christopher Highley, *Shakespeare, Spenser, and the Crisis in Ireland* (Cambridge: Cambridge University Press, 1997).

18. See, e.g., Robert Weimann, *Shakespeare and the Popular Tradition in the Theater*, ed. Robert Schwartz (Baltimore and London: Johns Hopkins University Press, 1978), 169–77, and Walter Cohen, *Drama of a Nation: Public Theater in Renaissance England and Spain* (Ithaca and London: Cornell University Press, 1985). Peter Womack argues further that, by involving audiences in the reconstruction of a collective "national"; past, the Elizabethan theater invited them "not merely to contemplate the 'imagined community' but to *be* it" ("Imagining Com-

munities: Theatres and the English Nation in the Sixteenth Century," in *Culture and History 1350–1600: Essays on English Communities, Identities and Writing*, ed. David Aers [New York and London: Harvester Wheatsheaf: 1992], p. 138).

19. Joel Altman, " 'Vile Participation': The Amplification of Violence in the Theater of *Henry V*," *Shakespeare Quarterly* 42 (Spring 1991): 7.

20. This formula basically sought to adapt received humanistic notions of historiography to a theatrical context. According to sixteenth-century authorities such as Thomas Lanquet and Thomas Blundeville, the writing and reading of history was profitable because it preserved the fame of great rulers and commanders of antiquity, thereby providing a storehouse of instructive *exempla*, both positive and negative, of the arts of governance and warfare that would "sturre [readers] to vertue, and . . . withdrawe them from vice." Of course such a theory is hardly able to encompass the diversity of approach that actually characterized English historical drama in this period; besides overlooking historical romances like Greene's *James IV*, it offers an inadequate definition of the chronicle play proper, which rarely followed such a straightforwardly didactic and hagiographic agenda.

21. According to A. D. Smith, the "myth of descent" is among the most potent of the ethnic myths, symbols, and traditions that constitute the bedrock of any nation. In invoking an heroic ancestry it provides the aspirant nation with a model of identity and a charter for "regenerative collective action," as its people seek to recreate the spirit of a "past golden age" (*Myths and Memories*, chap. 2).

22. Thomas Heywood, *An Apology for Actors* (1612), ed. Richard H. Perkinson, (New York: Scholars' Facsimile, 1941), B3^r.

23. Heywood, *Apology for Actors*, F3^r. Cf. the implied concession to the illiteracy of some sections of the audience in the opening lines of the chorus to act 5: "Vouchsafe to those who have not read the story / That I may prompt them" (5.0.1–2).

24. Heywood, *Apology for Actors*, F3^r.

25. *Pierce Pennilesse his supplication to the Divell* (1612), (Menston, England: Scolar Press, 1969), H2^r.

26. *Pierce Pennilesse*, H2^r.

27. Cf. Pugliatti, *Shakespeare the Historian*, 60–62.

28. Heywood, *Apology for Actors*, B4^r.

29. See "Ideology and Ideological State Apparatuses," in Louis Althusser, *"Lenin and Philosophy" and Other Essays*, trans. Ben Brewster (London: 1961), 121–76. Despite the usefulness of Althusser's theory of interpellation for my purposes, this essay stops short of subscribing to its deterministic and totalizing implications. As many critics have noted, by positing the subject as a simple *effect* of ideology, Althusser seemingly precludes the possibility of individual agencies resisting its operations. (See, e.g., Claire Colebrook, *New Literary Histories* [Manchester: Manchester University Press, 1997], 158–62). Drawing on recent work that critiques such monolithic narratives of ideology, culture, and the formation of self, I attempt to show how the contradictory ways in which characters and audience are interpellated in *Henry V* result in a proliferation of subject positions, thereby opening up a space for political contestation.

30. It cannot be coincidental that Heywood's comments on the instructive value of the history play are followed by a ringing affirmation of the ideological orthodoxy of the theatre in general: "Plays are writ with this ayme, and carryed with this methode, to teach the subjects obedience to their King, to shew the peo-

ple the untimely ends of such as have moved tumults, commotions, and insurrections, to present them with the flourishing estate of such as live in obedience, exhorting them to allegeance, dehorting them from all trayterous and fellonious stratagems" (F3ᵛ, cf. Nashe, H2ᵛ–H3ʳ).

31. See Taylor's introduction to the Oxford edition, 11.

32. The play abounds in promises or exhortations to rouse oneself to action. In addition to the instances discussed below, cf. 1.2.122–4, 273–75, 309–10; 2.2.36–38; 2.3.3–5; 2.4.69–72; 3.0.17–18; 3.1.1–2; 3.2.1; 3.5.48–53; 4.5.16–17; 4.7.56–60; 5.0.8–9; 5.1.9–12.

33. One might assume that "history" refers here to the chronicles, twice cited in the play (1.2.163, 4.7.89), once by Fluellen, whose excessive reverence for, and comic misuse of, historical precedent is one of the ways in which the practice of invoking an exemplary past is ironized in the play. However, the personification of history as "speak[ing]," along with the allusions to funerary monuments, seems to encompass more popular (oral and visual) forms of historical commemoration.

34. Raphael Holinshed, *Chronicles of England, Scotland and Ireland*, rev. ed. (London, 1587), 3.546.

35. Rackin, *Stages of History*, 94.

36. The intervening figure of Hotspur, whose self-dedication to the obsolete code of "bright honour" is represented as both laudable and ludicrous, is the clearest index of this shift of perspective.

37. For an excellent analysis of the ideological appropriation of heroic exemplars sanctioned by humanist tradition, see Timothy Hampton, *Writing from History: The Rhetoric of Exemplarity in Renaissance Literature* (Ithaca and London: Cornell University Press, 1990). As Hampton notes, Shakespeare's attitude to this practice is consistently sceptical (though he confines his study to the latter's handling of classical models): "[His] use of the exemplar theory of history works both to celebrate the power of the past and to undermine attempts to appropriate its authority for political ends. Shakespeare demystifies the relationship between politics and history and demonstrates the extent to which all use of the past in guiding public action is shaped by rhetoric" (206).

38. See Michael Goldman, *Shakespeare and the Energies of Drama* (Princeton: Princeton University Press, 1972), 58–73.

39. Such contrarieties emerge not only from the diction, imagery, and other rhetorical devices of particular speeches, but between speeches. A much less flattering image of the common soldier as an inhuman and immoral brute is delineated by Henry at 3.3.90–121, and 4.1.152–59.

40. See, e.g., Helgerson, *Forms of Nationhood*, 231, and Anne Barton, "The King Disguised: Shakespeare's *Henry V* and the Comical History" (1975), rpt. in *Essays, Mainly Shakespearean* (Cambridge: Cambridge University Press, 1994), 207–33.

41. Jonathan Baldo, "Wars of memory in *Henry V*," *Shakespeare Quarterly* 47 (1996): 132–59.

42. Again we are alerted to the mystification of social relationships by the existence of alternative images. At 3.6.70–83, Gower offers a less romantic "take" on the veteran who exploits his supposed intimacy with the "great commanders" to defraud gullible "ale-washed wits." In actuality, the ordinary conscripts could expect to suffer acute social and economic hardship on their return from the wars (see Pugliatti, *Shakespeare the Historian*, 229–32).

43. For exceptions, see Holinshed, *Chronicles,* 3.551, 565. But, equally significantly, there is no equivalent in Holinshed for the exchanges between Henry and individual foot soldiers in 4.1 and 8, which (as with 3.2) do, briefly confer both an identity and a voice on the recalcitrant conscripts.

44. See, e.g., Weimann, *Shakespeare and the Popular tradition,* 214–15.

45. See, esp., Stephen Orgel, "Making Greatness Familiar," in *The Power of Forms in the English Renaissance,* ed. Stephen Greenblatt (Norman: University of Oklahoma Press, 1982), 41–48, and David Scott Kastan, "Proud Majesty Made a Subject: Shakespeare and the Spectacle of Rule," *Shakespeare Quarterly* 37 (1986): 459–75.

46. Although the relative proportion of "priviliged" versus "non-privileged" spectators estimated to have attended the public playhouses in this period is still vigorously debated, Andrew Gurr's conclusion that the citizen and artisanal classes provided the staple audience has been widely accepted (see *Playgoing in Shakespeare's London* [Cambridge: Cambridge University Press, 1987], 64).

47. For the evidence of women frequenting the commercial theatres, see Gurr, *Playgoing,* 55–63. The question of how their experience of plays and playgoing might have been differently inflected by their gender is addressed by Jean Howard in *The Stage and Social Struggle in Early Modern England* (London: Routledge, 1994), 76–92, and (with Rackin) in *Engendering a Nation,* 32–36.

Anachronistic Italy: Cultural Alliances and National Identity in *Cymbeline*

Peter A. Parolin

When the two princely brothers, Guiderius and Arviragus, first appear in Shakespeare's *Cymbeline,* they evoke geography and eating habits to lament their own potential barbarism. Bemoaning that they have lived their whole lives in a "pinched cave" in Wales, Arviragus complains, "We have seen nothing. / We are beastly: subtle as the fox for prey, / Like warlike as the wolf for what we eat."[1] In comments like this one, Shakespeare makes the interplay between a feared barbarism and a desired civility into one of *Cymbeline*'s central themes. Denied access to activities that could establish their civil status, Guiderius and Arviragus feel themselves to be nonentities. Jodi Mikalachki argues that "what the brothers protest is their exclusion from history. They have seen nothing; they are barbaric."[2] Excluded from history, the brothers are excluded from processes that permit individuals and nations to assert their power and relevance on an international stage. They are excluded as well from the historical records that could memorialize their achievements. Throughout *Cymbeline,* the brothers' fears of barbarism are also Britain's: as a remote Roman colony waging war to avoid paying Rome its yearly tribute of £3,000, Britain endangers its claim to civil status on the twin fronts of its sheer distance from and its opposition to Rome, the center of European civilization.

So crucial in the ancient world of *Cymbeline,* the question of British civility was equally alive in English culture at the time of the play's first performance. Situated on the margins of Europe, England in the early seventeenth century could not take its own historical importance and cultural civility completely for granted. London may have been among the largest cities in Europe in 1600, but the centers of political, economic, and cultural power remained continental. One historian bluntly characterizes late sixteenth-century England as a country "on the fringe of Europe and at best a second-rate power."[3] In 1588, the Italian political theorist Giovanni Botero noted that except for London "there is not a city in [England] that deserves to be called great."[4] English texts of the period repeatedly questioned the nature and origin of English civilization, especially in light of the sixteenth-century historiographical reorientation that dislodged such grandiose national myths as the founding of Britain by the Trojan exile Brutus.[5]

This paper will explore Britain's efforts to banish its own potential barbarism in *Cymbeline,*and in Jacobean culture. *Cymbeline* seeks to dispel British barbarism by appropriating the mantle of Roman civilization, just as James I was doing at the time of the play's initial performance. The play's first London audience might have found Britain's opposition to Rome strange, given that their own king represented himself so thoroughly in terms of the iconography of the Roman Empire and modeled so much of his political identity on Roman precedents. Any confusion would have dissipated before too long, though, because by the end of the play Britain, despite having won the war, enters into a respectful partnership with Rome and agrees to pay the disputed tribute. The mechanism by which *Cymbeline* enables this concluding alliance between ancient Britain and ancient Rome is the anachronistic interpolation of a decadent contemporary Italy into the action.[6] Scenes that according to the play's ancient time frame should be taking place in Rome are clearly placed in contemporary Italy, while Iachimo, the most characteristic denizen of this Italian space, has an Italian rather than a Roman name and is repeatedly called "an Italian," a "false Italian," and an "Italian fiend" (2.1.35; 3.2.4; 5.4.210). Since *Cymbeline* represents contemporary Italy as the antithesis of Roman virtue, the way is free for Britain to assert its own status as the implicit heir to Roman civilization and imperial power.[7]

But if *Cymbeline* stages the impetus to enter history, it also exposes some of the problems with this desire. Many commentators stress that in *Cymbeline,* Britain lays claim to ancient Rome's imperial legacy, but I will argue that the play ultimately dismisses as fantasy the idea that cultural alliances can be easily manipulated to produce a desired national identity. The play shows that alliances, even with a culture as celebrated as Rome's, necessarily hybridize identity, producing not only triumphalist prophecies about future national greatness but also anxieties about national vulnerability and failure. For me, the presence of contemporary Italy is the factor that most clearly indicates the problematic complexities of *Cymbeline*'s Anglo-Roman alliance. Contemporary Italy stands as the polity that ancient Rome degenerated into, so that even as Britain works toward an alliance with Rome, Italy insists on Rome's vulnerability, on its degradation over the course of history. Through the anachronistic presence of Italy, *Cymbeline* raises the disturbing possibility that Britain may not end up resembling Rome after all, but rather Italy, that it may not be seen as exclusively masculine but also as feminine, and that it may not be defined exclusively by military strength but also by weakness.[8] *Cymbeline* foregrounds the fact that once on the historical stage no nation can control the way it is written into the historical record. In its continual fluctuations, history works against any nation's desire to control and stabilize its preferred identity. Exploring the dangers of history, then, *Cymbeline* does not simply write Britain into the historical narrative, but also insists on the ways in which unpredictable historical processes challenge Britain's desired identity as the proper heir of ancient Rome.

Exploring ancient Britain's attempt to control its historical identity through contestation and war, dynasty building, and alliance, *Cymbeline* stages tactics that James I and the political classes of his new English nation were experimenting with in the years after the king's accession. Trying to fashion a post-Elizabethan identity for the nation, they were in effect trying to determine what the nature and extent of the nation's historical engagement should be.[9] Most critics have argued that *Cymbeline* constructs the nation's relationship to history in accordance with James's desires, but I argue that the play presents a much more complex view of history.[10] *Cymbeline* reads historical processes disruptively, deconstructing rather than confirming tenuous Jacobean fantasies about the leading historical role Britain might play in Europe and the heightened state of civility such historical engagement might offer the nation. Situating Britain in relation to both ancient Rome and contemporary Italy, *Cymbeline* explores the potential dangers a nation faces when it tries to define itself by allying with or appropriating foreign cultures.

What my reading of *Cymbeline* proposes, then, is a reorientation of the dominant argument that the play registers James's early seventeenth-century political desires in idealized form. By finding political ambivalence in *Cymbeline,* this reading can also stand as a case study in the range of attitudes that plays could express about Britain's proper place in history and, more broadly, about the crucial work of history-making itself. For far from seeing history—even a history in which Britain appropriates the prestige of Rome's imperial mantle—as an unbroken narrative of enhanced power and status, *Cymbeline* insists on the unpredictability of the alliances and the fragility of the assumptions necessary to sustain such a narrative. *Cymbeline* undoubtedly registers Britain's early seventeenth-century desire for historical significance but it registers just as strongly the difficulties getting in the way of this goal. Perhaps it registers, too, the climate of failure surrounding James's own attempts to make a mark on history. Yearning to figure importantly as a European statesman, James enjoyed a limited measure of success as a diplomatist, but increasingly he experienced frustration in his major goals of uniting the kingdoms of England and Scotland and of successfully mediating Europe's religious conflicts. I contend that *Cymbeline* engages with James's failures, skeptically interrogating the alliance-making that characterized the king's political approach.

The primary act of cultural interaction that *Cymbeline* scrutinizes is Britain's appropriation of Rome's legacy. Here the play is glancing at James I, who attempted to manipulate historical thinking through an intense engagement with the iconography and the historical figures of ancient Rome. For James, the Roman link ratified his image as a founder—of peace, of civility, of a united Great Britain; to this end, one of the Roman figures with whom he identified was Brutus, the legendary founder of ancient Britain. James saw himself as a "second Brutus," a leader who would fulfill ancient prophecies and revive the former unity of Great Britain.[11] After he succeeded to the English throne, James made the unification of Britain one of his major priorities; indeed, James styled himself not king of England and Scotland, but "King of Great Britain, France, and Ireland."[12] Speaking to his first Parliament, James described the proposed union of the kingdoms as "the second great blessing that GOD hath with my person sent unto you," ranking it only after peace with Spain as an important gift to his people.[13] In the same speech, James claims to exceed the achievements of his ancestor Henry VII, so feted in Tudor histories for uniting the warring houses of Lancaster and York: "But the Union of these two princely Houses, is nothing comparable to the Union of two ancient and famous Kingdomes."[14] Given James's determination to revive the ancient union of England and Scotland, Glynne Wickham asks "what better title to being the second Brutus could anyone claim than James himself?"[15] In addition to the mythic Brutus, James's Roman identifications extended to the historical Emperor Augustus. Leeds Barroll points out that Augustus was "for the Elizabethans, the ideal Roman Emperor";[16] Wickham shows that James self-identified as a "British Augustus."[17] The basis of James's comparison of himself to Augustus was their common commitment to peace, a commitment that, within the play, is shared by another British king, Cymbeline, a contemporary of Augustus who can also be seen as an avatar of James.[18]

Echoing contemporary cultural politics, the numerous identifications between Britain and Rome in *Cymbeline* work to craft a desirable British identity along the lines proposed by James. Britain overcomes its initial resistance to Rome, ultimately banishing its own potential for barbarism through its respect for the cultural authority of the empire. Here it is worth remembering that the *OED* defines "barbarian" in relation to recognized sites of civilization: "One living outside the pale of the Roman Empire and its civilization, applied especially to the northern nations that overthrew them." In other words, when Britain opposes Rome, it jeopardizes its own desired status as a civilized nation; perhaps for this reason, *Cymbeline*'s British characters so carefully stress their connections to Rome. For example, at the very moment when Cymbeline defies Augustus's ambassador Lucius and makes war with Rome inevitable, he still acknowledges his own debt to Caesar and by implication to Rome: "Thy Caesar knighted me; my youth I spent / Much under him; of him I gathered honour" (3.1.67–69).[19] Even when Britain is at odds with Rome, it relies on Rome as an important source of national self-definition. As Coppélia Kahn notes, Britain's relationship with Rome "expresses both identification and rivalry."[20] This mixture of impulses is also visible when war becomes inevitable and Posthumus predicts that the fighting Britons "will make known / To their approvers that they are people such / That mend upon the world" (2.4.17, 24–26). Here Rome is necessary both as the source of value against which British strength will be measured and as the judicious authority that will ratify Britain's new stature.[21] At the end of the play, Cymbeline establishes the union between Britain and Rome based on the commitment to peace that he shares with the historical Augustus. In the final speech of the play, Cymbeline repeats the word "peace" three times, insisting on his own identity as peacemaker. The link to Augustus through the focus on peace also forges a connection between Cymbeline and James: Cymbeline is the British king whose respect for Augustus prefigures James's own.[22] As James in seventeenth-century England, so Cymbeline in Shakespeare's play stands for the value of uniting Britain and Rome.

Roman precedents also undergird British identity in the case of Posthumus, another figure who unites British and Roman values in himself. Patricia Parker notes numerous similarities between Posthumus and that quintessential Roman hero, Aeneas, such as their eventual attainment of long-delayed happiness.[23] Other critics have argued that Posthumus anglicizes Roman values so that far from losing their force, they are enhanced when the mantle of empire passes from Rome to Britain.[24] Attending to the pun in *Cymbeline*'s notion of "paying tribute," Coppélia Kahn argues that Shakespeare himself is ultimately the figure who has always most thoroughly merged Roman and British qualities: "in this play, Shakespeare pays tribute to Rome as a cultural model for Britain and specifically, as source and inspiration for his own Roman works, acknowledging his own form of emulation."[25] *Cymbeline* comes to stand, then, for the way that Britain and writers like Shakespeare appropriated Rome's value to assert British cultural identity in the early seventeenth century.

The play brings together ancient Roman, ancient British, and contemporary British most strongly in the repeated reiteration of "Milford Haven," where the battle is fought and the peace concluded. Milford Haven also had contemporary importance in that it was the place where Henry VII's army defeated Richard III to usher in the Tudor-Stuart dynasty.[26] Rome and Britain thus fly their flags of friendship in the very spot from which James derived his political legitimacy. Through this network of Roman allusions and associations, *Cymbeline* participates in the cultural politics of early Jacobean England, reinforcing the notion that a strategic appropriation of Roman models can greatly enhance Britain's stature. Yet I shall argue that *Cymbeline* does not unequivocally celebrate the project of installing Great Britain as a latter-day Rome and its king as a modern Augustus. For me, what keeps getting in the way is the anachronistic presence of contemporary Italy. Although Posthumus ostensibly leaves Britain for Rome, he arrives in what is clearly contemporary Italy: talking to his companions, Posthumus refers to "your Italy"; Iachimo is repeatedly identified as "an Italian"; and Imogen worries about the influence of the "shes of Italy" (1.4.90; 2.1.25; 1.3.30).[27]

One dominant argument, which I will seek to complicate, holds that Britain successfully claims Rome's legacy in *Cymbeline,* with the anachronistic presence of contemporary Italy justifying and guaranteeing the northerly passage of empire. This argument maintains that *Cymbeline* splits Rome itself into two entities, creating contemporary Italy as a new site of barbarism against which Britain can assert its civil status.[28] By splitting Rome into ancient Rome, represented by the virtuous Lucius, and contemporary Italy, represented by the vicious Iachimo, *Cymbeline* promotes Britain over Italy as the legitimate heir to Roman virtue and power.[29] From the Soothsayer's final characterization of "the radiant Cymbeline, / Which shines here in the west" (5.4.476–77), it is clear that Cymbeline's and Britain's fortunes are in the ascendant, and that Britain will carry Rome's mantle forward into the Jacobean future and beyond. As Patricia Parker argues, the play accomplishes "a passing of the true Roman virtues not from Rome to a later Italy but from Rome to the Britain symbolized by Posthumus and Imogen and by the king's recovered heirs."[30] J. M. Nosworthy argues that "the Britain–Rome union . . . transfers to Cymbeline's kingdom the virtues of Augustus' empire," bypassing "the corrupt Italy of the Renaissance."[31] And most evocatively, G. Wilson Knight finds Italy's significance in the Soothsayer's vision of "Jove's bird, the Roman eagle" passing "from the spongy south to this part of the west" (4.2.349–50):

> the word "spongy" suggests softness and also, perhaps, an enervating, clammy heat, as though the imperial eagle were leaving a soft, effete, decaying land for one more virile; and indeed shows the precise relation within our drama of Renaissance Italy to ancient Rome, whilst indicating why their synchronization was forced: as the Roman virtue sinks to the level of Iachimo, the heritage of ancient Rome falls on Britain.[32]

Here Knight anticipates later critics by assuming that anachronism moves unidirectionally: ancient Rome devolves into contemporary Italy; ancient Britain rejects contemporary Italy; *Cymbeline* evokes Italy in order to use it and contain it. Nowhere in Knight's schema does the anachronistic element, contemporary Italy, exert a power of its own, but it seems to me that it must. To read *Cymbeline* as a play that easily coopts Italy to forge a seamless alignment of Britain and Rome is effectively to ignore the power of anachronism and to overlook the disruptive potential in the juxtaposition of ancient Rome and contemporary Italy.

Just what is contemporary Italy doing in a play about ancient Britain and Rome? I would suggest that in *Cymbeline,* Shakespeare deploys anachronism to subvert a straightforward nationalistic narrative, just as, at the end of *Henry V,* he undercuts an intensely nationalistic view of history by anachronistically gesturing to his previously written *Henry VI* cycle. Phyllis Rackin has demonstrated the new relevance of anachronism to Renaissance thinking, attributing it to a growing historiographical awareness of the difference between past and present.[33] In its insistence on historical alienation, Rackin argues, anachronism jars contemporary consciousness:

> anachronisms that disrupt the historical context to create direct confrontations between past and present are . . . radical in their effect. The very essence of history is that it deals with the past, with events that have already taken place. Therefore, any invocation of the present in a history play tends to create radical dislocations: it invades the timeframe of the audience, and its effect is no less striking than that of a character stepping off the stage to invade the audience's physical space or addressing them directly to invade their psychological space.[34]

In *Cymbeline,* the anachronistic coexistence of ancient Rome and contemporary Italy has just the disruptive effect Rackin describes. Anachronism explosively activates a new historical moment, in *Cymbeline*'s case a contemporary historical moment. And because historical moments carry powerful symbolic charge, to evoke a new historical moment inevitably deploys a new set of symbolic meanings that cannot be reduced to the service of a single ideological agenda. In *Cymbeline,* the anachronistic presence of Italy complicates what might otherwise seem a straightforward celebration of the Anglo-Roman alliance and the subsequent British revival under James. The play shows that when ancient and contemporary Britain engage with Rome, they must also engage with Italy, and with forms of cultural exchange that the British might prefer to suppress. When Posthumus encounters the recognizably italianate Iachimo, for example, the play activates contemporary English discourses about the dangers of Italy and about the deeply disturbing relationship between Italy and contemporary England. With James I envisioning a more international stature for Great Britain, the English were increasingly interacting with Italy in the early seventeenth century, but many English observers worried that English travelers were being harmed by exposure to undesirable Italian characteristics. To inject contemporary Italy into *Cymbeline* thus challenges rather than confirms Britain's status as the new Rome and indicates a deep ambivalence about the process of using other cultures to gain access to the historical stage.

Even as Britain attempts to appropriate ancient Rome's legacy, *Cymbeline*'s anachronism associates Britain with contemporary Italy, suggesting that the move toward civilization is always haunted by more than the mere shadows of that which is imagined as barbaric. Despite Guiderius and Arviragus's initial frustration that they are excluded from history, the central concern of *Cymbeline* may not be Britain's potential barbarism after all, but rather the dangers that beset its desired civility. In Wales, the brothers lament their rude eating habits, but in the end their asceticism protects them from the excesses of civilized life. In Rome, by contrast, Posthumus dines with a cosmopolitan group of men and is almost immediately goaded into wagering on Imogen's fidelity. Iachimo later describes the setting for this scene as "a feast" (5.4.155): unlike the barbarous Welsh eating that the brothers describe, this Italian feast is civilized and polished, but also malicious. While *Cymbeline* stages the desires that move Britain inexorably toward an alliance with Rome and an engagement with history, it also registers its anxiety over what those desires might mean and where they might lead.

One of the places those desires lead is Italy. In the conventional cultural politics of the early seventeenth century, English texts routinely demonized Italy but, as I will show, they also registered Italy's seductive appeal to English readers and its power to transform English minds. The most famous vilification of Italy occurs in Roger Ascham's *Scholemaster,* where Ascham treats Italy as a place that can stand for the danger of history, much as Shakespeare does in *Cymbeline*. When he looks at Italy, Ascham sees both ancient Rome and contemporary Italy simultaneously; in this sense, he may be said to see historical process in telescoped form:

> tyme was, whan Italie and Rome have bene, to the greate good of us that now live, the best breeders and bringers up of the worthiest men, not onelie for wise speakinge but also for well doing, in all Civill affaires,

that ever was in the worlde. But now that tyme is gone, and though the place remayne, yet the olde and present maners do differ as farre, as blacke and white, as vertue and vice.[35]

For Ascham, contemporary Italy represents history's power to undo Empire: Italy's mere presence, where Rome once stood, evokes history's power to destroy civilizations. The anachronistic presence of Rome's past intensifies Ascham's disgust at Italy's current barbarous state: he condemns the Pope for tolerating brothels in Rome, and reports that Venetians "waulter with as litle shame in open lecherie, as Swyne do here in the common myre."[36] For Ascham, behavior that puts humans on a par with animals marks the Italian barbarism that supplanted Roman civility.

Like Ascham, Robert Greene reflects on the relationship between ancient Rome and contemporary Italy in *A Quip for an Upstart Courtier* (1592). Greene's *Quip* is a contestation between Cloth-Breeches and Velvet-Breeches and the values they represent. Cloth-Breeches stands for "the old and woorthye customes of the gentilitie and yeomanrie of Englande," while Velvet-Breeches stands for newfangledness originating in Italy.[37] Attacking Velvet-Breeches, Cloth-Breeches charges that "the imperiall state, through thy pride, hath decayed, and thou hast, like the yonge pelican, peckt at thy mothers brest with thy presumption, causing them to lose that their forefathers with true honor conquered; so hast thou beene the ruine of the Romane empyre, and nowe fatally art thou come into Englande to atempte here the like subuersion."[38] In Greene's book, Italy—or, more precisely, values that he labels Italian—are responsible for ruining the Roman Empire and are now threatening to ruin England. Casting the Roman Empire and England as parallel representatives of virtue under siege, Greene implicitly compares them; in *Cymbeline,* Shakespeare pushes a step further to substitute England for Italy as ancient Rome's proper heir. Yet in both Shakespeare and Greene (and in Ascham, too), England is under siege from within by the very Italy it attempts to denigrate.

While anti-Italian writers labor to differentiate between Italy and England, they also betray a concern that the boundaries between the two countries may be permeable and that Italy may appeal to English travelers. In this line of thinking, Italy represents a diversion from history and serious masculine purposes, recalling places like Carthage in *The Aeneid* and the Bower of Bliss in *The Faerie Queene.* Ascham as usual establishes the template in arguing for the particular kinds of degradation available in Italy:

I know diverse noble personages and many worthy Jentlemen of England, whom all the *Siren* songes of *Italie* could never untwyne from the maste of Gods word . . . [b]ut I know as many or mo, and some sometyme my dere frendes, for whose sake I hate going into that countrey the more, who partyng out of England fervent in the love of Christes doctrine and well furnished with the feare of God, returned out of *Italie* worse transformed, than ever was any in *Circes* Court.[39]

Ascham's allusion to Circe's influence over Odysseus's men suggests that the danger he fears is the willing self-transformation of English travelers; he senses that Italy appeals to them by promising self-indulgence free from subjection to English authorities. Similarly, Thomas Palmer warns travelers to avoid Italy on the grounds that it will transform them: he speaks of "the infinite corruptions, almost inevitable, that invest Travailers after small abode there [in Italy]; as it is reported, I know not upon what ground, of the Realme of Ireland."[40] Linking Italy's corruptions with Ireland, Palmer leaves room for England to claim the space of civility, yet since both Italy and Ireland hold a power over the English, he inadvertently raises the question of just how strong this English civility will be. Given the context of the English campaign in Ireland, Palmer implies that both Ireland and Italy entice the English to seek pleasure and "corruptions" rather than to train their minds on the imperial business of conquering and controlling foreign countries.[41]

The dynamics of attraction and repulsion that characterize Italy in much English writing of the sixteenth and seventeenth centuries appear prominently in *Cymbeline*. The play certainly constructs a barbarous contemporary Italy to define by contrast Britain's place within the rubric of Roman civilization, but Italy's role has other dimensions as well. Anachronistically present in the play, Italy repeatedly functions as an alternative to Rome as an object of British allegiance, suggesting that once situated in history, Britain might find itself just as easily following the model of Italy as the model of Rome. Italy exerts a hold on English imaginations; Italy is the historical endpoint of the Roman Empire; all in all, Italy is hard to resist, no matter how stridently English polemicists might seek to demonize it. In this way, the Italian anachronism introduces a profoundly discordant note that relates to *Cymbeline*'s ambivalent attitude about history and undermines a purely heroic sense of Britain.

Although *Cymbeline* has been persuasively called "Shakespeare's last Roman play,"[42] it might equally be called one of his last *Italian* plays because it depends so strongly on the early seventeenth-century English stereotypes of Italy. Italy's impact on Britain can be marked by the speed with which it transforms Posthumus's concept of identity from something that is stable to something that is infinitely changeable. He goes to Rome promising Imogen that "I will remain / The loyal'st husband that did e'er plight troth" (1.1.96–7), but by the end of his first scene in Italy, he swallows Iachimo's bait and wagers on Imogen's fidelity. In Britain, Posthumus was described as a source of absolute virtue, "a creature such / As, to seek through the regions of the earth / For one his like, there would be something failing / In him that should compare" (1.1.19–22). Knowing no national bounds, Posthumus's virtue seems to mark him with the cultural prestige of an international empire like Rome's. In Italy, however, Posthumus embraces a system of national differences and quickly accepts an Italian worldview where stable moral absolutes do not exist: "Spare your arithmetic, never count the turns. / Once, and a million," he cries in response to Imogen's supposed adultery (2.4.142–43).[43] When Imogen hears about Posthumus's transformation, she quickly blames Italy: "Some jay of Italy, / Whose mother was her painting, hath betrayed him," she cries (3.4.49–50); elsewhere, she simply says "My lord, I fear, / Has forgot Britain" (1.6.113–14). This line stands for the fear, current in English thinking since *The Scholemaster,* that the English will be transformed in Italy. In *Cymbeline,* the first-century Posthumus has anachronistically become Ascham's sixteenth-century *inglese italianato,* the Italianate Englishman who travels to Italy and forgets his homeland.

Italy also troubles definitions of Britishness through the ease with which Iachimo insinuates himself into the minds and attitudes of his British targets. He poses such a frightening threat because he works on his victims through undefended entry points like their ears and their bedroom doors. He works on Posthumus through the ear: When Pisanio first reads of Posthumus's suspicions against Imogen, he exclaims, "O master, what a strange infection / Is fall'n into thy ear! What false Italian / As poisonous tongued as handed, hath prevailed / On they too ready hearing?" (3.2.4–6). Iachimo's assault on the ears evokes Ascham's writing about Italy: citing Ulysses's encounter with the Sirens, Ascham warns that the traveller to Italy needs "to stop his ears with wax";[44] failing to defend the ears suggests the desire to hear the Sirens' songs. The ear is perhaps only the most prominent of orifices vulnerable to Italian assault in *Cymbeline;* the door to Imogen's chamber is another. Scholars have rightly noted that when Iachimo enters the chamber, explicitly evoking Tarquin's rape of Lucrece, he is metaphorically raping Imogen.[45] Standing in Imogen's darkened bedchamber, cataloguing all the parts of her body, the contents of her book, and the tapestries with which she has adorned her room, Iachimo insinuates a deep knowledge and even mastery of Imogen's most private self.[46] Penetrating the chamber, Iachimo literally embodies *Cymbeline*'s fears of the Italian within. Iachimo watching over the sleeping Imogen is a nightmare image for Britain; the fact that Britain seems to have left its ears and its doors unguarded against Iachimo suggests the possibility that the British may be complicit in their own Italian seduction.[47]

The British court seems from the outset to have embraced behavior associated with the Italian so that to posit a British identity wholly hostile to or innocent of Italianate vice is impossible.[48] Dominated by the queen and her son Cloten, the British court is a place of machiavellian scheming receptive to Iachimo's deceitfulness. Where Iachimo is metaphorically called a "false poisonous Italian," the queen traffics in literal poison. "Now Master Doctor, have you brought those drugs," she asks Cornelius; and she later gives Pisanio a cordial meant to kill him and Imogen both (1.5.4). The queen's penchant for "[s]trange ling'ring poisons" creates an Italianate atmosphere: Italians were renowned in England for the poisons that they treacherously administered to their enemies. Stories of poisoned Italian popes, cardinals, dukes, and duchesses circulated widely in England and frequently found their way into the plays of the period.[49] Fynes Moryson sums up the prevailing view when he says that "the Italyans aboue all other nations, most practise revenge by treasons, and espetially are skillfull in making and giuing poisons."[50] He adds that "In our tyme, it seemes the Art of Poysoning is reputed in Italy worthy of princes practise," which is in keeping with the situation in *Cymbeline,* where it is the Italianate queen herself who brings poison to the very heart of the British court. *Cymbeline* activates an English discourse of Italianism in act 1, scene 4, which takes place in contemporary Italy; significantly, the play sustains rather than counters this discourse in act 1, scene 5, when the action returns to Britain and the queen hatches her plan to poison Imogen. Through his juxtaposition of scenes, Shakespeare stages the moral poison of Italy not in order to contrast it to a morally pure Britain but to show Italianism already at work in Britain.

Cataloguing Italian vices, Robert Greene mentions "vaine-glory, self loue, sodomie, and strange poisonings."[51] If the strange poisonings apply to the queen, then the vainglory and self-love apply to Cloten, so completely infatuated with himself that he cannot comprehend Imogen's preference for "that base wretch" Posthumus (2.3.110). When he is scorned by Imogen, Cloten vows, "I'll be revenged," and plots a nasty attack in which, disguised as Posthumus, he will brutalize Imogen: "With that suit upon my back will I ravish her . . . [W]hen my lust hath dined . . . to the court I'll knock her back, foot her home again" (3.5.134–40). Cloten's desire for an outrageous revenge intensifies the Italianate nature of the British court, because the Italian thirst for revenge was legendary in English writing about Italy. Moryson claims that "if an Italyan be wronged, he is very likely to take revenge, and that very deepe beyond the quality of the offence"; here Moryson's description of an Italian fits Cloten equally well.[52] Throughout the court scenes, then, Cloten and the queen serve to remind audiences of Britain's proximity to Italy and its distance from the Roman virtues it seeks to emulate.

On a number of levels, *Cymbeline* calls attention to the ways in which Britain, claiming a place on the historical stage through alliance with Rome, risks losing control of its own desired identity. Focusing on the dangers of claiming a role in history, *Cymbeline* points to tensions within its contemporary historical context: given the dissonances in *Cymbeline*'s treatment of history, it seems more likely that the play is engaging with the challenges and failures of Stuart politics rather than celebrating the royal family, as most topical readings maintain. From this perspective, Cymbeline's decision to pay Rome the disputed tribute, so often interpreted as the culmination of the play's politics of union, can be more plausibly read as an instance of serious, if subterranean, political tension. With his sons having led Britain to a spectacular victory over Rome, Cymbeline surprisingly submits to Rome's initial demand for tribute. By embracing Rome, Cymbeline in effect gives away what his sons have won, and his act can be seen as an assertion of his political will over and against their achievement.[53] "My peace we will begin," Cymbeline announces, and with the possessive he emphatically reasserts control over his own foreign policy, shifting focus from the sons whose martial feats have already captured the popular imagination (5.4.460).[54] In the divergence between Cymbeline, angling for peace, and the young princes, eager to prove their martial prowess, *Cymbeline* also identifies the emerging disagreements between King James and his son, Henry, prince of Wales, over Britain's proper place in Europe.[55]

Instead of celebrating the military victory over Rome, the play focuses on Cymbeline's desired union and on Britain's role as Rome's successor; here again, problems unsettle the move toward historical greatness. Specifically, the union with Rome can be seen to comment on James's cherished proposal to unite the two kingdoms of England and Scotland, a proposal that became the most spectacular failure of his early years in London.[56] James saw the proposed union as an opportunity both to reassert the island's Roman heritage and to enhance his own prestige as the bringer of internal peace. Designed to leave a mark on history, the union project failed largely because of English ambivalence about allying themselves politically and culturally with another country. Far from seeing this kind of historical change as unequivocally beneficial, members of Parliament worried that if the union went ahead, closer ties with Scotland would threaten the integrity of English identity and undermine the English constitution. Barry Coward has noted the difficulty James faced in England in proposing any political reform along the lines of the union of the kingdoms:

> [I]nherent in the concept of the "ancient constitution" was the assumption that the existing framework of government was perfect. There was therefore a possibility that anyone who proposed reform was in danger of being smeared as a dangerous "innovator" who was undermining the framework of the "ancient constitution" and therefore threatening traditional values.[57]

In essence, many of James's English subjects saw the union project as an illegitimate tampering with England's historical identity. Although the project was designed to enhance the country's stature, it could easily blur the distinction between England and Scotland, which for the English was unacceptable. As one MP said of the Scots' turbulent political history, "They have not suffered above two Kings to die in their Beds, these two hundred Years. Our King hath hardly escaped them."[58] By the parliamentary session of 1610, James's union project was a dead letter. The fear that union with Scotland would undermine Englishness is a potent context for the movement in *Cymbeline* whereby alliance with Rome leaves Britain vulnerable to the depredations of Italy.

In light of the rejection of the union proposal, Cymbeline's climactic announcement of the Romano-British peace may be as troubling as it is triumphalist. Cymbeline says "Let / A Roman and a British ensign wave / Friendly together" (5.4.480–82); as Coward notes, one of the few concrete changes to emerge from the union project was a union flag that flew on British ships for twenty-seven years.[59] The final image of the united flags may thus express contemporary apprehension about James's union project and his pacifism.[60] In the image of the two flags flying together, Britain risks losing the distinctness of its independent identity.[61] Through the peace and the united flags, Britain's future becomes bound up with Rome at the same time that *Cymbeline*'s Italian anachronism continually reminds audiences that imperial Rome degenerated into contemporary Italy. Shadowed by Italian anachronism, the final celebration in *Cymbeline* is less complete than it seems. Britain achieves its civility and its place at the table of history, but at the cost of the very alignment with Italy that the play had been seeking to avoid.

While Italian degradation seems an inevitable aspect of the British union with Rome, the play nevertheless explores in different settings the possibility of achieving the union without the taint of Italy. In particular, the play constructs Wales as an insular place where it remains possible to imagine the foundation of a classically virtuous British civilization "untainted" by interaction with contemporary cultures.[62] As critics have pointed out, this Anglo-Roman space is imagined as predominantly if not exclusively masculine. Jodi Mikalachki memorably refers to the "masculine romance of Roman Britain," and on multiple levels this masculine romance takes shape in Wales.[63] The only female character in the Welsh scenes is Imogen, but she is disguised as the boy Fidele for most of the time. The strong social bonds, on the other hand, as well as the significant choices characters make, primarily center attention on the male characters. In Wales, for example, Posthumus resumes his British identity for good, rejecting Italy symbolically by changing his clothes: "I'll disrobe me / Of these Italian weeds, and suit myself / As does a Briton peasant" (5.1.22–24); additionally, in Wales the "Briton peasant," Posthumus, roundly defeats the Italian Iachimo, who freely acknowledges the superiority of the British: "If that thy gentry, Britain, go before / This lout as he exceeds our lords, the odds / Is that we scarce are men and you are gods" (5.2.8–10). After the battle, Iachimo confesses his treachery and submits to British justice; with Italy defeated, Britain and Rome conclude their peace.

The Welsh scenes also complete Imogen's transformation from the active, public, verbally dexterous heir to the throne to the symbolic, less politically powerful figure that she becomes at the end of the play.[64] Imogen was first introduced as Cymbeline's daughter "and the heir of's kingdom" (1.1.4), but now, with her brothers having moved ahead of her in the line of succession to Cymbeline's throne, Imogen's political power is transformed into the symbolic power that guarantees Jupiter's prophecy for Britain. This prophecy mentions a time when "a lion's whelp shall, to himself unknown, without seeking find, and be embraced by a piece of tender air" (5.3.232–34); at the end of the play, the Soothsayer interprets that tender air as Imogen:

> the piece of tender air thy virtuous daughter,
> Which we call *'mollis aer';* and *'mollis aer'*
> We term it *'mulier',* which *'mulier'* I divine
> Is this most constant wife, who even now,
> Answering the letter of the oracle,
> Unknown to you, unsought, were clipped about
> With this most tender air.
>
> (5.4.447–53)

Embracing Posthumus, Imogen is the disembodied British air that symbolizes his return to proper British identity.[65] Her symbolic value can be seen as well in the transformation of Iachimo, who is also affected by the British air: "The heaviness and guilt within my bosom / Takes off my manhood. I have belied a lady, / The princess of this country, and the air on't / Revengingly enfeebles me" (5.2.1–4).

From the construction of male bonds to the disempowering of Imogen, Wales seems to serve as a model whereby the Anglo-Roman alliance creates the pure civilization—all-male, all-virtuous—that points to the greatness of Britain's future identity. While Guiderius and Arviragus may denigrate Wales as a remote outpost that excludes them from the historical process, the very remoteness of Wales protects the brothers from corruption and allows their innate nobility to shine. Of their surrogate father Belarius, Arviragus asks, "What should we speak of / When we are old as you? When we shall hear / The rain and wind beat dark December, how / In this our pinching cave, shall we discourse / The freezing hours away?" (3.3.36–39). Belarius champions Wales, insisting that the court, with its Italianate focus on sartorial excess, is the true site of barbarism: "O, this life / Is nobler than attending for a check, / Richer than doing nothing for a bauble, / Prouder than rustling in unpaid-for silk" (3.3.21–24). Despite Belarius's argument, Guiderius and Arviragus face a difficult paradox: absence from the historical stage protects their innate virtue, but only participation on the historical stage will allow them to exercise their virtue; to enact their virtue thus threatens the conditions that enable it in the first place.

As the paradox suggests, the image of Wales as a space purged of hybridity is a nostalgic fantasy that cannot be sustained. The historical world inevitably imposes itself on Guiderius, Arviragus, and the Welsh setting.[66] With their military success against Rome, Guiderius and Arviragus help usher in British history and British civilization. To this extent, their upbringing in Wales does not so much exclude them from history as prepare them for it. Yet the concluding partnership with Rome implicates Wales, too, in *Cymbeline*'s exploration of the problematic aspects of alliance making, in particular the hybridity that accompanies it. Most crucially, the feminine reenters the ostensibly all-male political landscape of Wales in that once the battle is concluded, Imogen emerges from behind the costume of Fidele. Imogen has certainly been diminished over the course of the play, but she has not been erased. Despite the effort to dissolve Imogen into "tender air," she retains a physical presence on stage. When she tries to reveal herself to Posthumus in the final scene, for example, he strikes her, in a theatrical transaction that exploits the actors' physicality. Later, when Posthumus finally understands who she is, he cries, "Hang there like fruit, my soul, / Till the tree die" (5.4.263–64). Again, these words suggest Imogen's physical presence, not to mention her reproductive capability.[67] Even as the men ratify their concluding peace, Imogen remains a body on the stage, a reminder that the all-male nature of the conclusion is a misrepresentation that depends on the repression of the disruption that the woman's body makes possible. After all, Iachimo could cause so much trouble because he was able to gain access to Imogen's chamber, where he could catalogue not only the physical objects that adorn her room but also the private marks of her physical body. Imogen's physicality stands as a firm reminder that the "masculine romance of Roman Britain" is an illusion, and that Britain can never be the exclusively masculine Roman terrain that it fantasizes about becoming.

Interestingly, the play also questions the assumed masculinity of Rome itself. Like Imogen, Rome is imagined in both symbolic and physical terms. Symbolically, characters see Rome as the pinnacle of civilization, but physically it is a body subject like any other to invasion and decay. In *Cymbeline,* Rome is vulnerable to British arms and to other fighting forces as well. Cymbeline says, "I am perfect / That the Pannonians and Dalmatians for / Their liberties are now in arms, a precedent / Which not to read would show the Britons cold" (3.1.71–74). In a sense, Rome in *Cymbeline* is repeatedly wounded by the attacks of its subject peoples. Coppélia Kahn reminds us that "[t]he Latin word for wound is *vulnus,* the root of 'vulnerability,'" and she draws out the gender implications of this connection: "In an obvious sense, wounds mark a kind of vulnerability easily associated with women: they show the flesh to be penetrable, they show that it can bleed, they make apertures in the body."[68] Rome is subject to this kind of penetration in the play; indeed, Linda Woodbridge argues that Rome's symbolism as a besieged polity seems to have been as charged as its symbolism as an Empire at the height of its power:

> A binary image of Rome, almost Levi-Straussian in its precise mirror inversion, haunted the European imagination for almost a thousand years: Rome the implacable invader, thrusting its masculine armies deep into the virgin territory of the Goths, its soldiers raping the queen of Britain's daughters; and Rome the invaded, the sacked city, ravaged by Goths.[69]

The drive in *Cymbeline* to fashion a masculine polity based on the alliance between Britain and Rome requires the suppression of this second image of Rome, vulnerable and bleeding. Yet the play clearly evokes the image of Rome under attack, complicating Britain's emulation of Rome. Insofar as Rome is the model to which Britain aspires, Roman wounds evoke potential future British ones. The image of an invaded Rome positions Britain in the unpredictable flux of history and defeat. Perhaps Britain's unexpected submission to Rome is designed to shield Rome from the full impact of the wounds it receives, thus protecting the imperial position that Britain itself aspires to occupy.

Kahn notes, of course, that the wound is never exclusively the site of the feminine: it also marks and calls forth virtue that is figured as masculine. What makes the wound so troubling is that in its own indeterminancy it points to the indeterminacy of all gender categories: "Poised, as it were, between 'warriors' (men locked in agonistic structures of rivalry), and 'women,' the wound in [Shakespeare's Roman plays] is always a site of anxiety and indeterminacy; a point at which it is possible to identify an ideology of gender difference in process."[70] In *Cymbeline,* to expose an ideology of gender difference in progress threatens to reveal the coercion through which the all-male political order takes shape. As well, it undermines the privileged site (a Rome conceived of as masculine) against which British identity measures itself. The insistent presence of the feminine is thus a symptom of Britain's failure to appropriate the mantle of an invulnerable, all-male Rome; this failure is also stressed in the anachronistic presence of contemporary Italy, which serves as a constant reminder of Rome's inescapable vulnerability to historical change.[71] Britain may appropriate a certain version of Rome but, with Italy and the feminine as integral parts of the exchange, Britain gets more than it bargained for.

In suggesting the desire to banish Italy from constructions of Britishness, *Cymbeline* is at odds with trends in the Stuart court. Among James and Charles's greatest courtiers, interest in Italy was on the rise. In the second decade of the century, for example, great aristocrats like the earls of Somerset and Arundel and the duke of Buckingham were aggressively scouring Italy to procure the paintings and statues that would enhance their cultural prestige at home.[72] Early in the reign of Charles I, Peter Paul Rubens, in London as Philip IV's envoy, praised the excellence of English culture by explicitly comparing it to its Italian counterpart: "Certainly in this island I find none of the crudeness which one might expect from a place so remote from Italian elegance."[73] *Cymbeline* certainly thematizes the crudeness that one finds far from Italy, but it rewrites this crudeness as the ancient virtue that Britain shares with Rome; British civility depends on the alliance with Rome and the rejection of an Italian model of civilization. Yet the intimations of connections between Britain and Italy, such a source of anxiety in the play, become increasingly overt in Stuart culture, so that when Rubens wants to praise England he does so by likening it to Italy. Rubens's comment can serve as an ironic historical coda to a play that powerfully expresses the British desire to ground its national identity in an identification with Rome but not with the Italy that Rome became. But perhaps the coda is not so ironic after all in that the play suggests the difficulty—even the impossibility—of constructing "desirable" forms of national identity purged of unwanted elements. The disruptive principle of anachronism is essential to *Cymbeline,* undermining easy confidence in cultural appropriation as a tool of national identity formation, whether in the ancient Britain of the play or the revived Great Britain of King James's desires.

Notes

I am very grateful to Rebecca Bushnell, Leigh Edwards, Mary Floyd-Wilson, Susan Frye, Phyllis Rackin, Cedric Reverand, and Valerie Wayne for their generous and insightful responses to earlier drafts of this article.

1. *Cymbeline,* ed. Roger Warren (Oxford: Oxford University Press, 1998), 3.3.39–41. All further references are to this edition.

2. Mikalachki, "The Masculine Romance of Roman Britain: *Cymbeline* and Early Modern English Nationalism." *Shakespeare Quarterly* 46 (1995): 314–15.

3. J. A. Sharpe, *Early Modern England, A Social History 1550–1760,* 2nd ed. (London: Arnold, 1997), 12.

4. Quoted in Sharpe, *Early Modern England,* 78.

5. John Curran argues that work by sixteenth-century English historians and antiquarians necessitated the revision of "the notion, intrinsic to the time-honored Galfridian Brute myth, that Britain maintained a glorious lineage as old as the Trojan war." In place of the distinguished mythic history, classical history revealed the ancient Britons to be "a wild band of naked, painted heathens, as unacquainted with architecture and agriculture as they were with civilized sexual mores" ("Royalty Unlearned, Honor Untaught: British Savages and Historiographical Change in *Cymbeline.*" *Comparative Drama* 31 [1997]: 279). Mikalachki notes the impact of this shift in historiographical thinking: "One of the great intellectual stumbling blocks to the recovery of national origins in sixteenth-century England was the absence of a native classical past on which to found the glories of the modern nation" ("Masculine Romance," 302). Curran locates the native past in Guiderius and Arviragus, who allow their audiences "to reevaluate standards for judging the past—to locate virtue in savage forbears and obscure origins." He adds that the princes point toward "the new conception of wild but yet noble ancient Britons" ("Royalty Unlearned," 278; 286).

6. Two very fine articles on *Cymbeline*'s use of Italy have just appeared in *Shakespeare Yearbook*'s edition on Shakespeare and Italy. See Thomas G. Olsen, "Iachimo's 'Drug-Damn'd Italy' and the Problem of British National Character in *Cymbeline,*" *Shakespeare Yearbook* 10 (1999): 268–96 and Michael J. Redmond, " 'My lord, I fear, has forgot Britain': Rome, Italy, and the (Re)Construction of British National Identity," *Shakespeare Yearbook* 10 (1999): 297–316. Although we are all interested in the same nexus of problems, our emphases and some of our conclusions differ. Olsen unpacks *Cymbeline*'s Italianate context to argue that the play's use of Italy helps ensure the smooth alliance between Britain and Rome "by dramatizing and neatly resolving the conflicts surrounding union" (282). I argue, in contrast, that the play uses Italy disruptively in order to trouble the alliance

with Rome. Redmond persuasively claims that the play uses the British alliance with Rome to challenge the Anglo-Scottish union. Where Redmond finds that the Italian anachronism, symbolized by Iachimo, "creates interpretive confusion" (313), I explore the function of the Italian anachronism in detail, arguing that it exposes the pressure points in the alliance with Rome and indicates the incompatibility between a politics of alliance and any stable definition of national identity. I have included in subsequent footnotes some of the three essays' important points of intersection and departure.

7. Mary Floyd-Wilson suggests the impact of Britain's adoption of the Roman imperial model: "once interpreted as cultural advancement, ancient Britain's submission to Rome became a model in the logic of 'progress,' which dictated, in turn, that the Anglo-Britons would transmit this civility by eradicating the residual barbarism of Scotland and Ireland" (Floyd-Wilson, "*Cymbeline*, the Scots, and the English Race," forthcoming, in *British Identities and English Renaissance Literature*, ed. David Baker and Willy Maley [Cambridge: Cambridge University Press, 2002]).

8. For Jacobean Britain, the importance of identifying with Rome rather than Italy is suggested in Lisa Hopkins's wonderful argument that Italy occupies the position of the colonised in early modern English thinking, as opposed to imperial Rome, the coloniser: "[I]f colonizing classical Rome was able to look at, record, and even name that which it saw . . . its successor, Renaissance Italy, was not the coloniser, but the colonised, fought over and occupied by both France and Spain . . . Moreover, Italy's reputation as the foremost artistic center of the world further constructs it as a locus of things to be seen, rather than as itself a possessor of the gaze" (" 'It is Place which Lessens and Sets Off': Perspective and Representation in *Cymbeline*," *Shakespeare Yearbook* 10 [1999]: 256–57).

9. In the form of the Union question, this process included raising a question as fundamental as whether the king's nation would be one nation or two.

10. For historical readings of *Cymbeline*, see the following: G. Wilson Knight, *The Crown of Life: Essays in Interpretation of Shakespeare's Final Plays* (London: Methuen, 1947); Emrys Jones, "Stuart Cymbeline," *Essays in Criticism* 11 (1961): 84–99; David Bergeron, "*Cymbeline:* Shakespeare's Last Roman Play," *Shakespeare Quarterly* 31 (1980): 31–41; Robert Miola, *Shakespeare's Rome* (Cambridge: Cambridge University Press, 1983); Linda Woodbridge, "Palisading the Elizabethan Body Politic," *Texas Studies in Literature and Language* 33 (1991): 327–54; Mikalachki, "Masculine Romance"; Curran, "Royalty Unlearned"; and Olsen, "Iachimo's 'Drug-Damn'd Italy.' " Most of the critics who adopt historical approaches argue that *Cymbeline* celebrates Britain and offers optimistic, ideologically coherent solutions to the problems of British history. For example, Linda Woodbridge finds unity and equilibrium in *Cymbeline*'s use of history, despite her exploration of the play's fraught national and sexual boundaries: "Shakespeare had always identified England with Rome, and his last Roman play unites them. . . . Toward the end of his career, Shakespeare, living in a charmed moment in a changing culture, envisioned a society neither invaded nor invader, neither raped nor rapist, neither polluted nor polluter" ("Palisading," 348). While I share these critics' historicist project, I argue that the play engages much more contentiously with history than others have claimed in the past. One critic who has identified profound tensions in *Cymbeline*'s use of history is Leah Marcus. Identifying in the play an "unease of topicality" that is really an "unease with Jacobean textuality,"

Marcus brilliantly argues that *Cymbeline* puts forward "a series of arresting, even jarring visitations which impose a relentless textuality upon the flow of events and which, through their resistance to assimilation in the action, undermine the very political message they seem designed to communicate" ("*Cymbeline* and the Unease of Topicality," in *The Historical Renaissance: New Essays on Tudor and Stuart Literature and Culture,* ed. Heather Dubrow and Richard Streir [Chicago: University of Chicago Press, 1988], 138; 136). Michael J. Redmond, too, argues against the notion that Shakespeare in *Cymbeline* "is aiming at a consistent expression of a single idea" (Redmond, "My Lord, I Fear," 310).

11. Patricia Parker, "Romance and Empire: Anachronistic *Cymbeline*," in *Unfolded Tales: Essays on Renaissance Romance,* ed. George M. Logan and Gordon Teskey (Ithaca: Cornell University Press, 1989), 193.

12. Barry Coward, *The Stuart Age* (London: Longman, 1994), 137.

13. Charles Howard McIlwain, ed., *The Political Works of James I, Vol. I* (Cambridge: Harvard University Press, 1918), 271.

14. McIlwaine, *Political Works of James I,* 271.

15. Wickham, "From Tragedy to Tragi-Comedy: 'King Lear' as Prologue," *Shakespeare Survey* 26 (1973): 39.

16. Barroll, "Shakespeare and Roman History," *Modern Language Review* 53 (1958): 341. Discussing Augustus's reputation, Barroll says "whether the Romans praised Augustus for ending civil disaster, whether the Christians honoured him because Christ enrolled as a citizen under the head of his temporal kingdom, or whether he was remembered for restoring the laudable institution of kingship, the varying attitudes only reinforced each other" (343).

17. Wickham, "From Tragedy to Tragi-Comedy," 37, 42.

18. On peacemaking as James's link to Augustus, see Bergeron, "Shakespeare's Last Roman Play," 33, and Woodbridge, "Palisading," 343. Iconographically, James used his accession medal to style himself emperor of the whole island of Great Britain. The medal depicts James dressed as a Roman Emperor; the significance of this iconography is suggested by Linda Levy Peck's comment that "James was the first British monarch to portray himself on his coinage as a Roman Emperor" ("The Mental World of the Jacobean Court: An Introduction," in *The Mental World of the Jacobean Court,* ed. Linda Levy Peck [Cambridge: Cambridge University Press, 1991], 5). Jonathan Goldberg summarizes James's Roman ambitions: "From the start, then, the king who declared his marriage to his nation, proclaiming himself the peacemaker and uniter of Scotland and England into Great Britain, restorer of pristine unity to the realm, presented himself in the Roman image, stamped with the Roman stamp" (*James I and the Politics of Literature* [Baltimore and London: Johns Hopkins University Press, 1983], 46).

19. Reading this speech, Meredith Skura argues that in important ways, Rome can be said to have "generated [Cymbeline] and his ideals" ("Interpreting Posthumus' Dream from Above and Below: Families, Psychoanalysts, and Literary Critics," in *Representing Shakespeare: New Psychoanalytic Essays,* ed. Murray M. Schwartz and Coppélia Kahn [Baltimore: Johns Hopkins University Press, 1980], 213).

20. Coppélia Kahn, *Roman Shakespeare: Warriors, Wounds, and Women* (London and New York: Routledge, 1997), 161. Here Kahn is referring specifically to the description of Posthumus's father, Sicilius, as one who "did join his honour / Against the Romans with Cassibelan" (1.1.29–30).

21. Posthumus's prediction of future British greatness also evokes the contemporary Jacobean scene in which many of the important political figures desired to show the world a new and secure Britain, whether this was the new Britain envisioned by James, a peacemaker amid the competing factions of Europe, or the new Britain increasingly linked to Prince Henry, an aggressive supporter of European Protestantism. Frances Yates argues that *"Cymbeline* would reflect the time just before Prince Henry's death when great adventures were planned by the Prince, acting in concert with his sister's future husband. After some bold, successful venture of a military character, a wide solution of universal peace would be established, an ending of the 'jars' in religion. . . . The great peace is not King James's idea of a peace of appeasement through marrying one half of his family into the Spanish-Hapsburg side. It is Prince Henry's idea of a peace to be achieved through defeating that side and afterwards arranging a universal religious peace, an ending of all religious jars" (*Shakespeare's Last Plays: A New Approach* [London: Routledge and Kegan Paul, 1975], 53–54).

22. Alexander Leggatt notes that "Cymbeline's extraordinary act of submission shows that he is in tune with the new age of peace" ("The Island of Miracles: An Approach to *Cymbeline*," *Shakespeare Studies* 10 [197]: 207).

23. Parker, "Romance and Empire," 193.

24. David Bergeron argues that "both in name and in character Posthumus Leonatus seems the most Roman of the British characters" ("Shakespeare's Last Roman Play," 36). Robert Miola claims that Posthumus learns to "reconcile his British heart with his Roman arms," a process which Miola sees as crucial because he believes that "in the best of [the British characters] Roman pride is balanced by humility, Roman courage by the qualities of mercy and forgiveness, Roman constancy by a capacity for flexibility, growth, and change" (*Shakespeare's Rome*, 212; 207).

25. Kahn, *Roman Shakespeare*, 161.

26. Leah Marcus points out that "James's descent from Henry gave him the right to the English throne; his identification with the first Tudor was so intense that when he died he was, at his own wish, buried in Henry VII's tomb" ("Unease of Topicality," 148).

27. For a good discussion of the Italianate features of the scene that ostensibly takes place in ancient Rome, see Olsen, "Iachimo's 'Drug-Damn'd Italy,' " 273–75; Olsen calls the scene "one of the least specific and most over-determined Italian settings in Shakespeare's *oeuvre*" (274).

28. Reading *Cymbeline* against the backdrop of Rome's vexed position in early modern British historiography, Olsen argues that Italy serves as a scapegoat for Roman vice: "the Roman cultural pollution with which the historiographers contended, whether Julius Caesar's subtlety or the invaders' general love of luxury, attachees itself instead to Iachimo and 'drug damn'd Italy' " ("Iachimo's 'Drug-Damn'd Italy,' " 282). I differ from Olsen here in my contention, outlined above beginning on p. 195, that the Italian anachronism, far from containing Italian vice, unleashes it on both Britain and Rome.

29. For a rich discussion of Jacobean England's sense of itself as heir to the Roman Empire, see Woodbridge, "Palisading," esp. 342–45.

30. Parker, "Romance and Empire," 206–7.

31. *Cymbeline*, ed. J. M. Nosworthy (London and New York: Routledge, 1969), xlv.

32. Knight, *Crown of Life*, 165–66.

33. Comparing the Renaissance sense of the past to that of earlier periods, Rackin argues that "what distinguishes the Renaissance is the *sense* of anachronism, the recognition of temporal distance that alienated a nostalgic present from a lost historical past" (*Stages of History: Shakespeare's English Chronicles* [Ithaca: Cornell University Press, 1990], 91).

34. Rackin, *Stage of History*, 94.

35. *The Scholemaster*, ed. John E.B. Mayor (London: Bell and Daldy, 1863; rpt., New York: AMS Press, 1967), 69.

36. *Scholemaster*, 88.

37. *A Quip for an Upstart Courtier; or, A Quaint Dispute Between Veluet-Breeches and Cloth-Breeches*, in *The Harleian Miscellany*, vol. 2 (London, 1809), 216.

38. *Quip*, 222.

39. *Scholemaster*, 73–74.

40. Palmer, *An Essay of the Meanes how to make our Travailes, into forraine Countries, the more profitable and honourable* (London, 1606), 44. The reference to Ireland is relevant. Like Italy, Ireland was one of the oppositional sites against which English identity took shape in the early seventeenth century. It is not surprising that these places, designed to create by antithesis a heightened awareness of English superiority, should also threaten to dissolve English identity, or to reveal it as inextricably connected to that which it seeks to deny. Ireland's "savagery" and Italy's "hypercivility" are characteristics that the English abhor in themselves and project outward. As Peter Stallybrass and Allon White suggest, the Other originates in and can never be wholly separated from the agent that invents and demonizes it: "A recurrent pattern emerges: the 'top' attempts to reject and eliminate the 'bottom' for reasons of prestige and status, only to discover, not only that it is in some way frequently dependent upon that low-Other . . . but also that the top *includes* that low symbolically, as a primary eroticized constituent of its own fantasy life. The result is a mobile, conflictual fusion of power, fear, and desire in the construction of subjectivity: a psychological *dependence* on precisely those Others which are being rigorously opposed and excluded at the social level" (*The Politics and Poetics of Transgression* [Ithaca: Cornell University Press, 1986], 5).

41. For a further discussion of the discursive links between Italy and Ireland in English thinking, see Ann Rosalind Jones, "Italians and Others: Venice and the Irish in *Coryat's Crudities* and *The White Devil*," *Renaissance Drama* 18 (1987): 101–19.

42. The phrase is David Bergeron's, in the title of his article.

43. Patricia Parker shrewdly contextualizes this scene in terms of an Italian mercantile rhetoric that represents the world as comprised of negotiable commodities. "Iachimo himself is a patently Italian Renaissance merchant disguised as Roman nobility, as all his language of trade and 'diseased adventures' (in both senses) suggests" (*Literary Fat Ladies: Rhetoric, Gender, Property* [London: Methuen, 1987], 134–35).

44. *Scholemaster*, 73.

45. Discussing rape in a number of Shakespeare texts, including *Cymbeline*, Georgianna Ziegler persuasively outlines a representational tradition that identifies woman as her private room, with the result that "the man's forced or stealthy

entry of this room constitutes a rape of her private space" ("My lady's chamber: female space, female chastity in Shakespeare," *Textual Practice* 4 [1990]: 73). Woodbridge is also excellent both on Iachimo's metaphorical rape of Imogen and on the more general concern with the permeability of various kinds of boundaries in *Cymbeline* (see "Palisading," esp. 333–35).

46. Arguing that Iachimo's intrusion has major significance for Imogen's control of her own identity, Susan Frye convincingly demonstrates that the textiles in Imogen's bedchamber "function as emblems of her identity and agency": "the play stages the way in which privileged women surrounded themselves with texts and textiles as the means to articulate their identity both for themselves and for the limited audience of those who might enter these interior spaces." Frye argues that while textiles permit Imogen to articulate a rich sense of selfhood, they also "ask us to consider the extent to which the male appropriation and interpretation of women's textiles silences the women of the plays and allows men violent access to the female bodies that they seek to possess" (Frye, forthcoming).

47. Speaking of Iachimo's appearance in Imogen's chamber, Alexander Leggatt notes a comic dimension to the scene: "I have seen four productions of *Cymbeline*, and on each occasion Iachimo's emergence from the trunk was greeted with laughter. For a modern audience, he suggests a jack-in-the-box; for a Jacobean audience, he would probably have suggested a comically old-fashioned devil popping up through the trap door" ("Island of Miracles," 195). To me the laughter associated with this scene can be understood as a response to the perceived threat of the Italian within. Yet as my notion of complicity suggests, the threat of the Italian points to English traits, or in this case to a recognition that Iachimo's misogyny can stand as well for Posthumus's actions and desires.

48. For a discussion of the queen as the Italianate Machiavel and Cloten as the English Ape figure, see Olsen, "Iachimo's 'Drug-Damn'd Italy,' " 287–90.

49. See plays by Webster, Middleton, and Ford, for example.

50. Fynes Moryson, *Shakespeare's Europe* (London, 1903, rpt., New York: Benjamin Blom, 1967), 405.

51. *Quip*, 222.

52. Moryson, *Shakespeare's Europe*, 404.

53. Ronald Boling argues that Cymbeline is primarily concerned with protecting the cultural capital that accrues to Britain through association with Rome: "Cymbeline ultimately desires reconciliation with Rome and offers concessions to gain it" ("Anglo-Welsh Relations in *Cymbeline*," *Shakespeare Quarterly* 51 [2000]: 51).

54. Meeting Posthumus right after the battle, the Lord has already popularized the sons' exploits into a pithy saw: "This was strange chance: / A narrow lane, and an old man, and two boys" (5.3.51–52).

55. Scholars agree that from around 1610 to Henry's death two years later, James and Henry were associated with different ideas about the role Britain should play in Europe. James aimed to be the pivotal figure who would engineer peace first between England and Spain and then between Europe's warring Catholic and Protestant factions. Henry, by contrast, was associated with those who favored more active British involvement on the side of European Protestantism. David Bergeron says that "those disgruntled with James, those yearning for a Protestant union of Europe, those itching for war—all rallied to the cause and hope of Henry" (*Royal Family, Royal Lovers: King James of England and Scotland* [Colum-

bia and London: University of Missouri Press, 1991], 97–98). Frances Yates notes the prince's extraordinary cultural appeal: "[T]here was . . . in this early Jacobean period a movement which might be called an Elizabethan revival, and which was particularly associated with James's eldest son, Prince Henry" (*Shakespeare's Last Plays*, 19). Contemporary reports suggest that James was less than wholly enthusiastic about the adulation of the Prince of Wales. During the celebrations for Henry's investiture as Prince of Wales, Henry was not permitted to ride on horseback into London; according to the Venetian ambassador, "The reason is the question of expense or, as some say, because they did not desire to exalt him too high" (*Calendar of State Papers, Venice, Vol. XI, 1607–1610*, 507).

56. For compelling scholarship reading *Cymbeline* in the context of the debate on Anglo-Scottish union, see Redmond, " 'My Lord, I Fear,' " and especially Floyd-Wilson, "Cymbeline, the Scots, and the English Race."

57. Coward, *The Stuart Age* (London: Longman, 1994), 106.

58. *The Parliamentary or Constitutional History of England*, V (1763), 178. The quotation is also reproduced in Coward, *The Stuart Age*, 137.

59. Coward, *The Stuart Age*, 138.

60. Michael Redmond also notes the significance of the united flags in an anti-union context. See " 'My Lord, I Fear,' " 307–8.

61. Roger Lockyer has suggested that in some quarters, the Anglo-Scottish union plan was seen as a type of conquest of the kingdom that would in fact abrogate the ancient constitution and give all legislative power to the king. Lockyer quotes an anti-union pamphlet that argues, "the change of style will be, as it were, the erecting of a new kingdom, and so it shall be, as it were, a kingdom conquered, and then may the King add laws and alter laws at his pleasure" (*James VI and I* [London and New York: Longman, 1998], 56).

62. Mikalachki calls Wales "the last preserve and final retreat of pure Britishness" (*The Legacy of Boadicea: Gender and nation in early modern England* [London and New York: Routledge, 1998], 105).

63. Mikalachki's phrase comes from the title of her *Shakespeare Quarterly* article, and is reproduced as a chapter title in her book.

64. Mikalachki genders the origin of British civilization by reading it alongside the disempowerment of Imogen. Extending Phyllis Rackin's insight that "the incorporation of the feminine represents the end of the historical process," Mikalachki argues that "in the romance of national origins, the dis-incorporation of the feminine is the place where history starts" ("Masculine Romance," 321, n.62). On Imogen's transformation, Janet Adelman notes that "the Imogen [Posthumus] leaves behind is a powerful and powerfully passionate woman, the only heir to a king; the Imogen he returns to is the faithful page of a defeated soldier, about to lose her kingdom to her brother" (*Suffocating Mothers: Fantasies of Maternal Origin in Shakespeare's Last Plays, Hamlet to The Tempest* [New York and London: Routledge, 1992], 209). Adelman powerfully argues that the disempowerment of Imogen is a function of the play's deep suspicion of the feminine; she sees it as compensation for the initial "loss of masculine identity through excessive trust in women" (194).

65. Discussing "mollis aer," Mary Floyd-Wilson suggests that it represents the civilizing power of Britain, symbolized by Imogen, and that Posthumus is "clearly identified as the object of Britain's civilizing embrace" ("*Cymbeline*, the Scots, and the English Race," forthcoming).

66. As Bergeron notes, once Cloten and the Roman army bear down on Wales, "the world starts reaching in to touch the lives of the Belarius household" (*Shakespeare's romances and the Royal Family* [Lawrence: University Press of Kansas, 1985], 153).

67. Valerie Wayne suggests that her physicality is here being marshaled into the service of a procreative marital economy. I agree, and would stress that the sexual generativity of these lines opens up the issue of the female body's disruptiveness to a masculinist polity. As Rackin notes, the woman's role in bearing the children who will inherit political legitimacy and power disturbs many early modern patriarchalists: "Authorized by the principle of patrilineal inheritance, patriarchal society depended for its very existence on the wives and mothers within whose bodies that inheritance was transmitted from father to son" (*Stages,* 160). In *Cymbeline,* even as Britain seems poised to embark on an all-male historical journey, Imogen's physicality represents the (not so) repressed knowledge that historical enterprises depend on women's bodies. Through her physicality, then, Imogen will always trouble the masculine political order that worked to disincorporate her. In my thinking about Imogen's insistent physicality, I am indebted to Valerie Wayne's thought-provoking comments and questions.

68. Kahn, *Roman Shakespeare,* 17.

69. "Palisading," 329.

70. Kahn, *Roman Shakespeare,* 18.

71. The inevitability of change over time is evident in the death of Fidele and in the earlier death of the boys' mother Euriphile. As the brothers say in their dirge for Fidele, "The scepter, learning, physic, must / All follow this and come to dust" (4.2.269–70). Although Fidele is later restored to the brothers in the form of their long-lost sister Imogen, nothing brings back their dead mother or alters the fact of mortality. The transience of human power lingers as a potent context in the very Welsh scenes where access to human power is being furiously contested.

72. For a discussion of Stuart grandees, particularly Robert Carr, as collectors, see A. R. Braunmuller, "Robert Carr, Earl of Somerset, as collector and patron," in *The Mental World of the Jacobean Court,* 230–50. For Arundel as a collector, see David Howarth, *Lord Arundel and his Circle* (New Haven and London: Yale University Press, 1985).

73. See Ruth Saunders Magurn, trans. and ed., *The Letters of Peter Paul Rubens* (Evanston, IL: Northwestern University Press, 1991), 321–22. The excerpt is from a letter of August 9, 1629.

REVIEWS

A Feminist Companion to Shakespeare
Edited by Dympna C. Callaghan
Oxford: Blackwell Publishers, Inc., 2000

Reviewer: Lisa Hopkins

The idea of a feminist companion to Shakespeare is an attractive one, and it has resulted in an attractive volume, pleasingly substantial and handsomely packaged. Dympna Callaghan sets the tone strongly in her introduction, where she comments that "this volume aims to push ahead with uncomfortable questions rather than to offer reassuring answers" (xiii), and concludes by observing that the last essay of the volume, Philippa Berry's "Between Idolatry and Astrology: Modes of Temporal Repetition in *Romeo and Juliet*," suggests the distance feminism has traveled from 'images of women' " (xxix). Indeed, what primarily characterizes these essays is their diversity and the extent of the terrain they traverse: feminism is by no means all that is touched on here.

It is a pity that Callaghan, a very fine critic, did not provide an essay herself, but there is still much to enjoy. The best essays are driven not by ideology but by close, detailed observations of individual texts, and paradoxically tend to offer arguments that look, at the outset, like the precise inverse of those more traditionally associated with cruder and earlier kinds of feminist criticism. Thus, Katherine M. Romack's subtle "Margaret Cavendish, Shakespeare Critic" argues that Cavendish herself was in fact antifeminist, and Phyllis Rackin in "Misogyny is Everywhere" refreshingly and provocatively argues that "reminders that women were expected to be chaste, silent, and obedient probably occur more frequently in recent scholarship than they did in the literature of Shakespeare's time" (44). Mihoko Suzuki observantly compares the treatment of gender and class in *Much Ado Abut Nothing* and *Twelfth Night* with that in *Arden of Faversham* and *A Warning for Fair Women*, while Rachana Sachdev interestingly analyzes travel writings in

220   Reviews

conjunction with medical knowledge, particularly that centered on the practice of female circumcision, with special reference to *The Tempest*. Her argument ultimately becomes tendentious, but this is full of fascinating incidental facts and observations. Susan Zimmerman is equally fascinating on corpses and corpse lore in relation to *Macbeth*, and M. Lindsay Kaplan neatly and suggestively reads Jewishness and femininity against each other in *The Merchant of Venice*.

Other essays form pairs, and though it is clear that in some cases this cannot have been originally intended, it nevertheless leads to some suggestive conjunctions. Thus Margo Hendricks's " 'A word, sweet Lucrece': Confession, Feminism, and *The Rape of Lucrece*," which has a particularly interesting section on confession, forms a neat twin with Joyce Green MacDonald's wide-ranging and subtle "Black Ram, White Ewe: Shakespeare, Race, and Women," and Jyotsna Singh's analysis of gift-giving in *The Merchant of Venice* sits well alongside Ania Loomba's stylish and sophisticated discussion of "The Great Indian Vanishing Trick—Colonialism, Property, and the family in *A Midsummer Night's Dream*." And there is a neat irony in having Denise Albanese's attack on Jude Kelly's photonegative *Othello* followed by Juliet Dusinberre's suggestion of universal cross-dressing. In conjunctions like this, this volume becomes more than the sum of its parts.

Theatre and Humanism: English Drama in the Sixteenth Century
By Kent Cartwright
Cambridge: Cambridge University Press, 1999

Reviewer: Sheila T. Cavanagh

Kent Cartwright's *Theatre and Humanism: English Drama in the Sixteenth Century* is a detailed and erudite volume that provides an intriguing reassessment of English drama in the century preceding

Shakespeare. Cartwright begins his study with a familiar but important question, asking how this drama progressed so rapidly from being "allegorical, didactic, and moralistic," to being "censured as emotional, fantasy-arousing, and even immoral" (1). In his well-considered response, he suggests convincingly that "the excitement of the Tudor stage derives partly from a humanist dramaturgy that embroils feelings and emotions in the creation of meaning" (1). Although the argument that follows is often too dense to absorb without paying close attention, it rewards the patient reader with an abundance of information and a thought-provoking interpretation of a dramatic corpus that is often neglected. In sum, *Theatre and Humanism* offers a valuable accounting of sixteenth-century English drama that illuminates significant aspects of these plays that generally have been overlooked.

Much of Cartwright's argument focuses upon his reconsideration of the divide critics often locate between "popular" and "humanist" plays. Commonly, the former compositions have been perceived as being fairly inconsequential entertainments, while the latter plays have been considered dull and moralistic. Cartwright reexamines these responses, positing, a closer correspondence between the two forms than has generally been recognized and a richer theatrical content than standard conceptualizations of the drama would suggest. As his thesis unfolds, Cartwright provides detailed synopses of these plays, which are likely to help spark renewed interest in a number of these playwrights and their creations. In the aftermath of this vitalizing formulation, sixteenth-century drama should command deservedly increased attention.

The book consists of a lengthy introduction followed by eight meaty chapters and a short afterword. Although these sections work well as individual essays, they provide the most compelling presentation of Cartwright's thesis when read in their entirety. Each chapter highlights texts and authors that demonstrate how this drama defies simplistic characterization. Chapter 1, "The Humanism of Acting: John Heywood's *The Foure PP*," for instance, stresses the changes evident between medieval morality plays that "reproduce a system of allegorical correspondences [that] depend on straightforward acting" and "sixteenth-century drama's shift toward humanist and secular subjects [that] privileged ambiguity in a character's presentation" (25). Focusing on the ways that humanist tenets unexpectedly affected drama, Cartwright argues that "*The Foure PP* unfolds, principally, by shifting the spectator's attention from theology to character and performance" (29) and that *"The Foure PP* demands from its spectators increasing sophistication in discerning its characters' qualities and meanings" (32). By emphasizing, for example, the range of acting choices available in this play, particularly for the character of the Palmer, Cartwright begins to situate these productions in closer proximity to Elizabethan and Jacobean drama than is usually recognized.

Subsequent chapters expand the scope of this reorientation. The second chapter, for instance—"Wit and Science and the Dramaturgy of Learning"—discusses the strategies used in humanist drama "to encourage the spectators' emotional embrace of the transformative vision of education" (49). Drawing from a range of plays, by writers such as John Redford, John Rastell, John Skelton, and William Wager, Cartwright describes ways that these playwrights made learning "emotionally compelling" (50). Observing that these compositions cannot purport to offer the kind of irrefutable truths presented in morality plays, for example, he astutely argues that they instead seek "to heighten the audience's emotional engagement with the protagonist in his struggle for self-knowledge" (55). According to this argument, the incorporation into these plays of highly theatrical components, such as costumes, music, song, and dance, become effective means to achieve this kind of engagement with the audience. Although Cartwright admits that the focus of this chapter, John Redford's "Wit and Science," is primarily a "delightful and amusing schoolboy farce," he gives a convincing account of the play in the context of "the affective power of humanist dramaturgy" (74).

Chapter 3, "Playing Against Type: *Gammer Gurton's Needle*," explores what Cartwright terms "humanist playmaking's under-appreciated theatrical vitality and inventiveness" (75). Claiming that "didacticism now turns playfully ironic as the play explores theatre's emotional life" (75), he offers an interesting interpretation of *Gammer Gurton*'s methodology and achievements. This analysis also expands upon his overall thesis. Placing this play in the "interstices of Roman form" (76), for instance, he presents a compelling reading of *Gammer Gurton* that reveals the drama's delightful ambiguities, its "sense of openness and [its] ironic possibility" (99). By showing that *Gammer Gurton* resists "simple-minded didacticism" (99), Cartwright further demonstrates the complexity and theatrical sophistication that is often overlooked in drama from this era.

The remaining five essays offer similarly valuable revisions of traditional conceptualizations of sixteenth century drama. The middle chapters (4 and 5) discuss a number of plays within two broad topics: "Time, Tyranny, and Suspense in Political Drama of the 1560s" and "Humanism and the Dramatizing of Women." The last three chapters, in contrast, focus predominantly upon specific plays; namely, *Gallathea, Tamburlaine, Part 1,* and *Friar Bacon and Friar Bungay.* These chapters will prove useful to scholars working on a variety of early modern literary topics. "Time, Tyranny, and Suspense," for example, looks at the many intersections between political concerns and theatrical interests during the early years of Elizabeth's reign. Cartwright demonstrates that plays changed considerably during this period as "dramatic effect spill[ed] beyond didacticism to emphasize narrative complexity, psychological agitation, and Senecan sensationalism" (101). Discussing *Gorboduc, Damon and Pithias,* and a few related plays, he illustrates the increasing maturity of these dramas that accompanies the "infusion of humanist historical awareness into allegorical and mythic narrative" (133).

"Humanism and the Dramatizing of Women" then suggests that humanist drama has not been recognized for its contribution to "the achievement in Renaissance theatre of individualized women characters" (135). Providing an extremely valuable overview of the characterization of women in these plays, Cartwright gives his readers the historical accounting they will need to best appreciate his fascinating chapter on *Gallathea.* This essay, in combination with its preceding chapter, not only offers a valuable corrective to many misapprehensions about the representation of women in these plays, it also successfully advances Cartwright's contention that standard distinctions between humanist plays and those termed popular stem from inadequate understandings of the intersections between these interrelated dramatic forms. Although this chapter focuses specifically upon John Lyly, therefore, it engages with a wide range of issues. As Cartwright remarks: "Moving Lyly back from the margins of dramatic history and toward popular Elizabethan theatre, moreover, hints at the larger possibility of integrating Renaissance intellectual values with the appreciation of the theatre's material life" (193).

The final two chapters similarly perform double duty, by expanding our understanding of *Tamburlaine, Part 1* and *Friar Bacon and Friar Bungay,* respectively, at the same time that they address a host of broader questions. Thus, the Marlowe essay considers numerous issues involving spectatorship, both within the play and in Elizabethan England, and the last chapter uses *Friar Bacon and Friar Bungay* to demonstrate "how commercial drama in the late 1580s could exploit humanist techniques of imitation, allusion, and analogy to attract repeat playgoers to an emergent fixed-venue theatre" (222). While this final chapter may not prompt revivals of Greene's play, it provides a fittingly thoughtful culmination to Cartwright's impressive volume. By the time the reader has completed these chapters, s/he will find it difficult to approach any of these plays again without being influenced by the insights and arguments presented here. Although the text's prose is often hampered by the necessary inclusion of multiple citations from these largely unfamiliar plays, *Theatre and Humanism* is an important study of this topic. Kent Cartwright deserves our gratitude for providing such a thoughtful, learned, and provocative work.

Whores of Babylon: Catholicism, Gender, and Seventeenth-Century Print Culture
By Frances E. Dolan
Ithaca: Cornell University Press, 1999

Reviewer: Jeffrey Knapp

If Frances Dolan had not called her first book *Dangerous Familiars*, she might well have used that title for her new effort, *Whores of Babylon: Catholicism, Gender and Seventeenth-Century Print Culture*. Both books concern domestic perils in Renaissance England: for *Dangerous Familiars*, the hazard at issue is crimes committed by ostensible subordinates, which is to say, wives and servants; for *Whores of Babylon*, the internal threat is English Catholicism. Compellingly, Dolan refuses to cordon off one danger from the other: fear of enemies who neither looked nor sounded different from friends often caused Protestants, in Dolan's account, to "associate

Catholic conspiracy with the intimate rebellion of a wife within the household rather than with the invasion of a rival foreign power" (56). *Whores of Babylon* focuses on the "paradoxical" efforts of seventeenth-century English anti-Catholics to demonize "a church run by powerful, celibate men by associating it with the feminine" (60).

Dolan is extremely well-informed about half of this relationship between religion and gender in seventeenth-century England. One could hardly imagine a more thorough and judicious survey of the scholarship on gender in the period than *Whores of Babylon* supplies. Yet, aside from its discussion of the Virgin Mary in chapter 3, the book tells us almost nothing about the religious beliefs that inflamed Protestants against Catholics in the first place. Dolan appears to have decided that she could overlook these beliefs because her subject is the anti-Catholic "imagination," in particular the "fantasies and representations" that "linked Catholics and Catholicism to disorderly women" (4). But, surely, perceived differences in ecclesiology and doctrine must have crucially affected how Catholics represented themselves and how they were represented by Protestants. To exclude theology from a study of a "cultural imaginary" (157) has the further negative effect of implying that "fantasies and representations" played no part in the doctrinal debates of the period.

At times in *Whores of Babylon*, Dolan seems inconsistent about what counts as imaginary and what as real. She begins the book by explaining that, whereas she had once viewed court records as "reliable" evidence, she now regards them as " 'representations' that we must read with caution" (2–3). Dolan urges scholars to exercise the same "suspicion" when examining historical events such as the "purported" Gunpowder Plot (3); taking her skepticism still further, she argues that, since there is no accessible " 'real problem' " behind representations, we should turn our attention to the "representational process" (84) itself. But this last, extreme position leads her into contradictions. For instance, to maintain as she does that English law was "no less fictional" a form of anti-Catholicism than other "stories England told itself about who its enemies were" (32) is to assume (unsuspiciously, from the Protestant perspective) that no English Catholics represented any real threat to England whatsoever. Conversely, Dolan wants to disagree with the historians who "dismiss [Queen] Henrietta Maria as more interested in people than in politics" (130), but if all evidence is merely representational and therefore fictional, on what grounds can she dispute such an interpretation?

The more difficult problem Dolan faces in *Whores of Babylon* is how to avoid reaching predictable conclusions about the imagination of gender in seventeenth-century England. As she notes, the Protestant "strategy of representing difference and disorder through the person of the unruly woman [was] hardly unique to reformers or, later, anti-Catholic polemicists" (52). Over the course of her book, therefore, Dolan offers a variety of reasons for believing that the anti-Catholic scapegoating of women deserves special attention. Perhaps the weakest of these rationales is Dolan's claim that "debates around Catholicism brought to the fore contradictions in the prevailing ideologies of gender, sexuality, and the family" (49). Since we now take these contradictions for granted, it is not clear why we should be interested in some previously unremarked expressions of them. This is a problem that particularly besets Dolan in her chapter on Elizabeth Cellier, the midwife charged in the Meal-Tub Plot with conspiring to turn Protestants against Presbyterians rather than Catholics. Cellier's story is a fascinating one: thanks almost exclusively to her own efforts, she was acquitted of treason; she then wrote a book about her trial, *Malice Defeated*, which she distributed from her own home; the book caused her to be tried once again, and this time she was convicted of libel. Unfortunately, Dolan can find nothing in Cellier's life to suggest that Cellier was able to change or broaden her culture's "options for representing women as agents and authors" (164): in Dolan's account, Cellier was simply pushed "to the limits of the available options" (173).

A stronger approach for Dolan is her argument in chapter 3 that Catholic defenses of the Virgin Mary and her devotee, Henrietta Maria, "countered the sweeping misogyny of Protestant writers, creating the possibility of a positive discussion of women's contributions" (116). Yet Dolan provides us little more than her assertion that Protestant writers were more misogynistic than Catholics; at the same time, the obvious exceptionalness of Mary and the queen makes it difficult for us to envision what kind of "possibility" these two figures created for other women. Although Dolan insists that Catholic "defenses of the Virgin Mary and Henrietta Maria undermined Protestant England—with all its purported investment in spiritual equality and companionate marriage—more successfully than Guy Fawkes could do with his barrels of powder" (131), the claim seems dubious on at least four counts: first, Dolan had earlier asked us to doubt whether Fawkes had even been involved in the Gunpowder Plot; second, his barrels never exploded, so they represent a fairly empty standard of action or influence; third, Dolan never undertakes the project of determining whether Protestants generally, not just in regard to the Virgin Mary or Henrietta Maria, supported spiritual equality and companionate marriage less or more than Catholics did; and most important, Dolan never provides any evidence that the defenses in question actually shook the faith of any English Protestant on any issue.

The most illuminating section of Dolan's book is her discussion in chapter two of "Jacobean Penal Laws and the Problem of the Recusant Wife." As Dolan impressively demonstrates, Protestants grew increasingly concerned about the power of Catholic women to teach Catholicism in their households and otherwise support Catholic evangelism; yet, Dolan asks, how could English law hold English wives responsible for their religious dissidence "without dismantling the legal fiction of coverture, which had become the model of right relations not only in the household but in the nation and the cosmos" (136)? This is truly absorbing scholarship, and Dolan improves upon it with her account in chapter 3 of Elizabeth Cary, whose life illustrates "the problem of the recusant wife" so remarkably.

Whores of Babylon does not often relate its findings on Catholicism and women to the imaginative literature of the period. The major exception is Dolan's brief analysis of *Macbeth* and *Antony and Cleopatra,* which begins very promisingly: Dolan points out that scholars who invoke the Gunpowder Plot in their account of *Macbeth* never ask why the play "dramatizes treason not as a conspiracy among men but as a collusion between husband and wife" (77). Dolan's own responses to the question prove too abstract and allegorical to be convincing, however: for instance, she maintains that Antony's "inability to reconcile" his ties to Rome and Egypt "resembles" the "dilemma of Catholic subjects in a Protestant country" (82), yet, at such a level of generality, one might make the same claim about any representation of divided allegiance in any play. Dolan's readings of Shakespeare and inquiries into seventeenth-century Christianity may not be richly detailed, then, but her historical research on gender certainly is, and *Whores of Babylon* deserves attention on that count.

Showing Like a Queen: Female Authority and Literary Experiment in Spenser, Shakespeare, and Milton
By Katherine Eggert
Philadelphia: University of Pennsylvania Press, 2000

Reviewer: Coppélia Kahn

This is a big, impressive book, rich in implications for how we read the canon—how we conceive the gendered entitlements that underpin early modern authorship and conceptions of poetic and political power. Eggert takes her starting point from the prevailing critical tendency to read political imperatives as aesthetic imperatives, to make "the pervasive cultural presence of the queen" (as Louis Adrian Montrose phrased it) the determining and also disabling factor for male writers. Acknowledging that Elizabeth's anomalous power produced a discourse of "anxious masculinity" in the works of those who sought her patronage, as Montrose and many others have persuasively argued, Eggert declares that "it is time to go further." She does so by sidestepping the one to one alignment of ascribed gender with authority (the female ruler) and authorship (the male writer). Instead, she attends to gender as figurative and dynamic, produced by discursive constructions and above all by the kinds of transformations that gifted literary imaginations can effect.

"Femininity, for the Renaissance," she declares, "is a state of mind: a mind that is . . . disorderly, unstable, unwilling to remain within acceptable bounds or to focus upon acceptable aims" (10). In this view the feminine, especially the "pervasive cultural presence" of Elizabeth's feminine rule, provided a fertile environment for literary experimentation, for the re-imagining of both genres and genders: "For the authorial voice can escape the very conditions of hierarchy if it imagines itself not solely as *reversing* the circumstances of queenly rule over men . . . but rather as *inhabiting* the circumstances of queenly rule, so that the authorial voice dwells within and embraces the feminized form, becoming itself master-mistress of authorial presence" (13).

Not that in treating gender as a discursive or imaginative formation Eggert fails to pay attention to "the circumstances of queenly rule over men"; quite the opposite. She is fully alert to the "tension between historical circumstance and literary form" (20), weaving into her interpretation of the latter numerous ironic, oblique, revealing instances of the former. Her chapter on *Hamlet,* subtitled "Queenship, Succession, and Revenge Tragedy," presents an excellent example of this dual astuteness. Pausing at Claudius's familiar epithet for Gertrude, "imperial jointress," Eggert explores the legal privileges conferred by, and the political implications of, jointure (by which a widow was entitled to the use of more than the customary one-third of her deceased husband's lands and income, and could be surer of holding onto it than she could a dower). Ironically enough, beginning in Henry VII's reign, Eggert explains, the queen consort could "administer her own jointure lands, maintain her own household, preside over her own Council, and make use of her own royal seal" (105). Thus, rather than Claudius it is Gertrude as jointress who has "popp'd in between th'election" and Hamlet's hopes, obstructing and complicating the succession, which can no longer be the "closed, well-knit, concise" compact of male-male inheritance but has been put "out of joint" for Hamlet by the woman who is not only his mother but who, "conjunctive to [his uncle's] life and soul," has in effect conferred the state of Denmark upon him by bringing him her jointure in marriage. In a double sense, Eggert argues, "Hamlet's identity lies not within an inheritance from his father . . . but in his being the subject of a queen" (110)—a queen who is, nonetheless, the occasion for his famous subjectivity, "that seething, melancholic, basically formless morass of grief, bitterness, and despair that is brought on by her marriage" (112). Forced by this morass to meditate on the revenger's role rather than carry it out, Hamlet winds up reinventing the revenge tragedy, "in the space opened up by the suspension of masculine rule" (115). Eggert adds yet another dimension to Hamlet's invention of a new literary form by viewing it in the light of the boys' companies' revivals of old revenge tragedies (including *The Spanish Tragedy* around 1600, which was then owned by Shakespeare's company). She provocatively suggests that in writing a new kind of revenge tragedy Shakespeare is competing not against Kyd but rather against the boys, "troupes in an eternal state of adolescence" something akin to Hamlet's arrested development as son and revenger (124). Thus, in seeking out new discursive figurations of female authority, Eggert remains closely in touch with social and historical formations of female and feminized authority.

Yet as fresh and illuminating as these new figurations are, to some extent Eggert too works from the same paradigm of politics determined by aesthetics, in constructions linked directly to the queen's overt, inescapable gender identity and heavily infected by conventionally masculine devaluations of the feminine. For example, the chapter on Book 5 of *The Faerie Queene,* which addresses the question of why that book swerves away from romance into a historical allegory that most critics have found artistically unsatisfying, identifies the same dynamic of bewitching, emasculating female power and male recoil that preoccupies Montrose et al. Romance, like the feminine, is diffuse, inconclusive, meandering, effeminizing—all terms that evoke the aging Elizabeth's womanish willfulness and maddening ambivalence as a ruler. Thus, Eggert suggests, Spenser seeks in historical allegory an escape from both the inconclusiveness of romance and of the queen he serves. Book 5, then, seems the worst-case scenario of Eggert's argument: the feminine provokes a literary experiment that fails. She maintains, however, that it's not so much a failure as a illustration of the futility of trying to make allegory impose a univocal closure on the "messy and conflicting nature" of what the poem is trying to represent (49).

A key concept in the book is "ravishment"—the association of femininity with the kind of theatricality that "is fundamentally rapine, creating in its audience an absence of male self-possession, then . . . transferring its own licentious nature into the gap it has created" (60). Here, in one of Eggert's characteristically original and illuminating gender-bends, it is the females who ravish: notably, Joan of Arc, whose theatrical skill in verbal performance seduces her male audiences and renders them effectively impotent. In a further twist, Eggert sees Joan's ravishing performances reinvested in Richard III, who "integrates feminine theatrical method, in all its sexual bewitchment, into his own modus operandi" (71). Finally, it is the unimpeachably "masculine" Henry V who appropriates that originally feminine ravishment on behalf of an England purged of the feminine, to create "a legend of himself that . . . recalls the puissance of his forebears," a legend he embodies and projects, in ravishing fashion, into the minds of his countrymen and his audience (89).

The book's final chapter, on Milton, makes the most paradoxical (or as Eggert herself says, "eccentric") claims for the shaping presence of Elizabeth's rule and iconography in the divorce tracts, *A Mask at Ludlow Castle,* and *Paradise Lost.* Eggert persuades me of these claims, but even if she hadn't, in a larger sense she proves the limitations of treating Milton's (or Shakespeare's or Spenser's) idea of femininity according to ascribed, explicit, or conventional gender. Eggert constructs a Miltonic genealogy of the feminine in which "a virgin queen becomes a virgin Lady becomes an enfranchised husband becomes a free-thinking Eve" (180), a genealogy culminating in a reading of *Paradise Lost* that centers on "the contradictory character of Eve, who unlawfully usurps sovereignty within her marriage but who also inaugurates a future of human choice" (182). Consonant with Eggert's aim throughout the book, questions of femininity are closely bound up with questions of genre and literary experiment. Rejecting Spenserian romance not only for the well-known dangers of the genre per se, but also as the celebration of a female monarch who fashioned her court on the model of Arthurian romance, Milton evokes (and rejects) that celebration in Satan's ravishing address to Eve as "Goddess among Gods." Thus he prepares readers for Eve's unseemly sovereignty over the unwitting Adam. The poetry—even the prosody—of Eve's "Virgin Majesty," Eggert demonstrates, resonates strongly with tropes of the Virgin Queen. Nonetheless, Milton grants to Eve the queenly power to choose and to decide, and the heroic privilege of having her virtue tested. Here Eggert joins in the extended debate over whether Eve is Adam's equal at the same time that she is subject to his authority, or whether "her subjection is a necessary condition of her subjectivity" (193). Taking neither position, she argues instead that "Adam's subjectivity . . . comes into being . . . only because female will has *ab origine* been given away. . . . What there is of outward- and onward-directed human motion in the poem is entirely at Eve's instigation—not only the human fall into sin, but also their apprehension of choice, possibility, and even joy" (195).

This is an ambitious book that realizes its ambition: "to marry a new-historicist account of literature as a cultural form to a literary-historical account of the succession of texts" (20). Eggert's assimilation of scholarship in three vast fields—Shakespeare, Spenser, and Milton—is deep, generous, and thoughtful. It is equalled by her originality in discerning and bringing to light the counter-patriarchal fantasies of feminine power, both political and poetical, that animate some great works of Renaissance literature.

Early Modern Visual Culture: Representation, Race, and Empire in Renaissance England
Edited by Peter Erickson and Clark Hulse
Philadelphia: University of Pennsylvania Press, 2000

Reviewer: Jerry Brotton

This is an extremely ambitious collection of essays by some of the most distinguished scholars working in the field of early modern English studies. Editors Peter Erickson and Clark Hulse begin by arguing that "much of the innovative work being done in literary studies is undergoing a transformation toward the visual," at the same moment that art history has moved "toward the study of the social meaning of visual images" (1). So as much as the collection looks forward to new interpretative possibilities in the analysis of early modern visual culture, it also remains enmeshed in the critical fallout of the redefinition of the disciplinary boundaries of both art history and literary studies.

It is noticeable that the key contributors to this collection are all primarily trained as literary scholars, including the editors as well as Steven Mullaney, Valerie Traub, Harry Berger Jr., Stephen Orgel, and Kim Hall. This is in itself indicative of the critical energy that emanates from literary studies within the current field of Renaissance, or early modern studies, but at certain points *Early Modern Visual Culture* also reveals the limitations of literary critics colonizing the terrain of art historians. In most cases, this is an excellent group of essays, which show an impressive dialogue across each other. Steven Mullaney's "Imaginary Conquests: European Material Technologies and the Colonial Mirror Stage" represents some of Mullaney's most interesting work in recent years. Contrasting the material and visual culture of Northern European and the New World, Mullaney develops a provocative approach to the Americas as "a world with no history, meaning no history in relation to us; it was there for the taking, and the taking advantage of, on a scale of colonial plunder so unprecedented that it provided the surplus capital necessary . . . for the emergence of capitalism itself" (21).

This globalizing imperative is taken up by Valerie Traub in a critical discourse of "Mapping the Global Body," where the incorporation of figural representations on the borders of seventeenth-century maps "enacted a powerful universalizing logic" (85). However, the collection also offers a series of critical strategies for reading against the grain of these globalizing tendencies. Karen Dalton analyzes the classical, imperial connotations of the figure of the black emperor in the Drake jewel in "Art for the Sake of Dynasty." In one of the collection's most thoughtful essays, "Object into Object? Some Thoughts on the Presence of Black Women in Early Modern Culture," Kim Hall surveys a range of images of black women, which she ultimately sees "not as anonymous bodies on display for the pleasure of European men or as passive recipients of male wisdom, but as women who resist, talk back, and test the patriarch with 'hard questions'" (376).

There are some other fascinating contributions, including Stephen Orgel's elegant account of artistic connoisseurship in mid-seventeenth-century England, Ernest Gilman's detailed analysis of Anthony Van Dyck's so-called "Madagascar Portrait" of Thomas Howard, the earl of Arundel, and Clark Hulse's deft reading of Holbein's portrait of Cromwell (1532–33). The irony of the collection is that the weakest articles involve a closer interrogation of literary rather than strictly visual artifacts. Susan Frye's "Staging Women's Relations to Textiles in Shakespeare's *Othello* and *Cymbeline*" argues that in these plays "women tend to *become* the cloth rather than its producers and consumers" (221). This is a terrific idea but simply unsustainable through recourse to the plays, as Frye goes on to show by straining the texts to extravagant lengths. A basic distinction has to be made between large, narrative tapestry that hangs in Cymbeline's room (and pervades Spenser's *Faerie Queene,* which Frye neglects to mention) and the kind of intimate textiles (handkerchiefs and purses) used in *Othello.* Frye puzzlingly avoids any discussion of how *Cymbeline* is part of an *ekphrastic* tradition that unties literary and imperial dimensions that seem to be a more promising avenue of enquiry than the one pursued here. Similarly the very title of Peter Erickson's contribution, "'God for Harry, England, and Saint George': British National Identity and the Emergence of White Self-Fashioning," reveals lazy anachronism. Saint George is of course the patron saint of *England,* not Britain, as any closer inspection of either contemporary right-wing English political rhetoric or Hal's speeches in *Henry V* would quickly reveal.

Erickson's putative argument is that "Saint George gradually becomes racialized as it is applied to new commercial ventures in a widening international frame of reference. Under the pressure of this global outreach, Saint George as the symbol of British nationhood comes to be associated with racial whiteness" (314). Apart from a quotation from Michael Neill's discussion of the display of a Saint George banner in Java in 1604, there is little specific historical evidence for these grand claims. Both Carpaccio and Spenser's representation of Saint George in painting and literature of the sixteenth century suggest that George was much more a contested figure East and West between Christians and Muslims, a complication of issues of "race" and "ethnicity" that the better articles in this collection begin to "juggle" (to use Margaret Ferguson's suggestive phrase) more productively. This distinction captures the productive tension of *Early Modern Visual Culture*. Its better articles are alive to the complexities of *history* as much as visual culture, and if the study of visual culture is to blossom, then it is surely by addressing historical issues rather than retrenching back into literature.

Desiring Women Writing: English Renaissance Examples
By Jonathan Goldberg
Stanford, CA: Stanford University Press, 1997

Reviewer: Judith Butler

A characteristically elegant work, Jonathan Goldberg's *Desiring Women Writing* offers what might be taken to be a lesbian reading of some writings by women, or writings whose authorship may or may not be a woman's. It is a wonderful work precisely because Goldberg takes up some of the most important questions about authorship, sexuality, and reading in a knowing and innovative way, not only asking the question of what women's writing is, or whether or not a woman wrote a particular text, but showing us, in his refusal to answer, the difficulty that makes any easy answer impossible. I'm nevertheless more than tempted to say that this is a great work of lesbian scholarship. Goldberg's approach to these questions not only permits me to say it, but challenges his reader to think more than twice about reducing readings to identity positions. If this is great lesbian scholarship, then that does not mean that Goldberg is a lesbian, or it does not mean that precisely. His writerly voice becomes, in the manner he describes in the Renaissance women writers considered here, an occasion and vehicle for cross-gendered identification and desire. That his text, his writing, can become the vehicle for desires that Goldberg may or may not have makes the point rhetorically as well as thematically—that writerly voice is not only equivocal, but productively so, and that it is not reducible to sociological position or presumed gender identity. To the degree that one is tempted, too tempted perhaps, to say that this is a lesbian text, the seduction is partly Goldberg's fault—or, indeed, his virtue. He can and does read for lesbian desire not as the secret or final content or cipher of any of the texts he carefully considers here, but as that which is conditioned and "vehiculated" by the peregrinations of voice and perspective in the text itself.

The "vehicle" is no simple matter here, since the vechicle is not an empty vessel, a form that is indifferent to what it carries. On the contrary, Goldberg's work shows how certain desires are staged precisely through taking on a vehicle that would appear to dissimulate them, but where the vehicle itself turns out to be more resonant and equivocal than usually thought. In an analogous way, his own text bears a set of desires that may or may not be "his," but more importantly, his text trains us away from the habit of trying to find a univocal truth for authorial desire. The vehicle or the articulation is not ancillary to the desires in question. There is no psychological truth to which the textual production is reducible. As a result, the vehicle for desire becomes part of the very constitution of desire. And in this sense, his text becomes an exemplary instance of lesbian desire itself, showing us in particular how desire itself is fashioned through mechanisms of substitution and displacement.

I am ill-equipped to judge the scholarship of the period here, since I am not a reader of English Renaissance texts. But I would suggest that the framework and the readings provided brought me into an engagement with texts I did not know, and produced in me a desire to know them better. I hope this serves as a sign of the importance of this book not only, clearly, to the study of Renaissance women writers which others have and will surely confirm, but of the theory and practice of reading gender and sexuality that Goldberg so deftly and persuasively provides. Although not a moment of apologetic self-consciousness is ever displayed in these pages, at some point the reader has to remark that Goldberg, a "man," spends page after page considering in detail the writings of contemporary women scholars who have tried to understand what status to accord to English Renaissance women writers and how the legible voice is related to the problem of desire. He offers no self-justifying moves in this reading, which comes as a welcome relief. On the one hand, I am tempted to say, "what an incredible work of scholarship by a man," and then, I have to stop myself—for what am I assuming about Goldberg the author? Surely, his voice is also a site of enunciation for a complex set of identifications and desires.

Goldberg probes judiciously and incisively the questions of whether one can know or presume the desires of women on the basis of what they write, whether one can assume their dispossession and erasure, what the writing itself signifies about their capacity to assume power through voice, whether they are readable within contemporary feminist frameworks, how and in what way these writings compel us to rethink the relation between gender, desire, politics, and writing. His approach to contemporary scholars in this area is enormously respectful, but it also assumes that no defense of his own "position" is warranted or necessary. This way of proceeding constitutes a significant breath of fresh air. The presumption is—and the thesis for which he argues explicitly—is that there is more "crossing" than is generally understood, and that we ought not to presume an equivalence between social position and the range encompassed by authorial perspective. He cautions us, for instance, against the great-woman approach not only because of its uncritical relation to canonization, but because "women" are represented in these texts in a highly complicated interaction with the canon and with presumptive male authority.

He makes this point concretely in Part Two of the text, which is concerned explicitly with translation and, in particular, the secondary status of women as translators. That section begins with Florio's introduction to his translation of Montaigne, "all translations are reputed femalls, delivered at second hand." The identification of femaleness with secondariness, however, is not an historical constant, much less the occasion for a transhistorical frame. As Goldberg argues, "the opposition between original and secondary or imitative works is a categorical opposition largely absent in the Renaissance, the notion of original writing became valorized only later" (83). Here he works effectively with Patricia Parker's early work, engaging as well some of the disputes that followed the publication of Tom Laqueur's *Making Sex,* in which he tracks the historical shift from the one-sex to the two-sex "system." Laqueur treats this shift as a straightforward historical transition, claiming that there was once one sex and then came two—or, at least, a medical vocabulary that permitted for the recognition of a "twoness" in which female was not simply a (failed) permutation of male. Goldberg builds on some of the existing criticisms of this transition to argue that "the one" was only retrospectively made possible by virtue of the emergence of the second, the female, as its own specificity. Similarly, given the identification of translation with femininity and feminine practice, the very emergence of the "one" and its primacy is an effect made possible by the latter emergence of the "two." The "one" was, then, always a certain effect of doubling, in which case what takes place historically "later" becomes the ground for what is posited as earlier. In the same way, the degraded status of translation only came about once original writing was valorized, but the modes of authorship in the English Renaissance did not valorize the single author, according to Goldberg. As a result, the historically later valorization of single-authored literary production emerges against the background of an historical field it denies, one in which, we might speculate, translation is not only the norm of authorship, but the very means by which texts are produced by several hands.

When Florio makes his claim about translations reputed to be female, he is also reputing himself, as a translator, to be female in some sense or, rather, to function as a passage between male and female, a labile form of identification that in some ways belies the fixity of the gendered terms in question. In this sense, translation, and cross-identification, are the condition of the binary between male and female, its presupposition, preceding and exceeding male and female precisely by being the passage between them.

Goldberg takes the text as "vehicle" for identification and desire quite seriously, offering both a theoretical elaboration of a point made elsewhere by Eve Sedgwick and a host of engaged and detailed readings that rewrite the theory for him. If Sedgwick showed in unprecedented ways that male-male desire could and did take place through an apparent depiction of a heterosexual scene, with the woman, as it were, functioning as the conduit or vehicle for homoeroticism (the "sign" in the Lévi-Straussian sense), Goldberg shows us how women's desire in its equivocity—its hetero- and homo- possibilities—makes use of masculine narrative voice and structure as its vehicle. Over and against those who would consider the substitution of the male voice or figure for the feminine to be the sign of a sure and fatal effacement, Goldberg shows, persuasively, how substitution and displacement become the vehicle for a range of desires, not all of which are commensurable with one another or fully discrete from one another.

In the poetry of Aemilia Lanyer, for instance, he writes that "it is virtually impossible to separate hetero- and homoerotics in the bedroom scene" (39)—these crossings become the vehicle for class crossings as well. He considers at length the scholarly, mainly feminist, readings of her poem, "To the Ladie *Lucie,* Countesse of Bedford," and notes that the figure of Christ offered up by Lanyer is clearly feminized, and further suggests that this is an instance of cross-identification worth reading. In Goldberg's argument, extending and revising (if not radicalizing) the readings of Wendy Wall, Lorna Hutson, and Suzanne Woods, "some of the similes used to describe [Christ] are attached to the body of the bride in Canticles. . . . The dark lady in this poem is Lanyer's Jesus" (34).

In his reading of Aphra Behn, Goldberg shows us that there is no reason to think that gender was any more stabilized in Behn's time than it is now. On the one hand, he disputes those who would find lesbian desire to be the unspeakable and the deep truth of the poem (60). On the other, he argues vigorously that for Behn, multiple gender and sexual possibilities exist simultaneously. The poem to Clarinda, for instance, juxtaposes hetero- and homosexual desire in such a way that neither is figured as free from danger. It makes no sense to try and discover or fix the "true" mode of address here, since the simultaneous existence of the incommensurable seems to be the measure of the text's desire. Goldberg usefully cites Margaret Ferguson in this regard, who underscores the necessity of paying more attention to "modalities of identification and difference." With respect to the controversial place of Behn's gender and racial politics, and the question of their reconciliability, Goldberg advises us to live with the incommensurability. Over and against a feminist framework that would presume the asymmetrical heterosexuality of desire and situate the positions of dominance and subordination within that frame, Goldberg offers feminism a more nuanced framework in which the representation of heterosexuality is read with reference to its site of enunciation. Hence, when Behn desires the ravishing of Imoinda, "he omitted saying nothing to this young maid, that might perswade her to suffer him to seize his own . . . she was not long resisting those Arms," Goldberg asks a key question: "where is Behn in this moment?" (66).

Behn's narrator hosts the "enunciation of 'male' desire as her own, an identification across gender that allows for the vicarious enjoyment of Imoinda." Indeed, it is not possible to "fix" Behn or, indeed, the narrative perspective there, for the narrator, in Goldberg's view, participates vicariously from both positions, at once subject and object of desire. But here a question is raised for me, from the perspective of gender theory perhaps. Is cross-identification what charts the mechanisms of displacement and substitution in desire? Or is it also the mechanism by which gender is assumed? If we make sense of cross-identification through referring to gender as what we know and can assume—a woman cross-identifies as a man, for instance—then do we stabilize gender in order to destabilize and render equivocal desire? What if the mechanism by which desire is constituted, through substitution and displacement, is also the mechanism by which gender itself is assumed? Does Behn, for instance, exercise the textual possibility of lesbianism when she takes up the position of the ravisher within the text? Or does she also become a man? The risk here is that we will think that if desire for a woman is articulated, that a man must be its object, and so ratify the heterosexual presumption that seeks to lay claim to sexual desire. That would clearly be a mistake. But perhaps some separation of these issues, the formation of desire, the formation of gender, might be worth more theoretical attention, especially as the two work to render each other equivocal.

In Part Two of the text, Goldberg offers a chapter entitled "The Countess of Pembroke's Literal Translation" in which he considers the conflicted scholarship that seeks to give an account of Mary Sidney's accomplishments. Her literal translations of Petrarch call to be read somehow (118). If she was a woman writing as a man, that must mean some fundamental betrayal of and to her gender? Wouldn't such conclusions ascribe to the original a determinate power that might itself fall into question even in this most literal of translations—if, that is, one were to argue that even literally to rewrite the poem could locate the countess's hand at a site of original duplication?

For Sidney to have written again Petrarch's poem, to write it faithfully word for word is "to take up the position of writing her own demise, to find voice only at the point of death." Relying on Wendy Wall's similar reading of Isabella Whitney's "Wyll and Testament," Goldberg makes a distinction between *representing* a site of dispossession and *identifying with* it. This site, he elaborates, "is moreover so riven with contradictions about person, place, and time—since one speaks, and yet is dead, since one takes possession at a moment of dispossession, since one occupies a temporary split between a future that one will never occupy and a present one is evacuating—that the contradictions, rather than being annihilative, are productive" (119). He makes this very clear when he considers the instability of the "I" in this text, and the way this very instability conditions desire: "lines of cathexis are opened up here that heighten a female-female erotics to be found from the very opening lines of the poem in which the "I" of the poem may be read as a woman speaking of and to other women as her "chosen mates." This displacement along the lines of same-sex identification furthers the scandal of crossing and cross-identification that the poem undertakes" (128). Goldberg clearly wants to insist on the capacity of the pronoun to elude gender fixity when he writes, redoubling "insistence" in his own sentence: "It gets marked again, insistently so, as the second part opens, when the 'I' of the poem refuses to call itself man, but is insistently and only 'I.' "

Section Three is titled playfully, perhaps self-consciously, as "Writing as a Woman." This is Goldberg's title and, hence, according to his own critical framework, his enunciation. In the chapter he is at once speculative, theoretical, and programmatic, having clearly earned the license to all of these through his painstaking readings. He writes, for instance, and rightly: "what is needed is first of all to break the deadlock between the construction understood as an evaporation of lived reality and essentialism as rooted in the supposition of a transhistorical and universalization of gendered inequity and female suffering" (137). This is surely the task for both feminist and sexuality studies, as well as one site for the potential and productive alliance. He cautions us against relying on "sexual difference" as an assumed framework, since so often it not only encodes a nonproductive essentialism but constrains desire in heterosexual directions by virtue of its logic. He asks us to consider, for instance, that when a woman writes, in a text, "we men," she may not be performing her self-erasure but facilitating, through substitution and displacement, a new trajectory for desire (139).

His insistence that we begin to approach questions of politics, gender, and sexuality without assuming the marital bond as the constraining context for desire is crucial and timely.

In his elegant chapter, "Mary Shelton's Hand," Goldberg shows how reading for desire can and does take place when the "I" cannot be fixed in terms of its authorial referent. Whether or not Mary Shelton wrote the text "O Happy dames," Goldberg argues, "the presumed hetero desire in the poem also vehiculates male-male desire" (156). Indeed, to show what a text "vehiculates" does not require access to the author precisely, for what is produced here is a text with its own sets of possibilities. Whereas Jonathan Crewe sees Shelton as performing her own self-erasure by assuming the voice of a man, Goldberg suggests that substitution is not reducible to negation (and, in this sense, he coincides with the psychoanalytic readings for which substitutability is a condition of desire). She is placed, in Goldberg's view, "in a locus of substitution that is not the same thing as the erasure of difference" (162).

In his final chapter on Elizabeth Cary's "Tragedy of Mariam, the Fair Queen of Jewry," Goldberg offers his most deconstructive reading. If, in the previous chapter, Mary Shelton, the presumed author, could not be secured referentially, then here, the figure at issue, eludes referentiality more radically as the unspoken and unwritable region that becomes the source of transgression. He finds utopic and egalitarian desires, for instance, in the play's character "Graphina," a name that functions effectively as a signature for women's writing generically. According to Goldberg's reading, Graphina's mark, he calls it, designates a region in which gender hierarchies are transgressed through a move that reoccupies the conventionally masculine domain in order to resignify female-male equality through the position of male-male friendship (181).

Here again, substitution is not simply erasure but vehiculation. And we see that complex negotiations are made possible through instantiating narrative voice and character as fundamentally equivocal. This is not a reading for the sake of a celebratory equivocity, but one that proceeds from a complex understanding that to read gender, desire, politics, and writing together, as they are implicated in class and race as well, is to regard the text as a dense site of multiple articulations. It is because the map of desire and power are so complex, and demand nonreductive readings from us, that we are asked to become alert to the incommensurable and multiple directions for desire that can follow from the simplest pronoun. It is Jonathan Goldberg's singular brilliance to cast his net so widely and to come up, always, with something so indisputably fine.

The Place of the Dead: Death and Remembrance in Late Medieval and Early Modern Europe
Edited by Bruce Gordon and Peter Marshall
Cambridge: Cambridge University Press, 2000

Death in England: An Illustrated History
Edited by Peter C. Jupp and Clare Gittings
New Brunswick, NJ: Rutgers University Press, 2000

Reviewer: Katherine O. Acheson

Although the back cover of *Death in England* says that in the present age we are in the process of discarding "the taboos surrounding death," it is clear from today's news that the cultural conflicts crystallized by attitudes towards death and the dead that these books address are, if you will, alive and well. A contemporary example, set far from the geographic mandates of these books, will show what I mean. In the summer of 1999, at the foot of a glacier in Tatshenshini-Alsek Park in the northwest region of British Columbia, three sheep hunters discovered the frozen remains—a body with skin, hair, and flesh, clothing and implements—of what turned out to be a 550-year old body of a human in his twenties. Because the remains were found in its traditional territory, the Champagne and Aishihik First Nation assumed authority over the use and disposition of the body. The first nation called the body Kwaday Dän Sinchì, meaning "long ago person found," and came to an agreement with the British Columbian government under which tests were run and samples collected for future research. The body was returned to the band in July 2001, and cremated on 21 July.

On the day of the cremation, the Canadian national newspaper *The Globe and Mail* ran an editorial entitled "Knowledge to Ashes." The editorial raises two of the enduring questions about the dead: first, who owns or has jurisdiction over remains, and second, what priorities should govern their disposal or use? The editorial characterizes the conflict over the body as, first, property-based: it begins with the question "Who owns the dead?" While the first nation is said to have "quickly decided that Kwaday was their property," the editorial's writer asks, "Do priceless remains of such antiquity not belong to everyone, rather than to one native band?" Second, the conflict is represented as being between the priorities of different belief systems: "Scientific inquiry and its hunger for information often chafes against other, more spiritual priorities, which in general deserve respect. What's unfortunate here is that after so many centuries, the Iceman could not have been preserved a little longer before being consigned to the wind. The loss is irretrievable."

In addition to situating the conflict over Kwaday's remains in terms of these two persistent questions, the editorial also implicitly inserts the problem within sets of competing contemporary political and social discourses, revealing the significance of the problem of the dead to larger issues. It uses the language of traditional rights and collective property entitlement, which are the hallmarks of the discourses of native rights in Canada, in order, ironically, to assert the rights of "all" to the knowledge that "belong[s] to everyone." Another echo of the discourse of native rights is in the author's use of "irretrievable," which, in the context of native history in Canada, has an inescapable moral resonance, marking as it does the fate of so much of first-nations culture—including the remains of the dead—since contact. In effect, the writer is insinuating that the Champagne and Aishihik have violated their own beliefs and history in their claim to and disposal of Kwaday's remains; in the editorial, therefore, the band's use of Kwaday's remains signals the untrustworthiness and essential opportunism of native peoples in their dealings with non-native peoples and belief systems. The significance of such insinuations in an even broader political context is revealed by looking at the paper's front page, where a headline announces Prime Minister Chrétien's view on the placement of a northern gas pipeline, intended to deliver Arctic gas to southern markets. The Mackenzie Valley pipeline, which Chrétien endorses, has been opposed by native groups in the past, and will likely be opposed in the future. The contest over the proper disposal of Kwaday's remains links issues as disparate, then, as the ownership of a 550-year old woven cedar hat, found on a melting glacier, with twenty-first-century North American energy consumption and policy. The dead, it seems, are never just the dead.

The two books under review make amply clear that the dead have never just been dead, and that struggles over their disposal, social status, and posthumous significance have always been intimately linked with philosophical, epistemological, economic, cultural, political, medical, and scientific priorities, conflicts, and beliefs. *Death in England* ably achieves its intention to map out the "whole history of English death" (1) for the last half a million years. The book is aimed at the general reader, although all of the chapters are fully situated within contemporary scholarship, the footnotes are generous, though not completely comprehensive, and some of the research appears original to the authors of individual chapters. It is amply illustrated in black-and-white and color, and will be of use not only to the general reader but to those teaching survey courses in literature or history, and for those seeking creditable information to supplement or undergird arguments about death in literature and culture.

For the readers of this periodical, the most interesting chapters will probably be the two concerned with the late medieval and early modern periods. Philip Morgan's chapter, "Of Worms and War: 1380–1558," begins at the end of a period of extremely high mortality rates—first from famine, then from the plague—at a time when the existence of purgatory and the community of saints were firmly established in doctrine and practice, and when the rituals that comprised the good death and effective memorialization were widely accepted. It ends at the beginning of a period during which mortality rates were substantially lower, the existence of purgatory was officially denied, and the ritual and material practices attending death altered significantly. Of greatest importance to the meaning of death in this period was purgatory: "The rise of Purgatory and the ensuing social and religious significance of intercession on behalf of those held there created enormous bonds of obligation between the living and the dead" (132). These bonds were severed by the rejection of purgatory, which at least doctrinally brought about a "sudden and cathartic transformation" (141) of the relationships between the living and the dead. Morgan concludes the chapter with a literal example of such a transformation: in 1549, "Edward, duke of Somerset, one of the architects of the Edwardian reforms, ordered the demolition of the pardon cloister on the north side of St. Paul's cathedral, famous for its tombs, monuments and depiction of the *danse macabre,* and employed the now 'found materials' to build his new house on the Strand" (143). There are few more stunning signs of early modern "modernity" than Somerset's transubstantiation of the stones of memory into the rock of real estate.

During the period of Clare Gittings's chapter, "Sacred and Secular: 1558–1660," "Protestants of all persuasions agreed that the fate of the soul was sealed with death" and that "the actions of the living could have no effect on the dead" (153). In consequence, funerals and memorial practices became much more secular than religious, and individual rather than social. The medieval doctrine of the "good death" was maintained, but its objectives mingled the material "ordering of affairs" with the conventional "ordering of the soul." The control of the state over the rituals and social meanings of funerals and memorial rites was also reduced by James I's disregard of the role of the College of Heralds, which asserted the genealogical relationship between the aristocratic living and dead by acting out the transfer of titles in the name of the monarch. One of the most significant effects of the privatization of death that Gittings describes was the intensification of individual mourning, particularly by spouses, and the acceptance of increasingly "modern" expressions of grief and loss by survivors. Gittings's essay is, to my mind, the best in the collection, as she supplements the objective, historical description of her topic with fine, but somewhat more speculative, interpretation of representations of death, particularly of memorial portraits.

The other book under review, *The Place of the Dead,* is more conventionally academic in tone; the essays are argumentative, they present original research, and they are by-and-large narrowly conceived in their topics but widely significant in their findings. The topics include plague, prayer and commemoration, ghosts and spirits, the geographies of the afterlife, burial disputes, church architecture, will-making, funeral sermons, the uses of death in propaganda, infant baptism, and the representation of monstrous births. All of the essays aim to contribute to what the introduction calls a "social history of death," and particularly address questions such as what was the status of the dead, what obligations towards, or relationships with, the dead were maintained by the living, how were the dead exploited for political or social ends, and how were the dead, as emblematic of the "past," instrumental in the construction of the sense of history in the societies with which the scholars are concerned.

The essays in the collection are all very good, although some are better suited for specialists in the cultures and periods of the titles of the essays, while some generate insights of more general use to the medieval or early modern scholar of other times and places. Among those that offer broader insights are Samuel K. Cohn, Jr.'s "The Place of the Dead in Flanders and Tuscany: Towards a Comparative History of the Black Death," which compares testamentary instructions in regions that are conventionally claimed to have had starkly different "Renaissances," and finds both striking similarities and phenomena that contradict the Huizingan and Burkhardtian models usually applied to the regions; Penny Roberts's "Contesting Sacred Space: Burial Disputes in Sixteenth-Century France," in which "burial disputes . . . represent a crucial barometer of relations, and tensions, between the faiths within French communities during an intense period of civil and religious strife" (148); Vanessa Harding's "Whose Body? A Study of Attitudes Towards the Dead Body in Early Modern Paris," which reads the social and epistemological dimensions of struggles for the jurisdiction over individual corpses; James M. Boyden's "The Worst Death Becomes a Good Death: The Passion of Don Rodrigo Calderón," which interprets the extraordinary manipulation of the codes of good dying by a man whose execution was intended to assert the authority of the Spanish crown over corruption and malefaction; and Philip M. Soergel's "The Afterlives of Monstrous Infants in Reformation Germany," which uses the tools of visual rhetoric, in tandem with social history, to analyze the representations of severely deformed infant corpses.

There are several essays on English topics, including ones by Clive Burgess on late medieval prayer and commemoration, Peter Marshall on Reformation controversies over the spatial contours and dimensions of the unseen worlds, J. S. W. Helt on women's will-making in Elizabethan England, and Will Coster on infant baptism, which charts a shift from the view that infants were corrupted with original sin to the view that they were innocent vessels. The latter two are especially interesting to those interested in gender history; Helt persuasively argues that women's bequests were more strongly oriented towards caring for the poor and especially poor women than men's, and Coster provides indirect evidence of the diminishment over time of the sense that women's bodies were containers of sin. Another very fine article is by Andrew Spicer on the development of burial aisles and other changes in Scottish church architecture that reflect doctrinal and social changes due to the Reformation.

There are no essays on Ireland or Wales, and none on the Low Countries other than Flanders, which would have rounded out the Western European orientation of the collection, and provided further matter of interest to scholars who work on British literature and culture. But there is much more to be done in this field: there are also no essays in this collection that deal with the sorts of confrontations between belief-systems that occurred during the Crusades, or in the exploration and colonization of the New World, or with the experience of epidemic disease by participants in both, or which deal in any substantial way with celebrity death, with suicide, and with wartime death. But the notes on the contributors to both volumes indicate that much more work by "death scholars" (*Death in England,* 3) is forthcoming, and that we can look forward to these and other topics being addressed in due time. As the example of Kwaday's remains shows, the afterlife of death is of importance to us all, not only in our scholarly pursuits, but in the issues that form our presents and shape our futures.

Shakespeare's Noise
By Kenneth Gross
Chicago and London:
University of Chicago Press, 2001

Reviewer: *Marshall Grossman*

"This book pursues a vision of the work of words in Shakespeare's plays" (1). So begins Kenneth Gross's remarkable exploration of "violent and disorderly forms of speaking: slander, defamation, insult, vituperation, malediction, . . . curse . . . Rumor and gossip" (1) in *Hamlet, Measure for Measure, Othello, Coriolanus,* and *King Lear.* On first reading, the peculiarity of the sentence slides by unnoticed. But after reading a chapter or so—enough to get a sense of the texture of Gross's current thought—one realizes that the sentence, with its alliterative and synaesthetic promise of a *"vision* of the work of words" means exactly what it says. The effects that occupy Gross's attention are very much sound effects: mutterings, howls, shouts, rhythms of breath, half-heard whispers, and the inhuman noises of wind, thunder, and battle, that Shakespeare's characters, on occasion, may take or mistake for articulate speech. But the book works to see how these sounds shape what the characters see and what the audience sees and how they—characters, audience, readers—feel about what they see. The compression of that first sentence, then, sets out the scope and pressure of the argument, but it also signals that this book asks to be read, and understands that reading is a commitment beyond that of following an argument. Learned, smart, appropriately skeptical of his own ideas, Gross writes literary criticism, which is to say that this book—at once argument and meditation—is both critical and literary. To succeed in this combination the literary aspect of the writing must not be something added to the critical. Rather, to avoid pretension, it must result from the necessary persistence of thought at the limit of critical articulation. The literary quality should result from an effort—to take a phrase from the preface of Gross's previous and similarly meditative book, *The Dream of the Moving Statue* (1992)—"to speak about what cannot be spoken about" (xiii). In an engaged effort to understand subtle things and to articulate clearly, subtle thoughts, Gross risks a style of writing more highly wrought and more verbally attentive than that of most academic criticism. Because he succeeds both intellectually and aesthetically, his writing consistently affords pleasure as it provokes and unsettles thought.

Shakespeare's Noise engages its subject on (at least) three levels, offering a chapter each on five of Shakespeare plays, a serious meditation on the vulnerability of the ear and the effects of slanderous speech on both perpetrator and victim, and an attempt to assess the particularity and sources of the power of live theater. The two larger themes grow intimately out of and into the specific exploration of the plays: "Writing this book, I became increasingly aware of how Shakespeare's preoccupation with these extreme forms of human speech grows out of their power to animate the stage. . . . I have indeed felt at times as if all proper theater were a theater of noise" (4).

Gross's chapter titles identify four of his chosen plays with a somewhat different style (if that may be the right word) of noise: A chapter on rumor in *Hamlet* is followed by one called "The Book of the Slanderer," which attempts a historical understanding of attitudes toward slander at the beginning of the seventeenth-century; a chapter on *Measure for Measure* is concerned with styles of hearing, attending to, or avoiding noise. Gross then turns to denigration in *Othello,* the noise of war in *Coriolanus,* and curse in *King Lear.* A finely written "coda," entitled "An Imaginary Theater," concludes the book with the general thought that theater per se is animated by and as noise.

The idea of *animation,* reached at the end of this book, figures importantly also in *The Dream of the Moving Statue,* and in both books *animation*—not simply movement, but bringing to life— tends to arrive together with the word *wound.* The twinned notions of animation and wound place both books in the context of a large, if implicit, project. To trace the outline of this project and indicate what I take to be the scope of the book, before saying a little more about the contents of Gross's chapters, I am going to quote a rather lengthy passage from the concluding meditation in which he offers a revised formulation of the book's "central theme":

> Physical gesture can devour the spoken word onstage, subjecting words to an entirely visual or bodily idiom . . . But the opposition between gesture and words feels false to the degree that the word itself lives onstage as a gesture, a site of passage and translation, exposure and secrecy. It is here that I can return to what has been the central theme of this book: the wounding presence of the word. In Shakespeare's plays, after all, the spoken word often carries dramatic weight just through becoming an entity in its own right. Launched into the air, the spoken word can be fought over, marred, remade, juggled with, or buried, thrown back at speakers with changed force. For a dark wit like Hamlet, any word (say "son" or "king") becomes a prop, a tool, a weapon. Words bind the actors together through forms of violence or contamination. Individual words and phrases wander, often taking up a habitation in speakers who know little of their history; each character is made to speak for many others, even in their isolation. Words hide their sense, or get caught up by darker systems of noise and murmur, like Cordelia's

"nothing." What must have been unsettling as well as compelling for Renaissance audiences, even in plays by writers other than Shakespeare, was the spectacle of an actor's ability to make himself up onstage exactly out of such ungrounded words, words subject to such a conflict of employments. (200)

Hamlet is reading a book. Polonius asks "What do you read my lord?" and Hamlet replies "Words, words, words." Polonius tries again: "What is the matter, my lord?" and Hamlet asks "Between who?"[1] What more concise gloss than Hamlet's can there be on Gross's passage? What more expansive gloss than his passage can there be on Hamlet's lines? The presence of actors (or statues) is all surface. The eye plays over them: until they speak. As we are constantly reminded in Hamlet, words enter us: they can abuse our ears or stick in them like daggers. They are the matter that is between Hamlet and Polonius, and as Hamlet goes on to say, they are "slanders." We can close our eyes but not our ears. At the same time, theatrical words are gestural, ungrounded; and like all the gestures in Hamlet's listing of "the suits and traps of woe," "they are actions that a man might play." Cordelia's "nothing" fills the theater of Lear's court and the theater in which *King Lear* is played. It says that she will not speak and that her sisters' copious speech is nothing. Entering all ears, proclaiming silence out loud and silencing what has been said, it exemplifies what Gross means by noise that animates and wounds:

> The rumors at work in Shakespeare's plays are no vague muddle of sense, but possibilities sharp enough to penetrate the mind and lodge themselves inescapably within memory, even if only half understood, carrying as the do echoes of our most primitive cries. The plays show us what it means to build so many selves, so many sensuous worlds, precisely of speech that troubles hearing and out of hearing that transforms what is spoken, making it speak in a different voice, making sense out of what is not heard, or heard wrongly. (207)

At its highest level of generality, Gross's *noise* resembles Derrida's logic of the supplement in which representation cancels its own original, and, at a slightly lower level of generality, Lacan's understanding of the speaking subject alienated by the subject of its own utterance. But Gross does not choose to work at this level of generality. He is more interested in understanding the animating wound through close description of Shakespeare's noise and the effects its produces. His observations of words subject to "a conflict of employments" also owes an acknowledged debt to Harry Berger's ideas about the "complicity" among characters and their language in Shakespeare's plays, though his concerns are more general and more speculative than Berger's. The relationship is clear in Gross's opening discussion of *Hamlet,* which, after a brief but useful historical discussion linking *slander* to more general notions of *fame* and *noise* in the Renaissance, turns to the dispersal of Hamlet's language among the various characters of the play:

> Hamlet ... says things that make others think, or suspect, he has knowledge of them, especially of their implication in matters criminal or sinful. This means that Hamlet's knowledge is in part something others project onto him (by which they betray themselves, in both senses of the word). It also means that his assumed knowledge is a reflex of other people's desperate, thwarted desire to know Hamlet, to divine for themselves his dark interior. (21)

But Gross's revisiting of the peculiar verbal mirrors in which the characters of *Hamlet* see themselves superposed pushes toward a broader and more risky consideration of "the situation of slander in the troubled domain of hearing" (18). Gross reaches his central theme of the animating wound when he finds in representations of slander contemporary with *Hamlet* "hints of a violence and a shame that inhabit speaking and hearing in general ... point[ing] to a perilous pleasure and a mode of knowing that are strangely beyond government, by turns fantastic and commonplace" (19).

In the following chapter, "The Book of the Slanderer," Gross pursues this unsettling immixture of violence, shame, and pleasure into "the period's larger preoccupation with damaging words" (33), examining contemporary readings of the Book of Psalms, pamphlets, and treatises by Richard Allestree, Nicholas Breton, and William Vaughan, among others. Considering anxieties about slander that surface in theatrical representations, letters, emblem books, and theology (notably Calvinist) as well, this chapter extends "the mirror structure of slander" to the function of detraction as a mirror or mimic of the law. Thus, while deepening the historical description of slander, the chapter also forms an apt bridge between *Hamlet* and *Measure for Measure,* the next object of Gross's attention. The focus of this chapter, "A Disturbance of Hearing in Vienna," is less on what is said than on what is heard or not heard, and by whom. Observing that "the Duke moves through the play as an isolated, occulted ear, in flight from both public praise and slander from the relentless murmuring that fills his city" (69), Gross notes that the Duke is deaf to the emotional distress of others and that his "peculiar deafness represents a kind of zero point within the play's picture of the Duke's knowledge, suggesting how voices can become, for this particular listener, a kind of unaccountable noise, nothing but 'a thousand escapes' of falsifying wit" (79). A very careful reading of the play's problematic final scene leads back to the paradoxical resemblance of slander and law. "The Duke's involvement in the scene makes the legal forms of accusation . . . feel at once inescapable and arbitrary" (96), and:

> the silences at the end of *Measure for Measure* are abortive rather than pregnant. They lie in cold obstruction, silences silenced, eaten up, neither cursed nor blessed. There is nothing to hear. Speech is buried alive, as Antigone is buried alive. If these silences are filled with anything it is with the weight of an undischarged debt that has been accumulating since the Duke first reentered the kingdom he had pretended to leave. (99)

Like the Duke in *Measure for Measure,* Iago "never sets himself at risk before another's inner life or lets himself be transformed by his effects on others" (108). Shakespeare's noise in this chapter is represented by Iago's "disguised battle" (120). Iago conjures suspicions by precisely *not* adding hidden meanings or double entendres. In an interesting and malevolent turn on Cordelia's "nothing," the vacuity of Iago's words, their lack of precise meaning or reference, induces his victims to fill the empty space of meaning with their own dark fantasies.

Near the beginning of his chapter on *Coriolanus,* Gross, reacting to the opacity of the central character, remarks that Shakespeare, after having written "his central tragedies of the mind," seems with this play to have "set out to write the tragedy of someone with no interiority" (134). Coriolanus represents, for Gross, something like a terminal disturbance of hearing. Like Hamlet he has an ear for slander and feels too acutely the power of words to reduce him to a shadow of what is represented about him. Although Gross does not pursue the link, a Lacanian might say that Coriolanus, as Gross describes him, cannot accept the name of the father. This would also explain something about his inability to relinquish the maternal objects—Volumnia and Rome. War gives Coriolanus a name earned rather than inherited, and its noisy chaos is his respite from the slander of naming: "The noise of war is . . . a freedom associated with a realm of physical risk and violence, but also one of clear knowledge and action." It "suggests a private language . . . that no skepticism dare call in doubt" (146). If he lacks interiority, it is because to protect his ears from the animating wound, he produces the blocking noise of war—a howl of rage.

Howling is, of course, also what *King Lear* is about. In his chapter on *Lear,* Gross explores the tension the play maintains between two senses of *curse*: "curse as a contingent utterance and curse as an inescapable truth" (162). The tension between curse as a verbal performance and as a condition of being (cursedness?) with its cross-coupling of subject and object, curser and cursed plays out also on the more familiar ground of "the fate of those banished from clear systems of curse and blessing" (165). The most complex and subtle in this complex and subtle book, the chapter on Lear is a tour de force in which an acute reading of the play is combined with a deft shaping of the book to prepare for the "reformulated statement of its central theme" offered in the conclusion: "The curse or blessing of the world in *King Lear* is that no one can ever become nothing, any more than one can finally say nothing; no one can die when he wants to, or fully alienate an inalienable humanity" (182). The wound of noise is also its animating substance.

My description of these chapters cannot and does not expect to do them justice. Rather it is intended to suggest the design and scope of the book and to make clear that *Shakespeare's Noise* is theoretically informed, but it is an empirical rather than a theoretical book. It is grounded in Shakespeare's texts and the experience of theater. It offers sustained, insightful, and original readings of the five plays it discusses and a thoughtful exploration of the power of theater and its noise. Informative, insightful and provocative, it is also a great pleasure to read.

Note

1. *Hamlet,* ed. Harold Jenkins, *The Arden Shakespeare* (London: Methuen, 1982), 2.2.191–94.

Sexuality and Form: Caravaggio, Marlowe, and Bacon
By Graham L. Hammill
Chicago and London: University of Chicago Press, 2000

Reviewer: Denise Albanese

In *Sexuality and Form: Caravaggio, Marlowe, and Bacon,* Graham Hammill has offered a demanding, intensely absorbing, and at times elusive series of readings in early modern culture, with the aim of intervening in the apparent impasse between queer theory, derived as it is from Foucault, and the Freudian-inflected models of ego-formation that would seem to be queer theory's antithesis. Hammill aims to disarticulate sexuality from representation and identity both, the better to place it at the center of cultural production, as a motive and alibi, as minor subjectivity and conjuration of the body. Via case studies, and via initial and concluding chapters that offer inventive and flexible theoretical meditations on the problem of reading sexuality as it discloses itself in time, *Sexuality and Form* argues for a model of the sexual that is nonidentical with either the Foucauldian characterization of it as social thought or with the discourse of performativity characteristic of subsequent queer theory. Instead, (queer) sexuality takes its being from a historically precise albeit durable interplay between aggression and the force of civilization, in which the former finds creative pleasure, enabling it to extend itself beyond the dominant and regulative via a aestheticized modeling of the body. This extensive modeling, which Hammill deems a "poiesis," necessitates a "historically minded phenomenology of sexualities" (8), a provocative analytical turn by which Hammill means to counter the tendency of psychoanalytic interpretation to bracket the social.

One of the book's overall strengths is the variety of its arguments, the fact that each chapter pursues a nuanced, even acrobatic set of analyses bringing together a wide range of discursive possibilities. These analyses themselves also shift in scale, moving from attempts to explain the political, aesthetic, and disciplinary terrain of Renaissance Florence via discussions of perspective, conduct books, and city-state regulations, to the more narrowly focused exemplary reading of his chapter on *Dr. Faustus*. Throughout, Hammill is not interested in sexuality per se, either discursively or representationally, but in the way that cultural dominants embodied in texts—the mannered, disciplined body; the aesthetic and the literary, temporality, Christianity, and historical time—are haunted by the possibility of a queerness that in one way or another history seeks not to know. The chapter on Caravaggio, in this regard, is particularly incisive: it acknowledges the cogency of reading the paintings in light of a queer aesthetic, but it takes great pains to account in psychoanalytic terms for the anachronism of that mode of reading—not because Caravaggio could not have been "queer" or that depicting the homoerotic could not have been his intention (both alternatives are irrelevant to Hammill), but because the theatricalization of pictorial space characteristic of the artist figures forth a psychic void that both provokes and negates historical recognition of queer subjectivity. Although his general practice is not text-driven, Hammill's reading of these images is deft and persuasive; he offers useful concretizations of an argument that could easily fly into abstract theorizing. And he handles the specificity of medium skillfully, reading the line of drawing and the telling splash of color with as much ease as he handles textual artifacts elsewhere in his study. Hammill's subsequent reading of *Faustus*, for instance, tellingly addresses the sodomitical valence in the homosocial exchanges between the scholar and Mephistopheles—who promises an endless stream of courtesans but proffers a devil in a dress when he brings on Helen to further cement their bond. In Hammill's account, it is the representational logic of sodomy and its uncanny doubling of orthodox friendship that matters, rather than the fact of its being hinted at through the screen of costume: its socially and psychically ambiguous mode links imaginatively with Faustus's imbrication in a series of elusive, yet all-determinative, bargains and substitutions. And Hammill's challenging account of Bacon uses the texts' repeated emphases on bringing a new epoch of experimentation into being (a promise of futurity undermined by Bacon's repeated stress on "purging" the idols of the past) in order to position the Baconian body as both index of and subject to an experimental regime. This chapter, which moves confidently through Augustine, Elizabethan juridical and political discourse, Hans Blumenberg's analysis of the temporal structure of modernity, Protestant hagiography, and an array of Baconian texts, is the book's most rhetorically persuasive. Moreover, it forges a highly convincing link between the Baconian imperative towards programmatic novelty in the making of knowledge and a Protestantism that similarly must break off from Catholic superstition, the better to reinstate a mode of probative truth that nevertheless depends on a continual rehearsal of difference from its point of departure.

Although topics such as temporality within the regime of Christianity and the sexed body (uniformly although not avowedly male in his readings) recur throughout *Sexuality and Form,* the chapters' relative discreteness makes it difficult at times to assess the cumulative power of Hammill's argument. Indeed, while much potentially depends on the introductory staging of the psychoanalytic against the discursive, or on his analysis of aesthetics, manners, and war in Florence, little overt connection is offered between these earlier moments and subsequent analyses. While it is a point of admiration that Hammill does not set up an initially mechanistic model through which he grinds a series of texts, it is also the case that he offers comparatively little in the way of rhetorical continuity—both between and within chapters. The Caravaggio chapter, for instance, initially suggests that Christian typological reading, in its substitution for the particularized embodiment of Jewish identity the universalizing possibilities of Christianity, provides a useful analogue for reading the paintings. Since, in effect, Hammill himself argues that the paintings offer a forecast of future queerness (even as he complicates the mode of ego-formation and the operations of desire in its relation to the material world), it is disappointing that he never returns to typology as a way to bring together the providential history represented in many of the pictures he examines with the historically emergent queer spectatorship upon whose existence his reading depends. Toward the end of this same chapter, Hammill notes that the perilously angled sword in *David with the Head of Goliath* reveals the giant-killer's insouciance at the threat of castration, born of a hypermasculinity secure about the flesh because it possesses the phallus. But the blade could as well be read to index circumcision, a distinction between Jew and Philistine important to the Jewish "carnality" with which Hammill's typological analysis engages at the outset. Recognizing the coalescence of signification here would render his claim usefully concrete, and establish a typological relationship of its own (however thwart) between Christian teleology and Lacanian subjectivity in the Symbolic order.

As this example indicates, the chapters sometimes tend to the centrifugal. To take another, small, point as further illustration: Is it argumentatively necessary to stipulate that *Faust*'s relationship to literary culture depends on print culture rather than on the distinction between orality and literacy? Not that Hammill doesn't make inventive use of the connection between print culture and an increasing freedom of interpretation precisely responsive to literariness understood as suspending disbelief: it is that the grounding in the play-text he offers, via citations to acts of reading, do not in themselves allow for restrictions of these acts to printed media. I am not suggesting he misreads or that the claim should not be further pursued—I found his subsequent argument about *Faustus* well worth suspending my own concern for detail over. Rather, it is that the density of potential approaches leaves certain questions begging, certain claims, here and elsewhere in the study, only gestures. (Later in the same chapter, I was coaxed into seeing how Marx on labor might interarticulate with a more historically nuanced economy of homosocial exchange even if not, as he argues, with the Faustian soul read as commodity—but nothing in Hammill's initial step had forecast that turn in the argument, nor rendered it strictly necessary.) A ready analogy might be drawn between the search for argumentative closure and the elusiveness of desire in Lacan, but that is not, I think, Hammill's design. Rather, I take the multiplication of topics, of ostensibly ad hoc strategies of apprehension, to be evidence of the fecundity of his encounters with the material with which he has chosen to work. If at times the proliferation of local readings and methods tends to obscure the destination of the argument as a whole and makes for difficult parsing, that proliferation is also what renders the book so stimulating.

I wonder, too, given his concern for particularity, whether Irigaray's positioning of women in the gaps of "between-men history" (170) can so readily be mapped onto the dilemma of the queer: however crude the distinction might appear in this formulation, there is a difference yet worth preserving between being written out of history altogether and a queerness, understood as a resistance to judgment, which occupies the "spaces in between the repetition of social thought" (5). After all, Hammill reads no texts claimed specifically as instances of feminist identity before the fact, as Bacon, Marlowe, and Caravaggio have been claimed for a universalizing gay studies that Hammill rightly critiques. Of course, noting that he does not read women's texts is not meant to discipline him, but rather to suggest that in their canonicity his exemplary figures confirm the very historical distinction his optimistic reading of Irigaray obscures. However, that sexuality and the queer, the sexed body and the male body—all terms that Hammill uses—sometimes collapse into one another analytically seems a problem worth anticipating, especially also given his concern with the blind spots "identitary time"—which places the self in time as a social institution—can produce when it looks elsewhere than at itself.

But these criticisms nevertheless leave much to admire in Hammill's study. In all, the bracing intelligence, energy, and inventiveness everywhere characteristic of *Sexuality and Form* make it a text to be reckoned with. Even if Hammill does not (and could not single-handedly) settle the question of Lacan's and Freud's pertinence to queer discourse understood in relation to temporality and historical difference, he has introduced a vigorously destabilizing set of terms and problems into the discussion.

Scare Quotes from Shakespeare: Marx, Keynes, and the Language of Reenchantment
By Martin Harries
Stanford, CA: Stanford University Press, 2000

Reviewer: John Drakakis

In what has become a controversial essay, Stephen Greenblatt, in defence of his own, often maligned and sometimes misunderstood critical practice, admitted: "If I do not approach works of art in a spirit of veneration, I do approach them in a spirit that is best described as wonder." While conceding that "wonder" has tended to be associated with literary formalism, he expressed the wish to extend its concerns "beyond the formal boundaries of art, just as I wish to intensify resonance within those boundaries."[1] He defined the terms "resonance" and "wonder" as "the power of the object displayed to reach out beyond its formal boundaries to a larger world, to evoke in the viewer the complex, dynamic cultural forces from which it has emerged and for which as metaphor or more simply as metonymy it may be taken by a viewer to stand," and "the power of the object displayed to stop the viewer in his tracks, to convey an arresting sense of uniqueness, to evoke an exalted attention."[2] "Resonance" is the evocation in the viewer of the metaphoric or metonymic status of the cultural object, but "wonder," which Greenblatt takes great care not to identify too closely with the Kantian "sublime," remains as a stubborn testimony to the transhistorical cultural significance of art. Part of Greenblatt's critical apparatus may be read as a defence of the anecdotal, as well as a commitment to the synchronic relations that exist between the elements of culture. Applied to the realm of literary quotation, it activates a series of interesting questions.

In a footnote near the end of Martin Harries's new book, *Scare Quotes From Shakespeare,* another Greenblatt text is invoked to suggest that communication with the past is a process akin to the occult and suggestive of haunting (175–76, n. 26). In a concentrated introductory chapter he describes the traditional work that quotation performs as a process of decontextualization that facilitates the reinforcement of the "naturalness" of a world that occludes the conditions of its own construction (3). By contrast, what he calls the "scare quote" functions to estrange "the appearance of the natural" (3), so that quotation as "second nature" then "becomes a symptom of the faults in its [nature's] carapace" (4). According to this logic, the "scare quote" in general and the Shakespearean "scare quote" in particular, discloses a faultline "in a cultural solution that is only apparently stable" (4). Harries contends that certain kinds of Shakespearean quotation are deployed habitually in texts by Marx and Keynes as means of engaging with areas of experience that reveal fissures in the carapace of Enlightenment rationalism. Or to put the matter another way, materialism itself is forced into an oblique acknowledgment of a spectral otherness that "haunts" it and against which it has sought, differentially, to define itself. The "specter" will be no stranger to readers of Marx's and Engels's *Communist Manifesto,* where it is identified as a "Communism" that was, in the nineteenth century, haunting Europe. More recently Jacques Derrida has inverted the logic of this claim to assert that in the modern "post-Marxist" world it is Marxism itself, like the ghost of Hamlet's father, that now exerts a "spectral" pressure upon the political anxieties of the human subject in its attempts to come to terms with the past.

These historically overdetermined entanglements with an absent, allegedly constitutive, metaphysics that Harries associates, pace Slavoj Žižek, with ideology itself (7), are of particular significance to students of Shakespeare for whom the spectral presence of an authorizing force raises a series of complex methodological question that knee-jerk allusions to Althusserian Marxism, and to fashionable phrases such as "cultural capital" do not fully explain. Moreover, the projection of Shakespearean quotation into the domain of the ideologically charged phantasmagoric that is usually, and more properly, associated with the Gothic, directs our attention both to those psychic processes that are ultimately subsumed into the practice of writing itself, and to a critical practice that Harries associates with the location and reading of "historical allegory" (9). The latter is a practice that those familiar with the opening chapter of Richard Halpern's *Shakespeare Among The Moderns* (1997) will recognize, and implied in Harries's methodology is Halpern's identification of an "articulation of the contemporary and the historical."[3] It is within this context that Shakespeare provides what Harries calls "a privileged language for the perception of re-enchantment" (9). The "scare quote," then, is no mere appeal to a cultural authority, rather its appearance is symptomatic of those moments when later writers encounter "blind spots in their analyses of critical moments in European history" (7).

The subtitle of Harries's book is "Marx, Keynes and the Language of Re-enchantment," and he begins by rehearsing the nineteenth-century preoccupation with mechanically produced phantasmagoria, and especially the "invention" of one Henry Dircks that came to be known as "Dr. Pepper's Ghost" and who is offered as "an allegorical representative of the 'enlightenment' encounter with re-enchantment" (26). Harries acknowledges briefly the work of, among others, Terry Castle, whom, he notes, have been instrumental in recent years in seeking "to restore the phantasmagoria's material past, to remind us that behind the term lay an apparatus and a technological history" (96). He rehearses part of this history in a first chapter that begins with Thomas Carlyle's claim in *Past and Present* that "the expectation of rationalisation and disenchantment is ... simply stupidity; only the duped expect the rational" (24), and that "the prevailing nightmare of Enchantment leaves no possibility for *re*-enchantment" (24–25). Carlyle and Weber are opportunistically invoked simply as opposing means of throwing into relief Harries's thesis, derived, in part, from Castle,[4] involving the re-emergence in the discourse of reason of an "enchanted" past that hovers spectrally over the present and haunts its rationality. It is "the latent irrationalism haunting, so to speak, this rationalist conception of mind"[5] that the history of phantasmagoria discloses, and that Harries attempts to locate in texts such as Marx's *Eighteenth Brumaire of Louis Bonaparte* and John Maynard Keynes: *Economic Consequences of the Peace*. Indeed, he argues that if the mechanical production of ghosts was aimed at debunking superstition, then the process ends, paradoxically, "in an encounter with the stubborn recalcitrance of the supernatural" (26). The impact on the viewer is akin both to Greenblatt's sense of "wonder" before the work of art, but also to Lyotard's revision of Kant's conception of the "sublime" as that "contradictory feeling [of] pleasure and pain, joy and anxiety, exaltation and depression."[6] For Castle the effect is the consequence of the annulment of "the supernatural," which is a "strange rhetorical recoil" that forces "the spirit-world of our ancestors" to become relocated "in our theory of the imagination."[7]

What interests Harries is the extent to which the mechanically produced "supernatural" becomes, for Henry Dircks (and "Dr. Pepper's Ghost"), "the centre of a growing vibrant economy" that "forgets both enlightenment and superstition in his celebration of the production of capital in the representation of ghosts" (36). Both the theatricalization and the commodification of the supernatural represents a bifold attempt to reduce it to a position in a system in which commodities are given a relative value. But as Jean-Joseph Goux has brilliantly observed, the value of capital is, like "the emergence of the Father," dependent upon the conversion of the commodity into monetary form that assumes "the position first of a fetish, then of a symbol, of an idealised standard and measure of values," before functioning as the murdered or expelled "Father" "which is simply the phantasmatic (or metaphysical) aspect of a purely syntactic moment belonging to the very structure that constitutes the general equivalent, that is, its necessary exclusion from the relative form of value." But what for Goux is a logically excluded, transcendentally endowed sovereign measure of value, for Harries is the unrepresentable fetishization of the commodity that is the "irrational" core that "assures the rationalisation of the economy" (15). It is this, quasi-Lacanian figure of "the real" of which, Harries contends, the "scare quote" is a symptom.

Harries brings into alignment Dircks's dream, of using his phantasmagoria to "stage" Shakespeare, with the cultural afterlife of

Shakespearean texts that, he argues, "provided the privileged vocabulary for intimations of the supernatural in this period" (41). He works towards a theory of Shakespearean quotation in which the circulation of "a privileged rhetoric for the history of the Ghost" (41) parallels to some extent the circulation of commodities whose value is determined by the absent "ghost" of Shakespeare himself. The "scare" quote for Harries, then, with its propensity to repetition, projects the afterlife of the cultural artifact into the lurid Gothic world of psychic disturbance, subterranean vaults, and displaced energies that may have something to contribute to the methodological procedures of materialism itself.

Preeminent among the representations of the supernatural in Shakespearean texts is the figure of the ghost of Hamlet's father, "the paradigmatic English apparition" (42), although Harries contends that Dircks's "invention" was explicitly designed to supply a lack in Shakespeare's own imperfect realisation of the supernatural in plays such as *Hamlet* and *Macbeth* (43). Dircks's attempts to demystify the supernatural by producing it mechanically represents an act of rationalization that itself became both subject to theatrical burlesque; and also "the centre, even genesis, of a world of mystery, as an irrational enchanting instrument of dispossession" (53). In this way, so Harries argues, the rational world of the Enlightenment became the inadvertent means whereby a hitherto diminished enchantment with the world of the supernatural re-entered rationalist discourse. And the paradigmatic case turns out to be the recirculation of Shakespearean formulations of the supernatural divorced from their originating historical context and rearticulated as part of a rationalist discourse haunted by an excluded spectrality.

Harries's reading of Marx's *Eighteenth Brumaire of Louis Napoleon,* which takes up chapters 2 and 3 of his book, begins with the issue of commodity fetishism and the connection between "magic" and "money" (54). His claim is that Marx's text imagines itself, like Dircks's phantasmagoria, as "a disenchanting one" (56), but that even though he recognized himself as a "critic of enchantment" (57) he fully recognised the "irrational" that "the progress of reason brought into being" (57). For Marx, unlike for Hegel, the repetitions of history contribute to "an unreal, questionable, and theatrical" existence (61), a way of articulating the concerns of the present that incorporates the discursive models of the past in a caricatured form. Hence the theatrical metaphors in which Marx describes Louis Napoleon's rise to power, but also the context within which that rise is articulated: "Men make their own history, but not of their own free will; not under circumstances they have chosen but under the given and inherited circumstances with which they are directly confronted."[9] In addition to the presence of residual, dominant, and emergent ideologies that Marx's own empirically based account uncovers, Harries seeks to draw our attention to Marx's investment in the allusive power of the Shakespearean text in general, and of the figure of the ghost of Hamlet's father in particular. This potent theatrical image of a supernatural past, that operates from *beneath* the stage of history (71) begs the question of whether there can be "a disenchanted language for the real *ground* of history" (72), or whether critical language can ever be "either completely enchanted by or completely liberated from the fantasies of ideology" (73).

These are, of course, large questions from which neither Marx, nor commentators such as Martin Harries, are entirely free. The attempts to demystify ghosts presuppose their existence (74) and it is the dialectic that undermines a rational critical language to the extent that it can never be entirely free from the enchantment that it seeks to explain. If *The Eighteenth Brumaire* inaugurates what he calls a "Gothic Marxism," of which Derrida's *Spectres of Marx* is a continuation (77), then Harries's reading of Marx (and possibly Derrida) reading *Hamlet* is subject to precisely the same interpretative processes, and there is no guarantee that he will himself, ever reach "the 'real' ground of history" (79). This is a serious methodological problem considering that Harries sets himself up as a politically enlightened "Ghostbuster" for whom the supernatural is both a projection of cultural anxiety as well as an appropriation from the past of a spectral epiphenomenon, to whose existence a causal logic can only be applied retrospectively. The ghost of Hamlet's father, in this argument, becomes a figuration of "underground history" (79), though not in any pure sense since in the analogical discourse of *The Eighteenth Brumaire* "revolution" does not find a "pure" or finally grounded expression, but, rather, "its forms are parodic or allusive" (81). What is important about Harries's argument is that his symptomatic reading of *all* revolutionary energy (which is what he takes to be the substantial burden of Marx's text) finds its paradigmatic articulation in the complex overdetermined figure of the ghost of Hamlet's father. It appears to offer an allusive "contrary language," but one that can never be fully severed from the past (85). Implicit in Harries's argument is the pessimistic conclusion that all attempts at demystification are inadvertently caught up in the very specters they seek to explain, and that "re-enchantment" is consequently smuggled in through the cellarage, so to speak. Harries appropriates Raymond Williams's categories of the "internal dynamic relations" of social process, particularly the interactive connections between the "residual," "dominant," and "emergent" elements of culture. Williams is careful to distinguish between a residual past that remains active in the present, and the "archaic" as a past "which is wholly recognised as an element of the past, to be observed, to be examined, or even on occasion to be consciously 'revived.' "[11] It is in the space between the categories of the "archaic" and the "residual" that Harries seeks to position the figure of the Ghost (91–92), and he claims that this is the position that it already occupies in Shakespeare's play (92). This leads to a difficulty, since having eschewed the utilization of quotation as a means of reinforcing Shakespearean cultural authority in favor of an emphasis upon Marx's allusive reading of Shakespeare, the specter of an originary authority peeps through the curtain of Harries's densely-woven argument.

But Harries's quarry is multifaceted and he labours diligently to recuperate the Shakespearean Ghost of the dead father for Marx's own Enlightenment project. He contends that "*Hamlet* provides a vivid image of the 'hidden ground of history' Marx and Engels described in *The German Ideology*," and he then proceeds to juxtapose, tendentiously, both the activity and the predicament of Shakespeare's Gravediggers with Marx's description of France in *The Eighteenth Brumaire* (94). The Gravediggers, compelled to live under an antiquated system, know that they do so, and as in the case of Napoleon III, what appears to be the dawn of a revolutionary advance is nothing other than the projection of a "defunct epoch" that functions to proliferate an existing social formation (95). For Harries this moment in Marx's text "introduced not a workers' revolution but a revolution in the workings of capitalism," and this "illuminates a similar contradiction between the archaic and the emergent in *Hamlet*" (95). It is at moments like this in the argument that we glimpse Harries, reading Marx, reading Shakespeare, reading the emergence of capitalism, and doing so all at the level of the symptom.

Harries insists that focusing attention on the "mine" beneath *Hamlet*, discloses "a peculiarly phantasmagorical play" (97). Thus, the Ghost in the mine, which is, *pace* Adorno, "the site of modernity's re-enchantment" turns out to be "an archaic face for a nascent world of economic exchange" (97). Although this argument is not without its ingenuity, there is some lack of clarity in the juxtaposing of the phantasmagorical significance of the Ghost and the historically overdetermined *structures* of power in which the figure of the absent father may be rearticulated and recontextualized. Harries's argument would sit more comfortably with the example of the figure of the Jew in *The Merchants of Venice,* who is an archaic demonized stereotype but who is, in effect, the harbinger of a capitalist future. To suggest that the Ghost in *Hamlet* represents capitalism since it is both "authoritative" and demonic" (104), simply because it is associated in the play with the "cellarage," which is in turn associated with the "mine" (106–8) is not convincing. The logic that suggests that "the cellarage scene arouses fears related to the rising hegemony of capitalist forms of value" (108) demands that we accept Harries's account of Marx's alleged reading of *Hamlet.* Perhaps the matter needs to be put a little differently, since both Shakespeare and Marx seem to be concerned with the past and with history as active forces in the present, so that the Ghost may be thought of as one side of a dialectical encounter whose contours have, at the end of the sixteenth century, yet to be realized. We may wonder at Harries's chiliastic formulation that the first part of the play "supernaturalises authority" as opposed to the second part that "authorises the supernatural" (111), and particularly at the rather too convenient way in which he draws the theater, money, authority, and the supernatural together, in a formulation that owes much to Jean-Joseph Goux: "The nexus of theatricality, money, authority and the supernatural surfaces in a concentrated dialogue" (112). Again, at issue here is the question of the historical specificity of the structure of social formations, and while Harries is quite correct to draw our attention to the investment that the material world continues to have in the spectral, it is difficult to distinguish between his claim that Marx was engaged in an "allusive" reading, and the possibility that he, like Harries himself, may have simply appropriated a text. This is a little different from Marx's own claims concerning Louis Bonaparte's strategy in *The Eighteenth Brumaire,* but it is up to Harries to show us more clearly what the difference is. Simply to talk of "the monetarisation of the world of the Ghost" (113) seems rather too economistically reductive, nor is it sufficient to condense these complex issues into a series of rhetoric questions which elide historical issues that require to be kept distinct from each other: "What gives a ghost authority? What gives value to money?" (116).

Even though it is possible to query some of Harries's own discursive strategies, the issues with which he has chosen to deal are of central importance. It is, perhaps, axiomatic that modernity is predicated upon repression, and, again, following Adorno, Harries believes that repression within the modern is "the hallmark of phantasmagoria" (118), and that "*Hamlet* stages a phantasmagorical narrative" (118–19). Unquestionably, *Hamlet* can be read in this way, and clearly, Marx was aware of that excess that "reason" could not articulate. But whether the "archaic summons" that the Ghost bears makes him "the figure of an important subterranean ground to the growing capitalist economy," and whether "Marx summons this phantasmagorical *Hamlet*" (119) is more questionable. The difficulty here lies with the assumption that certain Freudian categories, such as "repression" can be applied uncontroversially to the play, and to particular readings of it. That the "strange weird spell" within whose aegis the productive promise of plenty can be "turned into sources of want" (Marx, quoted in 119) may well allude to "the phantasmagorical conditions of the nineteenth century," but to imply, as Harries does, that Shakespearean allusions provided a systematic entry to those conditions is to force the evidence. In a quotation from Marx's "Speech at the Anniversary of the *People's Paper*," the figure of Robin Goodfellow is thought to be the "old mole," who is "that worthy pioneer—the Revolution" (120), and this is glossed by Harries as a "revision" demonstrating Marx's discontent with "the questionable appropriateness of associating the revolution with the feudal Ghost of King Hamlet" (120). What this explanation does not quite elucidate is the suppleness of Marx's capacity for Shakespearean quotation and allusion; clearly, too programmatic a reading would filter out the contradictions, but could it be that these composite allusions are, as Harries suggests, indicative of a political imagination that encounters difficulty "in picturing the future" (121)? To suggest uncertainty in what for a number of Marx's critics has long been thought to be a mechanically predictive methodology, all but recuperates Marx for a postmodernist uncertainty. But it also raises, in dense and intelligent form, some serious questions about what we might call the theory of quotation and allusion.

Harries's reading of Marx's reading of the historical events that comprise *The Eighteenth Brumaire*, in part, through a series of allusions to Shakespeare, offers richer pickings than his reading of John Maynard Keynes's deployment of quotation and allusion in his critique of the conditions of the Versailles treaty, *The Economic Consequences of The Peace* (1919). In the preface to his *Essays in Persuasion* (1931) Keynes professed himself a reluctant economist, and expressed the wish that with the proper use of resources the Western world would be capable "of reducing the Economic Problem which now absorbs our moral and material energies, to a position of secondary importance."[12] Harries begins this part of his analysis with a reference to the early pages of R. H. Tawney's *The Acquisitive Society* (1920) and with an affirmation of the distinction between "quotation" and "allusion"; he argues that "[q]uotation, like psychoanalysis, provokes the articulation of that which speaks only in mute symptoms," whereas [a]llusion is, then, a counter-symptom, showing the awareness of such unknowing and potentially destructive historical regression" (126). His quarry in the final two chapters of the book is Keynes's deployment of quotation and allusion to *Macbeth,* although Harries argues that "allusive awareness of re-enchantment saturates the work of many of its strongest critics," especially during the period following the First World War (125). Beginning with R. H. Tawney's allusion to the New Testament epistle of St. Paul to the Romans, he suggests that as in the case of *The Eighteenth Brumaire,* allusion may be used as "a tool for the critique of historical regression" (126). His assumption—and hence his preoccupation with the Ghost of Hamlet's Father—is that all allusions to such specters herald symptomatically both an acknowledgment of, and a reinvestment in, the sphere of the supernatural. Except that even for Marx, the weight of the past is perceived not exclusively in its truly spectral form but in its material effects, and even in Shakespeare's *Hamlet* the Ghost has a solidity that the nineteenth-century Gothic imagination interpreted differently, as any reader of Walpole's *Castle of Otranto* can testify. This is not to deny Harries's identification of phantasmagoria as "a disguise under which culture hides the new" (129), but it is to raise a question about the reinstatement of enchantment as a form of affective excess beyond the explanatory capacity of the discourse of materialism to account for. Here the difference between "quotation" and "allusion" may prove difficult to sustain, since the invocation of fragments of Shakespearean texts may just as easily constitute a desire to align a discourse that seeks to establish an explanatory authority for itself, with an existing cultural authority capable of transhistorical interpretation. Here quotation would then become *material* upon which the commentator extends a determinate labor. Harries half acknowledges this in his comment that both Tawney and Keynes "buttress" their analyses "with a supernatural superstructure, and in particular, with allusions to Shakespeare" (130).

Harries cites a newspaper skirmish of 1922 between Keynes and David Hunter Miller, who was a member of the U.S. delegation to the Treaty of Versailles conference, and he notes Keynes's deployment of references to *Macbeth* (132–33) as part of the rhetoric of this debate. Keynes's insulting reference to Miller as a "commissionaire" (the Porter from *Macbeth*) and his "recourse to the supernatural" indicate, according to Harries, the thoroughness of his imagination" of the world in which he might have influence as enchanted"; Keynes, he argues, "claims occult agency in the face of an occulted world" (135). There is no mention here of Shakespeare as the "national" poet whose meanings are inaccessible to outsiders, a factor that looms far larger in this exchange between the "knowing" English commentator and his incredulous American counterpart than the issue of "occult agency." Clearly what is required here is a much more detailed account of the contexts for such quotation as something that is readily available as a yardstick of lived experience. Here the question of the "currency" of quotation becomes a matter of some importance insofar as it functions phantasmagorically as a medium of exchange capable of projecting an image that is separate from itself, and hence, erecting, as Goux observes, a transcendent criterion of value. What Harries seems to be charting here is less a symptom of Keynes's residual preoccupation with the supernatural per se, than of the reification and the naturalization of some of the features of the spectral world of *Macbeth* as it enters the secular universe of early twentieth-century politics. What is off-putting in the quotations he selects is the mention of "spectres" and haunting"—in short, the rhetorical deployment of the vocabulary of the Gothic—in order to describe the dynamic interaction of historical forces. There is more to be investigated here, particularly the association between "sorcerers, ghosts and spooks" (135) and the connection between enchantment, haunting, and psychological control that Daniel Pick has investigated in his recent book *Svengali's Web: The Alien Enchanter in Modern Culture* (2000). Harries's own strategy here is to begin with the symptoms, which he analyzes deftly, but then to collapse it into thematic study. Thus, Keynes's preoccupation with the *economic* advisability imposing the conditions of the Treaty of Versailles upon Germany, and the transformation of French locations, especially Paris, into the "unreal" cities of the modernist, Eliotean imagination, is used as a peg on which to hang a comparison between equivocation in *Macbeth* and the political equivocation of statesmen separated from "real" events that are happening elsewhere.

Harries's insistence upon "the intermingling of political and supernatural influence figured by *Macbeth* in later works by Keynes" (150) need not imply a process of "re-enchantment" no matter what work they may perform at the level of the symptom. Perhaps Greenblatt's deliberately anti-aesthetic account of "wonder," which is not a mark of the sublime, might have been of more use here. Harries is absolutely correct in his insistence that we give these quotations from Shakespeare a detailed scrutiny, and the value of his argument for cultural historians lies in the brave attempt that he makes to provide a discursive framework for distinguishing and discussing them. Of course, at the end of the day, the specter that haunts modern culture may be none other than the ubiquitous ghost of Shakespeare himself, who functions as the absent father, against whose authoritative and paternalist utterance the value of modern experience is being constantly weighed. That is the mesmeric power that needs rigorous cultural analysis. Moreover, at the end of the day all quotation must be "scare" quotation in that it points to an act of creative ventriloquism within whose aegis the speaker her/himself becomes the phantasmagoria, the image of a national identity, but one who also bears the marks of an educational ideology. We may readily agree with Harries reading of *Macbeth* as a play in which "the language of the witches [*sic*] form the supernatural nexus where questions of 'historical' causation and the 'natural' meet" (161). But why reading Keynes involves seeing the play as "an allegory of the scare quote" because the play "returns this question of the scare quote to the 'natural' " (161–62) is not quite clear. There is much in the final chapter of Harries's book that involves a wider reading of *Macbeth,* particularly concerning the question of the play as a "history" play, though some of his conclusions are less disciplined than they could have been.

Perhaps, a conclusion in which "the end of the scare quote" (182) is proclaimed is a shade disingenuous. Notwithstanding Pope's strictures against the attempts of critics to detect the movement of life, Harries's claim that our interest in the "scare quote" is a consequence of its having died, and his assertion that all quotation is now "most often deliberate" (182), smacks too much of the end-of-history argument that is a delusive figment of the American liberal imagination. And yet Martin Harries has produced a fascinating, detailed, and dense argument, whose own twists and turns themselves betray the continued existence of the principle of the "scare quote" as he defines the genre. Moreover, we wonder to what extent the specter of *Hamlet* (father and son) and the son's circumstantial transformation into the figure of Fortinbras, is destined to hover over the politics that govern the very geographical location from which Harries speaks.

Notes

1. Stephen Greenblatt, "Resonance and Wonder," in *Learning to Curse: Essays in Early Modern Culture* (New York and London: Routledge, 1990), 170
2. Greenblatt, "Resonance and Wonder," 170.
3. Richard Halpern, *Shakespeare Among The Moderns* (Ithaca and London: Cornell University Press, 1997), 9
4. See Terry Castle, *The Female Thermometer: Eighteenth-Century Culture and the Invention of the Uncanny* (New York and Oxford, Oxford University Press, 1995), 142–43.
5. Castle, *Female Thermometer*, 142.
6. Jean-Francois Lyotard, "The Sublime and the Avant-Garde," in *The Lyotard Reader*, ed. Andrew Benjamin (Oxford: Blackwell, 1989), 198–99.
7. Castle, *Female Thermometer*, 143
8. Jean-Joseph Goux, *Symbolic Economies After Marx and Freud*, trans. Jennifer Curtiss Gage (Ithaca and London: Cornell University Press, 1990), 18
9. Karl Marx, "The Eighteenth Brumaire of Louis Bonaparte," *Surveys From Exile,* ed. David Fernbach (Harmondsworth: Penguin, 1973), 146. All further quotations from "The Eighteenth Brumaire" are from this edition.
10. See Raymond Williams, *Marxism and Literature* (Oxford: Oxford University Press, 1977), 121–22.
11. Williams, *Marxism and Literature,* 122
12. John Maynard Keynes, *Essays in Persuasion* (New York: Norton, 1963), vii.

Adulterous Alliances: Home, State, and History in Early Modern European Drama and Painting
By Richard Helgerson
Chicago and London: University of Chicago Press, 2000

Reviewer: Clark Hulse

What do the following things have in common: Shakespeare's *Merry Wives of Windsor,* Dutch genre painting, Spanish Golden Age peasant drama, Molière's *Tartuffe?*

On the surface one might say, Nothing. Or worse yet, one might heave up some argument, too flabby to be tested, about the rise of the bourgeoisie in Europe in the early modern period. The ways in which such arguments get made in literary studies too often have the vices of the lumpers without the virtues of the splitters, with results that are laughable to any serious economic or social historian.

Richard Helgerson's answer, however, is a sophisticated and useful variation on that fuzzy old argument. All of these phenomena, he argues, though they appear in four different countries over a period of more than a century, share a set of characters and a plot. The scene in each case is the bourgeois home. It is intruded upon by a sexual predator, usually an upper-class or military figure, associated one way or another with the state. The state itself—in the form of the monarch or agent thereof—then resolves the problems created by its own intrusion, and in the short run the aristocratically-dominated national order is affirmed. In the process, though, bourgeois domesticity has turned out to be much more interesting than soldiers, courtiers, or aristocrats. The effect of that representation is to create new genres—domestic comedy, peasant comedy, genre painting, and so forth—that are alternatives to the heroic genres of the past, and that are the vehicles of emergent classes and their values. These genres are "the affective base for a new revolutionary order" (4). In short, there is a straight path from the humiliation of Falstaff to the guillotining of Louis XVI.

Helgerson's argument for this thesis is good precisely to the extent that he weighs carefully the specificity of each of his four disparate cases. He is accurate about plots, careful about dates, well-read in social history, and properly skeptical about his own readings of images, even as he gradually nudges each of his four components in the direction of the central and overriding thesis. All this is done concisely, and in that easy, lucid prose that the many readers of *Forms of Nationhood* have come to value. There are no great flights of eloquence in *Adulterous Alliances,* and only the occasional slip into the old cant by which this or that is "called in question" or is said to mark a site for the contestation of values. (Did we really talk that way not so long ago?) But neither is there the blather, silliness, or turgidity that too often appears in academic monographs where sentences should be.

The book, then, is valuable less for its thesis (*of course* nonheroic cultural forms emerge as alternatives to heroic and aristocratic forms and coincide with a challenge for control of the state) than it is for the proof that a sensible argument can be mounted for this thesis. *Adulterous Alliances* is a model for us all in several specific ways:

- It is about different countries and centuries. (At a time when humanist disciplines have become ridiculously overspecialized and insular—and none more so, punningly and tautologically, than English literary studies—Helgerson ventures to give a readable account of a broad swath of culture. The book can and will be reading by many.)
- It is respectful of the differences among those countries, centuries, and art forms.
- It is respectful of the findings of specialists who know a lot about those countries, those centuries, and those art forms.

In the process, Helgerson gives us serious discussions of the terms crammed into his subtitle. "Home" becomes a word that can be mentioned in polite company, defined of course in terms of gender but also economically and spatially. The "state"—or rather the four very different states of England, Holland, Spain, and France—comes under serious scrutiny precisely through this comparison, and emerges as an extremely fragile entity, blossoming somewhere between the (temporary) recession of the religion sphere, and the nascency of the economic sphere as a transnational category. "History" becomes narrowed as a term, reduced to an aristocratic and public category of representation, belonging to the state and separated from the home, until the new domestic representational forms lift their subject matter into contact with state and history. Most importantly, "early modern" becomes meaningful as a term precisely because Helgerson can connect up Shakespeare and Molière. As shy as we are about deploying the long-honorific language of "renaissance," it makes little sense to talk about the sixteenth century as "early modern" unless there is some plausible connection to the recognizably modern, circa the French Revolution.

Most of all, Helgerson makes a serious try at describing a significant relationship between drama and painting. For the most part, the relationship is defined through similarity of content. Dutch genre painting, especially in the 1650s and 1560s, is filled with imagery of soldiers encountering fair maidens in domestic settings. Helgerson does a splendid job of reading these images in relation to midcentury political events, and if the allegory is a bit fierce at times, it is self-consciously so. The counterargument can be made that we need to let up a little on *reading* the paintings and *look* at them, let them show off their ostentatious visibility and their alluring domestic surfaces and cavities. But that counterargument will simply turn us back to Helgerson's central point about the investment in the domestic that these art forms coerce from us.

It is therefore necessary for Helgerson to argue for a second significant relationship between drama and painting, at the level of artistic mode. Aristotle distinguished between narrative and dramatic (and lyric, too, but that's not to the point here), and the distinction resonates through our understanding of the aristocratic poetic modes of epic and tragedy. In terms of bourgeois representational modes, it is useful to add "descriptive" to narrative and dramatic. It is an established argument in art history (made especially by Svetlana Alpers in *The Art of Describing*) that Italian Renaissance painting is narrative and text-centered, while Northern (especially Dutch) painting is by the seventeenth century more descriptive, and thus properly visually centered. Within this dichotomy, the dramatic operates as something of a middle voice, mediating the aristocratic intrusion on the bourgeois in Shakespeare's *Merry Wives of Windsor*, just as it does in the vignettes and implied plots of paintings by de Hooch, Hoogstraten, or even Vermeer.

This modal analysis works well enough for Dutch genre painting, so long as it is bridled by Helgerson's good sense as an interpreter. It works splendidly with the works of the eighteenth-century

French painter Jean-Baptiste Greuze, where of course Helgerson has the brilliant work of Michael Fried to draw on. (Indeed, *Adulterous Alliances* and Fried's *Absorption and Theatricality: Painting and the Beholder in the Age of Diderot* would make great back-to-back reading.) It is at a theoretical level still hard to say *why* it works, though, since it rests finally on analogy: reading painting is not reading text, visual drama is not verbal drama, and painted narrative is not poetic narrative in the sixteenth or the eighteenth centuries.

The question points to the monster lurking at the ledge of the broad terrain that Helgerson maps in this book. It is a masterful accomplishment of cultural studies, traversing its disparate territories without flattening or scorching them. The likenesses appear to the scholarly beholder, just as they do to the spectator at a domestic drama or the beholder of a genre painting. We are, in the end, scholarly aristocrats of a sort, intruding on these textual and painted spaces, and reducing them to the monarchy of interpretation. It may be fair to say that the arts of the upper and lower classes are aggressive or resistant. But the drama of bourgeois domestic art may lie precisely in its serene indifference to our arguments.

A House in Gross Disorder: Sex, Law, and the 2nd Earl of Castlehaven
By Cynthia Herrup
Oxford and New York: Oxford University Press, 1999

Reviewer: *Richard Rambuss*

"No amount of archival digging and no special slip of parchment will ever tell us whether the 2nd Earl of Castlehaven was monster or victim or both; but that is not, in fact, the historian's best question" (6). This declaration of historical agnosticism is set forth early on in Cynthia Herrup's meticulous reconstruction of the infamous trial of Mervin Touchet, the 2nd Earl of Castlehaven, who was executed, along with two of his male servants, Giles Broadway and Florence Fitzpatrick, for rape and sodomy in 1631. Notwithstanding its author's declination of the question of whether justice had been served by the earl's conviction (a matter to which I will return), *A House in Gross Disorder* is an important and finely textured work of early modern cultural studies, one that surely will long hold its place as our central historical account of the Castlehaven scandal. And while Herrup warns away readers looking for a seventeenth-century whodunit, she has produced quite a page-turner, a nicely honed consortium of comprehensive archival research, supple interpretation, and engrossing narrative.

Her goal, Herrup writes, is to retell "a vaguely familiar story with new material and new purpose" (xiii). She succeeds on both accounts. The outline of this story is that Castlehaven had sex with several of his male servants; that he orchestrated the rape of his own wife by one of them; that he directed another to bed his teenage daughter-in-law (who was also his stepdaughter) and beget for him a new heir upon her; and that he sought to disinherit his own son, with the perverse aim of promoting his favorite servingmen over him. These sensational charges devolved from his son Lord Audley's complaint to the Privy Council—a grievance, Herrup interestingly points out, in which insinuations of sexual wrongdoing served at first only as backdrop to the dispute over inheritance. For evidence of paternal malfeasance, Audley referred to Castlehaven's inordinate generosity to his servant Henry Skipwith—a signal, as Audley saw it, of his father's propensity to elide "the difference between a servant and a son" (38). Castlehaven was apparently on no better terms with his wife, Anne Stanley Brydges, who was twelve years his senior and far his social better, even though his family had now grown more prosperous than hers. As Herrup puts it, "Castlehaven had grand estates, but little reputation; [she] little wealth, but considerable grandeur" (13). In the inquest that resulted from Audley's complaint, the countess reported that from the first week of their marriage (the second for them both) her husband had shunned her for the company of prostitutes and male servants. She further claimed that he had tried to couple her with several of his servants. Her refusal to take part in these domestic debaucheries occasioned her rape, the countess alleged, with her own husband holding her down while his man had use of her body. For his part, Castlehaven steadfastly denied all these charges, even after his conviction and sentencing. ("When the threat of losing access to communion did not draw a confession from him," Herrup recounts, "even the chaplains sent him by the King grew shaken" [92].) The earl insisted that he was instead the victim of familial treachery: of an impatient son "that would have his lands" and a reprobate spouse, of whom he maintained, "Tis too well known my wife has been naught" (76). Testimony heard at all three trials that the countess was both whorish and a murderous schemer revealed that Castlehaven's view of his wife had currency inside and outside their estate at Fonthill Gifford. Herrup reports that rumors of prior adultery and infanticide also dogged the countess during and after the trials.

Herrup suspends as irresolvable the question of whether Castlehaven was "monster or victim or both." Given the various strains of testimony that have come down to us from the trial, the question of whether Castlehaven's wife was monster or victim or both might also have been explicitly raised here, if only similarly to be deferred. In any case, Herrup urges us to comprehend the trial as speaking to more than simply "the cruelty of humans to one another, and to tragedies of unhappy families" (xiii). This is not hard to do. No English peer had been tried for felony in a generation, and Castlehaven was one of the few aristocrats ever to be executed for sexual misconduct. His is also, Herrup notes, the earliest secular English prosecution for sodomy for which we have extensive documentation. Nonetheless, this book works to recast Castlehaven from his "starring role in most histories of male homosexuality in England" (1), repositioning him instead as the principal in a cautionary tale that reflects "quotidian struggles in more 'normal' households over how to live within the accepted prescriptions of early modern English culture" (xiii). What his sensational trial and its legacy reveal about early modern social organization (and its pressure points and fault lines) is thus for Herrup "the historian's best question." That is, it is a better question than Castlehaven's guilt or innocence, or for that matter the guilt or innocence of his wife, or his son.

Herrup may indeed be right to leave all this as a conundrum. Yet nearly every detail of the legal proceedings she painstakingly recovers and explicates points (despite her demurrals) toward Castlehaven's exoneration, toward a sense that he was a man more sinned against than sinning. At very least, this study points to the recognition that Castlehaven, given the circumstances of the trial and the quality of the evidence presented against him there, was improperly convicted. Many times Herrup remarks that the case made against the earl was "technically flawed" (5), that "technically sound evidence was thin" (47), that "the technical evidence for both rape and sodomy was imperfect" (65), that "neither Castlehaven's nor Fitzpatrick's actions fit the prior legal definition of sodomy and Broadway's may not have fit the technical threshold of rape" (145). (What work is the repeated modifier *technical* doing here?) Herrup also discovers little corroboration among witnesses. In Audley's original complaint against his father, his stepmother figured not as the victim of sexual assault but as a sexual wanton. Moreover, Skipwith, the servant whom Audley first identified as having risen to an unnatural place in his father's affections, and thus become a rival for Audley's due inheritance, was never indicted, despite reports that he was Castlehaven's special favorite and did "often lie in bed with the Earl" (40). Herrup surmises that, along with the testimony he supplied against the earl, Skipwith's ongoing relationship with Lady Audley, Castlehaven's stepdaughter/daughter-in-law, may have been what spared him. Two other male servants never mentioned by Audley, Broadway and Fitzpatrick, instead became Castlehaven's codefendants. Broadway confessed that he had attempted to rape the countess at Castlehaven's prompting, but he maintained that the attempt was unsuccessful. Broadway also acknowledged engaging in mutual masturbation with his master, who, he further attested, had on occasion "used his body as a woman" (46). He insisted, however, that there was no penetration. (What does this mean? Frottage? Herrup does not say.) Broadway later repudiated his deposition, saying that he did not understand its implications when it was elicited from him. Fitzpatrick likewise acknowledged an intimate relationship with Castlehaven, but he too later retracted his testimony, claiming that it had been suborned under a false promise of immunity. Although Herrup remarks that his confession was "damagingly graphic" (46), again she does not specify the intimacies enjoyed by Castlehaven and his footman. But she does emphasize that Fitzpatrick also disavowed the occurrence of penetration. This is an important point. Herrup indicates that according to the antisodomy statue under which these men were tried, "penetration alone determined the felony" (28). During Castlehaven's trial, however, Sir Robert Heath, attorney general and one of the Crown's prosecuting lawyers, declared that the statue's general sense allowed for a definition of carnal knowledge that emission, not only penetration, would fulfill.

This impromptu reading, notes Herrup, stood "in contradiction to the tradition of construing capital offenses narrowly" (60). Indeed, she recounts that "the Earl, it was said, 'seemed much amazed' when the justices ruled that his actions constituted buggery" (89). Herrup adds that Castlehaven was not the only one who was astonished: "In 1632, the London attorney William Drake referred to the case as one in which 'that was made buggery which was never accounted so before' " (89).

In addition to being prosecuted for a crime that was redefined while he was being tried for it, Castlehaven faced other, probably insurmountable, obstacles. Herrup makes a persuasive case that probably no English monarch would have proven to be less sympathetic to the earl's situation than Charles I. She further speculates that Castlehaven might have served as an unwelcome reminder of the intemperance of the king's own father, James I, who likewise indulged a taste for male minions. Herrup also usefully outlines a series of previous adversarial encounters between the Crown and the Touchets that made manifest Charles's aversion for this family. Yet even though the Crown handpicked the jury that convicted Castlehaven, it failed to deliver a unanimous verdict on either count. Only a majority was needed for conviction, and that, Herrup reports, was fragile on the sodomy charge (fifteen in favor; twelve opposed). The split verdict would appear to indicate, despite Heath's makeshift ruling, that the meaning of sodomy was hardly clarified by this case.

With little direct evidence to prove what Castlehaven had in fact done, the prosecution, Herrup details, instead focused on who he was, on demonstrating that Castlehaven was the sort of man of whom such crimes could be expected. The taint of Catholicism and Ireland that hung over the Touchet family did not help matters for the earl. But the case against him principally turned on gender, on what Herrup, in one of the book's most thought-provoking sections, terms "the responsibilities of manhood" (70). Masculinity entailed mastery: self-mastery and mastery over one's household. Neither was evident at Fonthill Gifford. Fonthill Gifford was a disordered household not only because it was the reputed site of carnal debauchery, including voyeurism, exhibitionism, and group sex, along with the alleged rape and buggery; it was also such as a place where subordinates—wife, son, and servants—were found to be spectacularly out of place. Herrup stunningly shows that Castlehaven's self-defense—namely that he was the hapless victim of villains from within the household over which he was meant to govern—was "in many ways a transposition of the prosecution's own arguments" (85). Whether he appeared as victimizer or victim, Castlehaven's masculinity remained impugned, his decadent and disorderly instantiation of his own gender producing and presiding over (or not) a grossly disordered household. His, Herrup writes, was "an example that could not be allowed to stand unanswered" (77).

Herrup, as we have seen, maintains that the task of the historian is "to explain the verdict, not to test it" (8). Doing so, she contends, will allow us to rethink the scandal, "to understand what the story meant in its time, without disclaiming its ability to speak to ours" (8) and to recognize that "there need never have been a single dominant representation of the Earl; [that] his dynamism is one of the most historically significant things about him" (150). Yet it must be said that the Castlehaven who emerges from Herrup's book hardly resembles in the end a seventeenth-century English Sade, even if the book begins with the declaration of a Wiltshire historian that Mervin Touchet was "a name at which the world grew pale" (1). So how about this as a rethinking of the ever-dynamic Castlehaven? His principal crime—the only one for which satisfactory evidence could be marshaled—was his spectacular miscarriage as a patriarch. In his extreme waywardness, Castlehaven showed himself wantonly inclined to subordinate the claims of family and caste in order to indulge his fantasy of a counter kinship structure, one of homosocial and homoerotic affiliation. Castlehaven's wife testified that he had told her that "he loved John Anktill [one of his pages] above all the world" (74). Several other witnesses attested that the earl told Skipwith that "he had rather have a son of his begetting than by any man in England" (74). In these terms, Castlehaven, who clearly grew to prefer the company of men, could be seen to have been bent on creating (however loosely he may have conceptualized it) a same-sex family within the preexisting framework of his aristocratic household. In Castlehaven's male family, his heir would have been begotten not upon his wife in their marriage bed, but by one of his beloved servingmen. This was a form of intimate association that preferred elected, affective bonds to "natural" and natal ones: what we might take to be a nascently homosexual alternative to the emerging nuclear family.

Of course this rendering restores Castlehaven his starring role in histories of male homosexuality in England; indeed, it has lineaments of hagiography, the earl cast, with an eye toward our own times, as a proto-gay martyr. (Edward Hyde, visiting Castlehaven on the eve of his beheading, found the earl, according to one early account cited here, "as full of pity as ever any martyr was, and as void of passion" [93].) But why not? If "the enigma of Castlehaven's guilt or innocence is irresolvable" (97), this sexual libertine may be as available for gay canonization as a lover of men and a martyred sodomite as he is for incrimination as an abettor of rape. Herrup maintains that nothing in her researches ever "persuaded me that the Earl was innocent, but they did lead me to ponder why almost no one in the past 370 years seemed to have seriously explored the possibility" (5). It must be obvious that I wish that Herrup in her own way had not herself so readily set aside that possibility. My dissatisfaction on this account is not to insinuate that Herrup's historiography should have taken a turn toward advocacy and special pleading, much less positivism. Her appreciation of the strangeness of the past, as well as our inability ever to render and know it fully, is salutary. Yet some sustained exploration of the possibility that Castlehaven may indeed have been innocent of capital crimes would be in order in such a book as this, I think, if only to give more play to the other kinds of stories, both about his culture and our own, that might have been opened up via just such a testing of the verdict against him.

It may be instructive, in conclusion, to compare the avowed historical agnosticism of Herrup's treatment of Castlehaven to Frances Dolan's *Dangerous Familiars,* another fascinating and learned study of early modern legal and literary representations of domestic crime.[1] In its often sympathetic, sometimes even redemptive, accounts of women who kill, Dolan's book displays little overt concern with questions of actual guilt and innocence. Nor does her indifference on this account inhibit Dolan from implicitly inviting us "to imagine, . . . sympathize, [and even] identify with" her female felons, with women who in their own households "suffer frustrations and annoyances so great that they turn to violence," including husband murder and infanticide.[2] The ultimate culprit here, Dolan makes clear, is patriarchy. Just as it arguably is in the earl's case. Of course, the reframing of the Castlehaven domestic crime scandal I have sketched above (admittedly only one narrative that could be derived from it) is underwritten with an antihomophobic perspective and not necessarily a feminist one—but also, I would argue, not an antifeminist one either. The second "axiom" propounded in Eve Kosofsky Sedgwick's *Epistemology of the Closet* is that "antihomophobic inquiry is not coextensive with feminist inquiry."[3] I find that the Castlehaven scandal emerges from Herrup's rich and provocative study as a pressure point for testing the relations between feminist and gay studies, a site where we may find that these analytic projects are not always to be entirely correspondent, even with respect to what they have to say about gender, sexuality, eroticism, subjectivity, and power, or in their critiques of patriarchy. In the case of Herrup's book, the disjunctions between feminist and gay studies may be more legible because of the unusual pairing (at least to us) of crimes—sodomy and rape—of which Castlehaven was accused. Would the prospect of more fully entertaining the possibility—even the probability—that Castlehaven was wrongly convicted, that this disorderly outsider was himself a casualty of the patriarchy, have come more readily for Herrup if no charge of rape were involved? Such critical counterfactuals might seem beside the point to many positivist historians, but they signal the trials that lay ahead for gender scholarship.

Notes

I am grateful to Michael Elliott, Patricia Cahill, Jonathan Goldberg, and Charles O'Boyle, Jr., for the opportunity to discuss so fruitfully with them a number of the issues I raise in this review.

1. Frances E. Dolan, *Dangerous Familiars: Representations of Domestic Crime in England 1550–1700* (Ithaca: Cornell University Press, 1994).

2. Dolan, *Dangerous Familiars,* 32, 31. Indeed, it is hard not to imagine a sympathetic treatment being accorded to these female felons, given Dolan's particular interest here in "violent resistance as one means by which women could be constituted and recognized as subjects in the early modern period" (57). For Dolan's own, markedly unsympathetic treatment of the Earl of Castlehaven, see pp. 79–87, in which she dismisses his self-defense as "machinations" (84).

3. Eve Kosofsky Sedgwick, *Epistemology of the Closet* (Berkeley: University of California Press, 1990), 27.

"The Tempest" and Its Travels
Edited by Peter Hulme and William H. Sherman
Philadelphia: University of Pennsylvania Press, 2000

Reviewer: Bruce Avery

To precisely chart all of *The Tempest's* performative and critical travails one would need to muster an army of Mercators, but Peter Hulme and William H. Sherman, in *"The Tempest" and Its Travels,* have produced something like cubist map of the play, by collecting writers from "diverse geographical and disciplinary backgrounds" (xii) whose multiple perspectives shed light on much of its extraordinary landscape.

This is all to the good. Perhaps no other play in the canon has inspired as much commentary on the practices of colonialism in Shakespeare's age. Much of that discussion has sought to exert pressure on old distinctions between high and low culture, center and periphery in geographic space, and savagery and civilization. To give form to the political import of these critical positions, the editors record voices from both inside and outside traditional positions of authorized pronouncement. There is, to be sure, a clutch of tenured professors—about whom more in a moment—but the volume also contains work by essayists, poets, novelists, and an employee of two non-governmental organizations (NGOs) involved in postcolonial policy.

That employee is named Lucy Rix, and her essay, "Maintaining the State of Emergence/y: Aime Césaire's *Une tempête*," focuses on Césaire's adaptation of the Shakespeare play (the volume also prints two scenes from Césaire's work in translation). For Césaire, *The Tempest* is "essentially about the master slave relation" (237) in multiple contexts, and Rix notes that his adaptation "is as open to a variety of times and locations as Shakespeare's text [is]" (237). Yet, as her essay convincingly shows, *Une tempête* is rooted in Césaire's Martinique experience, his conception of *negritude,* and his desire to create a specific space for black expression amid the overwhelming presence of Eurocentric culture.

Whatever her duties at her NGOs, Rix deploys a methodology of interpretation and citation to arrive at her destination, so while her voice might come from outside the academy, her practice is very much a product of that world. Hence her essay differs little in form from that of, say, the erudite discussion by academician John Gillies in "The Figure of the New World in *The Tempest*." Gillies shows how the play both uses and subtly alters the trope of the New World as it was employed in Shakespeare's age. While giving appropriate attention to Caliban, Gillies traces the play's fascination with Miranda as the "rich and strange" object of European attention, thus preserving the New World trope's element of wonder, yet emptying that trope of its native component: Ferdinand goes exploring and finds an "exotic" girl just like the girl who married dear old dad.

True to its multidisciplinary design, the collection gives space to poems, images, and three performance-oriented discussions. Philip Crispin's translation of *Une tempête,* staged at The Gate theater in London in 1998, is represented by two scenes. Ric Allsopp gives an account of *Tempest(s)* as it was performed in Copenhagen in 1999. Raquel Carrió's essay on her own *Otra Tempestad,* written with Flore Lauten for Cuba's Teatro Buendía, is excepted here as well. In Carrio's play, Prospero is an explorer on a voyage financed by Shylock.

Wait, there's more:

> The encounters and enchantments controlled by Sycorax create a labyrinth in which the characters "do not know if they are dead or asleep." Prospero confuses Elegguá with the Ariel of his lost kingdom; Hamlet hallucinates Oshún as Ophelia; Othello re-encounters Desdemona; Oyá seduces Macbeth through her transformation into Lady Macbeth; and Miranda and Caliban fall in love in a curious subversion of their play's plot. (158)

"Curious" is perhaps excessively understated, but no matter. What this citation demonstrates is that, in *"The Tempest" and Its Travels,* Hulme and Sherman have succeeded in their goal of charting the manifold visions readers and audiences find in and around the play by assembling a suitably baroque collection of essays, poems, images, and appropriations. Like the cartography that proliferated in Shakespeare's era, these pieces reflect back to us our continuing preoccupation with race, conquest, and rebellion, and have as much to tell us about our own failure as about Shakespeare's wonder.

Renaissance Clothing and the Materials of Memory
By Ann Rosalind Jones and Peter Stallybrass
Cambridge: Cambridge University Press, 2000

Reviewer: Frances E. Dolan

This erudite, substantial, and engaging book scrupulously documents how Renaissance attitudes toward cloth and clothing sharply differed from our own. In the sixteenth and seventeenth centuries, the authors show, clothes were both enormously costly and valuable possessions and animate, constitutive of identity, saturated with history, meaning, and memory. As a consequence, focusing on Renaissance clothing opens to challenge basic oppositions between inner and outer, surface and depth, subject and object. For what this book reveals, above all, is a self subsequent to its clothes. This version of the subject does not assume its clothes but is instead created by them. By focusing on garments, *Renaissance Clothing and the Materials of Memory* recreates a world in the process of disavowing the material as "mere things" to be accumulated and appraised rather than loved. In doing so, it offers a fresh perspective both on the sixteenth and seventeenth centuries and on our own assumptions. At its best, the book offers exhilaratingly unsettling reminders that it has not always been so, and is not inevitably so. Throughout the book, the authors assess a way of valuing cloth and clothing that they locate first in the Old Testament, but that culminates in sixteenth and seventeenth century Europe, where it is under increasing pressure. The authors outline their central arguments in an extremely helpful introduction, concluding with the summation: "Our argument is that fabrics were central both to the economic and social fabrication of Renaissance Europe and to the making and unmaking of Renaissance subjects" (14).

What interests Jones and Stallybrass most about the sixteenth and seventeenth centuries is that it is a period of massive transition in which clothes bear double meanings: they are "material mnemonics" as well as circulating commodities. Many of the book's claims are dialectics or paradoxes: fashion is change but also " 'deep' making," as in the phrase "clothes make the man"; livery materially marks its wearer's indebtedness to and dependency on others yet is also a highly valuable form of compensation; clothes permeate and shape the self and become in turn imbued with meaning and memory, but are also interchangeable, transferable, prosthetic. This is the central paradox of the book: "clothes as material memories, constitutive of the subject; clothes as a currency whose circulation unmakes and remakes the subject" (269).

Jones and Stallybrass are highly adept at putting a practice such as spinning or weaving, or a garment such as a ruff, into a richly evoked cultural context, always attentive to the operations of gender, race, and class/status, always considering the massive changes underway in the early modern world (conquest, colonization, and slavery; reformation and subsequent religious conflict; industrialization and the rise of capitalism). For instance, the opening discussion of the process by which Europeans came to demonize some objects, especially those highly valued by others, as fetishes ultimately argues that this contempt for other cultures' attitudes towards objects

> implied a new definition of what it meant to be European: that is, a subject unhampered by fixation upon objects, a subject who, having recognized the true (i.e. market) value of the object-as-commodity, fixated instead upon the transcendental values that transformed gold into slaves, slaves into ships, ships into guns, guns into tobacco, tobacco into sugar, sugar into gold, and all into an accountable profit. What was demonized in the concept of the fetish was the possibility that history, memory, and desire might be materialized in objects that are touched and loved and worn. (11)

Throughout the book, the authors show how a reverence for and identification with (and through) objects once widely shared came to be displaced onto the socially and intellectually different (and supposedly inferior), and thereby to be demeaned and rejected.

The book is organized into three parts and ten chapters, plus an introduction and conclusion. The first part, "Material Subjects," considers "the function of clothes in the constitution of Renaissance subjects" (11). It includes chapters on livery, portraits, and the complex cultural meanings that were condensed around yellow ruffs. Part two, "Gendered Habits," examines the relations between women's work—spinning, weaving, and needlework—and ideological constructions of feminine virtue. It includes chapters on Velázquez's painting *Las Hilanderas* (The spinners), Renaissance transformations of the stories of Penelope and of the Three Fates, and the relationship between needle and pen for Renaissance women. As the authors show, while poor women's spinning was the first step in all textile production, that labor was devalued and erased; furthermore, spinning was recast as crucial to an "ideological program for the production of virtuous femininity across class lines" (110). The chapter on women's needlework effectively undoes an opposition between the needle and the pen, private and public, showing that "women stitched themselves into public visibility by negotiating among the ideological and commercial versions of needlework that they found in diverse and often conflicting sources . . . thread and cloth were materials through which they could record and commemorate their participation not in reclusive domestic activity but in the larger public world" (134). Thus, enjoined to take up their needles elite women turned their needles into pens, transforming domestic industry into a means of political commentary and participation.

Part three, "Staging Clothes," considers the function of clothing in the English professional theaters. It begins with a chapter on how important the accumulation and circulation of clothes were in the development of a professional theater, going so far as to make the theater, like the subject, subsequent to its clothes: "the theater was a new and spectacular development of the clothing trade" (176). There are also chapters on boy actors and how scenes in which the boy playing a female character undresses reveal an understanding of gender as so prosthetic that clothes not only make the man but can make the man a woman; on various versions of the Griselda story and the fascinating differences among them; and on ghosts and their clothes on the Renaissance stage.

Along the way, *Renaissance Clothing and the Materials of Memory* assembles and presents far more fascinating information than I can do justice to here. The reader learns about the astonishing value of clothes, the procedures and economics of textile production, and the brisk trade in secondhand clothes in which everyone in the culture seems to have participated. The chapter on portraits teaches you to break the habit of focusing on the sitter's face to consider his or her clothes. Jones and Stallybrass show that portraits commemorate both an occasion and the clothes commissioned for it, more than a radiant subjectivity prior to and extending beyond this sitting, this suit of clothes. The portrait itself often cost less than the clothes worn for it; the clothes were more distinctive and required more skills to render than the sitter's face. The discussion of ruffs demonstrates that neither the genitals nor the coverings of the lower body (breeches vs. skirt) were the sole focus of gender identity and anxiety. As Gail Paster has shown that the heart is gendered, so Jones and Stallybrass show that the head is as well. Their focus is on prosthetic devices, such as the hat and the ruff, and how these circulate. The book also offers acute and arresting insights into a whole range of visual and verbal texts, including *Twelfth Night, Hamlet,* and *The Roaring Girl* among many others.

Renaissance Clothing and the Materials of Memory counters the disavowal of objects with a marked affection for them. This can sometimes lead to a superabundance of detail and description. The authors frequently refer back to their central claims sometimes to the point of overkill. Their movement across time, space, and genre, while wonderfully thought-provoking and unpredictable, occasionally muffles the specificity of the historical claims. These are, however, minor quibbles. This book materializes the pleasures and power of collaboration—two sets of eyes, two ranges of expertise, two habits of thought, two sets of research skills and energies. It is, as a result, remarkably wide-ranging (from the Old Testament to Richardson's *Pamela*), deeply learned, and also quirky in the best sense. You cannot predict where the authors will turn next, what kinds of evidence they'll bring in, what they'll teach you in the next chapter. While the authors generously facilitate selective reading, by providing a helpful introduction and informative titles for chapter subsections, this is a book that repays reading cover to cover.

Shakespeare after Theory
By David Scott Kastan
New York and London: Routledge, 1999

Reviewer: Kiernan Ryan

The nub of David Scott Kastan's latest book is to be found in the introduction and the opening chapter, from which the volume takes its title. "The great age of theory is over" (31), proclaims Kastan, so the million-dollar question is plainly, "What should Shakespeareans do next?" And the answer, according to Kastan, is equally plain: head for the past and go back to reading Shakespeare historically. Our aim henceforth should be to "restore Shakespeare's artistry to the earliest conditions of its realization and intelligibility: to the collaborations of the theater in which the plays were acted, to the practices of the book trade in which they were published, to the unstable political world of late Tudor and early Stuart England in which the plays were engaged by their various publics" (16).

But stay (I hear the reader cry), surely we have been here before, and more than once? The return to history Kastan recommends has already happened: the vogue for high theory surrendered to the sway of new historicism and cultural materialism back in the 1980s, and since then reading Shakespeare historically in one form or another has been the only game in town for upwardly mobile Bard-buffs. What Kastan seems to be touting as *le dernier cri,* moreover, is a one-way flight to the halcyon days before the advent of theory, when old-fangled scholarship still ruled the roost and hip historicists had yet to ride roughshod through the sleepy hollow of Shakespeare studies.

Kastan is too shrewd a cookie, of course, not to have anticipated these charges, and he makes a fair fist of defending himself against them. The new historicists clearly did steal his thunder some time ago by leading the retreat to the Rare Books Room, so it's crucial for Kastan to distance himself from his kissing cousins and justify the approach he advocates as a different kind of enterprise. Given his self-confessed debts to the wealth of work spawned by adepts of new historicism and cultural materialism, this proves no simple task. But in the end Kastan's quarrel with his corrivals boils down to the view that their thralldom to modernity makes them impervious to the strangeness of the past. Their readings turn out to be "too overtly self-interested to be compelling as historical accounts, more significant as records of our present needs and anxieties than as reconstructions of those of Shakespeare's time" (17).

That does not mean, Kastan hastens to add, that salvation should be sought in the arthritic embrace of "an older, untheoretical historiography" (40), the musty antiquarian positivism that helped start the stampede for theory in the first place. On the contrary: the history to which Kastan urges that Shakespeare studies be returned is, he insists, "a history that must itself be inflected by the theoretical initiatives that I've been discussing, aware that the approach to the past can neither be value-free nor immediate" (28). Nor does this imply, we are assured, any desire on Kastan's part "to reject literature for history or to reduce literature to history" (39). If Shakespeare's plays are best served in the twenty-first century "not by producing more theory but more facts" (31), it behooves us nevertheless to treat them, Kastan maintains, "no less as social facts than as aesthetic forms" (18).

At the level of theoretical assertion, in other words, the book affords few grounds for complaint. What every astute critic wants for Christmas is a way of tackling texts that brings their pastness into genuine dialogue with the dictates of the present, refusing to let either party hog the conversation; that strives to square a respect for historical fact with the vigilant mistrust of method and motive that theory demands; and that understands the subtle synergies that link literature to history, tracing the imprint of an era in the turn of a phrase without sacrificing the poetry to the politics. The problem is that Kastan's practice fails to jibe with what his theory prescribes. What principally absorb him are the material conditions under which Shakespeare's plays were originally produced as theatrical events and as printed texts. What turn him on are not their aesthetic qualities as unique configurations of language and form, but the tales they have to tell about the extraneous circumstances of their emergence, the pretexts they provide to expatiate on aspects of cultural and political history that immure them in an alien world.

As a result, *Shakespeare after Theory* conveys the impression of good old-fashioned scholarship crouching behind a theoretical rationale that has little purchase on its true concerns and frequently proves redundant. Thus chapter 3, "The Mechanics of Culture: Editing Shakespeare Today," musters poststructuralist pieties about the impotence of the author and the infinite determinants of the indeterminate text in order to remind us of the impossibility of establishing a pristine edition of any of Shakespeare's plays. Nor would this ploy matter, were it not that it serves the turn of an argument that drives us back to the very spot where it picked us up. "For years," Kastan recalls, "we just read whatever edition we happened to have at hand, confident that the text was accurate and authoritative" (60). Then the seeds of epistemological doubt were sown by editors wedded to the "social conception of textuality," as a result of which "there are no longer grounds on which one version of a text might be thought superior to another" (67). So where does that leave us? Not bothering to edit it all, "since the unedited text, even in its manifest error, is the only and fully reliable witness to the complex process of the text's production" (67)? Or floundering in hypertextual cyberspace, struggling to make sense of something that is "less an edition than an infinitely expandable and promiscuous archive" (69)? No prize for guessing that it leaves us exactly as before, leafing through whatever modern edition we have to hand, because there's no reason to regard one construction of the text as more definitive than another, and because both the other options are intolerable. "In truth," Kastan winds up conceding, "most of us will for the foreseeable future continue to read Shakespeare's plays and teach them in edited versions, in book form rather than off a computer screen, with spelling and punctuation modernized" (69). *Plus ça change.*

The following chapter, "Shakespeare in Print," pulls a similar superfluous stunt, rehearsing the familiar reasons ("All this is, of course, well known" [76]) for concluding that "the play that appeared in the bookstalls was always something other than the play Shakespeare wrote" (79)—which, in the absence of an authenticated manuscript, is naturally irretrievable. However intriguing one finds this indisputable fact, it's difficult to see what difference it makes to the only issue that matters: the sense we make of the modern edition selected for study. No one is going to suspend reading Shakespeare or ascribing the plays to him for want of cast-iron proof that he penned those very words in that very order.

Even when Kastan moves on to wrestle with the specific editorial problems posed by *1 Henry IV* in chapter 5, it still feels like

Groundhog Day for Shakespeareans. Kastan guides us expertly once more through the textual and historical arguments for restoring the name "Oldcastle" in place of "Falstaff," before arriving at the sensible conclusion that Shakespeare and his first editors, Heminges and Condell, were obviously happy to settle for the name that has stuck for four hundred years, so we would do well to do likewise. There's no doubting the quality of Kastan's scholarship or the range and depth of his historical knowledge; the question is why so much accomplishment should be deployed to so little purpose: to wit, taking the eccentric pedantries of the Oxford Shakespeare seriously.

Things perk up considerably when Kastan turns, in chapters 6 and 8, to the representation of authority and the impact of cross-dressing on the early modern stage. Kastan produces a splendid compendium of quotations from contemporary sources to prove that, whatever cynical modern critics may think, Shakespeare's fellow-citizens needed no persuading of the innately seditious drift of the drama. The playhouses, roundly denounced by Samuel Cox as "dangerous schools of licentious liberty," posed "a threat to the culture of degree" (154), claims Kastan, because they "unnervingly crossed class as well as gender lines; not only did boy actors play women but commoners played kings" (152). Indeed, Kastan mounts a plausible case for contending that the leveling impulse of the stage helped pave the way for the revolution and regicide that convulsed the nation a few decades after Shakespeare's death, and nowhere more effectively than in history plays that "placed the king on a scaffold before a judging public" (111). Unfortunately this contention is pitched into confusion in his final chapter on the closing of the theaters, where the historical evidence confirms that Parliament recognized "Publike Stage-plays" as crucibles of dissent, but theoretical correctness constrains Kastan to state, in baffling contradiction of his earlier assertions, "that the theater is itself constitutively ambivalent," that it is "never inherently *either* an agent of subversion *or* an apparatus of royal authority" (209).

Of course, the only way of settling the matter would be through a close reading of the plays, which is precisely what Kastan's sociological historicism steers him away from. Not the least objection to global statements about the Renaissance stage is that their remoteness from the verbal texture of the scripts performed upon it erases the distinction between one play and another. If the social and sexual cross-dressing intrinsic to the theater is a criterion of subversive intent, then *Perkin Warbeck* is as significant as *King Lear,* and *Love's Metamorphosis* as successful as *Twelfth Night,* a proposition to which only the most harebrained iconoclast would be apt to subscribe. What is the point of an approach to Shakespeare for which the poetry of the plays is beside the point? Why trawl the archives in search of secrets that can only be found in the form and phrasing of these startling masterpieces of dramatic art?

The problem with the contextual historicism Kastan commends is that its indifference to the formal grammar of the plays, to the way they are shaped and the way they are worded, blinds it to Shakespeare's most profound and arresting quality, and the reason why we remain enthralled by him today: his *anachronism,* his refusal to make complete sense in terms of his time, because his works are shaped as much by the pressure of futurity as they are by the world from which they sprang. To attend to the unpredictable twists of their diction and design is to discover their impatience with both the past in which they were penned and the present in which we encounter them. It is to recognize the futility of "restoring" Shakespeare's texts to contexts from which they have already looted all they need or which they have expressly ruled out as irrelevant to their purpose. It is to perceive those texts *as* history indeed—not in the retrospective, second-hand sense that Kastan intends, but in the sense that they are acts of historiography in their own right, rival imaginative versions of the past in which the prospect of transformation has been preserved.

The absence of this understanding mars what are otherwise the two best essays in the book, where Kastan offers readings of *Henry IV* and *Macbeth* that do undertake to engage with the texts. In chapter 7, " 'The King hath many marching in his coats,' or, What did you do in the War, Daddy?," Kastan rightly rejects accounts of *1* and *2 Henry IV* as ideologically orthodox, highlighting the way the plays unmask the manufactured origins of sovereignty. But the chief burden of proving their transgressive thrust falls implausibly, if unsurprisingly, upon Falstaff, whose "exuberance and excess will not be incorporated into the stabilizing hierarchies of the body politic" (136). The trouble with taking this tack is that in Falstaff those who rule behold their inverted mirror image, their alter ego, not their nemesis; the values he embodies are identical, not antithetical, to theirs, and to champion the cause of Falstaff against the dour disciplines of authority is merely to reverse the poles of the orthodox reading, leaving the plays' commitment to hierarchy uncontested. It is precisely through their structural and stylistic obsession with doubling, however, that *1* and *2 Henry IV* enact their endorsement of equality and demolish the foundation of difference upon which hierarchy is built.

Oddly enough, Kastan is admirably alert to the key role played by twinning and mirroring in Shakespeare's Scottish play. Chapter 9, "*Macbeth* and the 'Name of King'," takes its cue from Jonathan Goldberg's detection of "secular contamination" in the text and the confusion of heroes and villains discerned in the play by Harry Berger, and demonstrates how *Macbeth* confounds the moral authority of sovereignty itself. En route, moreover, Kastan makes acute points about Macbeth's habitual resort to euphemism and pronominal evasions, revealing how sharp a reader of Shakespeare he can be when he gives history books the elbow and fastens his mind on the work. But the past-bound gaze of historicism hobbles him here too, blocking out not only the democratic implications of doubling but also the egalitarian imagery of babies, blood, and "human kindness" that marks the tragedy's estrangement from its era, its contract with a dispensation whose advent we still await.

This has turned into a longer, more disgruntled review than I originally set out to write. I have no particular axe to grind with David Scott Kastan, who writes with elegance, lucidity, and wit, and whose plea for even more historicism than we've had already will doubtless be music to the ears of many Shakespearean scholars. It's simply that *Shakespeare after Theory* has brought home to me, by the patent belatedness of its appeal, how misguided the whole turn to history has been, how played-out its trademark routines now appear, and how urgent it is that Shakespeare studies move on and find new things to say about the plays as works of art.

In fact, I have a hunch that Kastan himself has cottoned on to this too, and that deep down his heart is not in the enterprise he endorses. In the title chapter he worries commendably, and justifiably, "that the approach urged here returns the study of literature to an elitism it has struggle to escape, demanding access to rare book collections and scholarly training"; and that "the focus on history, even the enabling conditions of literary activity, still deflects attention from the literary text itself" (41). In chapter 2, "Are We Being Interdisciplinary Yet?," he blows the gaff on the incompatibility of the literary and historical disciplines, which "often seem to belong to entirely different, if dependent, realms of being" (44)—as indeed they do, which is why it's such a waste of time trying to straddle them. "The commitment to interdisciplinarity," Kastan disarmingly admits, "has now become as reflexive and sentimental as was the commitment to disciplinary integrity. There may be something still to be said for traditional disciplinary interests and procedures" (47). Amen to that. Perhaps most telling of all, though, is what Kastan lets slip in the quip he enlists to distinguish his brand of scholarship from new historicism. "I have always understood my work as involved in a somewhat different, though clearly related, project," he writes, "something that Peter Stallybrass and I, usually gleefully, have come to think of as 'The New Boredom'" (18). I couldn't have put it better myself.

Shakespeare Jungle Fever: National–Imperial Re-Visions of Race, Rape, and Sacrifice
By Arthur L. Little Jr.
Stanford, CA: Stanford University Press, 2001

Reviewer: Richard Burt

Arthur Little Jr.'s *Shakespeare Jungle Fever: National–Imperial Re-Visions of Race, Rape, and Sacrifice* is a study of "the bodies of Lavinia, Othello, Antony and Cleopatra" (21). Each body—a "white female, black male, white male, and black female" (10)—gets a chapter, the last two chapters making up nearly half the book. After explaining that "jungle fever," the title of a Spike Lee movie, is used popularly and deprecatingly among blacks to mean interracial sex among whites and blacks, Little says that he wishes to use jungle fever "to point less to an interracial dynamic per se than to the cultural and multicultural anxieties giving rise to these scenes as sites and sights through which England as a nation and empire chooses to name and visualize itself" (15). Little focuses on Ireland and Africa rather than on the New World to argue that racial difference or Otherness was a means by which the English could maintain their identities. Once violated, women are made to sacrifice themselves so that national purity may be maintained. And the rapist is typically figured in early modern culture and drama as a racial Other, a black man. In Little's view, then, narratives of rape and sacrifice tend to serve the interests of a patriarchal, imperialist nation. In addition to *Titus Andronicus, Othello,* and *Antony and Cleopatra,* Little also discusses *The Rape of Lucrece* (Lucrece is a foundational figure for Little) and *Julius Caesar.* Little also ranges across some nonliterary discourses as well as visual discourses, including a number of paintings and prints. He profitably extends work on race in early modern English culture pioneered by Kim Hall, Lynda Boose, Ania Loomba, and Margo Hedricks, among others.

In chapter 1, Little argues that the rape and sacrifice of Lucrece and of Lavinia occurs in a racialized narrative. In chapter 2, Little argues that Othello's relationship to Desdemona cannot be separated from the discourse of rape. In chapter 3, Little argues that Antony has a leaky, female body, and that Antony tries to gain power by regendering himself as female, sacrificing himself like Dido, but that he fails to do so effectively. Antony, Little says, is queer, while Caesar's asexual heterosexuality makes it possible for Caesar to produce an ideological whiteness that triumphs over both Cleopatra's blackness and Antony's queerness. The fourth chapter is devoted to showing that Cleopatra redeems herself by exchanging her blackness for whiteness, and escaping the ideological whiteness of Caesar.

Little's book has no doubt made a contribution to the study of Shakespeare, race, and sexuality, particularly in the ways in which he draws attention to whiteness as a social construction and that whiteness is multiple, not one thing. Moreover, the range of plays and visual materials Little takes up is truly impressive. But I confess I found the book far less successful than it might have been in making its contribution. I sometimes found Little's arguments so abstract as to be beyond my comprehension. Consider: "The black presence in Shakespeare's play makes visible and then amalgamates and critiques those impolitic fictions that become engendered and intermixed in the name of cultural order.... The act of making fair fair and black black becomes itself a dramatic metaphor, hinting at the ways realpolitik uses metaphor in the spirit of literalness" (86). Or consider yet another example:

> To argue that "for spectators at the Globe, the stage Moor (a 'white' actor in blackface) was essentially an emblematic type," is to fail to appreci-

ate the ideological confluences between real African bodies and the very theatricality of blackness in early modern English culture. It is to miss the theatrical and metatheatrical cultural playfulness and seriousness when he offers Brabantio his rather desperate response—"If virtue *delighted* beauty lack, *I* Your son-in-law is far *more fair* than *black*" (1.3.2814–85; p. 100)

One might be forgiven for failing to appreciate and missing these points, given that they would be hard for almost anyone to find. The lack of a referent for "he" in the sentence above doesn't help matters, but the real problem is the sheer opacity of these and frequently similar formulations that are unfortunately all too typical of the book.

The book could also have been less repetitive. For example, in his summary of his final chapter, Little writes:

> Chapter 4, "(Re)posing with Cleopatra," draws on a rather dense repository of meanings, moving in and around the term *(re)posing*. The word works rather nicely to lay out what I argue is Cleopatra's polymorphous perversity, her *polyglossia*. Her place in Shakespeare's play moves from her posing to her posturing, from her posing (as in sitting to have one's picture taken) to her reposing, sexually stretched out in the barge; from her posing to her reposing, her repositioning of herself in response to a Western position of her; from sexual positioning to her sexual posturing, that is, her indulgence in the "preposterous" discourse of transvestism and sodomy. . . . Shakespeare's Cleopatra . . . uses her death to reposition the positioning of her in Roman narrative, particularly the fixing of her in Enobarbus's narrative. (24)

And in a section of chapter 4 called "Behind the Pornographic and Ethnographic Scene," the phrase "pornographic and ethnographic" (sometimes with small variations) is repeated nine times in a page and a half and eighteen times in seven and a half pages.

Apart from needing a good job of copyediting to make the prose clearer and the book more coherent and less repetitive, the substance of Little's book could also have been stronger. Little tends to homogenize early modern English culture, to create binary oppositions so that Othello or Aaron, for example, become rapists. And this leads him into self-contradiction. For example, Little says that "the black man has an almost omnipresent place in early modern rape drama but, not surprisingly, is never allowed to rape the white woman" (59). But he later adds that "Aaron is the play's real rapist" (63) and asserts that Othello is also a rapist "in effect" (what does the qualifier "in effect" mean here?). At later points, the "in effect" simply drops out. I wish Little had attended more closely to the contradictions in early modern English culture and in Shakespeare in particular.

I think the book would also have benefited greatly from more skeptical, resistant readers when it comes to the close readings Little offers (or Little would have done well to heed their advice, which they may well have given). Little admirably wants to do close readings of the plays, and faults New Historicism for not doing them: "New Historicism, in its overtly determined and self-proclaimed "turn away from the formal, decontextualized analysis that dominate[d] new criticism," has effectively shied away from offering extended close readings of its literary examples. Especially from the point of view of studying race and racial alterity in early modern culture, this move has been to its extreme detriment." (7). While I would say that Montrose, Goldberg, and Greenblatt have done plenty of close readings, I would agree with Little that it is certainly worthwhile to do them. Yet Little's own readings tend to strain credulity. Here are a few: "When Titus kills [Lavinia] he replays the sexual violence by masturbating her with his sacrificial knife and reenacts both the rape and the *raptus.* He incestuously steals back her chastity by stealing the place of Tamora's sons and Aaron, making himself the agent of Lavinia's rape, transforming it into his own orgasmic experience" (57); "Othello becomes in effect the first black rapist" (93); in Antony's funeral oration, "Caesar's body, with its multiplicity of 'dumb mouths,' gets dramatized as the victim of gang rape" (110); Antony "performs fellatio on Caesar's wounded corpse" (110); "the 'stones' in Antony's gendered narrative refer synecdochically to the phalluses, that is, the swords of Rome and hint simultaneously at the threat to them—that is, stones instead of / without penises" (112); we hear of the conspirators' "penetration of the male body, their homosexual trespasses" (118); Desdemona's marriage is *"obscene"* (82); "reading Antony as queer, culturally and sexually, is not lost on Shakespeare's play, in which the penetration of Antony's body is interwoven into suspicions about Antony as having been feminized by Egypt. From the very opening we get inklings of Antony who not only 'bends' in devotion but who bends over. We hear echoes of this accusation again when Antony imagines himself 'bending down' in 'penetrative shame.' Too, his arguing that he dies his student's student, conjures up and reverses the familiar language of sodomy within institutional pedagogy" (119); Enobarbus's description of Cleopatra on her barge first meeting with Antony offers "a virtual pornographic *ekphrasis*. . . . It moves more like a pornographic film replete with pan-eroticism, as it repeats (plays out) both the action and words of 'beating' and 'stroking' " (151); "[I]n effect, [Cleopatra] becomes Antony's rapist" (150); the first exchange between Antony and Cleopatra is, according to Little, a discussion of the size of Antony's member: "Along with the deed of sex, the pre-textually known emasculating Cleopatra tries to quantify—hence telling and reckoning—(if not shorten or cut off) the length of Antony's penis. Antony protests, insisting his sexual equipment is beyond measurement" (155–56).

Perhaps as a forecast of what is to come, Little characterizes his readings as "camp" (13) in his introduction, and I take it that the above quotations are examples of what he means by camp. I for one am happy to find and make bad puns and to find sex pretty much anywhere in a text or visual representation. But I have to wonder if Little really expects his readers to find his camp readings persuasive. One certainly would like to have fuller stage directions than those of the quarto or Folio editions of *Titus Andronicus* for Little's account of Titus masturbating with his sword and for his orgasmic experience. Why call Aaron the "real rapist," when he only plans it and Goths commit it? Why not consider the fact, as Francesca Royster has in an essay on the play in *Shakespeare Quarterly* (51:4), that Aaron does not rape Lavinia? Similarly, can Othello rightly be called a rapist when he has married Desdemona with her consent? It is not clear to me why Little rejects Ania Loomba's much more sensible suggestion that the image of the black rapist hovers around the marriage of Othello and Desdemona until Desdemona forcefully proclaims her consent and loyalty to Othello. Moreover, isn't it still debatable whether Othello and Desdemona ever actually have sex? Why call Cleopatra Antony's rapist? When does Antony ever refuse? Most readers would probably agree that the Enobarbus's description of Cleopatra's barge becomes highly sexualized and would accept a pun on "stroke." But does Little truly think that "beat off" meant masturbation for Shakespeare (as the words do now)? Although Little attacks conservative critics like Walter Jackson Bate and Brian Vickers, Little's readings are precisely the kind that get mocked in journalistic accounts of the MLA and literary criticism. Some readers might even wonder if Little isn't even offering himself up a martyr to the cause, inviting such attacks by making his readings as far-fetched as possible.

Like so many other political critics, Little claims his writing is motivated by passionately held extraliterary commitments (in this case to racial justice), and he takes to task, as have other political critics before, other kinds of critics for not being as political as he is. Little is typical, moreover, in claiming that there is a radical critique to be found in Shakespeare's plays, though Little is perhaps more vague about what "radical" means. Shakespeare, predictably, turns out to have been on the right side: "I propose as my most committed premise that Shakespeare positions himself as an 'alternative' reader of his culture's reading of alterity" (10). Little rings the changes on the current buzzwords along the way, such as "wound culture," "witness," "trauma," "hybridity," "performativity," and so on. And he touches all the bases of contemporary political criticism. He introduces the personal, noting that he writes "as a gay African American" (11) and "as an African American and gay man," (13). There is also the requisite attack on the New Historicism, this time for its "undertheorization of race and racial discourse in early modern England" (6) and for pushing "for an early world more idiosyncratic and arcane than comprehensible" (12). (It's interesting to see who drops out of Little's critical conversation: Greenblatt on *Othello* gets a single cite; the fine work by Timothy Murray, Edward Snow, Katherine Maus, and Carol Neely goes unmentioned. Perhaps this is another symptom of a new professionalism. Criticism now apparently has an increasingly short shelf life.) And Little adds an afterword wondering what the study of Shakespeare, race, and sexuality has to do with the present, and then mentioning the dragging to death of Texan and African-American William Byrd, Jr., the murder of gay man Matthew Shepherd, and the burning of O. J. Simpson's auctioned memorabilia before enthusiastic spectators on the steps of the Los Angeles County Courthouse.

Shakespeare Jungle Fever is hardly alone in being predictable and conforming to contemporary critical convention even as it makes the argument for its own and Shakespeare's transgressiveness and subversiveness. And I don't mean to fault it for doing what nearly everyone in the field also does. One could praise Little's camp readings as attempts to say something new, even if they fail to persuade. My point is that while Little's antiracist and antihomophobic politics are unobjectionable and will no doubt be shared by virtually all Shakespeareans who read his book, and while its predictability and conformism to critical decorum and convention will no doubt be lauded by similarly conformist political critics (who also view their own work as "oppositional"), *Shakespeare Jungle Fever* would have been a much stronger book if Little had delivered his readings with greater tact, texture, and persuasiveness and if he had made his argument more cogently, coherently, and clearly.

Maternal Measures: Figuring Caregiving in the Early Modern Period
Edited by Naomi J. Miller and Naomi Yavneh
Aldershot, England: Ashgate, 2000

Reviewer: Mary Beth Rose

Maternal Measures is a large collection of small essays. By large I mean in total size (comparatively speaking these days) and generosity: the collection includes twenty essays, all of which situate themselves proudly within existing scholarship. Further, rather than focusing on only one country or one discipline (English literature, e.g.) they encompass a variety of geographical areas and traditions and consider art history and music as well as social history and literature. By small I mean in analytic scope: the essays are short, and they contribute a great quantity of useful additional information to the store that exists, rather than, with some exceptions, offering new conceptualizations or arguments about motherhood and/or gender in the early modern period.

Editors Miller and Yavneh wisely have chosen essays that engage the broadest and most multifaceted conceptions of motherhood by focusing on a variety of roles that involve either caregiving and nurture, or their opposites, destruction and deprivation, the dreaded maternal antitype that seems to come with the territory of the idealized type. In addition the collection is unified by the almost universal concern of the contributors with motherhood as a site of contested cultural authority. Thus the essays feature "midwives and wet nurses, wise women and witches, polemicists and queens: many female positions of authority fostered definitions and comparisons that used maternity as a touchpoint or measure of validation or denigration. For each woman who claimed maternal measures as a strategy of power, one can find another woman who endeavored to stake out a position that extended beyond the purview of reproduction" (p. 19). The editors' focus on women's roles, laid out in careful detail in their introduction, tends to perpetuate an older model of gender relations in the Renaissance that clearly separates men and women and tends to rely on a binary analytic frame that assumes, or can lead to assuming, male oppressors and female victims. While there is no gainsaying the truth value of this model, recent scholarship has exposed it as insufficiently nuanced and, in some cases, unreflectively essentialist: it assumes that the normative conceptions of gender articulated by conservative thinkers in a variety of domains in the early modern world actually worked in empirical experience. Another related direction this model can take is toward a celebratory romanticizing of womanhood as conventionally defined. In contrast, more recent scholarship has clarified the complex and often ironic ways in which normative and prescriptive conceptions of gender intersect with a variety of sexualities, both in representation and in empirical reality. However, the editors clearly articulate a committed belief that viewing the maternal world of the past in terms of social roles and their demonic opposites, normatively defined, can greatly increase our knowledge. "Mothering others, for better or for worse, female caregivers in the early modern period participated in a spectrum of spectacles whose collective record, explored in part by the essays in this volume, offers an opportunity to measure our current understandings of women's voices and positions as mothers and others, both in the early modern period and our own" (p. 19).

The editors never explain precisely what they mean by "women's voices and positions"; nor do they theorize about ways in which the negotiation between the present and the past that they applaud is actually accomplished. However the best essays in the volume are concerned with the relationship of the maternal to power. The idea of early modern motherhood as a locus of cultural conflict and change is, of course, not new; but several of the essays bring fresh perspectives as well as novel and valuable information to our attention. In what follows I will deal neither with every essay in the collection, nor even with every good essay. Rather I will briefly discuss several of the essays that I feel best indicate the virtues and contributions of *Maternal Measures.*

In "Midwiving Virility in Early Modern England," Caroline Bicks focuses on ways in which "early modern midwifery and its female practitioners embodied specific concerns about how narratives that defined and underpinned male authority were produced" (p.49). Social historians have demonstrated that during the seventeenth century, particularly after the invention of the forceps, women's power as midwives was gradually taken over by the rapid professionalization of male doctors. Bicks focuses specifically and interestingly on the idea of the narrative power and valuable knowledge midwives had when birth was an all-female event. Discussing (with one particularly fascinating example of a midwife's rhetorical intervention in the queenship of Anne Boelyn) what she calls the competition between male and female tales of paternity, Bicks argues for the considerable and threatening "power of female narrative to tamper with male-authored genealogies of literary and monarchical figureheads" (p. 50). Female testimony, she contends, both subverts and affirms male narratives of power. This paradox constitutes the threat, and Bicks performs a worthy philological feat by demonstrating how the word "gossip," which had been a unisex term for a confidant in the sixteenth century, gradually becomes conflated with "midwife" as male medicine begins to defeat female power over the processes of birth during the ensuing century.

In " 'Players in your huswifery, and huswives in your beds': Conflicting Identities of Early Modern English Women," Mary Thomas Crane also performs a philological tour de force. Crane demonstrates that the word "housewife" in the seventeenth century developed as a separation from the term "hussy," indicating a connection with sexual anxiety. In an interesting move, Crane connects this anxiety specifically with female freedom and in particular with female labor and potential economic independence. To augment this argument she traces the evolution of the term "spinster" from a description of a woman (usually married) who was employed to spin to the pejorative term for a perpetually unmarried and childless woman. Crane quotes Herbert's *Outlandish Proverbs*—"she spins well that breedes her children"—as an example of the connection between woman as breeder and woman as income-producer, arguing, as do many of the essays in this volume, that the linkage between maternity and female power in other domains is both desired and feared. Because Crane's argument concerns female labor and the rising discomfort with it, her essay shores up the generally accepted thesis which contends that the gendered separation between public and private spheres in the seventeenth century gradually confined upper- and middle-class women to domesticity and isolation.

In " 'My Mother Musicke': Music and Early Modern Fantasies of Embodiment," Linda Phyllis Austern discusses with a focus on music the ways in which the liberal arts were represented as embodied women throughout early modern Europe, "based largely on a tradition of clothing abstract concepts in female flesh and on the complexities of an ancient and medieval heritage that held the idealized maternal body as an object of perfection, desire, and inspiration" (p. 240). Of all the arts, music particularly was associated with powers of creation and nurture, Austern explains, adding, in fascinating detail that, where vision had long been associated with masculine privilege, "hearing and vocality have been linked to women's interiority and irresistible invitation to comfort or seduction; the female body dissolves and is remembered in music, or becomes eroticized as an ear" (p. 243). Austern's essay is augmented by a wonderful series of illustrations, including both paintings and musical scores.

One of the most interesting essays in the volume, Frances Dolan's "Marian Devotion and Maternal Authority in Seventeenth-Century England," is reprinted from Dolan's recent book, *Whores of Babylon: Catholicism, Gender, and Seventeenth-Century Print Culture.* Dolan's emphasis on Catholic traditions leads her to present a new perspective on the relation of the maternal to female authority by focusing on the distinctive ways in which Catholics and Protestants view the Virgin Mary. "While Protestant writers tend to assume that women should be humble handmaidens, and that a woman elevated to the Virgin Mary's position in Catholic worship, is, of necessity, proud, ambitious, vengeful, and bossy, Catholic writers are less resistant to the very idea of female power," she writes (p. 282). Conversant with a wide variety of forms of writing, including medical, moral, and legal tracts (for example, witchcraft trial records), Dolan acknowledges that Catholic and Protestant writers alike subscribe to what she calls the "theological logic" that subordinates human to divine agency; and that all seek to curb female agency, which is often conflated with violence, particularly in the public sphere. Nevertheless she shows that through a series of subtle distinctions, Catholic writers contrast with Protestants who either deny female authority altogether or else acknowledge and then erase it. "Catholic defenders of Marian devotion suggest a third possibility—a male-authored discourse that assumes and even extends maternal authority" (p. 290).

Material London, ca. 1600
Edited by Lena Cowen Orlin
Philadelphia: University of
Pennsylvania Press, 2000

Reviewer: Cynthia Wall

This impressive collection of well-matched, well-crafted essays opens with particularly apt illustrations: first, "A Table of the chiefest Cities, and Townes in England" (1600), that *admits* the existence of other urban centers in England—but all from a bird's-eye-view of London; followed by another table that calculates the distance *to* London from Sites Elsewhere. The essays that follow themselves mark paths to and from the Renaissance city, along axes defined by the title: the various implications of "material" and "culture," the many contemporary meanings of "London," and the issues besetting the temporal assignment of "ca. 1600." The book is divided into five sections treating the meanings of "material" London, consumer culture, and the demography, diversions, and structures of the city. With some fifty illustrations, this volume offers historians, literary critics, and the general reader interdisciplinarity at its best, with an appeal far beyond the temporal boundaries of the Renaissance.

The well-known danger of a collection of essays is that it can't possibly create the same conceptual coherence or sustain the level of sophistication as a singly authored book. Orlin's introduction does a fine, clear job of surveying the textual territory, marking sites of overlap and not eliding differences in theoretical approaches, promising a compelling coherence-in-diversity. Orlin also provides a brief introduction to each section, linking subjects within the section and sections to each other. Each essay worthily resists simple generalizations or obvious agendas, paying close attention to historical nuances and textual details. More remarkable still: all the essays are not only learned (not surprising, given the impressive cast of characters) but also eminently readable.

In the first section, with essays by David Harris Sacks, Derek Keene, and Alan Sinfield, Orlin notes that while "the essays . . . seem [topically] disparate, they share space because, procedurally, they are so forthcoming" (19). The "disparate" topics are London as political capital, London as center of trade, and London as cultural capital—certainly London necessarily interconnected. Sacks's essay, "London's Dominion: The Metropolis, the Market Economy, and the State," analyzes London in terms of a materialism of "motion and change" through the historical anecdotes of the earl of Essex's rebellion and of Will Kemp's dance from London to Norwich, to show that "it was not merely trading commodities that spread along the highways to and from London but ideas, values, habits, and practices—the elements of a way of life centered on exchange and consumption which drew more and more of England into its web" (41–42). Derek Keene's "Material London in Time and Space" challenges the whole assignment of significance to "ca. 1600" ("it is at least arguable that the decisive stage in the development of the city as the focus of national power and expenditure was in the late thirteenth century rather than in the sixteenth" [58]). But the conditions for noticeable change abounded in 1600—in the doubling of population, the increase of foreign goods, and the increased manufacture of, among other local things, beer-brewing. Alan Sinfield worries about "the Marxian political edge . . . slipping away" from studies of materialism into a focus on "thinginess" (75) and includes a critique of "new historicists and cultural materialists" who have just "picked up bits and bobs from Natalie Zemon Davis and Christopher Hill." Sinfield uses Jonson's *Poetaster* (1601) to look at writing under pressure in 1600, claiming that the play "is not documenting the author function, it is helping to constitute it" (82).

The second section, "Consumer Culture: Domesticating Foreign Fashion," incorporates essays by Joan Thirsk, Jane Schneider, Ann Rosalind Jones and Peter Stallybrass, and Jean E. Howard, on the role of the provinces, the complex codes of colors and dyes in seventeenth-century fashion, and gendered spaces. Thirsk's essay, "England's Provinces: Did They Serve or Drive Material London?" argues: *both*. She looks at the new taste for vegetables and fruits, local knitting traditions, the drive to create employment, the standardization of skills, and the preservation of cultural individualities, to show the interdependent developments of imported tastes by the gentry and aristocracy and the local reproductions (and nationalizations) of those tastes. Schneider's particularly fascinating essay links the Elizabethan reproduction of black and white clothing in aristocratic life and portraiture to a nationalist resistance to the (superior) dyeing capabilities of the Mediterranean—until the English dyers learned the trade properly; upon which "the Venetians retreated to their terra firma, [clothing] themselves ever more cautiously in black, [and] Londoners had their colorful coming out" (122)—including the defining red of Britain's imperial armies. Jones and Stallybrass also take up the issue of color and cloth, marking the inconsistencies (not to say hypocrisies) of the English attitude towards the yellow Irish mantle. The mantle is at some points reviled as a sign of "the 'looseness' and 'idlenesse' of the Irish in general" (133) but was later "redefined as a necessity for the 'civil' colonizing army" (135). This essay finally argues that the English court—composed of Scots and English, Catholics and Protestants—was fashioned "quite literally by London's international trade in the silks, satins, velvets, gold thread, cochineal, and indigo of the high-fashion Irish mantle and in the saffron, starch, linen, and lace of ruffs and cuffs" (146). In "Women, Foreigners, and the Regulation of Urban Space in *Westward Ho*," Jean Howard looks at "two categories of outsiders: those from beyond the city walls and those from beyond the seas" (151) to argue that Dekker's and Webster's play ferrets out national identity less in terms of a monarch than of a subject's relationship to "certain places, values, customs and institutions" (153). Urban hybridity could be both acknowledged and resisted; "Englishness" is not just geographical location but a cultural accommodation (164).

"Subjects of the City" looks at shopping, medicine, and vagrancy as categories of urban habitation. Ian W. Archer begins with the breathtaking catalog of goods for our "lacke" from Jonson's entertainment written for the opening of the New Exchange, and tracks the shift from morality plays to commercial displays in various cultural realms. He looks at changes in shop sizes, guild codes, and the schizophrenia of Elizabethan and Jacobean attitudes towards the

City's mercantile success. Conspicuous consumption, he notes, was lavished more on "plate and linenware, elements which stressed their hospitable role" (187) rather than for the sake of display alone; "collective values retained a powerful hold in London" (187). Gail Kern Paster's piece, "Purgation as the Allure of Mastery: Early Modern Medicine and the Technology of the Self," at first glance seems odd-essay-out, but in fact argues that purgation—the medical recommendation for good health—stands in as a "signifying practice upon the social body as a whole" for early modern culture (195), as in fact another form of conspicuous consumption. While Paster looks at the innard world, Patricia Fumerton investigates the underbelly. She suggests that the traditional *literary* constructions of an underworld network didn't map on to any reality. Rather, because "the master-servant bond was . . . at best insecure and at worst subject to gross violations," apprentices and servants—which included Younger Sons of gentry—were "[unmoored] from any secure social, economic, or physical space" (211). The conceptualization of early modern subjectivity must itself, argues Fumerton, become "vagrant or multiple" (221), arguing from another angle an ever-earlier sense of subjectivity as "mobile and inconsistent" (222, invoking Katharine Eisaman Maus).

"Diversions and Display" explores power structures created by houses, theaters, and the spaces of collections. Alice T. Friedman sees the grand new country houses as ways of counteracting the new freedoms and mobility that the city offered women by more or less immuring them architecturally, geographically, and therefore socially. Andrew Gurr's essay makes a case for "The Authority of the Globe and the Fortune"—which in conventional thinking had no authority whatsoever, but which "helped to develop the ultimate paradox: the most anti-authoritarian system of management that ever ran in early modern England, with the king's own name as its cover" (266). And Linda Levy Peck charts the building, buying, and collecting trends of the Jacobean court that "laid the basis for the creation of a European court culture in Britain" (285). All three essays continue the discussions of consumerism, exchange, shopping, and thinginess begun in the previous section.

I have had trouble coming up with the reviewer's obligatory criticism of this volume; the best I can do is to wish that "Building the City" had come earlier as a grouping of essays, so I would have had a better literal grounding for these issues. On the other hand, John Schofield, Peter W. M. Blayney, and Lena Cowen Orlin pick up the spatial discourses of "Diversions and Display" very (but not too) neatly. Schofield's "The Topography and Buildings of London, ca. 1600" clearly and succinctly lays out the neighborhoods, walls, civic and religious spaces, houses, industries, and surrounding areas, concluding implicitly with Derek Keene that London, despite its rapid growth, was still "a medieval city on the edge of spectacular expansion in the century to come" (319). From Schofield's overview we move to Blayney's particulars: "John Day and the Bookshop That Never Was." In an exceptionally witty essay, Blayney dismantles the assumption that St. Paul's Churchyard resembled a marketplace by showing how the bookseller John Day tried to slip in the thin end of a wedge with an appeal to build a bookshop there—and was firmly thwarted by the City's "traditional rights and privileges in Paul's Cross Churchyard" (339). Orlin also peers closely; her concluding essay focuses in great detail on Ralph Treswell's London surveys to show how "many boundaries had been determined not by a logic of space but instead through a process of negotiation and redistribution" (353), such that boundary disputes could not be resolved by common sense or uniform criteria. Spaces were shared, borders were moveable, and Coke's ruling in 1605 that "the house of every one is to him his Castle and Fortress" in fact most likely expressed a frustrated cultural "yearning for clear boundaries and impregnable perimeters" (372).

Each of these essays resists the temptation to construct clear boundaries and impregnable perimeters; separately and together they present a fluid, complicated, contradictory, paradoxical, never-fully-assimilable city, marking not only its uniqueness in time and place, but also the ways in which it was *not* particularly exceptional in relation to its neighboring centuries, its neighboring nations. This volume has proved a joy of summer reading: a model for collective scholarship, an exemplar for interdisciplinarity, and an ideal for editorialship. I enthusiastically recommend *Material London, ca. 1600* to the world of Early Modern Studies.

The Vanishing: Shakespeare, the Subject and Early Modern Culture
By Christopher Pye
Durham, NC: Duke University Press, 2000

Reviewer: Scott Wilson

Christopher Pye's *The Vanishing* is a welcome contribution, in Shakespeare studies, to the debate concerning early modern subjectivity. Situating itself in relation to New Historicism and cultural materialism, the book offers a robust defense of the importance of psychoanalysis in thinking about the construction of the "subject" of modernity in some of its earliest textual traces. Furthermore, it intervenes on the New Historicists' "home ground," as it were, discussing a selection of Shakespeare's plays in relation to a range of popular topics such as the market, demonism, witchcraft, sexuality, and anatomy. The most important juxtaposition, however, concerns reading Shakespeare in relation to visual culture in the Renaissance, particularly fifteenth-century Italian representations of the *Annunciation* (the book is generously illustrated).

In contradistinction to an "austere variant of cultural materialism" that allegedly finds no trace of any subject at all in the early modern period (1), and the kind of New Historicism that would "materialize" the subject as a contingent, culturally embedded thing, Pye reaffirms the Lacanian (and Hamletian) assertion that the subject is a thing of nothing, but a nothing that is hollowed out by a signifier and denoted as a subject for another signifier, or indeed a battery of other signifiers. The subject is brought into being by a signifier that immediately places that being under erasure, its existence evident only in the trace of its disappearance. This is "the vanishing": "the fading or detouring of the subject in the very movement of its coming forth" (10). This formulation sounds strange and paradoxical, but it is useful in understanding how different forms of subjectivity arise at moments of historical and social transition. For example, it is widely supposed in materialist criticism that the Elizabethan and Jacobean theater stage a shift in value from the symbolic (feudal) to the economic, and that men and women are reduced to the value of commodities. No longer tied to the land (often forcibly due to enclosures), "free men" found their value measured in exchange-value. For Pye, however, rather than disclosing the absence of a subject, this change betrays the emergence of a recognizably modern subject precisely as an effect of the anxiety produced by the destruction of one's symbolic value in commodification. Modern "individualist" subjectivity is the retroactive effect of the instability and crisis in identity during the break up of the feudal order. Pye discusses this process in relation to Shakespeare's history plays, but it is evident everywhere, particularly in the romantic and urban comedies. This is because, since the modern subject has no positive content, it needed a detour in order to emerge, an image in which to recognize itself negatively. For early modern dramatists, this was more often than not the daughter who refused to be exchanged in marriage, thereby challenging family and dynastic ties and affirming her value in excess of them; or, conversely, the prostitute, the whore who becomes the mirror of the male subject in the market, selling her labor to whomever will pay. It is in relation precisely to this negative image, then, the point where social value seems to vanish in abjection, that the value of the subject qua individual comes into being. As Pye argues, the subject "emerges not as a commodified being in a system of exchange but at the more radical and unstable point where economy establishes itself as a system" (14).

The thematic of the subject that emerges as an effect of its "vanishing" is investigated across a range of texts and scenes. In his reading of the *Annunciation* images, which are taken to be "the ur-instance of symbolic interpellation in the Western tradition" (14), Pye reads "a pictorial structure that articulates the modern subject as defined in relation to its own negation" in the vanishing point of Albertian perspective (15). This structure is then discussed in relation to the famous "Dover Beach" scene in *King Lear* where "once again subjectivity is visibly constituted or reconstituted, around the determinate infinity of the vanishing point" (15). As Pye attempts to show throughout the book, this structure opens out not only the space of the state, modern politics, and the market economy but also the temporality of historicity itself. An account of the early modern subject can never be, Pye insists, just one account among others of historicizing the subject, "it would be more accurate to say that historicism and the early modern subject derive from the same ground" (11). Appropriately, Pye seeks negative support for this position in Stephen Greenblatt's contention that "the subject of psychoanalysis—'our' subjectivity—is ultimately *a product of* the Renaissance," interpreting it as a "provocative, camp-forming argument against bringing psychoanalysis to bear on the Renaissance" (Greenblatt, cited in Pye, 12). For Pye, however, this is precisely what makes psychoanalysis so revealing in relation to early modernity and, working in relation to its own "vanishing point," is therefore better able to adumbrate the horizon of modernity from within.

While this "insight" is certainly expressed by Greenblatt in the essay cited, I had always associated it with Joel Fineman, where, certainly, its implications are more powerfully and positively explored. In *Shakespeare's Perjured Eye* (1986), Fineman argues, as the guiding principle of his project, that "modernist—and for that matter, postmodernist—theories of the self are not so much a theoretical account or explanation of subjectivity as they are the conclusion of literary subjectivity initially invented in the Renaissance. . . . Shakespeare marks the beginning of the modernist self and Freud . . . its end, the two of them thus bracketing an epoch of subjectivity."[1] Of course Fineman was a colleague of Greenblatt's at Berkeley, so I expect the topic came up. It is a surprise, however, that Pye nowhere acknowledges Fineman's book in his, assuming of course that he has read it. If he has not, then he should. Fineman's text, as a sustained Lacanian rhetorical analysis of Shakespeare's sonnets, anticipates his whole thesis. Fineman's argument is essentially that Shakespeare introduces a more recognizably modern form of poetic subjectivity through disclosing, in the opacity of linguistic complexity, the disappearance of the poetic ideality of previous sequences whose poetic personas glitter in the reflected glory of the objects they praise. Shakespeare marks a turning point because instead of being a reflection of an "ideas mirror," poetic subjectivity becomes an effect of a different vision of beauty, in which "beauties" are "vanishing, or vanish'd out of sight" (see Sonnet 30). In a way that breaks with sonnet tradition, Fineman argues, Shakespeare's poet "notices that there is something missing in the mutuality of his panegyric self-reflection, and that there is therefore something empty in the self discovered through such praise."[2] The reflective image recedes because of the insistence of the signifier in poetic language, beauties vanish, but they are replaced by the duplicitous seduction of the "dark lady" of writing itself. A new poetic subject emerges, therefore, as an effect of its disappearance in a void both veiled and signified by writing, its "I/ eye" betrayed, perjured in and by language.

It is disappointing, therefore, that there is no reference to Fineman in Pye's book, since it would have particularly illuminated his negotiation with New Historicism, for example. Of course it is not possible to read or cite everything, but *Shakespeare's Perjured Eye* is not an obscure text produced somewhere outside the U.S. This is Berkeley in 1986, at the very heart of the New Historicist beast. Fineman's text is at least the equal of *Renaissance Self-Fashioning*, and the history of Shakespeare criticism might have been different were it not for his untimely death. Though it is also no doubt the case that Fineman's rhetoric analysis, that seemed to owe much to de Man and the Yale School, went out of fashion partly because of the revelation of de Man's wartime journalism. It is historically interesting, therefore, how Pye's argument so closely resembles Fineman, while his style, juxtaposing apparently unrelated texts and issues, owes so much to Greenblatt.

Pye also omits other psychoanalytic readings of Shakespeare that would seem to be quite central to his concerns. The reading of the "Dover Beach" scene in *King Lear*, for example, that is really the major illustration of Pye's argument with regard to Shakespeare, is largely anticipated in a more detailed reading of the scene in Philip Armstrong's 1994 essay in *Textual Practice*.[3] This and other omissions suggest that psychoanalytical critics of early modern history like Pye could strengthen or at least nuance their arguments if they researched, a little more widely, other work deploying psychoanalysis in the Renaissance.

Nevertheless, this is an excellent book that deserves to be read by Shakespeareans whether not they have an interest in psychoanalysis. I hope it renews interest in psychoanalytic approaches to Shakespeare. But further, it may even be possible to pursue Pye's central trope of the "vanishing" beyond the epoch of subjectivity delimited by Shakespeare, Freud, and psychoanalysis. As Félix Guattari said, "I'm not at all sure that the concept of the 'a' object in Lacan is anything but a vanishing point, an escape, precisely, from the despotic character of signifying chains."[4] The concept of the *objet petit a* is that little extimate motor of subjective alterity that produces the vanishing point that, for Pye, supports the subject. For Guattari, on the other hand, it is a machine for moving beyond the subject of post/modernity into different forms of subjectification.

Notes

1. Joel Fineman, *Shakespeare's Perjured Eye* (Berkeley: University of California Press, 1986), 47.
2. Fineman, *Shakespeare's Perjured Eye*, p. 216.
3. Philip Armstrong, "Uncanny Spectacles: Psychoanalysis and the Texts of *King Lear,*" *Textual Practice* 8, no. 2 (1994): 414–34. See also my commentary on this piece in relation to the vanishing point, anamorphosis and the change of perspective with regard to the Dover Beach scene in Scott Wilson, *Cultural Materialism* (Oxford: Blackwell, 1995), 161–65.
4. Félix Guattari, *Chaosophy* (New York: Semiotext(e), 1995), 107.

Dead Hands: Fictions of Agency, Renaissance to Modern
By Katherine Rowe
Stanford, CA: Stanford University Press, 1999

Reviewer: *Talia Schaffer*

What do we get when we consider the severed hand as a literary trope over the last five centuries? As Katherine Rowe's fascinating book reveals, we get a new grasp on notions of agency, identity, legal, political, and religious paradigms. Rowe reveals the multiple meanings that have accrued to the hand in each era, and does a dazzling job of showing how each severed hand invokes its period's most fundamental uneasiness. This is possible because the hand is a unique type of body part. It is an instrument of the body's will, yet can be severed to act with a kind of ghostly instrumentality of its own, or twisted to another's purpose. It therefore raises serious questions about the nature of will, the extent to which our identities are coherent and controllable. Moreover, its status has shifted from the Renaissance, when it was considered the most perfect body part, to the nineteenth century, when it was associated with debased manual labor. In fantasies of the severed hand, then, we can see both idealizations of the human relationship to God and terror of an industrial corpus coming back to haunt us, as well as questions about whether our bodies are indeed ourselves.

In chapter 1, Rowe explores depictions of the hand in anatomical textbooks of the sixteenth century. In the late medieval period, the hand was associated with manual rituals in the church and feudal realms. Anatomists who dissected corpses were concerned about the body as the site of dark chaos, but they developed a distinct tradition about the exquisite beauty of the hand, the locus of God's intentions in the body. Rowe's marvelous readings of illustrations, primarily in Crooke's *Microcosmographia,* focus on the iconography of the hand. Eventually, Rowe explains, "cut tissue and cutting hand become a symbolic unit, signifying effective, voluntary action and the unity of parts" (42). The dissected hand is drawn to look as if it is inviting the knife, encouraging the anatomist's own hand, engaging in its own dissection. The chapter offers multiple readings of the hand: dark chaos, divine beauty, sign of the corpse's participation in its own dissection, sign of the anatomist's artistry, the sign of God's creative agency. Rowe draws each layer separately as its own tissue, layering them over each other to make up a body of interpretation in itself.

A similar technique is visible in chapter 2, about the dismembered hands of *Titus Andronicus.* Here Rowe turns her attention from the religious iconography of the anatomy texts to the political problematics of the Renaissance body politic. *Titus* implies that capacity for action "inheres not in persons, but in the objects and instruments of an action" (54). This idea predates the Hobbsian belief that the capacity to act is "an essential faculty of the body." Instead, *Titus* problematizes what it means to act and who acts. Rowe demonstrates the play's fears about agency by showing us what hands meant to the sixteenth century, and consequently what audiences saw in scenes of the hand interrupted, severed, lopped off. For instance, when Lavinia carries Titus's hand in her mouth, she becomes a human version of the iconography of justice, a scepter topped with a hand (73). The severed hands also function as grotesque interruption and reworking of the handclasps accompanying gift exchange, marriage, and fealty. Maimed Lavinia "functions in *Titus Andronicus* as a space where the political distribution of the signs of agency is worked out. She blurs the boundaries between instrument and principal, actor and prop in disturbing but compelling ways" (73). Rowe makes a strong argument that in reading Lavinia we should focus on the specifically manual significance of her dismemberment, not leap to a tempting post-Freudian paradigm of castration and fetishism. Because handclasps signified the completion of political and marital alliance, the severed hands of *Titus* "symbolize the horror of a lost fiction of continuous, redemptive history" (83).

Chapter 3 traces the severed hand into Jacobean drama, asking why these scenes of spectacular dismemberments acquired such interest. Although the hand continues to emblematize agency and marriage, Rowe now adds two more realms: witchcraft and contractual identity. She analyzes the "Hand of Glory," a felon's severed, treated, and flaming hand that supposedly rendered the witch invisible. In witchcraft prosecutions, the "Hand of Glory" exemplified the difficulty of determining cause or assigning blame. In *The Duchess of Malfi,* Rowe suggests that Webster is particularly fascinated by the notion of what a contract—particularly a marriage contract—means for the bodies involved. She points out that in the seventeenth century, a new model of rational self-interest embodied in contracts challenged the older idea of social obligation determined by status. Bosola, for instance, oscillates between loyalty due to status and acting in his own interest, thereby expressing Ferdinand's conflicting inner impulses. Contracts present a difficult problem: can one voluntarily subject oneself? What happens when self-interest clashes with duty? How does one control an agent? And because a handclasp seals a contract, the severed hand problematizes contractual bonds. Rowe demonstrates that when Ferdinand offers the dead hand to the Duchess, it is a marvelously overdetermined movement that evokes the allegory of the "body marital," literalizes the gift of hands in marriage, and challenges "couverture" (the legal fiction that the wife merges into the person of the husband) (94). Similarly, when the Duchess's hand is described as an "engine," the word means a trick, stage machinery, and a self-running mechanism, a complex of contradictory and disturbing meanings that exemplify the problem of contracts in this play.

At this point, Rowe introduces a chapter on the long nineteenth century, running from the 1790s through the 1930s. Chapter 4 traces stories about the ghostly clutching hand. Rowe begins with a discussion of "mortmain," the medieval legal code in which an agent could posthumously exercise control of property. Keats's "The Living Hand" depicts literary fame as the work of mortmain, as the poet's hand reaching directly for the reader to enforce a response. After swiftly reviewing Gothic novels, Rowe moves into "beast with five fingers" stories, stories in which severed hands scuttle around independently. She discusses how these stories embody a new kind of evolutionary awareness and how, by the 1880s, they frequently refer to labor accidents in factories, as if the much-despised factory "hands" are literally arising to take their revenge. In Sheridan Le Fanu's hand stories, Le Fanu overturns the usual understanding of masters issuing rational orders to servants by inventing ghostly, straying hands that produce arbitrary, incomprehensible directives. Le Fanu therefore locates anarchy in labor division itself, showing how the relative roles of master and servant can alienate characters—and readers—from rationality (148–49).

The modern emphasis continues in chapter 5, where Rowe discusses the appeal of fingerprints in the nineteenth and early-twentieth-century U.S., focusing on Mark Twain's *Pudd'nhead Wilson*. She traces the way fingerprinting was constructed as an involuntary, unbiased, infallible confession in which the criminal's own hand testified against himself, a notion with which J. Edgar Hoover was particularly enamored. Since fingerprinting demands major infrastructure to produce, manipulate, and store records, it facilitated crime-fighting's movement away from local police towards major federal bureaucracies like the FBI. However, fingerprints leave a trace of an action, but not a trace of an intention (165). Rowe analyzes several Twain stories in which agency and intention are severed, for the crime is committed by a prosthetic appendage, a conjoined twin, or a person who is technically a piece of property. Can a person who is not legally a person be held responsible for actions? Rowe points out that the dispossession of the individual "mirrors the social dispossessions of slavery" (203). She also notes that in spite of fingerprinting's supposed infallibility, it is almost always accompanied by oral confession; stories are needed to confirm and claim the fact of the fingerprint. Finally, a brief epilogue both takes us into the contemporary world and returns us to the study's medieval beginnings, as Rowe does an ingenious riff on the pointing finger of the computer cursor and its relation to the maniculae, the pointing hands in the margins of medieval manuscript.

On the whole, Rowe's characteristically scintillating arguments work brilliantly when her readings can flicker across a single central text, *Titus Andronicus* or *The Duchess of Malfi*. The reader can keep a single image in mind—the iconic severed hands of Titus, Lavinia, or Ferdinand—and watch in fascination as Rowe reveals more and more readings of it, until it radiates with the era's political, legal, economic, and emotional concerns. But in chapter 4, Rowe's erudition sometimes overwhelms her own argument. She chooses to write about multiple short stories ranging from the 1830s through the 1930s, originating in France, Great Britain, and the United States, not to mention Gothic fiction and Romantic poetry, while simultaneously producing close readings of Carlyle, Darwin, George Eliot, E. P. Thompson, Freud, and Engels, carrying through the medieval idea of "mortmain," reminding us of the "Hand of Glory," and introducing new concerns about Irish poverty and evolutionary and industrial thought. Each reading is dazzling, but each appears disconnected from each other in ways Rowe does not resolve. Surely Rowe does not want us to assume that Carlyle's ideas really apply to a French story from the 1830s and an American tale from 1902 in the same way, but if not, what does she want us to understand by juxtaposing them?

Rowe explains that she decided not to include a chapter on the eighteenth century because she wanted to sharpen the contrast between the early modern and modern paradigms (xii). The problem is that, without such a chapter, Rowe lacks the space to work out important and culturally specific nexuses that really belong to the long eighteenth century. For instance, her analysis of Locke is now rather confusingly relegated to the end of the chapter on Webster where we are explicitly told it does not apply yet. Rowe's work on the Gothic happens far too fast, connecting quite different texts and papering over the differences between the Gothic, horror fiction, ghost stories, and science fiction; she dashes through so many versions of the genre that when she mentions "the end of the century" and "beginning of the century" it is unclear which centuries she means (126–27). And she is forced to make pronouncements she has no space to demonstrate, like this one, ascribed to Keats: "the general condition of Romantic writing [is] a posthumous, alienated, and oppressive legacy" (116). There's just no room to do justice to anything before 1830. The stress produces a curious chronological flexibility. At one point Rowe mentions "contemporary fiction, from *Pamela* to *The Turn of the Screw*" (152), as if two centuries' worth of fiction were all produced simultaneously. Only a few pages later, however, she claims that the slave economy was "still vestigially present in the 1890s" (159), when of course it was more than vestigially present just a generation after the Civil War.

Such a chapter might also have given Rowe a chance to explore how the hand works in epistolary novels. Handwriting is raised in *Dead Hands,* but very briefly. I wondered whether Rowe would read the handwritten letter as another alienated aspect of identity, and how she would answer the fascinating question of whether the agency of the written subject coincides with that of the writing subject. The problem of whether Pamela can indeed be herself and yet a character in her own narrative seems to me to have interesting affinities to the issue of the dissecting/dissected hand in chapter 1.

But these are the faults of an extraordinarily ambitious and impressive project; trying to do too many things at once almost necessitates that some will be done better than others, but that is no reason not to try. It is a remarkable achievement to produce an authoritative text that covers four centuries and three nations, political philosophy, drama, medicine, poetry, and fiction. As Rowe herself sums up, "viewed longitudinally, such conventional dismemberments stretch our understanding of the essentialist strategies that underwrite Western concepts of autonomous, dependent, and corporate action" (206–7). The rather charmingly eccentric topic of the severed hand turns out to point the way to a new understanding of political and personal agency in Anglo-American culture.

Shakespeare's Sonnets: Critical Essays
Edited by James Schiffer
New York and London: Garland Publishing, Inc., 1999

Reviewer: Lynne Magnusson

Shakespeare's Sonnets follows a different—and more useful— agenda than the announced program of the Garland series. Not tasked to do the impossible—provide a representative sampling both of the most influential early criticism and of contemporary interpretations—James Schiffer focuses instead on a wide range of contemporary or 1990s perspectives, including reprints of four influential essays and sixteen newly commissioned essays, many by authors who have already had an important impact on sonnet criticism. This accent on the 1990s leads one almost inevitably to ask of the volume, What impact has the historical and social turn in Shakespeare studies had on reading the sonnets?

The key emphasis turns out to be reception and textual history, so that the early commentary Schiffer appears to have omitted is in fact richly present as one of the volume's main topics. Margreta de Grazia's 1991 *Shakespeare Verbatim* led the way in making culturally situated textual study, or "Editing as Cultural Formation" (the title of Peter Stallybrass's lead essay), central to the reading of Shakespeare's sonnets. Stallybrass revisits the cultural site of Edmond Malone's late eighteenth-century editorial work and the debate with George Steevens to which his Sonnet editions served, in a sense, as an answer. Stallybrass concurs with de Grazia that Malone essentially "invented" the modern-day "Shakespeare" when he jettisoned the editorial interventions of Benson's 1640 edition, restoring the organization of the 1609 Quarto and introducing a story of four "characters": the poet Shakespeare, a fair young man, a rival poet, and a dark lady. "Shakespeare," a national poet at once gentle, admired, decent, and "normal," arose, in Stallybrass's argument, out of reading strategies motivated by and responsive to a crisis. The crisis was enflamed by Steevens's denunciation of the Sonnets—with their passionate affection expressed for a "lovely boy"—as disgraceful and his proclamation that even "the strongest act of Parliament . . . would fail to compel readers into their service" (78). What so stirred up Steevens was the potential recognition that England's national poet might turn out to be a "contaminator and corrupter of youth" (79), a "sodomite" and a "pederast" (77). Hence, "cultural hysteria" guided the defensive reading strategies over the next century, for example, the neo-platonizing of the male "friendship," strategies of denial that set Shakespeare "straight," and, Stallybrass asserts, had an even wider impact in helping to produce the post-Enlightenment "narratives of 'normal' and 'deviant' sexualities" (86) that still shape modern-day sexual identities.

Stallybrass's storytelling is so compelling and so readily cribbed and simplified that it is easy to imagine many twenty-first century teachers, despite Bruce R. Smith's claim later in the volume that people still resist seeing homoerotic desire in the Sonnets, reversing the Victorian lesson plan: don't get blinded by cultural hysteria into thinking Shakespeare was straight. But according to the complex and subtly nuanced essay by Margreta de Grazia included in this volume, which reviews much of the same ground as Stallybrass's, that would be to make a category mistake. She argues that the last two centuries of critics have spent much of their energy denying what all along would have been a misrecognition—their own anachronistic projection of homosexuality onto the sonnet story. If the sonnets in their own time were playing with fire, were flirting with anything associated with degrading sexual practices, it was not in their show of "pederastic" love, the kind praised in E. K.'s notes to Spenser's *Shepherdes Calendar* and aligned in the Sonnets with socially sanctioned efforts to sustain social hierarchy by "reproducing the fair values of the dominant class" (102). It was in what E. K. derides as "gynerasty," that is, the overzealous lust for women. This is, indeed, what the sonnet speaker clearly labels the "worser" love, representing in it Sonnets 127–154 as deranging to the sufferer and as collapsing distinctions on which social order depends, such as truth and falsity, fair and black. According to de Grazia, the scandal of the sonnets is "hidden" right on the surface—it is the perverse and anarchic womb-lust that the speaker admits to in the "dark lady" sonnets, confounding class distinctions. Furthermore, it may well be that the mistress's characterization as "black" is best read in its plainest sense, thus also exposing, de Grazia suggests, the added social peril of "abhorred miscegenation" (107).

It is interesting to find that each of the three challenging and influential opening essays offers what Heather Dubrow explicitly calls a "map of misreading" (128). Indeed, each essay, to some extent, pulls the ground out from under the previous one. Dubrow's interpretive agnosticism challenges the bipartite division at Sonnet 126 between "fair youth" and "dark lady" sonnets. De Grazia had carefully acknowledged how Malone, constructing this division, obscured the number of sonnets in which the addressee's gender is not made explicit, even while she chose to structure her historicist reading around this division. In an essay aptly titled "Incertainties now crown themselves assur'd," Dubrow rejects this assumed division, together with the usual working assumptions of critics about the Sonnets' basic story line and four characters. She is disinclined to accept Katherine Duncan-Jones's arguments that the 1609 Quarto was authorized by Shakespeare and speculates that we may actually have only a loose collection of poems in various stages of composition. Even if the Quarto does represent Shakespeare's plan, Dubrow suggests, we would be wrong to think that he meant to sketch out a coherent plot or specify the addressee of each poem. Dubrow illustrates how her position has the virtue of multiplying the possibilities for creative new readings: imagine "Shall I compare thee to a summer's day?" addressed to the Dark Lady, giving her a more complex mix of positive and negative qualities, or "How oft, when thou, my music, music play'st" addressed to the Friend, thus varying the aspects of homoerotic desire. Still, if criticism that assumes the standard story and specified addressee is, in Dubrow's judgement, so decidedly wrong, it is difficult not to ask, by what measure have these newly released meanings any clearer justification?

If we accept that we have been reading Malone's Sonnets rather than Shakespeare's and that the four "characters" and bipartite structure are the editor's construction, one wonders whether we will be moving towards new directions in sonnet reading or new inhibitions. David Schalkwyk has argued elsewhere that the overly emphatic rejection of biographical criticism did not merely silence conjectures identifying the dark lady with Mary Fitton or Lucy Negro, the fair youth with Southampton or Pembroke. It also had a further inhibiting effect, restricting Sonnet interpretation to "textually self-reflective and self-enclosed" readings to the neglect of readings attentive to the "historically situated embodiment of the Sonnets within a nexus that includes poet, addressee, and audience—each embroiled in complex political, sexual, and economic relations" (*Shakespeare Quarterly* 45 [1994]: 381–82). Paradoxically, the boldest move in this volume—historicizing early editing practices—if seen by scholars like Dubrow as entailing the rejection of even the most minimalist critical assumptions about the situations of utterance and the patterns of relationship in the Sonnets, might further suppress a culturally and historically situated sonnet criticism.

It is certainly true that this anthology is less vividly colored with Elizabethan life or with thick descriptions of early modern material culture than are similar anthologies about Shakespeare's plays. Nonetheless, the collection provides a number of interesting strategies for historical interpretation. It may be that Bruce Smith's essay responds most directly to the challenge of reading historically if one accepts that one has only indeterminate and shifting pronouns to "situate" the texts' renderings of desire. He asks why people acknowledge homoerotic desire in Shakespeare's plays and not the Sonnets, and answers that people make the sonnet "I" their own, filling the sonnet pronouns and their interrelations with their own sentiments and desires. Most people's investment in the speaker's "I," he argues, forestalls the speaker's alignment with same-sex desire, making the Sonnets "the last bastion of conservative critical thinking" (427). But Smith's complicated reading strategy is not simply aimed at critiquing a homophobic bias and getting people to say "yes" to same-sex desire in the Sonnets. By the logic of his argument, queering the "I," if it meant a presentist identification of the speaker's desire with any reader's same-sex desire, would misrecognize the culturally constructed "I," "he," "she" relationships produced by "early modern ways of marking gender and articulating sexual desire" (427). The tour de force of the essay is its illuminating glimpse into Elizabethan gender politics achieved by means of a close reading of pronoun interrelationships in various sonnets.

Most of the essays in the volume do work at finding fruitful strategies for connecting historical context and indefinitely situated texts. Religion supplies the context in two of the essays, Lisa Freinkel claiming that Shakespeare recasts "Petrarchanism within a Lutheran universe" (259) and John Klause arguing for Catholic allusion. Klause's detailed reading of Sonnet 124 identifies the "fools of Time" called upon to bear witness to the constancy, against accident and policy, of the speaker's "dear love" with Catholic martyrs as they are represented in prose texts of supplication and comfort by Robert Southwell. This essay does a good job of establishing how the difficulties of the poem seem to demand a specific identification or context and how disappointingly vague and abstract the closing lines are without it. At the same time, it is hard to see how Klause's detailed effort to match Shakespeare's words to Southwell's adequately pins down this identification.

Peter C. Herman and Joseph Pequigney argue convincingly for secular methods of contextualized close reading. Herman follows Thomas M. Greene's lead in exploring early seventeenth-century contexts for the economic metaphors of Sonnets 1–17, and Pequigney develops a more traditional formalist method in arguing that Sonnet 73 should be read in the context of a distinct grouping (71 to 74). For Herman, the negative and bourgeois associations of usury both in popular polemics and in Shakespeare's own plays pull against the ostensibly positive tenor of usury metaphors deployed to encourage the continuance of an aristocratic line. He is responding here to claims by Joel Fineman and others that linguistic doubleness emerges only with later complexities of the sequence: for Herman, commodification infects the poetry of praise with destabilized meanings from the outset. Pequigney's contribution also turns on what he regards as a verbal ambiguity or doubleness created by the unspecific uses of deixis ("this" and "that") in the couplet of Sonnet 73, a point of contradiction made legible when the very fact of Sonnet 73's artistic brilliance is read as a direct answer to the poet's self-derogation in the two preceding sonnets.

Essays by Olga L. Valbuena, Michael Schoenfeldt, and Naomi J. Miller proceed by reading clusters of sonnets whose imagery or diction can be aligned with a particular Elizabethan cultural practice or code. Valbuena's focus is on sonnets explicitly invoking the act and materials of writing, emphasizing how the early promise to eternize the friend's beauty through writing is unfulfilled, with the pen's blots becoming more prevalent in the sequence than the accomplishment of well-wrought lines. Shoenfeldt focuses on sonnets that explicitly invoke the "Galenic regime of the humoral self" (306) to establish the materiality of the inwardness being represented. On this basis he argues for a less ironic and more historical reading of the coldness praised in Sonnet 94 as a quality of the self-controlled figure. Miller's aim is to read the Sonnets' imagery of motherhood through "early modern codes of maternity" (350), and the essay brings a fresh perspective and prominence to Sonnet 143, in which "a careful housewife" alarms her baby by setting it down to chase after a runaway fowl.

Illona Bell contextualizes the Sonnets by showing how the indeterminate "I"—"he"—"she" relations might be read a little differently if the connections between *A Lover's Complaint* and the Sonnets were more fully recognized. The essay draws some convincing parallels between the situation of the Sonnet speaker and the female complainant, suggesting that their shared position as injured party to an arrogant and shameless young man is meant to function for a print audience that was not privy to circumstances shared with manuscript readers as a somewhat enigmatical "key" or commentary to the obscure Sonnet relationships.

Essays by Rebecca Laroche and Marvin Hunt extend the volume's treatment of reception history. Laroche explores the different ways in which Oscar Wilde negotiated his relation to literary history by way of the Sonnets in *The Portrait of Mr. W. H.*, in trial testimony, and in *De Profundis*. Hunt approaches the important and elusive issue of "how dark" is the dark lady by offering a fascinating look at traditions of interpretation: how particular "brown" readings (that is, as non-pale European) would be unravelled when the candidate was exposed as "white" and how even tentative "black" readings (that is, as having a discernable racial separation from the speaker) would, like the homoerotic readings Stallybrass discusses, evoke an almost hysterical labour of rebuttal. Speculating about the status of slaves brought into England in the late sixteenth century, Hunt situates a "shadow discourse on the circumstances of black people" (385) in the sonnets, though he leaves open-ended the question of whether it operates at a literal or figurative level. Whereas Hunt develops de Grazia's point about critical resistance to reading black as black, Valerie Traub develops the suggestion about gynerasty as scandal. Traub offers an interesting answer to the important question of why male homoeroticism of the Sonnets is linked to such a ferocious misogyny in terms of the amorphous definitions of sodomy within Shakespeare's culture. Taking seriously suggestions by Jonathan Goldberg and Margreta de Grazia that the sonnets end up portraying *heterosexual* relations as sodomitical, she argues that the misogyny arises as an ideological effect out of Shakespeare's strategic effort to authorize male homoeroticism by countering emerging legal discourses delimiting sodomy to sex between men.

Still other essays give more traditional themes a new turn, with Gordon Braden exploring Shakespeare's Petrarchanism and Joyce Sutphen memorializing strategies. Of the essays not primarily concerned with historical context, perhaps most striking and original is George T. Wright's meditation on the Sonnets as unsounded speech. He highlights their status as "sessions of sweet silent thought," exploring the relation between silent speech and interior consciousness. Seeking to particularize and situate the qualities of this unvoiced speaking, he identifies it, first, ahistorically, with the ruminative voice in T. S. Eliot's *The Waste Land* and, second, with our own silent reading practices and more generally, with our habituated apprehension of consciousness as a "continuous wordstream" (148). Nonetheless, even this essay takes care to raise the historical issue of whether or not Renaissance people read or thought this way. Working out of the differences that Anne Ferry posited between modern-day and Renaissance interiority, Wright aligns himself with the tradition that regards the inner voice as a new emergence in the lyrical poetry of Sidney and Shakespeare. When this continuous inner discourse migrated into Shakespearean drama in the early seventeenth century, Wright imagines, it might have seemed aberrant and dangerous—hence its association not only with the admired Prince Hamlet but with evil or disturbed characters, such as Lady Macbeth, Claudius, Iachimo, and Leontes. Indeed, Wright speculates that the "dangerous" inner discourse of the Sonnets may even explain why Shakespeare may not have authorized the publication of the Sonnets. Thus, we have a third candidate for the scandal of the Sonnets—the "epistemological" deviance of too loud thought rather than "sexual" deviance. Beyond Shakespearean drama, Wright traces the migration or "history" of silent speech throughout the English poetic tradition. Probing and speculative, this fine essay raises as many untreated questions as it answers, since, as Wright's own gesture at how reading practices change suggests, a persuasive history of silent speech could never be restricted to poetry as its solitary or even primary context. The addressee of Wright's silent speech is absent, but Lars Engle's thoughtful essay on shame offers a helpful complement, touching upon the extent to which the complex interiority of the Sonnet speaker has an intersubjective or dialogic cast.

Offering a rich and sophisticated gathering of up-to-date perspectives, Schiffer's volume may not fully serve the needs of students seeking a comprehensive overview but it will be invaluable to teachers and scholars looking for ways to situate themselves within the complex critical conversation on Shakespeare's Sonnets.

The Notorious Astrological Physician of London: Works and Days of Simon Forman
By Barbara Howard Traister
Chicago and London: University of Chicago Press, 2001

Reviewer: S. P. Cerasano

For reasons that require no explanation, readers are endlessly fascinated by the alchemist-magicians of early modern Europe. So, clearly, were our theatrical predecessors, who enshrined them in such plays as *Doctor Faustus* and *The Alchemist*. Moreover, their lives are not grist only for scholarly investigation. Giordano Bruno, John Dee, and Simon Forman all participated in the brand of Neoplatonic occultism that tweaks the popular imagination. As Peter Ackroyd's novel *The House of Doctor Dee* or Benjamin Woolley's recent book *The Queen's Conjurer* (2001) demonstrates, the amount of interest in Renaissance astrologers seems almost limitless.

Into this climate—a favorable one for biography, in general, and particularly for Renaissance subjects like Forman—comes Barbara Howard Traister's *Notorious Astrological Physician of London*. The expressed focus of Traister's undertaking is less "Forman the man than the cache of manuscripts that bears Forman's name." These papers, she notes, treat "medicine, astrology, alchemy, the theater, genealogy, giants, and creation" as well as gardening and a host of "incidental subjects" (xi). One of the book's strengths is that its author mines Forman's papers in order to augment our understanding of various aspects of medical and social history. Yet, as her narrative progresses, it is clear that any investigation of this type necessarily enters into the discussion surrounding the long tradition of Forman biography. It is impossible to discuss Forman's manuscripts without finally implying some judgment of the man and his reputation. In and amongst the many diverse topics presented in Traister's narrative is a much-needed adjustment of Forman's biography. While managing to produce an angular portrait of a man known to most readers largely through the lenses of others who have studied Forman's manuscripts, Traister raises important issues concerning the nature of biographical writing and the relationship between biographer and subject.

In the first half of her book Traister sets out to shift the emphasis from astrology to medicine, and in turn, to offer the most fundamental corrective to former accounts, such as that written by A. L. Rowse, which concentrate on Forman's other roles—amongst them, petty quack and sex maniac. Such a shift in emphasis brings with it significant consequences. Counter to the popular biographical mode dubbed "pathography" by James Atlas—a style of biography in which the author seems to undermine his or her subject—Traister (wittingly or not) ends up participating in an newly emerging form, perhaps conveniently thought of as "aristography" (from Greek *aristos,* i.e., "the best"), which seeks to realign or rehabilitate its subject both from former biographical treatments and even from the subject's own foibles. It is not an easy task, particularly in the case of Forman, who seems more than occasionally to have been his own worst enemy, simultaneously stirring up rancor amongst the London medical authorities and then standing for judgment as the victim of his own miscalculations. Although Traister's corrective is a welcomed addition to the growing complexity of Forman biography, the task she sets for herself is a difficult one. Finally, one wonders whether any "corrective" can be great enough, or whether it is possible to produce a quasi-objective portrait when some of the most controversial evidence for Forman's life was generated by Forman himself and preserved in his personal notebooks. Given this difficulty, Traister's task has to with larger questions in the field of biographical writing, most notably the debate concerning what level of sympathy an author ought to have with his or her subject.

The role of sympathy in biographical writing has been long debated by professional biographers. Leon Edel—who enshrined Henry James in more words than most readers can absorb in a lifetime, and who went on to become one of the most articulate theorists of biographical writing—argued persuasively that it was absolutely necessary for a biographer to be sympathetic with his or her subject. Yet other biographers argue (equally persuasively) that it is important to be skeptical of a biographical subject, suggesting that unless this is the case a biographer cannot achieve any level of objectivity. Atlas's "pathography" (intended as a term of opprobrium and an indictment of irresponsible biographical presentation) is an extreme form of such "skepticism," or so some practitioners would argue. Furthermore, for Atlas, it is the result of treating primarily the most unattractive, salacious, or unpleasant portions of a subject's life. Behind Atlas's complaint lies the sense that biographers who are willing to expose their subject's blemishes do so because that is what their readers "really want to know." Still, sometimes it is not that biographers choose the unattractive aspects of their subjects but that these are what their close-up lenses magnify. To cite a recent example, when Katherine Duncan-Jones published her treatment of William Shakespeare (2001)—intended not as a comprehensive biography but rather as "scenes from his life"—she found herself drawn to a neglected aspect of her subject, Shakespeare the "homo economicus." Unhappily for some critics, this slant produced trends that made the beloved playwright seem tight-fisted when it came to his own fortune and less than sympathetic to the starving classes. What emerged was a character who seemed inconsistent with the "sweet swan of the Avon" that Ben Jonson identified. Consequently, some reviewers have not taken kindly to Duncan-Jones's portrait, as if Shakespeare, a national icon, was somehow being defaced. Never were hard covers harder on their subject. (But perhaps not unnecessarily so, Duncan-Jones would argue. Shifting the gaze from Shakespeare-the-dramatist to Shakespeare-the-financial-being points up unattractive aspects of his life.)

In taking on a subject such as Forman, who brings with him such a checkered history, Traister's initial problem concerns the extant materials of Forman's life and whether they are to be trusted. How much of the portrait represented in his manuscripts is necessarily valid? How much should we trust a subject who so consistently sought the public's attention? The opening chapter ("A Self-Conscious Life") maps out the many ways in which Forman essentially wrote his own biography for posterity by manufacturing several coats of arms (all of them stretching the truth, if not purposely misrepresenting his lineage) and prose narratives recounting his life history. He also recorded his dreams and kept notes of his medical practice in addition to writing medical treatises. Whilst casting astrological charts, relating to himself, he wondered whether he would become a knight, lord, or earl (he didn't); whether he should seek a position as physician to James I (he never acquired it); and whether his philosopher's stone would prove to be lucrative (apparently it didn't). In Traister's overview, Forman was caught up in the mode of self-fashioning that has been discussed meticulously by Stephen Greenblatt and others. She concludes: "Forman's aspiration was not to achieve something unique or to change his society; instead he wanted to become as much like successful men as possible, to find a higher place that he was born to within the existing order" (26).

Hereafter, the book divides informally into two sections. The first contains two lengthy chapters (chapter 2, "Medical Theories: A Physician Evolves," and chapter 3, "Forman's London Practice") that culminate in a shorter discussion of "Troubles with the College of Physicians" (chapter 4). The final section reads Forman's occultism within the context of his medical practice (chapter 5) and treats, in chapters 6 and 7, a variety of related but more personal aspects of Forman's life: his book collecting, nonscientific writing and published writing, his relationships with women, his household, Forman's profile as a consumer, and his leisure activities. The final chapter reassesses Forman's activities within three areas of interest that commonly emerge in other accounts of his life—the Overbury trial, the New World, and political events such as the death of Elizabeth I. Traister also provides a useful handlist of Forman's Ashmole manuscripts (191–202), a much more user-friendly version of the Bodleian Library handlist.

Readers familiar with Traister's former work on medical history and the occult sciences will recognize her interests particularly in chapters 2 and 3, which "tease apart" Forman's interests in medicine and magic (31). In chapter 2 Traister traces—as well as one is able given the constraints of extant evidence—the evolution of Forman's engagement with medical theory and practice of the period. She discusses Forman's knowledge of surgical procedures, his methods for diagnosing conditions, and his grappling with the most authoritative medical theories of his time. She comments on the medical treatises that Forman copied for his own use (on plague, for instance) and sifts through his commentaries on madness, and concludes finally that, as a practitioner, Forman was far ahead of his time, despite the fact that his learning and application tended to be eclectic (50–51). Apparently his many clients recognized this, and responded to him positively as a caregiver. Forman's success, Traister notes, was a combination of what he thought of as "study (speculation), experience (practice), and inborn talent (natural inclination) to be the perfect physician" (55).

In chapter 3 Traister studies Forman's extant casebooks, which cover the period between March 1596 and November 1601. In the many names and details preserved there, Traister provides an overview of Forman's practice, which included many nonmedical consultations. Clients asked about travel, love relationships, marriage, and for assistance in making professional decisions. They purchased amulets and procedures to learn who had stolen their possessions. Nevertheless, "the backbone of Forman's practice was medical" (63). Forman attracted clients who lived throughout London, including many persons of rank and station, although it was a more diverse population than Rowse implied. Moreover, it was a practice that was frequented by many persons who returned repeatedly for assistance in a wide variety of ways. "By and large his therapies were conservative for the period," Traister writes. "Despite his frequent characterization as a quack, he was not an itinerant wanderer who preyed on a neighborhood and then moved on. Forman practiced in just two locations for over twenty years." In looking carefully at his casebooks, Forman has left "a fairly detailed picture of how a relatively ordinary urban medical practice functioned in the early modern period" (80). It is within this context that Traister reexamines Forman's well-known conflicts with the London College of Physicians (chapter 4). In her narrative the college's antagonism was based, in part, on the fact that they were interested in maintaining their exclusiveness, and Forman was not licensed by the College. Second, Traister suggests that Forman's sheer success in treating clients raised a red flag, that Forman was "competing very successfully with these elite physicians" (95). Despite this, and the fact that Forman was eventually licensed by Cambridge University, the College pursued Forman for almost twenty years, until his death in 1611, producing a long-lasting trauma and paranoia that Forman recorded in an autobiographical poem (92).

Because no study of Forman can ignore his interest in the occult sciences, chapter 5 is devoted to this topic. In this discussion it is Forman's typicality amongst his contemporaries that Traister emphasizes. In this he "resembled other men living in his century who were caught in similar intellectual crosswinds" (98). But although he knew John Dee, Forman had few friends who were practitioners of astrology. Like other occultists—all seem to have been highly competitive—Forman guarded his secrets well. Interestingly, what Traister perceives as Forman's feelings of inadequacy, present since his childhood, seem to emerge here as well: he "kept his distance from those who might make him feel inadequate or inferior" (99). Additionally, although he practiced alchemy occasionally and was familiar with the practices of witchcraft Forman was primarily involved in astrology and he was careful to distance himself from those who claimed to derive power from the devil (113).

Some of the most intriguing material presented in Traister's book appears in chapter 6, in which she discusses Forman's activity as a collector of books, his impressive library, his interests in giants and examination of a "giant's tooth." In chapter 7 these curiosities give way to "Forman in Society," in which Traister reevaluates Forman's violence toward women and what former commentators have seen as his promiscuous behavior. Readers who are interested in Forman's family will be attracted by the discussion of the Forman household ("a fairly easygoing, somewhat chaotic atmosphere," 161) and its inhabitants, along with the examination of Forman's profligacy and the many theater-related incidents that are encoded in his manuscripts. To no surprise, the final chapters provide an adjusted picture of Forman who, Traister concludes, was most likely not involved in the Overbury murder, and who was plugged in with the major political events of his time, but who seems to have been more interested as an observer than as a participant.

In her final paragraphs Barbara Traister reminds her reader that her goal has been to adjust the widely circulating image of Forman. "He wished to 'come to account,' to have a place in history, to reestablish the Forman name," she states. But:

> the "Forman" who lives on in print is largely the posthumous creation of a patriarchal culture, a demonic character who can shoulder the blame for the crimes of the nobility. And only occasionally the "silly fellow" first suggested by Jonsonian lampoons. "The astrological physician of Lambeth," Forman's favorite description of himself, has been totally eclipsed by "Forman the wizard" and "Forman the charlatan." (190)

To be sure, this is the case. *The Notorious Astrological Physician of London: Works and Days of Simon Forman* provides a useful realignment of Forman's image, and a broadly painted picture that reminds us of the many ways in which Shakespeare's age differed from our own.

Nevertheless, for all of Forman's typicality and the fascinating aspects of his practice that have been ignored by previous biographers, many questions remain, mostly those that arise from the fact that the bulk of what can be known about Forman emanates precisely from manuscripts that he created, and also because it appears that so many of his manuscripts were destroyed. (The latter is bound to make readers suspicious of his practices.) Was the Forman who wrote up a false genealogy, had his portrait painted, and who "wished to have a place in history" self-fashioning? Was he—alternatively—a liar, a parvenu who wished to follow in the model of John Dee, and who unhappily for Forman, never achieved Dee's fame, position with royalty, and public notoriety? Why precisely did Forman spend sixty weeks in prison in 1579, on the testimony of what appears to have been one man? (It was, after all, around the time when Forman claims to have taken up an interest in "prophecy and attempts to call spirits" [18]), and Forman claimed that "it took nine years after his release from prison before he was completely free of the paperwork and legal charges stemming from his arrest" [19].) What are we to make of Forman's claim that in 1588 he "practiced necromacy" (20)? Other assumptions concerning what might, or might not exist in lost papers undercut our confidence in the papers that do remain. To cite one example, Traister states "if Forman practiced this sort of illicit magic, however, he left little evidence in the papers that remain from this period [1603–11]" (23). But part of the constant harassment and imprisonment that Forman suffered at the hands of the College of Physicians, over so many years, included many occasions on which his papers were confiscated. Ultimately, while our attention is being drawn to what manuscripts still exist, we also question what has been lost. Perhaps what is missing would "readjust" the image of Forman in the direction of negativity that Traister has so carefully attempted to correct. Of course, given the state of affairs it is impossible to know. Certainly intimations of the negative aspects of Forman's personality and practice are hinted at in his extant manuscripts, though they are not nearly so pervasive as Rowse and others would have their readers believe.

    Therefore, despite the fullness of Traister's portrait it would seem that Forman is destined to swim eternally somewhere between polarities—the traditionally "notorious" astrologer of the book's title and Traister's fascinating multidimensional doctor whose success irritated the College of Physicians in London. Doubtless, readers will welcome the presentation of information Traister has culled from the Forman manuscripts; but they will simultaneously remember the necromancer, the believer in giants, and the sexual adventurer. There is, after all, something in us that enjoys Forman the "notorious" astrologer. It is in this way that he remains a curiosity in our time, even if he was not so in his own. More than many perhaps, Forman is a resistant subject who persists in being engagingly enigmatical; and in reading through the manuscripts he chose to create and preserve one wonders whether he didn't intend to leave us with precisely that impression.

Theaters of Intention: Drama and the Law in Early Modern England
By Luke Wilson
Stanford, CA: Stanford University Press, 2000

Reviewer: Constance Jordan

The relations of law to dramatic literature have preoccupied literary critics for some time now. First addressed in terms of reciprocal influence, they have more recently been studied for their illustrations of power and its deployment throughout the body politic. Wilson's study has the distinct merit of bringing into very close focus the processes by which play texts and legal texts represent what is surely the mental action that most constitutes what we know as consciousness—the intention do so something. His principal arguments attend to the ways in which theater simulates, that is, actually acts out as well as represents the kind of "purposive action" described in legal texts. (While it acts out a man who with malice aforethought stabs another man to death, it can be said to represent a murder.) Specifically, Wilson claims, by showing "routines of practical reasoning" in the process of being performed, theater redeploys legal processes of thought, particularly the fiction-making allowed in equitable jurisdiction. This redeployment is not, however, a case of influence, but rather the effect of a parallel intellectual development: as the institutions of theater and law were reciprocally reflexive, they employed similar methods of establishing reasons for and explanations of human behavior.

An important consequence of Wilson's approach to intention is his deft analysis of the idea of agency. As he notes, structuralist and poststructuralist criticism has largely dismissed the possibility of both intention and agency as far as the individual subject is concerned. They rather acknowledge as decisive the supervening structures of power that within a society permit no more than an illusion of the subject as thinking and acting independently of them. But by demonstrating how and with what subtle variations of tone intention is represented in action (as reported in play texts and legal texts), Wilson clearly establishes that the idea of an actor-agent and author-agent (indebted differently to the core notion of the Latin *agere,* to set in motion) constituted an early modern preoccupation. Both intention and agency gain thereby a central place in the cultural landscape of early modern England. To speak of the circulation of power *tout court* will no longer, I think, do full justice to ideas of the subject and subjectivity.

Hamlet provides the case study for the most fundamental understanding of intention, which Wilson defines as determined by what he calls the "hysteresis effect," in which action is evidenced or reported before the reasons for taking it are set forth and reviewed. The passage illustrating this effect is 2.2.584–90, in which Hamlet seems to discover the reasons for putting on "The Mousetrap" after he has arranged for the visiting players to add some "dozen or sixteen lines" from the "Murder of Gonzago." The trick or tic of reasoning supporting this atemporal sequence finds a parallel, as Wilson sees it, in Donne's "Satire III," in which the speaker consciously experiences his will, making its determination in the delay in which thinking takes place, as strangely following the doing of what it is about to determine to do. Thus, as Wilson states: "The self's sense of itself as agent, in my view, has less to do with epistemological certainty than with a practical familiarity with an image of oneself actually acting: it is acting as praxis, rather than a theoretical capability of knowing when or why to act, that is in question."

Directly relevant to *Hamlet* is the thinking apparent in the famous case of *Hales v. Petit,* in which the intention of Sir John Hales to commit suicide, that is, to act to kill himself, is entirely distinguished and separated from the action of suicide itself. This separation of intention from action permits a consideration of intention as independent of action (or praxis, as Wilson sometimes terms it), as, in fact, a mental event that can be situated in some zone or sphere whose relation to real events is problematic, a product of fictionalizing after the fact. The independence or "modularity" of intention affects particularly any appreciation of what constitutes interiority: in *Hales v. Petit,* the *mens rea* or state of mind intending suicide comes into being as a result of a "structurally retrospective construction of the act"; for the same reason Hamlet's state of mind, says Wilson, fashioned after the action he undertakes, is never quite "there."

Thus the weird reversal of what is generally understood as the sequence of thinking first and acting second permits a corollary activity of principal interest to both theater and law, that is, the construction of fictions designed to supply reasons and explanations for actions that have actually occurred but without apparent motivation. According to this way of thinking, intention is inherently retroactive, a fiction imposed upon an action to give it plausibility and color and to forge its connections to the desires and goals of the speaker. In law, such fictions are invoked to bring conflicts of interest to a resolution; they are justified by the equity that places responsibility for interpreting the law in particular cases on the judge, who must be persuaded that one or the other of the fictions produced by plaintiff or defendant yield the determination the legislator would have had in mind had he heard the case. In theater, they illustrate processes of practical reasoning, display interiority of character, and are perhaps most pointed in soliloquy.

I've rehearsed Wilson's understanding of intention in some detail, although without the really remarkable fund of knowledge of theater and law with which he supports it, because it sustains his arguments throughout his book. Intention is at the heart of the analysis of contract in *The Alchemist* and *Bartholomew Fair,* in which action develops from promises that may or may not result in the delivery of the thing promised. In distinction to the hysteresis effect illustrated in *Hamlet,* in which intention is read back into action, the promises made in Jonson's plays entail intention colored deeply by uncertainty: does the promissor mean to fulfil his promise or is he merely pretending that he will? The situations Jonson dramatizes reflect variously the doctrine of assumpsit as it was given a definitive form in Slade's case, in which a promise, or a stated intention to perform an action, was held to be knowable and binding upon the promissor. As Edward Coke described assumpsit in his report on Slade's case: "every contract executory imports in itself an assumpsit, for when one agrees to pay money, or to deliver any thing, thereby he assumes or promises to pay or deliver it." Does Subtle, taking Dapper's money, intend to give him a magical means to draw customers to his shop or merely to trick him into believing in such means and that they will be forthcoming?

The playwright's interest in promises becomes more explicit in the Induction to *Bartholomew Fair,* where at issue is the play itself, its interest and its pleasures—will it fail to satisfy the expectations of the playgoer, who has given up a consideration (the price of admission to the theater) upon the playwright's promise to entertain them? Important here, and especially to Wilson's understanding of the play, is the extent of the delay between the promise and the delivery: to Jonson, this delay is conditioned by the intention of the promissor, which may or may not be a mere pretense. *Bartholomew Fair* goes on to act out all kinds of contracts that entail promises, but shows a general preoccupation with the exchange of commodities that are human. To point up the political dimension of the play's various moments in which exchanges occur, Wilson considers debates in the Parliament of 1610 over the terms of the Great Contract and the status of wardship among other prerogatives of the king—they shadow the play's depiction of Grace Wellborn's courtship by implying its nature as a deal involving a human commodity.

The very considerable erudition displayed in this study of intention in theater and law also works to elucidate play texts and legal texts concerned with demonic exchanges, as in pacts with the devil, and with crimes for which there is either no person who can be charged or no person the prosecution wants to charge or the jury convict. In such a case, the culprit is Nobody, a fictional character who can be blamed but only in an explanatory mode. (Nobody did this or that.) Throughout these investigations, intention and agency remain the focus of attention; as Wilson says in his conclusion, his work has been to make "agency visible." In doing so, his book makes a major contribution to the literary history of theater and law as well as to historiography. The texts Wilson refers to are hard and the analytic tools he relies on to understand them are difficult to handle, but as a critical whole *Theaters of Intention* amply repays study.

Lanyer, A Renaissance Woman Poet
By Susanne Woods
Oxford and New York: Oxford University Press, 1999

Reviewer: Barbara K. Lewalski

This important study of the poet Aemilia Lanyer significantly advances a major scholarly enterprise of the past two decades—the recovery and analysis of literary and nonliterary texts by early modern women writers. Scholarship in this new field has now moved beyond general surveys of women's writing and introductory essays on particular authors and gender issues to the production of careful scholarly editions, book-length biographies, and penetrating critical studies of some of these writers, notably the Countess of Pembroke, Elizabeth Cary, Lady Mary Wroth, Margaret Cavendish, and Lucy Hutchinson. Susanne Woods has already made large contributions to this enterprise with a fine scholarly edition of Lanyer's poetry (1993) and through her ongoing work as chair of the executive committee of the Women Writers' Project, which is making available on-line a rich library of women's texts from 1350 to 1850.

The present study makes a methodological and critical breakthrough in regard to the still-vexed questions of how to locate these newly recovered women writers in their cultural and literary milieu, and how to evaluate their achievement. In contrast to their male contemporaries, few facts are known about the lives, education, intellectual pursuits, and literary associations of most of these women, and their works are not surrounded by a centuries-long tradition of scholarship and criticism. Because of this, and because their poetic and rhetoric practice sometimes departs from male canonical norms, women writers are often studied and taught as solitary voices or as a separate group defined by gender. Susanne Woods has found a way out of this bind. Making the not-unreasonable assumption that Lanyer, as a practicing poet, would more likely than not attend to some of the poetry of contemporary poets she had occasion to know or know of, Woods sets Lanyer's poetry over against that of Daniel, Drayton, Spenser, Shakespeare, Jonson,

Donne and others, exploring common (and differing) poetic strategies and the reasons for them.

The book begins with an incisive account of the known facts about Lanyer's life, and the conclusions that can readily be deduced from them: the musical education and the associations available to her through her Italian musician family (the Bassanos) and her husband's musical family (the Laniers); the classical education evident from the rhetoric of her poems and presumably supplied in the household of Susan Bertie, where she lived as a young woman; the cultural ambiance of Elizabeth's court, to which she had access as mistress of Elizabeth's powerful Lord Chamberlain, Lord Hunsdon; and the poets and writers she would come to know or know of during her residence at Cookham with Margaret Clifford, countess of Cumberland—especially Samuel Daniel, who was tutor to Margaret's daughter Anne. Woods points to passages in Lanyer's country-house poem, "The Description of Cooke-ham," indicating that Lanyer likely served as music tutor for Anne Clifford; and she adduces convincing evidence from Lanyer's treatment of Octavia, Rosamond, and Matilda in her passion poem, the *Salve Deus,* that Lanyer read Daniel's *Cleopatra, A Letter from Octavia,* and especially *Rosamond,* as well as Drayton's *Legend of Matilda.*

Subsequent chapters are less able to draw on known contacts and associations, but they offer suggestive inferences founded on textual comparisons. Woods argues, plausibly, that Lanyer may have learned from Spenser's dedicatory sonnets to the *Faerie Queene* and from *Colin Clout* something about imagining a community of patrons. She is also able to illuminate Lanyer's extended eulogy of Margaret Clifford in the *Salve Deus* by reference to Spenser's treatment of earthly and heavenly beauty and love in the *Foure Hymnes.* But I find less persuasive her argument that Lanyer's use of marginal (female) voices to center and decenter narrative action may owe something to Spenser's treatment of Una in the *Faerie Queene.* A central chapter on Lanyer and Shakespeare focuses on Shakespeare's narrative poetry. Woods points to a fascinating parallel in the structural uses of the courtly love colors, red and white, to describe Adonis in Shakespeare's *Venus and Adonis* and Christ in Lanyer's *Salve Deus,* and to a conceptual parallel between Lanyer's treatment of female agency in the face of male power and Shakespeare's *Lucrece.* This chapter also supplies a trenchent analysis of the unreliable evidence A. L. Rowse adduces from Simon Forman's diaries and Shakespeare's sonnets to support his claim that Lanyer was Shakespeare's Dark Lady—an identification, Woods forcefully demonstrates, that reaches "far beyond common rules of evidence and logic."

Woods grounds her suggestions of possible Lanyer–Ben Jonson associations in the family connections of Aemilia and her husband with the musicians Alfonso Ferrabosco and Nicholas Lanier, both of whom worked with Jonson on several masques. She points to interesting similarities and contrasts in the complex ways the two poets praise women's virtue—notably the virtue of the Countess of Bedford and Margaret Clifford—ways that "confound or at least extend cliches of gender." The revealing comparisons and gender-driven contrasts between Lanyer's *Cooke-ham* and Jonson's *Penshurst* have been explored in several articles and in many classrooms, but Woods finds a novel approach, inquiring what Jonson might have learned from Lanyer's poem (which was published first), as well as from his classical sources in developing what came to be the generic topoi of the seventeenth-century country-house poem. While there is no evidence that Jonson read Lanyer, it is salutary at least to consider the possibility that in this instance a woman's poem may have contributed something to the evolution of a new genre. The final chapter positions Lanyer among a number of English religious poets, Protestant and Catholic—Anne Lock, the Countess of Pembroke, Henry Constable, Robert Southwell, and especially John Donne—arguing that, like Donne, her theology is reformist while the physicality of her imagery links her with Counter Reformation spirituality. Most revealingly, Woods compares the idealized Elizabeth Drury in Donne's *Anniversaries* and the figure of Margaret Clifford in Lanyer's Passion poem, providing a new perspective on the authorizing strategies both poets employ. While Donne stands apart from his subject, Lanyer identifies closely with Margaret Clifford as the principal embodiment of that right understanding of Christ's Passion that her poem locates only in women.

Some of the parallels and contrasts Woods points to are commonplaces, and so some of the connections she proposes may seem doubtful. But this is not an influence study: Susanne Woods is careful not to claim facts of association or allusion that cannot be proved, and she offers her speculations as just that. This well-designed and eminently readable book certainly demonstrates its main thesis: that Lanyer "may have read, or probably read works by her contemporaries, [and] that in any case she produced her poems in conscious recognition of the poetry of her time. Whether

her awareness was in fact of these very poets or poems is in most instances unverifiable (although her list of narratives in *Salve Deus* 11. 209–48, provides strong evidence for a few), and it is not finally the point. What is important is that Lanyer be seen as part of the vigorous cultural production of Renaissance England" (117).

Index

Abell, Alice, 93–97
Acheson, Katherine O., 242–247
Adorno, Theodor, 45
Albanese, Denise, 220, 254–258
Alleyn, Edward, 103–105
Allsop, Ric, 283
Althusser, Louis, 171
Altman, Joel, 167
Anderson, Benedict, 165–171
Anne of Bohemia, 84–89
Anne of Denmark, 121
Archer, Ian W., 306
Aristotle, 48, 49
Ascham, Roger, 196–198
Astington, John H., 58–59, 106–110
Astley, John, 58–59, 106–110
Atlas, James, 327
Austern, Linda Phyllis, 303
Avery, Bruce, 282–284

Barroll, Leeds, 112
Barthes, Roland, 47
Bartolovich, Crystal, 25, 36–42
Bate, Walter Jackson, 298
Bawcutt, N. W., 129
Beal, Peter, 132
Beaumont, Francis, 130
Behn, Aphra, 238
Bell, Ilona, 323
Benfield, Robert, 115
Bentley, G. E., 55–61, 111–117, 120
Berger, Harry Jr., 232
Berry, Herbert, 56, 58, 93–98
Berry, Philippa, 219
Bertie, Susan, 338
Bicks, Caroline, 302
Blatherwick, Simon, 58, 74–83
Blayney, Peter W. M., 307
Bloom, Harold, 45

Blount, Charles, 122
Blumenberg, Hans, 255
Boose, Lynda, 295
Boyden, James M., 246
Braden, Gordon, 324
Brayne, John, 93–98
Broadway, Giles, 274–281
Brown, Cedric, 132
Brotton, Jerry, 232–234
Bruno, Giordano, 326
Brydges, Anne Stanley, 275
Buc, Sir George, 106–110, 134
Burbage, Cuthbert, 116
Burbage, James, 58, 99
Burgess, Clive, 246
Burt, Richard, 294–300
Butler, Judith, 234–242
Byrd, William, Jr., 299

Callaghan, Dympna, 9, 23–25, 219–220
Carleton, Lady Alice, 116
Carlyle, Thomas, 260
Carrió, Raquel, 283
Cartwright, Kent, 220–224
Cary, Elizabeth, 241, 337
Castle, Terry, 260
Castlehaven, second earl of, 274–281
Cavanagh, Sheila T., 220–224
Cavendish, Margaret, 219, 337
Cawarden, Sir Thomas, 107
Cecil, Sir Robert, 124
Cellier, Elizabeth, 226
Ceresano, S. P., 9, 55–61, 133, 326–327
Césaire, Aime, 282–284
Chamberlain, John, 114, 116
Chambers, E.K., 55–61, 120, 124
Chaytor, Miranda, 28–29
Chrysoloras, Manuel, 23
Cisson, C. J., 124–125

Index

Clifford, Lady Ann, 109
Clifford, Margaret, 339
Cohn, Samuel K., 246
Coke, Edward, 335
Condell, Henry, 115
Coster, Will, 246
Cotton, Robert, 142, 156
Cox, Samuel, 291
Crane, Mary Thomas, 302
Crawford, Patricia, 28
Crispin, Philip, 283
Crooke, Helkiah, 314

Daborne, Robert, 133
Dalton, Karen, 233
Daniel, Samuel, 337
Davis, Natalie, 27–28, 155, 305
Dee, John, 326, 330, 332
de Grazia, Margreta, 319–320, 324
della Mirandola, Pico, 23
De Malynes, Gerard, 156–157
de Man, Paul, 312
Democritus, 47
Derrida, Jacques, 31
Dircks, Henry, 260–270
Dolan, Frances E., 24, 26–30, 224–228, 280, 284–286, 303–304
Downton, Thomas, 103
Drakakis, John, 258–171
Drayton, Michael, 337–340
Dubrow, Heather, 320
Dudley, Lady Anne, 107
Duncan-Jones, Katharine, 132, 320, 328
Dusinberre, Juliet, 220
Dutton, Richard, 106–110
Dyson, Humphrey, 134

Edel, Leon, 327
Eggert, Katharine, 228–232
Eliot, T. S., 324
Elizabeth I, 143–158
Epicurus, 47
Erickson, Peter, 232–234

Fabyan, Robert, 85–89
Ferguson, Margaret, 28
Ferrabasco, Alfonso, 339
Ferry, Anne, 324
Field, Nathan, 130

Fineman, Joel, 311–312, 323
Fitzpatrick, Florence, 274–281
Fletcher, John, 130
Foakes, R. A., 59, 99–105, 133
Forman, Simon, 115, 326–333, 338
Foucault, Michel, 31, 44
Fracastoro, Girolamo, 48
Frederick, Prince Lewis, 115
Freeman, Arthur, 129–130
Friedman, Alice T., 307
Frienkel, Lisa, 322
Freud, Sigmund, 23
Frye, Susan, 233
Fumerton, Patricia, 307

Gilman, Ernest, 233
Gittings, Clare, 242–247
Goldberg, Jonathan, 234–242, 297, 324
Goldman, Michael, 175
Gordon, Bruce, 242–247
Goux, John Joseph, 261
Gowing, Laura, 28
Grafton, Richard, 85–89
Greenblatt, Stephen, 28, 258–259, 269, 297, 299, 311
Greene, Robert, 197
Greene, Thomas, 102, 121, 124, 322
Greenfeld, Liah, 165–166
Gresham, Sir Thomas, 143
Gross, Keneth, 247–254
Grossman, Marshall, 247–254
Gurr, Andrew, 112–117, 133, 307

Hall, Kim, 232, 233, 295
Halpern, Richard, 260
Hammill, Graham L., 254–258
Harding, Vanessa, 246
Harries, Martin, 258–171
Harrington, Sir John, 59, 108
Harris, Jonathan Gill, 25, 47–51
Hawarde, John, 33
Hays, James, 106
Helgerson, Richard, 162–167, 271–274
Helt, J. S. W., 246
Heminges, John, 115
Hendricks, Margo, 220, 295
Henry VII, 141–158
Henry VIII, 142–158

Index

Henslowe, Philip, 59, 74, 80, 99–105, 133, 162
Herbert, Henry, 111–117
Herman, Peter C., 322
Herrup, Cynthia, 274–282
Heywood, John, 221
Heywood, Thomas, 168–187
Hill, Christopher, 305
Hill, W. Speed, 129
Holinshed, Raphael, 85–89
Holland, Aaron, 60, 118–127
Honigmann, E. A. J., 128
Hopkins, Lisa, 219–220
Howard, Jean, 24, 305
Howard, Thomas, 233
Hulme, Peter, 282–284
Hulse, Clark, 232–234, 271–274
Hunt, Marvin, 323
Hutchinson, Lucy, 48, 337
Hyde, John, 93

Ingram, William, 56, 57, 59, 118–127
Ioppolo, Grace, 60, 128–136

James I and VI, 188–215
James, Henry, 327
Jameson, Fredric, 47
Johnson, Samuel, 39–42
Jones, Ann Rosalind, 284–286, 305
Jonson, Ben, 25, 36–42, 48, 107, 131, 305, 335–340
Jordan, Constance, 333–337
Jupp, Peter C., 242–247

Kahn, Coppélia, 193, 206, 228–232
Kaplan, M. Lindsay, 220
Kastan, David Scott, 129, 288–294
Katherens, Gilbert, 80
Keats, John, 316
Keene, Derek, 305
Kelliher, Hilton, 130
Kelly, Jude, 220
Kemp, Will, 305
Keynes, John Maynard, 258–270
Kirkham, Edward, 114
Klause, John, 322
Knapp, Jeffrey, 224–228
Knight, G. Wilson, 194
Knighton, Henry, 87–88

Knowles, James, 131
Knutson, Roslyn, 59, 111–117
Kyle, Chris R., 25, 31–35

Lacan, Jacques, 31, 171
Lancashire, Anne, 57, 84–92
Lander, Jesse M., 9, 137–161
Lanier, Nicholas, 339
Lanyer, Aemilia, 238, 337–340
Laroche, Rebecca, 323
Leucippus, 47
Lewalski, Barbara, 337–340
Lewkenor, Lewis, 107–110
Little, Arthur L., Jr., 294–300
Lock, Anne, 339
Loengard, Janet, 89
Long, William B., 133
Loomba, Ania, 220, 295
Love, Harold, 132
Lucretius, 47–48

MacDonald, Joyce Green, 220
Maclean, Sally-Beth, 58, 62–73
Magnusson, Lynne, 318–326
Maidstone, Richard, 84
Malone, Edmund, 111, 319, 321
Marcus, Leah, 132
Marshall, Peter, 242–247
Marx, Karl, 48, 258–270
Maus, Katherine, 299, 307
May, Stephen, 132
Meade, Jacob, 80, 103
Mendelson, Sara, 28
Meres, Frances, 40
Merriam, Thomas, 128–129
Middleton, Thomas, 129
Mikalachki, Jodi, 188, 203
Mildmay, Sir Humphrey, 114
Miller, David Hunter, 268
Miller, Naomi, 300–304, 323
Milton, John, 231
Molière, 271
Montaigne, Michel, 48–49
Monteagle, Lord, 66
Montrose, Louis Adrian, 228, 297
Morgan, Philip, 244
Moryson, Fynes, 200–201
Mueller, Janel, 132
Mullaney, Steven, 233

Index

Munday, Anthony, 128–129
Murray, Timothy, 299

Nashe, Thomas, 168–187
Neely, Carol, 299
Negri, Antonio, 137
Neill, Michael, 23, 234
Nelson, Alan H., 134
Norden, John, 74
Nosworthy, J. M., 194
Nungezer, Edwin, 120

Orgel, Stephen, 129, 180, 232
Orlin, Lena Cowen, 304–309

Parker, John, 25, 43–46
Parker, Patricia, 193, 194
Parolin, Peter A., 9, 188–215
Paster, Gail, 287, 307
Peck, Linda Levy, 307
Pequigney, Joseph, 322
Pick, Daniel, 268–269
Plato, 23, 49
Preston, Sir Richard, 106
Pye, Christopher, 309–313
Pym, John, 33
Pythagoras, 49

Rackin, Phyllis, 195
Rambuss, Richard, 274–282
Rastell, John, 222
Raylor, Tim, 130–131
Redford, John, 222
Rich, Penelope, 122
Richard II, 84–89
Richard III, 141
Rickert, R. T., 13
Rix, Lucy, 282–284
Roberts, Penny, 246
Romack, Katherine M., 219
Rose, Mary Beth, 28, 132, 300–304
Rowe, Katherine, 313–318
Rowse, A. L., 330, 338
Rubins, Peter Paul, 207
Rudick, Michael, 131
Rutter, Carol, 99–101
Ryan, Kiernan, 288–294

Sachdev, Rachana, 219
Sacks, David Harris, 305

Schaffer, Talia, 313–318
Schalkwyk, David, 321
Schiffer, James, 318–326
Schneider, Jane, 305
Schoenfeldt, Michael, 323
Schofield, John, 307
Sedgewick, Eve, 237
Shakespeare, William, 36–42, 48, 328, 337
—Plays: *Antony and Cleopatra*, 227, 294–300; *As You Like It*, 48; *Coriolanus*, 248–253; *Cymbeline*, 138, 188–215, 233; *Hamlet*, 229, 248–270, 287, 334–336; *1 Henry IV*, 130, 157–168, 290, 292; *2 Henry IV*, 48, 292; *Henry V*, 162–187, 233; *King John*, 141; *King Lear*, 248–253, 310; *Macbeth*, 112, 220, 227, 262–270, 292–293; *Measure for Measure*, 248–253; *Merchant of Venice*, 220; *Merry Wives of Windsor*, 271, 273; *Midsummer Night's Dream*, 220; *Much Ado About Nothing*, 219; *Othello*, 24, 112, 220, 233, 248, 294–300; *Richard II*, 112; *Romeo and Juliet*, 48–50, 219; *Tempest*, 220, 282–284; *Titus Andronicus*, 294–300, 314–318; *Twelfth Night*, 219, 287; *Troilus and Cressida*, 50, 157
—Sonnets, 318–326
Shelton, Mary, 241
Shepherd, Matthew, 299
Sherman, William, H. 282–284
Shershaw, Scott, 24
Shuger, Deborah, 44
Sidney, Mary, 239, 337
Sidney, Sir Robert, 108
Sinfield, Alan, 305
Simpson, O. J., 299
Singh, Jyotsna, 220
Skelton, John, 222
Slater, Martin, 58–61, 118–127
Smith, Anthony D., 166
Smith, Bruce R., 319–322
Snow, Edward, 299
Soergel, Philip M., 246
Somerset, Alan, 58, 62–73
Southwell, Robert, 322, 339
Sparkes, William, 93

Spenser, Edmund, 59, 108, 197, 229, 320, 337
Spivak, Gayatri, 42
Stallybrass, Peter, 284–286, 305, 319–320, 324
Steevens, George, 319
Stowe, John, 87–89
Stowers, Edward, 93–98
Suzuki, Mihoko, 219
Swinnerton, Thomas, 123, 125

Tanselle, G. Thomas, 132
Tawney, R. H., 267
Thirsk, Joan, 305
Thorne, Alison, 9, 162–187
Tillyard, E. M. W., 139
Traister, Barbara Howard, 326–337
Traub, Valerie, 232, 233, 324
Twain, Mark, 316
Tymme, Thomas, 155

Valbuena, Olga L., 323
Van Dyck, Anthony, 233
Vickers, Brian, 298
Voltaire, 39–42

Wager, William, 222
Walker, Garthine, 28–29
Wall, Cynthia, 304–309
Wall, Wendy, 240
Walsingham, Francis, 44
Warrison, Peter, 93, 95
Warrison, William, 93, 95
Werstine, Paul, 129
Whitney, Isabella, 240
Wickham, Glynne, 56, 188–193
Wilde, Oscar, 323
Wilson, Luke, 333–337
Wilson, Scott, 309–313
Woodbridge, Linda, 206
Woods, Susanne, 337–340
Woodward, Frances, 100
Woudhuysen, H. R., 132
Wright, George T., 324
Wright, James, 111, 115
Wroth, Lady Mary, 337

Yavneh, Naomi, 300–304
Yeandle, Laetitia, 134

Zimmerman, Susan, 220
Zizek, Slavoj, 40, 260